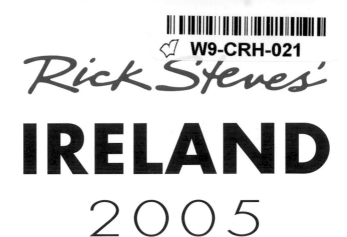

Rick Steves'

IRELAND

2005

Rick Steves & Pat O'Connor

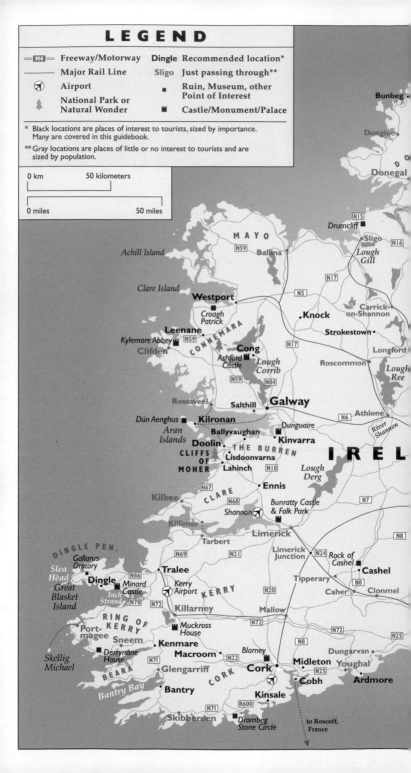

LEGEND

═M4═	Freeway/Motorway	**Dingle**	Recommended location*
——	Major Rail Line	Sligo	Just passing through**
✈	Airport	■	Ruin, Museum, other Point of Interest
🌲	National Park or Natural Wonder	♜	Castle/Monument/Palace

* Black locations are places of interest to tourists, sized by importance. Many are covered in this guidebook.

**Gray locations are places of little or no interest to tourists and are sized by population.

0 km   50 kilometers

0 miles   50 miles

Bunbeg

Dungloe

Donegal

DO

MAYO

Achill Island

Clare Island

Ballina

N59

Drumcliff

Sligo

Lough Gill

N15

N16

N5

N17

Carrick-on-Shannon

Westport

Croagh Patrick

Knock

Strokestown

Leenane

Kylemore Abbey

Clifden

CONNEMARA

N59

Cong

Ashford Castle

Longford

Roscommon

Lough Ree

Lough Corrib

N84

N59

N17

Rossaveel

Salthill

Galway

N6

Athlone

River Shannon

Kilronan

Dún Aenghus

IREL

Aran Islands

Ballyvaughan

Dunguaire

Kinvarra

Doolin

THE BURREN

CLIFFS OF MOHER

Lisdoonvarna

Lahinch

N18

Lough Derg

Ennis

N67

CLARE

N68

Bunratty Castle & Folk Park

N7

Kilkee

Shannon ✈

N8

Killimer

Limerick

Tarbert

Limerick Junction

N24

Rock of Cashel

Cashel

DINGLE PEN.

N69

N21

Gallarus Oratory

Slea Head

Dingle

Minard Castle

Tralee

Kerry Airport ✈

N86

Inch Strand

N70

Great Blasket Island

KERRY

Tipperary

Caher

Clonmel

N72

Killarney

Mallow

N20

N72

N25

RING OF KERRY

Port-magee

Sneem

Muckross House

N72

Derrynane House

Kenmare

Macroom

N71

N22

Blarney

Cork

Midleton

N25

Dungarvan

Youghal

Skellig Michael

BEARA

Glengarriff

N8

Cobh

Ardmore

Bantry

Bantry Bay

CORK

Kinsale

✈

N71

Skibbereen

R600

Drombeg Stone Circle

to Roscoff, France

Rick Steves'
IRELAND
2005

AVALON
TRAVEL

CONTENTS

Top Destinations in Ireland

INTRODUCTION

Flung onto the foggy fringe of the Atlantic pond like a mossy mill-stone, Ireland drips with mystery, drawing you in for a closer look and then surprising you. An old farmer cuts turf from the bog while his son staffs the tech help-line for an international software firm. Buy them both a pint in a pub whirling with playful conversation and exhilarating traditional music. Pious, earthy, witty, brooding, proud, and unpretentious...Irish culture is an intoxicating potion to sip or slurp as the mood strikes you.

This book breaks Ireland into its top big-city, small-town, and rural destinations. It gives you all the information and opinions necessary to wring the maximum value out of your limited time and money. If you plan three weeks or less for Ireland and have a normal appetite for information, this lean and mean book is all you need. If you're a travel-info fiend, this book sorts through all the superlatives and provides a handy rack upon which to hang your supplemental information.

Experiencing Irish culture, people, and natural wonders economically and hassle-free has been my goal for more than 25 years of traveling, tour-guiding, and travel writing. With this new edition, I pass on to you the lessons I've learned, updated for your trip in 2005.

Rick Steves' Ireland is a personal tour guide in your pocket. Better yet, it's actually two tour guides in your pocket: Rick's co-author/researcher for this guidebook is Pat O'Connor. Pat is the Ireland specialist and senior Ireland tour guide at Rick Steves' Europe Through the Back Door. Rick has enjoyed Ireland over 25 years of travel, but nobody has a more Irish name than Pat—whose travel passion has long been the Emerald Isle. Together, we will keep this book up-to-date and accurate (though for simplicity, "we" will shed our respective egos and become "I" from this point on).

The places covered in this book are balanced to include a

comfortable mix of exciting big cities and great-to-be-alive-in small towns. Note that this book covers the highlights of the entire island, including Northern Ireland. While you'll find the predictable biggies (such as the Book of Kells, Newgrange, and the Cliffs of Moher), I also mix in a healthy dose of Back Door intimacy (rope-bridge hikes, holy wells, and Irish traditional music pubs). I've been selective. On a short trip, visiting both the monastic ruins of Glendalough and Clonmacnoise is redundant; I cover only the best (Glendalough). There are plenty of great manorhouse gardens; again, I recommend just the tops (Powerscourt).

The best is, of course, only my opinion. But after spending half my life researching Europe, I've developed a sixth sense for what travelers enjoy. The places featured in this book will give anyone the "gift of gab."

This Information is Accurate and Up-to-Date

Most publishers of guidebooks that cover a country from top to bottom can afford an update only every two or three years, and rarely is the research done in person. Since this book is selective, covering only the top three weeks of sightseeing, I'm able to update it each year. The information in this book is accurate as of mid-2004—but even with an annual update, things change. Still, if you're traveling with the current edition of this book, I guarantee you're using the most up-to-date information available in print. For the latest, see www.ricksteves .com/update. Also at my Web site, check my Graffiti Wall (select "Rick Steves' Guidebooks," then "Ireland") for a huge, valuable list of reports and experiences—good and bad—from fellow travelers.

Use this year's edition. If you're packing an old book, you'll learn the seriousness of your mistake...in Ireland. Your trip costs about $10 per waking hour. Your time is valuable. This guidebook saves lots of time.

About This Book

This book is organized by destination, each one a mini-vacation on its own, filled with exciting sights and homey, affordable places to stay. In each chapter, you'll find the following:

Planning Your Time, a suggested schedule with thoughts on how to best use your limited time.

Orientation, including tourist information, city transportation, and an easy-to-read map designed to make the text clear and your arrival smooth.

Sights provides a succinct overview of Ireland's most important attractions, with ratings: ▲▲▲—Don't miss; ▲▲—Try hard to see; ▲—Worthwhile if you can make it; No rating—Worth knowing about.

Sleeping and **Eating,** with addresses, phone numbers, and Web sites of my favorite good-value hotels and restaurants.

Transportation Connections to nearby destinations by train or bus, and route tips for drivers.

The **Irish History and Culture** chapter gives you an overview of Irish history, a look at contemporary Ireland, and a taste of the Irish language.

The **appendix** has helpful information on telephoning, the climate, and festivals.

Browse through this book, choose the destinations that excite you the most, and link them up. Then have a great trip! You'll travel like a temporary local, getting the absolute most out of every mile, minute, and dollar. You won't waste time on mediocre sights because, unlike others, this guidebook covers only the best. Since your major financial pitfall is lousy, expensive hotels, I've worked hard to assemble the best accommodation values for each stop. And as you travel the route I know and love, I'm happy you'll be meeting some of my favorite Irish people.

PLANNING

Trip Costs

Five components make up your trip costs: airfare, surface transportation, room and board, sightseeing/entertainment, and shopping/miscellany.

Airfare: Don't try to sort through the mess. Find a good travel agent. A round-trip United States-to-Dublin flight costs $600–1,000 (even cheaper in winter), depending on where you fly from and when. If your travels take you beyond Ireland, consider saving time and money in Europe by flying "open jaw" (into one city and out of another; for instance, into Dublin and out of Paris).

Surface Transportation: For a three-week whirlwind trip of all my recommended Irish destinations, allow $250 per person for public transportation (train tickets and key buses), or $800 per person (based on 2 people sharing) for a three-week car rental, gas, and insurance. Car rental is cheapest if arranged from the United States. Since Ireland's train system has gaps, you'll usually save money by simply buying train and bus tickets as you go, rather than buying a railpass (see "Transportation," page 18).

Room and Board: You can thrive in Ireland on $100 a day per person for room and board (allow $120 per day for Dublin). A $100-per-day budget allows $15 for lunch, $25 for dinner, and $60 for lodging (based on 2 people splitting a $120 double room that includes breakfast). That's doable, particularly outside Dublin. Students and tightwads can do it on $50 ($25 for a bed in a hostel, $25 a day for meals—mostly cheap picnics—and snacks). But budget sleeping and eating require the skills and information covered below (and in greater detail in my book *Rick Steves' Europe Through the Back Door*).

Sightseeing and Entertainment: In big cities, figure $6–10 per

Irish Sightseeing Deals

Ireland offers two different passes (each covering a different set of sights) that can save you money. The first is smart for anyone, and the second works best for couples. Couples who love to sightsee should get both passes.

Heritage Card

The Heritage Card gets you into 99 historical monuments, gardens, and parks maintained by the OPW (Office of Public Works, formerly Dúchas) in the Republic of Ireland. It will pay off if you plan to visit half a dozen or more included sights over the course of your trip (€20, seniors age 60 and older-€15, students-€7.50, families-€50, covers free entry to all Heritage sights for 1 year, card comes with handy map and list of sights' hours and prices, purchase at any Heritage sight or Dublin's tourist information office on Suffolk Street, tel. 01/647-2453, www.heritageireland.ie). People traveling by car are most likely to get their money's worth out of the card.

If, instead of getting the Heritage Card, you pay for the sights individually, your costs will add up quickly. Adult entry prices range from €1.50 to €9.75. An energetic sightseer with three weeks in Ireland will probably pay to see nearly all 20 of the following sights (covered in this book): Dublin Castle-€5, Kilmainham Jail-€5 (Dublin); Brú na Bóinne-€9.75 (Knowth, Newgrange, and Visitors Centre in Boyne Valley); Hill of Tara-€2 (Boyne Valley); Mellifont Abbey-€2 (Boyne Valley); Trim Castle-€3.75 (Boyne Valley); Glendalough-€2.75 (Wicklow Mountains); Kilkenny Castle-€5 (Kilkenny); Rock of Cashel-€5 (Cashel); Reginald's Tower-€2 (Waterford); Charles Fort-€3.50 (Kinsale); Desmond Castle-€2.75 (Kinsale); Muckross House-€5.50 (near Killarney); Derrynane House-€2.75 (Ring of Kerry); Blasket Centre-€3.50 (near Dingle); Ennis Friary-€1.50 (Ennis); Dún Aenghus-€2 (Inishmore, Aran Islands); Connemara National Park-€2.75 (near Galway); and Glenveagh Castle and National Park-€2.75 (Donegal). This totals nearly €70; a pass saves you about €50 ($60) per person over paying entrance fees individually. Note that scheduled tours given by OPW

---

major sight (e.g., the Book of Kells at Trinity College-$9), $3 for minor ones (i.e., climbing church towers), $12 for guided walks, $30–40 for day-trip bus tours, and up to $60 for splurge experiences (such as the Dunguaire medieval castle banquet). An overall average of $25 a day works for most. Buying a discount pass can save you money—see the "Irish Sightseeing Deals" sidebar. Don't skimp on sightseeing and entertainment. After all, this category directly powers most of the experiences all the other expenses are designed to make possible.

Shopping and Miscellany: Figure $2 per postcard (including postage to U.S.), ice-cream cone, or cup of tea, and $4 per pint of guides at any of these sites are included in the price of admission, regardless of whether you have the Heritage Card.

Heritage Island Explorer Touring Guide

Ambitious travelers covering more ground should seriously consider the Heritage Island Explorer Touring Guide (€4), which does not overlap with the above Heritage sights and gives a variety of discounts (usually 2-for-the-price-of-1 entries, but occasionally 20 percent off) at sights in both the Republic and Northern Ireland. This is a great deal and a no-brainer for couples (just buy one Touring Guide for the 2 of you); you save the cost of the guide after only a couple of stops. Independent travelers might have to go to half a dozen sights before the discounts recover the initial €4. The guide can be bought at tourist information offices and participating sights, but study the full list of sights first (tel. 01/260-0058, www.heritageisland.com).

Sights mentioned in this guidebook include: Trinity College Library—Book of Kells and *Dublin Experience* (Dublin), Dublin City Hall, Dublinia (Dublin), James Joyce Cultural Centre (Dublin), Hugh Lane Art Gallery (Dublin), Old Jameson Distillery (Dublin), The Chimney viewing tower (Dublin), Guinness Storehouse (Dublin), GAA Museum at Croke Park (Dublin), Gardens of Powerscourt (Enniskerry), Bru Boru Cultural Centre (Rock of Cashel), Waterford Museum of Treasures (Waterford), Waterford Crystal Factory (Waterford), Hook Head Lighthouse (Waterford), *Dunbrody* Famine Ship (New Ross), Irish National Heritage Park (Wexford), Kinsale Regional Museum (Kinsale), Queenstown Story (Cobh), Old Midleton Distillery (Midleton), Blarney Castle (County Cork), Kerry the Kingdom Museum (Tralee), Siamsa Tire Theatre (Tralee), Galway Irish Crystal Heritage Centre (Galway), Clare Museum (Ennis), Glór Irish Music Centre (Ennis), Kylemore Abbey (Letterfrack), Ulster Museum (Belfast), W5 Science Centre (Belfast), Ulster Folk and Transport Museum (Cultra), Giant's Causeway (Portrush), Belleek Pottery Visitors Centre (Belleek), and Ulster American Folk Park (Omagh).

beer. Shopping can vary in cost from nearly nothing to a small fortune. Good budget travelers find that this category has little to do with assembling a trip full of lifelong and wonderful memories.

When to Go

July and August are peak season—my favorite time—with long days, the best weather, and the busiest schedule of tourist fun. Crowds don't go up as dramatically in Ireland as they do in much of Europe. Still, travel during "shoulder season" (May, early June, Sept, and early Oct) is easier and a bit less expensive. Shoulder-season travelers

Ireland's Best Three-Week Trip (By Car)

Day	Plan	Sleep in
1	Fly into Dublin, rent car, Glendalough	Kilkenny
2	Kilkenny, with side-trip to Cashel	Kilkenny
3	Waterford	Waterford
4	Explore County Wexford	Waterford
5	Cobh	Kinsale
6	Kinsale	Kinsale
7	Muckross House	Kenmare
8	Ring of Kerry	Dingle
9	Dingle Peninsula loop	Dingle
10	Blaskets, Dingle town (laundry and rest)	Dingle
11	Cliffs of Moher, Burren, Dunguaire banquet	Galway
12	Galway	Galway
13	Aran Islands	Aran Islands
14	Tour Connemara	Westport
15	Drive to Northern Ireland	Derry
16	Side-trip to County Donegal	Derry
17	Explore Derry, then drive to Portrush	Portrush
18	Explore Antrim Coast	Portrush
19	Belfast	Belfast
20	Drive to Boyne Valley sights, return car	Dublin
21	Dublin	Dublin
22	Dublin	Dublin
23	Fly home	

While this three-week itinerary (stretched to 23 days by using week-ends at each end) is designed to be done by car, you can do it by train and bus. For three weeks without a car, spend your first three nights in Dublin using buses and taxis. Cut back on the recommended sights with the most frustrating public transportation (Ring of Kerry,

get minimal crowds, decent weather, the full range of sights and tourist fun spots, and the joy of being able to just grab a room almost whenever and wherever they like—often at a flexible price.

Winter travelers find absolutely no crowds and soft room prices, but shorter sightseeing hours. Some attractions are open only on weekends or closed entirely in the winter (Nov–Feb). The weather can be cold and dreary, and nightfall draws the shades on sightseeing well before dinnertime. While Ireland's rural charm falls with the leaves, city sightseeing is fine in the winter.

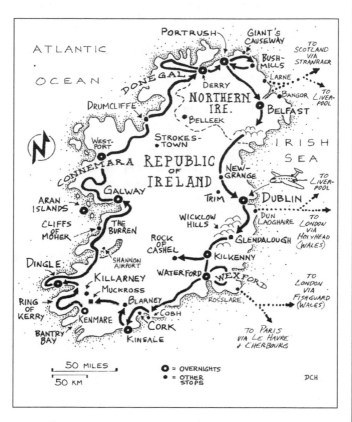

Boyne Valley, Connemara, and counties Wexford and Donegal). You can book day tours by bus for some of these areas at local tourist offices. For at least two people traveling together, taxis—though expensive—can work in a pinch, if bus schedules don't fit your plans (i.e., Cork to Kinsale, Waterford to New Ross, Dublin to Trim).

Plan for rain no matter when you go. Just keep going, and take full advantage of "bright spells." Conditions can change several times in a day, but rarely is the weather extreme. As the locals say, "There is no bad weather, only inappropriate clothing." Daily averages throughout the year range between 42 and 70 degrees Fahrenheit. Temperatures below 32 or over 80 degrees are cause for headlines (see the climate chart in the appendix). While sunshine may be rare, summer days are very long. Dublin is as far north as Edmonton, Canada, and Portrush is as far north as Ketchikan on the Alaskan panhandle. The summer sun is up from 5:00 until 22:00. It's not uncommon to have a gray day, eat dinner, and enjoy hours of sunshine afterward.

Sightseeing Priorities

Depending on the length of your trip, here are my recommended priorities:

3 days:	Not worth the trouble
5 days:	Dublin, Dingle Peninsula
7 days, add:	Galway and a day in Belfast
9 days, add:	County Clare/Burren
11 days, add:	Northern Ireland's Antrim Coast
15 days, add:	Aran Islands, Wicklow Mountains
19 days, add:	Kinsale, Waterford, Valley of the Boyne
23 days, add:	Ring of Kerry, Connemara, Derry, Donegal

(This includes everything on "Ireland's Best Three-Week Trip" map and itinerary on pages 6 and 7.)

Itinerary Specifics

Most people fly into Dublin and remain there for a few days. If you have a car rental set up at Dublin Airport, consider a mellower small-town start in Kilkenny or Trim. Then visit Dublin at the end of your trip, after you've turned your car back in at the airport. You'll be more rested and ready to tackle Ireland's greatest city. Dublin traffic has gotten clogged over the years, and visitors will find city sightseeing easier on foot, by bus (particularly the hop-on, hop-off tours), or by taxi. Spare yourself the traffic stress and parking expense of trying to drive in Dublin.

To give yourself a little rootedness, minimize one-night stays. It's worth a long drive after dinner to be settled into a town for two nights. B&Bs are also more likely to give a good price to someone staying more than one night.

Consider making the following travel arrangements before your trip:
- Reserve a room for your first night.
- If you'll be traveling in late June, July, or August and want to sleep in my lead listings, book your B&Bs (and the Dunguaire medieval banquet) as soon as you're ready to commit to a date.
- Confirm car rental and pickup plans with your rental agency (picking up a car on Sat afternoon or Sun can be difficult).

RESOURCES

Irish Tourist Office in the United States

Ireland's national tourist office in the United States—called **Tourism Ireland**—offers a wealth of information on both the Republic of Ireland and Northern Ireland. You can contact them at: 345 Park Ave.,

Rick Steves' Guidebooks

Rick Steves' Europe Through the Back Door
Rick Steves' Best European City Walks & Museums
Rick Steves' Easy Access Europe

Country Guides
Rick Steves' Best of Europe
Rick Steves' Best of Eastern Europe
Rick Steves' France
Rick Steves' Germany & Austria
Rick Steves' Great Britain
Rick Steves' Ireland
Rick Steves' Italy
Rick Steves' Portugal
Rick Steves' Scandinavia
Rick Steves' Spain
Rick Steves' Switzerland

City and Regional Guides
Rick Steves' Amsterdam, Bruges & Brussels
Rick Steves' Florence & Tuscany
Rick Steves' London
Rick Steves' Paris
Rick Steves' Prague & the Czech Republic*
Rick Steves' Provence & the French Riviera
Rick Steves' Rome
Rick Steves' Venice

*New in 2005

(Avalon Travel Publishing)

17th floor, New York, NY 10154, tel. 800/223-6470 or 212/418-0800, fax 212/371-9052, www.tourismireland.com, info@shamrock.org. Ask about the Ireland map, events calendar, and (based on your interests) golfing, outdoor activities, walking routes, horseback riding, and historic sights. Request a vacation planner packet.

Rick Steves' Books and Public Television Shows
Rick Steves' Europe Through the Back Door 2005 gives you budget-travel skills, such as minimizing jet lag, packing light, planning your itinerary, traveling by car or train, finding rooms, changing money, avoiding rip-offs, using mobile phones, staying healthy, taking great photographs, and much more. The book also includes chapters on 38 of Rick's favorite Back Doors, two of which are in Ireland.

Rick Steves' Country Guides, an annually updated series that covers Europe, offers you the latest on the top sights and destinations, with tips on how to make your trip efficient and fun.

My **City and Regional Guides,** freshly updated every year, focus on Europe's most compelling destinations. Along with specifics on sights, restaurants, hotels, and nightlife, you'll get self-guided, illustrated tours of the outstanding museums and most characteristic neighborhoods.

Rick Steves' Easy Access Europe, written for travelers with limited mobility, covers London, Paris, Bruges, Amsterdam, and the Rhine River.

Rick Steves' Europe 101: History and Art for the Traveler (with Gene Openshaw) gives you the story of Europe's people, history, and art. Written for smart people who were sleeping in their history and art classes before they knew they were going to Europe, *101* really helps Europe's sights come alive. However, this book has far more coverage of the European Continent than of Ireland.

Rick Steves' Best European City Walks & Museums (with Gene Openshaw) gives you self-guided tours of the major museums and historic neighborhoods in London, Paris, Amsterdam, Rome, Florence, Venice, and Madrid.

My public television series, *Rick Steves' Europe*, keeps churning out shows. Of 95 episodes (the new series plus *Travels in Europe with Rick Steves*), six shows cover Ireland.

Rick Steves' Postcards from Europe, my autobiographical book, packs more than 25 years of travel anecdotes and insights into the ultimate 2,000-mile European adventure.

Other Guidebooks

You may want some supplemental travel guidebooks, especially if you're traveling beyond my recommended destinations. I know it hurts to spend $25–35 on extra books and maps, but when you consider the money they'll save you and the improvements they'll make in your $3,000 vacation, it's money well spent.

While this book offers everything you'll need for the structure of your trip, each place you will visit has plenty of great little guidebooks to fill you in on local history. For cultural and sightseeing background in bigger chunks, Michelin and Cadogan guides to Ireland are good. The best budget travel guides to Ireland are the Lonely Planet and Let's Go guidebooks. Lonely Planet's guidebook is more thorough and informative, but it's not updated annually. *Let's Go Ireland* is updated annually and youth-oriented, with good coverage of nightlife, hostels, and cheap transportation deals.

More Recommended Reading and Movies

For information on Ireland past and present, consider these books and films:

Nonfiction: *A Short History of Ireland* (Richard Killeen); *How* *the Irish Saved Civilization* (Thomas Cahill); *Ireland: A Concise History* (Maire MacEntee O'Brien); *Traveller's History of Ireland* (Peter Neville); *Angela's Ashes* (Frank McCourt); *O Come Ye Back to Ireland: Our First Year in County Clare* (first in series of 4 by Niall Williams and Christine Breen); *Are You Somebody?: The Accidental Memoir of a Dublin Woman* (Nuala O'Faolain); *To School Through the Fields: An Irish Country Childhood* (Alice Taylor); *Round Ireland with a Fridge* (Tony Hawks); *The Back of Beyond: A Search for the Soul of Ireland* (James Charles Roy); *Culture Shock: Ireland* (Patricia Levy); and *Adapter Kit Ireland* (Steenie Harvey).

Fiction: *Trinity* (Leon Uris); *The Bódhran Makers* (J.B. Keane); Morgan Llewelyn's historical epics; Roddy Doyle's gritty portraits of working-class Dubliners; *Finbar's Hotel* (anthology of short stories by Irish writers); *Ladies' Night at Finbar's Hotel* (anthology of short stories by Irish women writers); and the works of masters, such as James Joyce, Oscar Wilde, Jonathan Swift, W.B. Yeats, G.B. Shaw, Samuel Beckett, Alexander Pope, Michael Comyn, Brendan Behan, Oliver Goldsmith, Thomas Kinsella, and Seamus Heaney.

Flicks: Classics include *The Quiet Man* (1952, John Wayne returns to his native Ireland) and *Odd Man Out* (1947, film noir about the early IRA, with a great scene filmed in the Crown Bar in Belfast). Fans of biographies will like *Michael Collins* and the thriller *Veronica Guerin.* Upbeat crowd-pleasers include *Far and Away, Circle of Friends, Evelyn, Into the West, The Matchmaker, Widow's Peak,* and *Waking Ned Devine.* For humor, check out *The Commitments, The Snapper, The Van,* and *Hear My Song.* For hard-hitting drama, look for *In the Name of the Father, The Boxer, The Field, My Left Foot, Some Mother's Son, The Magdalene Sisters,* and *Angela's Ashes.* The *Secret of Roan Inish* takes place in Donegal, and *Ryan's Daughter* was filmed on the Dingle peninsula. Other Irish-themed films are *Agnes Browne, Cal, The Dead, The Playboys, The Run of the Country* (romance), *Dancing at Lughnasa,* and *This Is My Father.*

Maps

The black-and-white maps in this book—drawn by Dave Hoerlein, who is well-traveled in Ireland—are concise and simple. Dave has designed the maps to help you locate recommended places and get to the tourist information office, where you'll find more in-depth maps of the city or region. The color map of Ireland at the front of this book shows the country's highlights.

Maps to buy in Ireland: Train travelers can do fine with a simple rail map (available as part of the free Intercity Timetable found at Irish train stations) and city maps from tourist information offices. (Get free maps of Dublin and Ireland from Irish Tourism before you go; see "Tourist Information," above.) If you're driving, get a detailed road atlas covering all of Ireland. Ordnance Survey, AA, and Bartholomew

Begin Your Trip at www.ricksteves.com

At ricksteves.com, you'll find a wealth of **free information** on destinations covered in this book, including fresh European travel and tour news every month, and helpful "Graffiti Wall" tips from thousands of fellow travelers.

While you're visiting the site, Rick Steves' **online Travel Store** is a great place to save money on travel bags and accessories specially designed by Rick Steves to help you travel smarter and lighter. These include Rick's popular carry-on bags (wheeled and rucksack versions), money belts, day bags, totes, toiletries kits, packing cubes, clotheslines, locks, clocks, sleep sacks, adapters, and a wide selection of guidebooks, planning maps, and *Rick Steves' Europe* DVDs.

Traveling through Europe by rail is a breeze, but choosing the right railpass for your trip (amidst hundreds of options) can drive you nuts. At ricksteves.com, you'll find **Rick Steves' Annual Guide to European Railpasses**—your best way to convert chaos into pure travel energy. Buy your railpass from Rick, and you'll get a bunch of free extras to boot.

Travel agents will tell you about mainstream tours of Europe, but they won't tell you about **Rick Steves' tours**. Rick Steves' Europe Through the Back Door travel company offers more than two dozen itineraries and 250+ departures reaching the best destinations in this book...and beyond. You'll enjoy the services of a great guide, a fun bunch of travel partners (with group sizes in the mid-20s), and plenty of room to spread out in a big, comfy bus. You'll find tours to fit every vacation size, from week-long city getaways (Paris, London, Venice, Florence, Rome), to 12- to 18-day country tours, to three-week "Best of Europe" adventures. For details, visit www.ricksteves.com or call 425/771-8303, ext. 217.

editions are available for about €12 in tourist information offices, gas stations, and bookstores. Drivers, hikers, and bikers may want more detailed maps for Dingle, Connemara, County Donegal, County Wexford, the Antrim Coast, the Ring of Kerry, and the Boyne Valley (easy to buy locally). Before you buy a map, look at it to make sure it has the level of detail you want.

PRACTICALITIES

Red Tape: You need a passport, but no visa or shots, to travel in Ireland.

Time: Like Great Britain, Ireland's time zone is one hour earlier than continental Europe. Ireland is also five/eight hours ahead of the East/West Coasts of the United States.

In Ireland, and in this book, you'll be using the 24-hour clock. After 12:00 noon, keep going—13:00, 14:00, and so on. For anything over 12, subtract 12 and add p.m. (14:00 is 2 p.m.).

Business Hours: Most shops are open Monday through Saturday (roughly 10:00–18:00), often with a late night on Thursday (until 19:00 or 20:00). On Sunday, when some stores are closed, street markets are lively with shoppers.

Holidays: Bank holidays bring most businesses to a grinding halt on Christmas, December 26, New Year's Day, Good Friday (March 25 in 2005), Easter Monday (March 28), and the first Mondays in May (May 2), June (June 6), and August (Aug 1). For a list of events and festivals—which can also enhance or complicate sightseeing plans—see page 324.

Discounts: While discounts (called "concessions" in Ireland) are generally not listed in this book, many Irish sights are discounted for seniors (loosely defined as anyone retired or willing to call themselves a senior), youths (ages 8–18), students, groups of 10 or more, and families.

Watt's up? If you're bringing electrical gear, pack along an adapter with three square prongs to plug into Ireland's outlets (which are just like Britain's), rather than the two-round-prong adapter you'd need for the rest of Western Europe. You might also need a converter to deal with the increased voltage. Travel appliances often have convenient, built-in converters; look for a voltage switch marked 120V (U.S.) and 240V (Europe).

MONEY

Exchange Rates

I've priced things throughout this book in local currencies. The Republic of Ireland uses the euro currency. Northern Ireland, which is part of the United Kingdom, has retained its traditional currency, the British pound sterling.

> 1 euro (€) = about $1.20
> 1 British pound (£1) = about $1.70

Republic of Ireland: Like dollars, one euro (€) is broken down into 100 cents. You'll find coins ranging from 1 cent to 2 euros, and bills ranging from 5 euros to 500 euros.

To roughly convert prices in euros to dollars, add 20 percent to Irish prices: €20 is about $24, €45 is about $55, and so on.

Northern Ireland: The British pound sterling (£), also called a "quid," is broken into 100 pence (p). Pence means "cents." You'll find coins ranging from 1p to £2, and bills from £5 to £50.

To roughly convert prices from pounds to dollars, add 50

percent to British prices: £2 is about $3, £6 is about $10, and 70p is about $1.20.

Northern Ireland issues its own currency, the Ulster pound, worth the same as an English pound. If you'll be traveling in Great Britain, note that English and Ulster pounds are technically interchangeable in both regions, although Ulster pounds are "undesirable" in Britain. Banks in either region will convert your Ulster pounds into English pounds at no charge. Don't worry about the coins, which are accepted throughout Great Britain and Northern Island.

Banking

Throughout Ireland, cash machines are the way to go. Bring an ATM or debit card (with a PIN code—numbers only, no letters) to withdraw funds from cash machines as you travel. Carry a few hundred American dollars as a backup (but bring smaller bills—banks in Ireland have had problems with phony $100 bills, and will not accept them).

Before you go, verify with your bank that your card will work, and alert them that you'll be making withdrawals in Europe; otherwise, the bank may not approve transactions if it perceives unusual spending patterns. Bring two cards in case one gets damaged.

Credit (or debit) cards are handy for booking rooms and transportation tickets over the phone, and necessary for renting a car. In general, Visa and MasterCard are far more widely accepted than American Express.

Traveler's checks are a waste of your time and money. Banks commonly charge a commission fee of €2.50–5 or even more. If you're relying on traveler's checks, it can pay to shop around if there are a few banks nearby. American Express exchange offices don't charge a commission on their checks or any others. The same goes for Thomas Cook checks at Cook offices. This can save you around 1.5 percent. But don't let this cloud your assessment of their exchange rates.

Note that you're charged fees to use ATMs; try to minimize fees by taking out the maximum amount allowable. Whether you use cash machines or banks, you'll save time and money by changing plenty of money at a time. Even in mist-kissed Ireland, you should use a money belt. Thieves target tourists, especially Americans. A money belt provides peace of mind. You can carry lots of cash safely in a money belt—and given the high bank fees, you should.

Damage Control for Lost or Stolen Cards

You can stop thieves from using your ATM, debit, or credit card by reporting the loss immediately to the proper company. Call these 24-hour U.S. numbers collect: Visa (tel. 410/581-9994), MasterCard (tel. 636/722-7111), and American Express (tel. 336/393-1111).

Providing the following information will help expedite the process: the name of the financial institution that issued you the card, full card number, the cardholder's name as printed on the card, billing address, home phone number, circumstances of the loss or theft, and identification verification, including a Social Security Number or birth date and your mother's maiden name. (Packing along a photocopy of the front and back of your cards helps you answer the harder questions.) If you are the secondary cardholder, you'll also need to provide the primary cardholder's identification verification details. You can generally receive a temporary card within two or three business days in Europe.

If you promptly report your card lost or stolen, you typically won't be responsible for any unauthorized transactions on your account, although many banks charge a liability fee of $50.

Tipping

Tipping in Ireland isn't as automatic and generous as it is in the United States, but for special service, tips are appreciated, if not expected. As in the United States, the proper amount depends on your resources, tipping philosophy, and the circumstance, but some guidelines apply.

Restaurants: Tipping is an issue only at restaurants and fancy pubs that have waiters and waitresses. If you order your food at a counter, don't tip.

If the menu states that service is included—generally about 10 percent—there's no need to tip beyond that. If service isn't included, tip about 10 percent by rounding up. You can hand the tip to the waiter together with the amount for the bill.

Taxis: To tip the cabbie, round up. For a typical ride, round up to a maximum of 10 percent (to pay a €4.50 fare, give €5; for a €28 fare, give €30). If the cabbie hauls your bags and zips you to the airport to help you catch your flight, you might want to toss in a little more. But if you feel like you're being driven in circles or otherwise ripped off, skip the tip.

Hotels: Hotels sometimes bill you for a service charge. I don't tip at hotels (whether or not a service charge has been tacked on), but if you're a tipper, give the porter about a euro for carrying bags, and leave a couple euros in your room at the end of your stay for the maid if the room was kept clean.

Special Services: Tour guides at public sites might hold out their hands for tips after they give their spiel; if I've already paid for the tour, I don't tip extra, though some tourists do give a euro, particularly for a job well done. In general, if someone in the service industry does a super job for you, a tip of a euro or two is appropriate...but not required.

When in doubt, ask. If you're not sure whether (or how much) to tip for a service, ask your hotelier or the tourist information office; they'll fill you in on how it's done on their turf.

VAT Refunds for Shoppers

Wrapped into the purchase price of your Irish souvenirs is a 21 percent Value Added Tax (VAT). If you make a purchase at a store that participates in the VAT refund scheme, you're entitled to get most of that tax back. Personally, I've never felt that VAT refunds are worth the hassle (especially if you're spending less than $100), but if you do, here's the scoop.

If you're lucky, the merchant will subtract the tax when you make your purchase (this is more likely to occur if the store ships the goods to your home). Otherwise, here's what you'll need to do:

Get the paperwork. Have the merchant completely fill out the necessary refund document, called a "Tax-Free Shopping Cheque." You'll have to present your passport at the store.

Get your stamp at the border. Have your cheque(s) stamped at your last stop in the European Union (e.g., the airport) by the customs agent who deals with VAT refunds. It's best to keep your purchases in your carry-on for viewing, but if they're too large or dangerous to carry on, then track down the proper customs agent to inspect them before you check your bag. You're not supposed to use your purchased goods before you leave. If you show up at customs wearing your new Irish sweater, officials might look the other way—or deny you a refund.

Collect your refund. You'll need to return your stamped documents to the retailer or its representative. Many merchants work with a service, such as Global Refund or Premier Tax Free, which have offices at major airports, ports, and border crossings. These services, which extract a 4 percent fee, can refund your money immediately in your currency of choice or credit your card (within two billing cycles). If you have to deal directly with the retailer, mail the store your stamped documents, and then wait. It could take months.

Customs Regulations

You can take home $800 in souvenirs per person duty-free. The next $1,000 is taxed at a flat 3 percent. After that, you pay the individual item's duty rate. You can also bring in duty-free a liter of alcohol (slightly more than a standard-sized bottle of wine), a carton of cigarettes, and up to 100 cigars. As for food, anything in cans or sealed jars is acceptable. Skip dried meat, cheeses, and fresh fruits and veggies. To check customs rules and duty rates, visit www. customs.gov.

TRAVEL SMART

Your trip to Ireland is like a complex play—easier to follow and really appreciate on a second viewing. While no one does the same trip twice to gain that advantage, reading this book in its entirety before your trip accomplishes much the same thing.

Reread entire chapters as you travel, and visit local tourist information offices. Upon arrival in a new town, lay the groundwork for a smooth departure. Buy a phone card, and use it for reservations and confirmations. You speak the language—use it! Enjoy the friendliness of the local people. Ask questions. Most locals are eager to point you in their idea of the right direction. Carry a pocket-sized notebook to organize your thoughts. Plan ahead for laundry, post-office chores, and picnics. Mix intense and relaxed periods. Every trip (and every traveler) needs at least a few slack days. Pace yourself. Assume you will return.

Design an itinerary that enables you to hit the various sights at the best possible times. As you read this book, make note of holidays and festivals (see page 324) and days when sights are closed. Sundays have pros and cons, as they do in the United States (special events, limited hours, closed shops and banks, limited public transportation, no rush hours). Saturdays are virtually weekdays. Popular places are even more popular on weekends—especially sunny weekends, which are sufficient cause for an impromptu holiday in this soggy corner of Europe.

Tourist Information

Virtually every town in Ireland has a tourist information center (abbreviated **TI** in this book). Take full advantage of this service. Arrive (or telephone) with a list of questions and a proposed sight-seeing plan. Pick up maps, brochures, and walking-tour information. In Dublin, you can pick up everything you'll need for Ireland in one stop at the TI in the old church on Suffolk Street. The general nationwide tourist information phone number for travelers calling from within Ireland is 1-850-230-330.

For all the help TIs offer, steer clear of their room-finding services (bloated prices, €4 booking fee, no opinions, and they take a 10 percent cut from your B&B host). If you're desperate, their nationwide room booking phone number for travelers calling from within Ireland is 1-800-363-626.

TRANSPORTATION

By Car or Train?

Cars are best for three or more traveling together (especially families with small kids), those packing heavy, and those scouring the countryside. Ireland's far-flung rural charms are most easily experienced by car.

Trains and buses are best for solo travelers, blitz tourists, and city-to-city travelers. Most rail lines spoke outward from Dublin, so you'll need to mix in bus transportation to bridge the gaps. Ireland has a good train-and-bus system, though departures are not as frequent as the European norm. Travelers who don't want (or can't afford) to drive a rental car find they still enjoy their travels using public transportation.

Rails, Wheels, and Wings

Schedules: The best overall source of schedules for public transportation in the Republic, as well as Northern Ireland—including rail, cross-country and city buses, and Dublin's DART and LUAS transit—is the Discover Ireland Web site: www.iol.ie/~discover /rail.htm.

Trains: Ireland's various passes offer a better value than BritRail's pricey "BritRail plus Ireland" pass (see chart on page 19). Irish railpasses can be purchased easily and cheaply in Ireland at major stations (Dublin info tel. 01/836-6222).

If you'd rather use point-to-point tickets, just buy your tickets in Ireland as you go. Fares are often higher for peak travel on Fridays and Sundays. To avoid long station lines in Dublin, you can book train tickets in advance in person or by phone with your credit card at the Iarnrod Éireann Travel Centre (35 Lower Abbey Street, Mon–Fri 9:00–17:00, closed Sat–Sun, tel. 01/703-4070).

Research options in advance by studying Irish train schedules at www.irishrail.ie or listening to a talking timetable at 01/805-4222.

Students are eligible for an **Irish Rail Student Travelcard** (which offers varying discounts per ride), but you have to plan a couple months ahead: Go to www.irishrail.ie, print the application form, get it stamped at your university student travel office, and mail it to Ireland (include 2 passport photos and €12, payable by credit card; they'll mail you the card in 4–6 weeks).

Buses: Buses are about 33 percent slower than trains, but they're also a lot cheaper. Round-trip bus tickets usually cost less than two one-way fares (i.e., Tralee to Dingle costs €9 one-way and €14 round-trip). The Irish distinguish between "buses" (for local runs with lots of stops) and "coaches" (long-distance express runs). On many Irish buses, pop music or sports games are piped throughout the bus; have earplugs handy if you prefer silence.

Railpasses

Prices listed are for 2004. My free *Rick Steves' Guide to European Railpasses* has the latest prices and details (and easy online ordering) at www.ricksteves.com/rail.

BRITRAIL PLUS IRELAND PASS

	1st class	2nd class
5 days out of 1 month	$515	$369
10 days out of 1 month	849	595

This pass covers the entire British Isles (England, Wales, Scotland, Northern Ireland, and the Republic of Ireland), including a round-trip Stena Line ferry crossing between Wales or Scotland and the Emerald Isle during the validity of the pass (okay to leave via one port and return via another). Reserve boat crossings a day or so in advance—sooner for holidays. One child (5-15) travels along free with each pass. Extra kiddies pay half fare; under 5 free.

DEALS ONCE YOU GET TO IRELAND:

These local specials are sold at major train stations in Ireland. €1.20 = about $1 U.S.

Ireland:
Approximate point-to-point one-way 2nd class fares in $US by rail (solid line), bus (dashed line), and ferry (dotted line). First class costs 50% more. Add up fares for your itinerary to see whether a rail and/or bus pass will save you money.

Pass Name	Version	Area	Duration	Price
Emerald Card	Rail & Bus	Republic & North	Any 8 days in 15	€198
			Any 15 days in 30	€341
Irish Explorer	Rail & Bus	Republic only	Any 8 days in 15	€176
Irish Rover	Rail only	Republic & North	Any 5 days in 15	€143
Irish Explorer	Rail only	Republic only	Any 5 days in 15	€116
Irish Rover	Bus only	Republic & North	Any 3 days in 8	€68
			Any 8 days in 15	€152
			Any 15 days in 30	€226
Irish Rambler	Bus only	Republic only	Any 3 days in 8	€53
			Any 8 days in 15	€116
			Any 15 days in 30	€168

SEALINK FERRIES AND CATAMARANS CONNECTING BRITAIN AND IRELAND

British port to...	Irish port	crossings daily	ferry/cat. hrs	ferry/cat. cost
Holyhead	Dun Laoghaire	3	3.5 / 1.5	$35 / $50
Fishguard	Rosslare	6	3.5 / 1.5	$30 / $40
Stranraer	Belfast	6	3.5 / 1.5	$35 / $40
London (RR + boat)	Dublin	1 direct	8.5	$85 / $90

See also www.seaview.co.uk. Dun Laoghaire is a 30-minute bus or train ride from Dublin. Travelers from London to Dublin may find it worthwhile to catch a quick $80 shuttle flight (see www.cheapflights.com). National Express (Britain's Greyhound bus service) offers great London-Dublin bus+ferry tickets for as low as $30 (restrictions apply).

Public Transportation in Ireland

— RAIL
--- BUS
••• BOAT

THIS MAP SHOWS MAJOR RAIL & BUS ROUTES FOR PLACES COVERED IN RICK STEVES' IRELAND BOOK. BUSES PARALLEL MOST RAIL LINES.

PORTRUSH
GIANT'S CAUSEWAY
DERRY
LARNE
TO STRANRAER & TROON (SCOTLAND)
BEL.- PORT. 9/DAY, 2 HRS
DONEGAL
BELFAST
BANGOR/ CULTRA
SLIGO
DUB - BEL 8/DAY, 2 HRS
DROGHEDA
WEST-PORT
DUB - SLIGO 3/DAY, 3 HRS
HOLYHEAD (N. WALES)
GALWAY
DUBLIN
GAL - DUB 5/DAY, 3 HRS
KILKENNY
DUN LAOGHAIRE
ARAN ISLANDS
ENNIS
LIMERICK
WICKLOW
DUB-TRA OR LIM 5/DAY, 4 HRS
DUB - ROS 5/DAY, 3 HRS
TRALEE
LIMERICK JUNCTION
WATERFORD
TO FISHGUARD (S. WALES)
DINGLE
KILLARNEY
BLARNEY CORK
ROSS-LARE
KENMARE
RING.
TO ROSCOFF
TO CHERBOURG (FRANCE)
KINSALE
ROS - TRA 1/DAY, 5 HRS.

Buses pick you up when the trains let you down. From Dublin to Dingle without a car, you'll need to take a train to Tralee and then catch a bus from there. From Dublin to Kinsale without a car, you'll need to take a train to Cork and then a bus from there.

If you're traveling up and down Ireland's west coast, buses are best (or a combination of buses and trains); relying on rail only here is too time-consuming.

Bus stations are normally at or near train stations. The Bus Éireann Expressway Bus Timetable comes in handy (free, available at some bus stations or online at www.buseireann.ie, bus info tel. 01/836-6111).

A couple of companies offer **backpackers' bus circuits.** These hop-on, hop-off bus circuits take mostly youth hostelers around the country super cheaply and easily, with the assumption that they'll be sleeping in hostels along the way. For instance, Paddy Wagon cuts Ireland in half and offers three- or six-day "tours" of each half (north and south) that can be combined into one whole tour connecting Dublin, Cork, Killarney, Dingle, Galway, Westport, Donegal, Derry, and Belfast (3 days/€139, 6 days/€269, 17 Westmoreland Street, Dublin, tel. 01/672-6007, www.paddywagontours.com); they also run one-day tours of Belfast from Dublin (€40, Sat, Sun, and Wed). Tír na nÓg Tours (TEER-nuh-ohg) operates similar three- or six-day trips (similar rates to Paddy Wagon, connecting Dublin, Kilkenny, Cork, Killarney, Tralee, Galway, Westport, Donegal, Derry, and Belfast; 57 Lower Gardiner Street, Dublin, tel. 01/836-4684, www .tirnanogtours.com).

Students can use their ISIC (International Student Identity Card) to get discounts on cross-country coaches (up to 50 percent). Children ages five through 15 pay half-price on trains, and wee ones under five go free.

Flights: If you're connecting Ireland with Britain or the Continent, look into cheap flights offered by Ryanair (Irish tel. 01/609-7878, www.ryanair.com), bmi (British Midland, Irish tel. 01/407-3036, U.S. tel. 800/788-0555, www.flybmi.com), and easyJet (flies in and out of Belfast only, Irish tel. 04894/484-929, British tel. 0870-600-0000, www.easyjet.com). Also consider www .cheapflights.co.uk. Round trips can be cheaper than one way—ask. To get the best prices, it's usually smart to book as soon as you have a date set (the best fares are generally available online, not by phone). Each flight has an allotment of cheap seats; these sell fast, leaving the higher-priced seats for latecomers. (Ryanair is the exception, offering promotional deals throughout the year.)

If you're flying within Ireland, try Aer Arann (Irish tel. 0818-210-210, British tel. 0800-587-2324, tel. from U.S. 011-353-61-704-428, www.aerarann.com). They fly from Dublin to Cork, Kerry, Galway, Knock, Sligo, and Donegal. Be aware that some of these smaller regional airports may not have car rental offices.

Car Rental

To see all of Ireland, I prefer the freedom of a rental car. Connemara, the Ring of Kerry, the Antrim Coast, County Donegal, County Wexford, and the Valley of the Boyne are really only worth it if you have wheels.

Touring Ireland by car is cheapest if arranged in advance through your hometown travel agent. The best rates are weekly, with unlimited mileage or leasing (possible for rentals over 3 weeks). You can pick up and drop off just about anywhere, anytime. But note that people over age 75 can't rent a car in Ireland or Britain.

For a trip that covers both Ireland and Britain, you're better off

AND LEARN THESE ROAD SIGNS

Speed Limit (km/hr)	Yield	No Passing	End of No Passing Zone
One Way	Intersection	Main Road	Freeway
Danger	No Entry	No Entry for cars	All Vehicles Prohibited
Parking	No Parking	Customs	Peace

with two separate car rentals, rather than one rental (because of high ferry costs). You can drive your rental car from the Republic of Ireland into Northern Ireland, but be aware of drop-off charges ($75–150) if you drop it off in the North. You'll pay a smaller drop-off charge ($25–50) for picking up the car at one place and dropping it off at another within the same country (even picking up in downtown Dublin and dropping off at Dublin Airport).

If you pick up the car and stay out of big cities, you're more likely to survive your first day on the Irish roads. Whether you drop the car off early or keep it longer, you'll be credited or charged at a fair, pro-rated price. Big companies have offices in most cities. (Ask

Driving in Ireland: Distance and Time

m = miles
h = hours

to be picked up at your hotel.) Small local rental companies can be cheaper but aren't as flexible.

The Ford 1.3-liter Escort-category car costs about $50 more per week than the smallest cars, but feels better on the motorways and safer on the small roads. Remember, minibuses are a great budget way to go for 5–9 people. An automatic transmission is going to add at least 25 percent to the car rental cost over a manual transmission. Weigh this against the fact that in Ireland, you'll be sitting on the right side of the car and shifting with your left hand...while driving on the left side of the road.

Ireland is tied with Portugal for the most traffic accidents in Western Europe. For peace of mind, consider CDW insurance (Collision Damage Waiver, about 25 percent extra). In case of an accident, CDW coverage offers a relatively low deductible (generally around $950). Some companies allow you to further buy down the deductible to zero (for about $12/day, often can be purchased in advance). It can be a better deal to waive the car rental company's CDW insurance entirely and opt instead for the coverage that comes

Tips on Driving

Driving gives you access to the most rural sights and is my favorite mode of transportation in Ireland. Here's what I've learned in the school of hard brakes and adrenaline rushes:

- The *Complete Road Atlas of Ireland* by Ordnance Survey (€12, handy ring-binder style, 1:210,000 scale) is the most useful Irish road map. It covers every road your car can wedge onto. Flipping to the next page of an atlas is easier to manage in a cramped front seat than wrestling with a large, ungainly folding map. Buy the atlas at the first TI or gas station you come to.

- Study your map before taking off. Know the areas you'll be lacing together, as road numbers are inconsistent.

- Road signs can be confusing, too little, and too late. There are three main kinds of signs: 1) Those with white lettering on a green background are found on major routes and give distances in kilometers. 2) Signs with black lettering on a white background are older and trickier: Distances shown with a "km" following it are in kilometers, while distances with nothing following it are in miles. (The plan is to phase out all signage in miles by the end of 2005 and go metric.) 3) Brown signs with white lettering alert drivers to sights, lodging, and tourist offices.

- Spend time figuring out your lights, wipers, horn, and radio before you're on the road.

- Adjust your sideview mirrors and get in the habit of using them. Many are spring-loaded to snap back into place (a pragmatic solution on narrow roads). Get comfortable with the sound of vegetation whisking the side of your car (it rarely scratches).

- Drive with your lights on all the time to make your vehicle more visible.

- Standard transmissions sip fuel and are much cheaper to rent than automatics. You'll get used to shifting with your left hand. Find reverse...before you need it. (I love the smell of burnt clutch in the morning.)

- Car travel in Ireland isn't fast. When planning your itinerary, estimate your average speed at 40 miles per hour (roughly two-thirds of a mile, or 1 km, per minute). Give your itinerary a reality check by finding distances between destinations on the driving map (page 23) or online (www.viamichelin.com).

• The shortest distance between any two points is usually the motorway (highway). Miss a motorway exit, and you can lose 30 minutes.

• Avoid driving in big cities whenever possible. Most have modern ring roads to skirt the congestion.

• Roundabouts are a snap. Take your time merging—yield to drivers already in the circle.

• When it comes to narrow rural roads, adjust your perceptions of personal space. It's not "my side of the road" or "your side of the road." It's just "the road"—and it's shared as a cooperative adventure. Locals are usually courteous, pulling over against a hedgerow and blinking their headlights to signal you to pass while they wait. Return the favor when you are closer to a wide spot in the road than they are. Pull over frequently—to let faster locals pass, to check the map, or to snap a photo.

• Keep an eye on the road ahead of you, and always expect that a hairpin turn, a slow tractor, a flock of sheep, a one-lane bridge, and a baby stroller are all just around the next blind corner. Honk when approaching blind corners to let oncoming drivers know you're coming.

• Tune in RTE One, the national radio station (89 FM), for long drives. Its interviews and music are an education in Irish culture, as well as just plain good company.

• Make your road trip fun. Establish a cardboard-box pantry of munchies. Keep a rack of liter boxes of juice in the trunk. Buy some Windex and a roll of paper towels for cleaner sightseeing.

• The biggest mistake is getting a late start, which causes you to rush, which makes you miss turns, which causes you stress, which decreases your enjoyment, which makes it feel less like a vacation.

• Travelers who want to use designated disabled parking spaces in Ireland can bring their Disabled Persons Parking Card from the United States (even though the Irish have a different card that they set on their dashboard). For more information, call the Irish Wheelchair Association at tel. 045/893-094 (from the U.S., dial 011-353-45-893-094).

with some credit cards (often with no deductible). MasterCard Platinum and Diners currently seem to be the only companies that allow this in Ireland. Ask your credit-card company how it works, and quiz them about deductibles and worst-case scenarios.

Driving

Your U.S. driver's license is all you need to drive in Ireland. Driving in Ireland is basically wonderful—once you remember to stay on the left, and after you've mastered the roundabouts. But be warned: Every year, I get a few cards from traveling readers advising me that, for

them, trying to drive in Ireland was a nerve-racking and regrettable mistake. To get a little slack on the roads, drop by a gas station or auto shop and buy a red "L" (new driver with license) sign to put in your window. An Irish Automobile Association membership comes with most rentals (www.aaireland.ie). Understand its towing and emergency-road-service benefits.

Gas (petrol) costs over $5 per gallon and is self-serve. Some pumps are unleaded. Seat belts are required by law. Speed limits are 50 kph (roughly 30 mph) in towns, 80 kph (approx. 50 mph) on rural roads (e.g., R-257, R-600, etc.); 100 kph (about 60 mph) on national roads (like N-8, N-30, and so on); and 120 kph (roughly 75 mph) on motorways (e.g., M-1, M-50, etc.). Be very careful with alcohol...the Garda (police) set up random checkpoints, and if you drink more than one pint, you're legally drunk in Ireland.

Parking is confusing. One yellow line marked on the pavement means no parking Monday through Saturday during business hours. Double yellow lines mean no parking at any time. Broken yellow lines mean short stops are OK, but you should always look for explicit signs, or ask a passerby.

Even in small towns, rather than fight for street parking, I just pull into the most central and handy "disk" parking lot I can find. Disks can be bought at nearby shops, and rates are reasonable by U.S. standards. You buy one disk for each hour you want to stay. Scratch off the time you arrived on the disk, and put it on your dashboard. I keep a bag of coins in the ashtray for parking meters and parking voucher machines (no change given for large coins).

COMMUNICATING

Telephones

Use the telephone routinely. You can make long-distance calls directly, cheaply, and easily, and there's no language barrier. Call ahead to reserve or reconfirm rooms, check opening hours, and confirm tour times.

Public Pay Phones: The Irish telephone system is great. Easy-to-find public phone booths are either coin- or card-operated. Phones clearly list which coins they'll take, and a display shows how your money supply's doing. Only completely unused coins will be returned, so put in biggies with caution. (If money's left over, rather than hanging up, push the "make another call" button.)

The more convenient phone-card booths are common. To avoid the hassle of carrying enough coins, you have the following two options:

1. Buy a Telecom Éireann **phone card** (€4, €7, or €15 at newsstands, TIs, and post offices). Insert the card into the phone and dial away.

2. Purchase a cheaper-per-minute **international calling card,** which works from any phone, including the one in your hotel room (see "International Calling Cards," below).

Calling Long Distance Within the Republic of Ireland or Northern Ireland: First dial the area code (which starts with 0), then the local number. You'll find area codes listed throughout this book, or you can get them from directory assistance (dial 11811 in the Republic, 192 in Northern Ireland).

Making International Calls: When dialing internationally, dial the international access code (00 if you're calling from Europe, 011 if you're phoning from the United States or Canada), the country code of the country you're calling, the area code (without its initial 0, if you're calling Ireland), and the local number. For example, Dublin's area code is 01. To call the recommended Harding Hotel in Dublin from the United States or Canada, dial 011 (our international access code), 353 (Ireland's country code), 1 (Dublin's area code without its initial 0), then 679-6500 (the hotel's number).

To call Northern Ireland from the United States, dial 011, 44 (the U.K. country code), 28 (Northern Ireland's area code without its initial 0), then the local number. To call Northern Ireland from the Republic of Ireland, dial 048, then the local number without any area code at all. To call the Republic of Ireland from Northern Ireland, dial 00, 353 (Ireland's country code), the area code without its initial zero, then the local number.

To call my office from anywhere in Ireland, I dial 00 (Europe's international access code), 1 (U.S. country code), 425 (Edmonds' area code), then 771-8303.

For a list of country codes and a handy European calling chart, see the appendix. Remember that Ireland's (and Britain's) time zone is one hour earlier than Continental Europe, and that Ireland is five/eight hours ahead of the East/West Coasts of the United States.

International Calling Cards: The easiest, cheapest way to make international calls from Ireland (figure 5 minutes per dollar to the United States) is by using a pre-paid international calling card, sold at most newsstands, exchange bureaus, and mini-marts. Since you don't insert these cards into the phone, you can use them from anywhere, including your hotel room, avoiding pricey hotel rates.

There are many different brands, so ask the clerk which one has the best rates to wherever you're calling. Because cards are occasionally duds, avoid the high denominations.

To use a card, scratch off the back to reveal your code. After you dial the access phone number, the message tells you to enter your code and then dial the phone number you want to call. To call the United States, see "Making International Calls," above. To make calls within Ireland, dial the area code plus the local number; when using an international calling card, the area code must be dialed even if you're calling across the street. International calling cards work only within the country of purchase, with the exception of some of the Spirit brand cards, usable in both the United Kingdom and the Republic of Ireland (confirm before buying).

To make numerous, successive calls with an international calling card without having to redial the long access number each time, press the keys (see instructions on card) that allow you to launch directly into your next call.

Calling Cards from American Companies: Calling cards offered by AT&T, MCI, and Sprint used to be a good value, until direct-dialing rates dropped and international calling cards appeared. Now it's much cheaper to dial direct using an international calling card—or even just coins.

Mobile Phones: Many travelers buy cheap mobile phones in Europe to make both local and international calls. (Typical American mobile phones don't work in Europe, and those that do have horrendous per-minute costs.) For about $75, you can get a phone with $20 worth of calls that will work in the country where you purchased it. (You can buy more time at newsstands, mobile phone shops, and most pharmacies.) For about $100, you can get a phone that will work in most countries once you pick up the necessary chip per country (about $25). If you're interested, stop by any European shop that sells mobile phones; you'll see prominent store-window displays. Depending on your trip and budget, ask for a phone that works only in Ireland or one that can be used throughout Europe. If you're on a tight budget, skip mobile phones and buy cheap international calling cards instead.

E-mail and Mail

E-mail: More and more hoteliers have e-mail addresses and Web sites (listed in this book). Some family-run pensions can become overwhelmed by the volume of e-mail they receive, so be patient if you don't get an immediate response. If you're leaving soon, don't be immobilized waiting for an e-mail response from a hotel. Give them a quick call to confirm your reservation...or at least find out if they're full, so you can look elsewhere. I've listed some Internet cafés in this book. Your hotelier or TI can steer you to the nearest Internet access point.

Mail: Get stamps at the neighborhood post office, newsstands within fancy hotels, and some mini-marts and card shops. To arrange for mail delivery, reserve a few hotels along your route in advance, and give their addresses to friends. If you have an American Express card, most AmEx offices will hold your mail for you for free. Allow 10 days for a letter to arrive. Phoning and e-mailing are so easy that I've dispensed with mail stops altogether.

SLEEPING

In the interest of smart use of your time, I favor accommodations (and restaurants) handy to your sightseeing activities. Rather than list hotels scattered throughout a city, I choose two or three favorite neighborhoods and recommend the best accommodation values in each, from $20 bunk beds to fancy-for-my-book $200 doubles. Outside of Dublin, you can expect to find good doubles for $80–100, including tax and a cooked breakfast.

I've described my recommended hotels and B&Bs with a standard code. Prices listed are for one-night stays in peak season, include a hearty breakfast (unless otherwise noted), and assume you're booking direct and not through a TI. Prices can soften off-season, for stays of two nights or longer, or for payment in cash (rather than by credit card). Teenagers are generally charged as adults. Little kids sleep almost free.

When establishing prices with a hotelier or B&B owner, confirm whether the charge is per person or per room (if a price is too good to be true, it's probably per person). In this book, room prices are listed per room, not per person.

Many places have three floors of rooms, steep stairs, and no elevator. If you're concerned about stairs, call and ask about ground-floor rooms. Remember that in Europe, the "first floor" is one floor above street level (what we would call the "second floor" back home).

In Ireland, virtually all rooms have sinks. Rooms with a private bathroom (toilet plus shower and/or tub) are called "en suite"; rooms that lack private plumbing are "standard." (If you want a room that contains a private bathroom, specify "en suite"; B&B owners sometimes use the term "private bathroom" for a bathroom down the hall, to which only your room has the key.) As more rooms go en suite, the hallway bathroom is shared with fewer standard rooms. If money's tight, ask for standard rooms.

"Twin" means two single beds, and "double" means one double

bed. If you'll take either one, let them know, or you might be need-lessly turned away.

Ireland has a rating system for hotels and B&Bs. These stars and shamrocks are supposed to imply quality, but I find that they mean only that the place sporting symbols is paying dues to the tourist board. Rating systems often have little to do with value.

Bed-and-Breakfasts

Compared to hotels, bed-and-breakfasts (B&Bs) give you double the cultural intimacy for half the price. In 2005, you'll generally pay €40–55 (about $50–65) per person for a double room in a B&B in Ireland. Prices include a big cooked breakfast. How much coziness, tea, and biscuits (and how many teddy bears) are tossed in varies tremendously.

If you have a reasonable but limited budget, skip hotels. Go the B&B way. If you can use a telephone and speak English, you'll enjoy homey, friendly, clean rooms at a great price by sticking to my list-ings. Always call first.

If you're traveling beyond my recommended destinations, you'll find B&Bs where you need them. Any town with tourists has a TI that books rooms or can give you a list and point you in the right direction. In the absence of a TI, ask people on the street for help.

B&Bs range from large guest houses with 15–20 rooms to small homes renting out a spare bedroom. The philosophy of the manage-ment determines the character of a place more than its size and the facilities offered. Avoid places run as a business by absentee owners. My top listings are run by couples who enjoy welcoming the world to their breakfast table.

The B&Bs I've recommended are nearly all stocking-feet com-fortable. I look for a place that is friendly (i.e., enjoys Americans); located in a central, safe, quiet neighborhood; clean, with firm beds; a good value; not mentioned in other guidebooks (and, therefore, filled mostly with Irish travelers); and willing to hold a room until 16:00 or so without a deposit (though more and more places are requiring a deposit or credit-card number). In certain cases, my rec-ommendations don't meet all of these prerequisites. I'm more impressed by a handy location and a fun-loving philosophy than by hair dryers and shoeshine machines.

A few tips: B&B proprietors are selective as to whom they invite in for the night. Very young children aren't always welcome (ask). Risky-looking people (2 or more single men are often assumed to be troublemakers) find many places suddenly full. If you'll be stay-ing for more than one night, you are "desirable." In popular weekend getaway spots, you're unlikely to find a place to take you for Saturday night only. Sometimes staying several nights earns you a better price—ask about it. If you book through a TI, it takes a 10 percent commission from the proprietor and a €4 booking fee from you. If you book directly, the B&B gets it all (and you'll have a better chance of getting a discount). If my listings are full, ask for guidance. (Mentioning this book can help.) Owners usually work together and can call up an ally to land you a bed.

B&Bs are not hotels; if you want to ruin your relationship with your hostess, treat her like a hotel clerk. Americans often assume they'll get new towels each day. The Irish don't, and neither will you. Hang them up to dry and reuse. Some B&Bs stock rooms with a hot-water pot, cups, tea bags, and coffee packets (if you prefer decaf, buy a jar at a grocery and dump the contents into a baggie for easy packing). B&Bs have plenty of stairs. Expect good exercise and be happy you packed lightly.

In B&Bs, no two showers are alike. Sometimes you'll encounter "telephone" showers—a hand-held nozzle in a bathtub. Many B&Bs have been retrofitted with plumbing, and water is heated individually for each shower, rather than by one central heating system. While the switch is generally left on, in some rooms, you'll have a hot-water switch to consider. Any cord hanging from the ceiling is for lights (not emergencies). Once in the shower, you'll find a multitude of overly clever mechanisms designed to somehow get the right amount and temperature of water. Good luck.

Cheap, Modern Hotels

Hotel chains, offering predictably comfortable accommodations at reasonable prices, are popping up in the centers of big cities in Ireland. The biggies are Jurys Inn (call their hotels directly or book online, reservations tel. 01/607-0000, U.S. tel. 800/423-6953, www.jurysdoyle.com), Comfort/Quality Inns (Republic of Ireland tel. 1-800-500-600, Northern Ireland tel. 0800-444-444, U.S. tel. 800/228-5150, www.choicehotels.com), and Travelodge (also has freeway locations for tired drivers, reservation center in Britain tel. 08700-850-950, www.travelodge.co.uk).

These super-convenient hotels offer simple, clean, and modern rooms for up to four people (2 adults/2 children) for €80–150, depending on the location. You'll likely save as much as €10 per room by booking online. Most rooms have a double bed, single bed, five-foot trundle bed, private shower, WC, and TV. Hotels usually have an attached restaurant, good security, and a 24-hour staffed reception desk. Of course, they're as cozy as a Motel 6, but they're great for families, and many travelers love them. You can book over the phone (or online) with a credit card, then pay when you check in. When you check out, just drop off the key, Lee.

Making Reservations

It's possible to travel at any time of year without reservations, but given the high stakes, erratic accommodation values, number of people traveling with this book, and the quality of the gems I've listed, I highly recommend calling ahead for rooms at least a few days in advance as you travel.

When tourist crowds are down, you might make a habit of calling your hotel between 9:00 and 10:00 on the day you plan to arrive, when the hotel knows who'll be checking out and just which rooms will be available. I've taken great pains to list telephone numbers with long-distance instructions (see page 319). Get a phone card, and use it to confirm and reconfirm as you travel. A hotel receptionist will trust you and hold a room until 16:00 without a deposit, though some will ask for a credit-card number.

Honor your reservations or cancel by phone: Trusting travelers to show up is a huge, stressful issue and a financial risk for small B&B owners. I promised the owners of the places I list that you will be reliable when you make a telephone reservation; please don't let them (or me) down. If you'll be delayed or won't make it, simply call in. Americans are notorious for reserving B&Bs long in advance and never showing up (causing B&B owners to lose money—and respect for Americans). Being late is no problem if you are in telephone contact. Calling long distance is cheap and easy from public phone booths.

While it's generally easy to find a room, a few national holidays jam things up (especially "bank holiday" Mondays) and merit reservations long in advance. Mark these dates in red on your travel calendar: Good Friday; Easter and Easter Monday (March 27 and 28 in 2005); the first Mondays in May, June, and August; Christmas; December 26; and New Year's Day. Monday bank holidays are preceded by busy weekends; book the entire weekend in advance.

If you know exactly which dates you need and really want a particular place, reserve a room before you leave home. To reserve from home, call, e-mail, or fax the hotel. To fax or e-mail, use the form in the appendix (or find it online at www.ricksteves.com/reservation). A two-night stay in August would be "2 nights, 16/8/05 to 18/8/05"—Europeans write the date day/month/year, and hotel jargon uses your day of departure. You'll often receive a message back requesting one night's deposit. Your credit-card number and expiration date will usually be accepted as a deposit, though you may need to send a signed traveler's check or a bank draft in the local currency. If your credit card is the deposit, you can pay with your card or cash when you arrive; if you don't show up, you'll be billed for one night. Reconfirm your reservations a few days in advance for safety (or you may be bumped—really). Also, don't just assume you can extend. Take the time to consider in advance how long you'll stay.

Hostels

Ireland has hostels of all shapes and sizes. They can be historic castles or depressing huts, serene and comfy or overrun by noisy school

Sleep Code

To help you easily sort through the accommodations listed, I've divided the rooms into three categories based on the price for a standard double room with bath.

$$$ **Higher Priced**
$$ **Moderately Priced**
$ **Lower Priced**

To give maximum information with a minimum of space, I use this code to describe accommodations listed in this book. Prices listed in this book are per room, not per person. You can assume a hotel takes credit cards unless you see "cash only" in the listing. Breakfast is included.

S = Single room, or price for one person in a double.

D = Double or twin room. (I specify double- and twin-bed rooms only if they are priced differently, or if a place has only one or the other. When reserving, you should specify.)

T = Three-person room (often a double bed with a single).

Q = Four-person room (adding an extra child's bed to a T is usually cheaper).

b = Private bathroom with toilet and shower or tub.

s = Private shower or tub only. (The toilet is down the hall.)

According to this code, a couple staying at a "Db-€90" hotel would pay a total of €90 (about $110) per night for a room with a private toilet and shower (or tub). The hotel accepts credit cards or cash as payment.

groups. Unfortunately, many of the International Youth Hostel Federation (IYHF) hostels have become overpriced, and, in general, I no longer recommend them. The only time I do is if you're on a very tight budget, want to cook your own meals, or are traveling with a group that likes to sleep on bunk beds in big rooms. But many of the informal private hostels are more fun, easygoing, and cheaper. These alternatives to IYHF hostels are more common than ever, and allow you to enjoy the benefits of hosteling.

If you're traveling alone, hosteling is the best way to conquer hotel loneliness. Hostels are also a tremendous source of local and budget travel information. And if you hostel selectively, you'll enjoy historical and interesting buildings.

Hostels of Europe (www.hostelseurope.com) and the Internet Guide to Hostelling (www.hostels.com) have good listings. Ireland's Independent Holiday Hostels (www.hostels-ireland.com) is a network of 145 independent hostels, requiring no membership and welcoming all ages. All IHH hostels are approved by the Irish Tourist Board.

You'll pay an average of €20 for a bed, €2 for sheets, and €3 for breakfast. Anyone of any age can hostel in Ireland. While there are no membership concerns for private hostels, IYHF hostels require membership. Those without cards simply buy one-night guest memberships for €2.50. You can book online for many hostels.

EATING

Ireland has long been labeled the "land of potatoes," but you'll find modern-day Irish cuisine delicious and varied, from vegetables, meat, and dairy products to fresh and salt-water fish. Try the local specialties wherever you happen to be eating.

The traditional breakfast, the "Irish Fry" (known in the North as the "Ulster Fry"), is a hearty way to start the day—with juice, tea or coffee, cereal, eggs, bacon, sausage, a grilled tomato, sautéed mushrooms, and optional black pudding (made from pigs' blood). Toast is served with butter and marmalade. This meal tides many travelers over until dinner. But there's nothing un-Irish about skipping the "fry"—few locals actually start their day with this heavy traditional breakfast. You can simply skip the heavier fare and enjoy the cereal, juice, toast, and tea.

Many B&Bs don't serve breakfast until 8:00. If you need an early start, ask politely if it's possible. While they may not make you a cooked breakfast, they can usually put out cereal, toast, juice, and coffee.

Picnicking saves time and money. Try boxes of orange juice (pure, by the liter), fresh bread (especially Irish soda bread), tasty Cashel blue cheese, meat, a tube of mustard, local eatin' apples, bananas, small tomatoes, a small tub of yogurt (it's drinkable), rice crackers, gorp or nuts, plain digestive biscuits (the chocolate-covered ones melt), and any local specialties. At open-air markets and supermarkets, you can get produce in small quantities. Supermarkets often have good deli sections, packaged sandwiches, and sometimes salad bars. I often munch a relaxed "meal on wheels" in a car, train, or bus to save 30 precious minutes for sightseeing.

At classier restaurants, look for "early-bird specials," allowing you to eat well and affordably, but early (around 17:30–19:00, last order by 19:00). At a sit-down place with table service, tip around 10 percent—unless the service charge is already listed on the bill (for details, see "Tipping," page 15).

Pub Grub and Beer

Pubs are a fundamental part of the Irish social scene, and whether you're a teetotaler or a beer guzzler, they should be a part of your travel here. Pubs, short for "public houses," serve as the community's living room and gossip center, as well as watering hole. Pub grub gets better every year and is Ireland's best eating value. For around $10–15, you can get a basic budget hot lunch or dinner in friendly surroundings.

Pub menus consist of a hearty assortment of traditional dishes, such as Irish stew (mutton with mashed potatoes, onions, carrots, and herbs); soups and chowders; coddle (bacon, pork sausages, potatoes, and onions stewed in layers); fish-and-chips; collar and cabbage (boiled bacon coated in bread crumbs and brown sugar, then baked and served with cabbage); boxty (potato pancake filled with fish, meat, or vegetables); and champ (potato mashed with milk and onions). Irish bread nicely rounds out a meal. In coastal areas, a lot of seafood is available, such as mackerel, mussels, and Atlantic salmon. There's seldom table service in Irish pubs. Order drinks and meals at the bar. Pay as you order, and don't tip.

I recommend certain pubs, and your B&B host is usually up-to-date on the best neighborhood pub grub. Ask for advice (but adjust for nepotism and cronyism, which run rampant).

When you say "a beer, please" in an Irish pub, you'll get a pint of Guinness (the black beauty with a blonde head). If you want a small beer, ask for a glass or a half pint. Never rush your bartender when he's pouring a Guinness. It takes time—almost sacred time.

The Irish take great pride in their beer. At pubs, long hand pulls are used to pull the traditional, rich-flavored "real ales" up from the cellar. These are the connoisseur's favorites: They're fermented natu-

rally, vary from sweet to bitter, and often include a hoppy or nutty flavor. Experiment with the obscure local microbrews (the best are at the Porter House in Dublin's Temple Bar). Short hand pulls at the bar mean colder, fizzier, mass-produced, and less interesting keg beers. Stout is dark and more bitter, like Guinness. If you don't like Guinness, try it in Ireland. It doesn't travel well and is better in its homeland. Murphy's is a very good, Guinness-like stout, but a bit smoother and milder. For a cold, refreshing, basic, American-style beer, ask for a lager, such as Harp. Ale drinkers swear by Smithwick's. Caffrey's is a satisfying cross between stout and ale. Try the draft cider (sweet or dry)...carefully. Teetotalers can order a soft drink.

Pubs are generally open daily from 11:00 to 23:30 and Sunday from noon to 22:30. Children are served food and soft drinks in pubs (sometimes in a courtyard or the restaurant section). You'll often see signs behind the bar asking that children vacate the premises by 20:00. You must be 18 to order a beer, and the Garda (police) are cracking down hard on pubs that don't enforce this. A cup of darts is free for the asking.

You're a guest on your first night; after that, you're a regular. A wise Irishman once said, "It never rains in a pub." The relaxed, informal atmosphere feels like a refuge from daily cares. Women traveling alone need not worry—you'll become part of the pub family in no time.

Craic (pron. "crack"), the art of conversation, is the sport that accompanies drinking in a pub. People are there to talk. To encourage conversation, stand or sit at the bar, not at a table.

The Irish government passed a law in 2004 making all pubs in the Republic smoke-free. Smokers now take their pint outside, turning alleys into covered smoking patios. An incredulous Irishman responded to the new law by saying, "What will they do next? Ban drinking in pubs? We'll never get to heaven if we don't die."

It's a tradition to buy your table a round, and then for each person to reciprocate. If an Irishman buys you a drink, thank him by saying, *"Go raibh maith agat"* (guh rov mah UG-ut). Offer him a toast in Irish—*"Slainte"* (SLAWN-chuh), the equivalent of "cheers." A good excuse for a conversation is to ask to be taught a few words of Gaelic.

Here's a goofy excuse for some *craic:* Ireland—small as it is—has many dialects. People from Cork are famous for talking very fast (and in a squeaky voice)—so fast, that some even talk in letters alone. ABCD fish? (Anybody see the fish?) DR no fish. (There are no fish.) DR fish. (There are fish.) CDBDIs? (See the beady eyes?) OIBJ DR fish. (Oh aye, be Jeeze, there are fish.) For a possibly more appropriate spin, replace the fish with "bird" (girl). This is obscure, but your pub neighbor may understand and enjoy hearing it. If nothing else, you won't seem so intimidating to him anymore.

Traditional Irish Music

Traditional music is alive and popular in pubs throughout Ireland. "Sessions" (musical evenings) may be planned and advertised or impromptu. Traditionally, musicians just congregate and play for the love of it. There will generally be a fiddle, a flute or tin whistle, a guitar, a *bodhrán* (goatskin drum), and maybe an accordion or mandolin. Things usually get going around 21:30 or 22:00. Last call for drinks is around 23:30.

The music often comes in sets of three songs. The wind and string instruments embellish melody lines with lots of tight ornamentation. Whoever happens to be leading determines the next song only as the song the group is playing is about to be finished. If he wants to pass on the decision, it's done with eye contact and a nod. A *ceilidh* (KAY-lee) is an evening of music and dance...an Irish hoedown.

Percussion generally stays in the background. The *bodhrán* (BO-run) is played with a small, two-headed club. The performer's hand stretches the skin to change the tone and pitch. You'll sometimes be lucky enough to hear a set of bones crisply played. These are two cow ribs (boiled and dried) that are rattled in one hand like spoons or castanets, substituting for the sound of dancing shoes in olden days.

Watch closely if a piper is playing. The Irish version of bagpipes, the *uilleann* (ILL-in) pipes are played by inflating the airbag (under the left elbow) with a bellows (under the right elbow), rather than with a mouthpiece like the Scottish Highland bagpipes. *Uilleann* is Gaelic for "elbow," and the sound is more melodic, with a wider range than the Highland pipes. The piper fingers his chanter like a flute to create individual notes and uses the heel of his right hand to play chords on one of three regulator pipes. It takes amazing coordination to play this instrument well, and the sound can be haunting.

Occasionally, the fast-paced music will stop, and one person will sing a "lament." Called *sean nos* (Gaelic for "old style"), this slightly nasal vocal style may be a remnant of the ancient storytelling tradition of the bards whose influence died out when Gaelic culture waned 400 years ago. This is the one time when the entire pub will stop to listen as sad lyrics fill the smoke-stained room. Stories—often of love lost, emigration to a far-away land, or a heroic rebel death struggling against English rule—are always heartfelt. Spend a lament studying the faces in the crowd.

A session can be magical or lifeless. If the chemistry is right, it's one of the great Irish experiences. The music churns intensely, while members of the group casually enjoy exploring each other's musical style. The drummer dodges the fiddler's playful bow with his half-ash cigarette sticking straight from the middle of his mouth. Sipping their pints, they skillfully maintain a faint but steady buzz. The floor on the musicians' platform is stomped paint-free, and barmaids scurry artfully through the commotion, gathering towers of empty, cream-crusted glasses. Make yourself right at home, "playing the boot" (tapping your foot) under the table in time with the music. Talk to your neighbor. Locals often have an almost evangelical interest in explaining the music.

TRAVELING AS A TEMPORARY LOCAL

We travel all the way to Europe to enjoy differences—to become temporary locals. You'll experience frustrations. There are certain truths that we find God-given and self-evident, such as cold beer, ice in drinks, sunshine, bottomless cups of coffee, and driving on the right side of the road. One of the benefits of travel is the eye-opening realization that there are logical, civil, and even better alternatives. A willingness to go local ensures that you'll enjoy a full dose of hospitality.

When updating this book, I hear over and over again that my

readers are considerate and fun to have as guests. Thank you for traveling as temporary locals who are sensitive to the culture. It's a joy to follow you in my travels.

Send Me a Postcard, Drop Me a Line

If you enjoy a successful trip with the help of this book and would like to share your discoveries, please fill out the survey at www.ricksteves .com/feedback or e-mail me at rick@ricksteves.com. I personally read and value all feedback.

Judging from all the happy postcards I receive from travelers who have used this book, it's safe to assume you'll enjoy a great, affordable vacation—with the finesse of an independent, experienced traveler.

Thanks, and happy travels!

BACK DOOR TRAVEL PHILOSOPHY
From *Rick Steves' Europe Through the Back Door*

Travel is intensified living—maximum thrills per minute and one of the last great sources of legal adventure. Travel is freedom. It's recess, and we need it.

Experiencing the real Europe requires catching it by surprise, going casual..."through the Back Door."

Affording travel is a matter of priorities. (Make do with the old car.) You can travel—simply, safely, and comfortably—virtually anywhere in Europe for $100 a day plus transportation costs (allow more for Dublin). In many ways, spending more money only builds a thicker wall between you and what you came to see. Europe is a cultural carnival, and, time after time, you'll find that its best acts are free and the best seats are the cheap ones.

A tight budget forces you to travel close to the ground, meeting and communicating with the people, not relying on service with a purchased smile. Never sacrifice sleep, nutrition, safety, or cleanliness in the name of budget. Simply enjoy the local-style alternatives to expensive hotels and restaurants.

Extroverts have more fun. If your trip is low on magic moments, kick yourself and make things happen. If you don't enjoy a place, maybe you don't know enough about it. Seek the truth. Recognize tourist traps. Give a culture the benefit of your open mind. See things as different, but not better or worse. Any culture has much to share.

Of course, travel, like the world, is a series of hills and valleys. Be fanatically positive and militantly optimistic. If something's not to your liking, change your liking. Travel is addictive. It can make you a happier American, as well as a citizen of the world. Our Earth is home to six billion equally important people. It's humbling to travel and find that people don't envy Americans. They like us, but, with all due respect, they wouldn't trade passports.

Globe-trotting destroys ethnocentricity. It helps you understand and appreciate different cultures. Travel changes people. It broadens perspectives and teaches new ways to measure quality of life. Many travelers toss aside their hometown blinders. Their prized souvenirs are the strands of different cultures they decide to knit into their own character. The world is a cultural yarn shop. And Back Door travelers are weaving the ultimate tapestry. Come on, join in!

REPUBLIC
OF IRELAND

Though a relatively small island, Ireland has had a disproportion-
ately large impact on the rest of the world. For hundreds of years,
Ireland's greatest export has been its friendly yet feisty people.
Geographically isolated in the damp attic of Dark Age Europe,
Christian Irish monks tended the flickering flame of literacy, then
bravely reintroduced it to the barbaric Continent. Later, pressure
from wars and famines at home (combined with opportunities
abroad) compelled many Irish to leave their island and scramble for
a better life in far-flung America, Canada, and Australia.

The Republic of Ireland is just over 80 years old, but its inhabitants proudly claim their nation to be the only modern independent
state to sprout from purely Celtic roots (the Romans never bothered
to come over and organize the wild Irish). Through the persuasive
and culturally enlightened approach of early missionaries, such as St.
Patrick, Ireland may also be the only country to have initially converted to Christianity without bloodshed. Irish culture absorbed the
influences of Viking raiders and Norman soldiers of fortune, eventually enduring the 750-year shadow of English occupation.

Just a few decades ago, Ireland was an isolated agricultural economic backwater that had largely missed out on the Industrial
Revolution. But membership in the European Union 30 years ago
began to turn things around, and the Irish government instituted far-
sighted tax laws to entice foreign corporations to set up shop here.

Today, the Republic enjoys a renaissance as its Celtic Tiger
economy—the strongest in the EU—attracts expatriate Irish and
new foreign investment. And as the only English-speaking country
to have adopted the euro currency, Ireland is an appealing place for
U.S. corporations to set up shop as a beachhead on European turf.
More than 40 percent of the Irish population is under 25 years old,
leading many high-tech and pharmaceutical firms to take advantage

Republic of Ireland

ATLANTIC OCEAN

50 MILES
50 KM

N

PORTRUSH   GIANT'S CAUSEWAY   TO EDINBURGH VIA TROON & STRANRAER SCOTLAND
DUNFANAGHY   BUSH-MILLS
DONEGAL   • DERRY
                NORTHERN   AIR-PORT
            OMAGH •   • BANGOR   TO LIVER-POOL
DRUMCLIFFE   IRE.   BELFAST
            BELLEEK •   MOURNE MTNS.
KNOCK   • STROKESTOWN   I R I S H
WEST-PORT   REPUBLIC   NEW-   S E A
                OF   GRANGE
CONNEMARA   IRELAND   • TRIM   TO LIVER-POOL
GALWAY   AIR-PORT • DUBLIN
ARAN ISLANDS   THE   TO LONDON VIA HOLYHEAD (WALES)
CLIFFS OF MOHER   BURREN   WICKLOW   DUN LAOGHAIRE
            C L A R E   MTNS.
              • ENNIS   • GLENDA-LOUGH
              SHANNON AIRPORT
            LIMERICK   ROCK OF CASHEL   • KILKENNY
• TRALEE • AIRPORT   • WATERFORD
DINGLE   • KILLARNEY   ROSSLARE
KERRY   AIR-PORT   • BLARNEY   • ARDMORE   TO LONDON VIA FISHGUARD (WALES)
   • KENMARE   • COBH
   • BANTRY   CORK
BANTRY BAY   KINSALE
                              TO PARIS VIA ROSSCOFF & CHERBOURG

DCH

of this young, well-educated labor force. Microsoft, Intel, Dell, Gateway, Apple, and IBM all have factories here (welcome to the "Silicon Bog"). Pfizer makes Viagra in Ringaskiddy, County Cork. And for the first time, Ireland has also become a destination for Third World emigrants seeking a better life...a switch from the days when Irish fled to start new lives abroad.

Other aspects of modern life are making inroads in traditional Ireland. In 2003, shops began charging customers 15 cents for plastic sacks for carrying goods, which has caused locals to conserve and re-use bags rather than litter. In 2004, smoking was banned in all Irish pubs. Some pubkeepers grumble about lost business, but the smokers seem happy to take their pints out onto the street (at least in summer).

How Big, How Many, How Much

- The Republic of Ireland is 27,000 square miles (slightly larger than West Virginia).
- The population is 4 million (148 per square mile, increasing slowly, 91 percent Catholic).
- 1 euro (€) = about $1.20.

The resilient Irish character was born of dark humor, historical reverence, and an optimistic, "we'll get 'em next time" rebel spirit. Though the influence of the Catholic Church is less apparent these days, it still plays a major part in Irish life. The national radio and TV station, RTE, pauses for 30 seconds at noon and 18:00 to broadcast the chimes of the Angelus bells. The country is small enough that radio broadcasts manage to cover traffic snarls nationwide, rather than citywide.

The vast majority of Irish people speak English, but you'll be treated to some Irish Gaelic if you venture to the western Irish fringe. Road signs everywhere are in both English and Irish.

At first glance, Ireland's landscape seems unspectacular, with few mountains over 3,000 feet and an interior consisting of grazing pastures and peat bogs. But its seductive beauty slowly grows on you. The gentle rainfall, called "soft weather" by the locals, really does create 40 shades of green—and quite a few rainbows as well. Ancient, moss-covered ring forts crouch in lush valleys, while stone-strewn monastic ruins and lone castle turrets brave the wind on nearby hilltops. Charming fishing villages dot the coast near rugged, wave-battered cliffs. Slow down to contemplate the checkerboard patterns created by the rock walls outlining the many fields. Examine the colorful small-town shopfronts that proudly state the name of the proprietor.

DUBLIN

With reminders of its stirring history and rich culture on every corner, Ireland's capital and largest city is a sightseer's delight. Dublin's fair city will have you humming, "Cockles and mussels, alive, alive-O."

Founded as a Viking trading settlement in the 9th century, Dublin grew to be a center of wealth and commerce second only to London in the British Empire. Dublin, the seat of English rule in Ireland for 700 years, was the heart of a "civilized" Anglo-Irish area (eastern Ireland) known as "the Pale." Anything "beyond the Pale" was considered uncultured and almost barbaric...purely Irish.

The Golden Age of English Dublin was the 18th century. The British Empire was on a roll, and Dublin was right there with it. Largely rebuilt during this Georgian era, Dublin—even with its tattered edges—became an elegant and cultured capital.

Then nationalism and human rights got in the way. The ideas of the French Revolution inspired Irish intellectuals to buck British rule, and after the Rebellion of 1798, life in Dublin was never quite the same. But the 18th century left a lasting imprint on the city. Squares and boulevards in the Georgian style (that's British for "neoclassical") gave the city an air of grandness. The National Museum, National Gallery, and many government buildings are in the Georgian section of town. Few buildings (notably Christ Church Cathedral and St. Patrick's Cathedral) survive from before this Georgian period.

In the 19th century, with the closing of the Irish Parliament, the famine, and the beginnings of the struggle for independence, Dublin was treated—and felt—more like a colony than a partner. The tension culminated in the Easter Rising of 1916, independence from Britain, and the tragic civil war. With many of its elegant streets left in ruins, Dublin emerged as the capital of the only former colony in Europe.

While bullet-pocked buildings and dramatic statues keep memories of Ireland's recent struggle for independence alive, it's boom time now, and the city is looking to a bright future. Locals are enjoying the strong "Celtic Tiger" economy, while visitors enjoy a big-town cultural scene wrapped in a small-town smile.

Planning Your Time

On a three-week trip through Ireland, Dublin deserves three nights and two days. Consider this aggressive sightseeing plan:

Day 1: 10:30-Trinity College guided walk; 11:00-Book of Kells and Old Library; 12:00-Browse Grafton Street and have lunch there, or picnic on Merrion Square; 13:30-Visit Number Twenty-Nine Georgian House; 15:00-National Museum; 17:00-Return to hotel, rest, have dinner—eat well for less during early-bird specials; 19:30-Evening walk (musical or literary); 22:00-Irish music in Temple Bar area.

Day 2: 10:00-Dublin Castle tour; 11:00-Choose between self-guided O'Connell Street Stroll or guided historical walking tour; 13:00-Lunch; 14:00-Kilmainham Jail; 15:30-Visit Guinness Storehouse brewery and finish with view of city; Evening-Catch a play, concert, or Comhaltas traditional music in Dun Laoghaire (DUN-leary).

ORIENTATION

(area code: 01)

Sprawling greater Dublin is home to over a million people—nearly a third of the country's population. But the center of touristic interest is a tight triangle between O'Connell Bridge, St. Stephen's Green, and Christ Church Cathedral. Within this triangle, you'll find Trinity College (home to the Book of Kells), Grafton Street (top pedestrian shopping zone), Temple Bar (trendy and touristy nightlife center), Dublin Castle, and the hub of most city tours and buses. The only major sights outside your easy-to-walk triangle are the Kilmainham Jail and the Guinness Storehouse (both west of the center).

The River Liffey cuts the town in two. Focus on the southern half, where nearly all your sightseeing will take place. Dublin's wide main drag, O'Connell Street, starts north of the river at the Parnell monument and runs south, down to the central O'Connell Bridge. After crossing the bridge, it continues south as the major city axis (as Westmoreland Street and then Grafton Street) to St. Stephen's Green.

The suburban port of Dun Laoghaire (described on page 79) lies south of Dublin, 20 minutes away by DART commuter train. Travelers connecting by ferry to Holyhead in Wales—or those just looking for a mellow town to sleep in outside of urban Dublin—can easily home-base here.

Greater Dublin

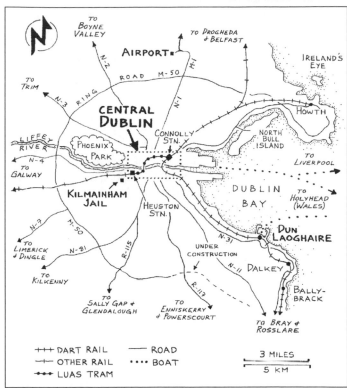

```
+++ DART RAIL        ──── ROAD
─┼─ OTHER RAIL       •••• BOAT
•••• LUAS TRAM
```

3 MILES

5 KM

Tourist Information

Dublin's main tourist information office (TI) is a big shop with little to offer other than promotional fliers and long lines (Mon–Sat 9:00–17:30, Sun July–Sept only 10:30–15:00, located in a former church on Suffolk Street, 1 block off Grafton Street, tel. 01/605-7700, www.visitdublin.com). It has a car-rental agency, bus-info desk, café, and traditional knickknacks. But perhaps its greatest value is the chance to peruse the rack opposite the info counter and pick up brochures for destinations throughout Ireland. There's also a TI at the airport (daily 8:00–22:00) and one at the Dun Laoghaire ferry terminal (Mon–Sat 10:00–13:00 & 14:00–18:00, closed Sun).

While you can buy the TI's lousy map for €0.50, its free newspaper, *The Guide to Dublin*, has the same one on its staple page. The handy *Dublin's Top Visitor Attractions* booklet has a small map and the latest on all of the town's sights—many more than I list here (€3, sold at TI bookshop without any wait). For a schedule of happenings in town, check the minimal calendar of events inside *The Guide to Dublin* newspaper (free at TI).

The excellent *Collins Illustrated Dublin Map* (€6 at TIs and newsstands) is the ultimate city map, listing just about everything of interest, along with helpful opinions.

Dublin Pass: This new sightseeing pass can be a good deal if you like to visit lots of sights quickly (€29/1 day, €49/2 days, €59/3 days, cheaper for kids, sold at all 3 TIs but not at sights, www .dublinpass.com). The pass might save you a little time, because it allows you to bypass ticket-buyer lines—though the lines at included sights generally aren't very long. It covers museums, churches, liter-ature-related sights, and expensive stops like the Guinness Storehouse and the Old Jameson Distillery, plus the Aircoach air-port bus (but not Airlink). However, the pass doesn't include the famous Book of Kells or any bus tours or walking tours, and many of the sights it claims to "cover" (such as the National Gallery and the Chester Beatty Library) are actually free.

Arrival in Dublin

By Train: Dublin has two stations. Heuston Station, on the west end of town, serves west and southwest Ireland (30-min walk from O'Connell Bridge; take taxi or bus #90 instead, see below). Connolly Station—which serves the north, northwest, and Rosslare—is closer to the center (10-min walk from O'Connell Bridge). Each station has a baggage-check facility and ATMs.

The two train stations are connected by the red line of the new LUAS commuter train (see "Getting Around Dublin," page 48) and by bus. Bus #90 runs along the river, linking both train stations, the bus station, and the city center (€0.85, 6/hr). When you're leaving Dublin and you want to reach Heuston Station from the city center, catch bus #90 on the south side of the river; to get to Connolly Station and the Busaras bus station from the city center, catch #90 on the north side of the river.

By Bus: Bus Éireann, Ireland's national bus company, uses the Busaras Central Bus Station next to Connolly Station (10-min walk or short bus ride to the city center; see bus #90 info in "By Train," above).

By Ferry: Irish Ferries docks at the mouth of the River Liffey (near the town center), while the Stena Line docks at Dun Laoghaire (easy DART train connections into Dublin, 4/hr, 20 min).

By Plane: The airport has ATMs, change bureaus, car-rental agencies, baggage check, a café, and a supermarket at the parking lot. Taxis from the airport into Dublin cost about €25, to Dun Laoghaire about €40.

Airport Buses: Consider buying a Rambler city-bus pass, which covers the Airlink bus into town (see "Getting Around Dublin," page 48)—but read this first to see if Airlink is best for you. To get to the recommended accommodations in the **city center,** take Airlink bus #748 (not #747) and ask the driver which stop is closest to your hotel (€5, pay driver, 2/hr, 40 min, connects airport with Heuston train station and the Busaras bus station, near Connolly train station). **Dun Laoghaire** is also served by Airlink (bus #746). But for the **St. Stephen's Green** neighborhood, the Aircoach is a better bet (€7, covered by new Dublin Pass but not Rambler city-bus pass, 4/hr, runs 5:30–22:30; pay driver and confirm best stop for your hotel, tel. 01/844-7118, www.aircoach.ie).

City Bus: To get from the airport cheaply to downtown Dublin, take the city bus from the airport; buses marked #16A, #41, #41B, and #41C go to O'Connell Street (€1.65, exact change required, 4/hr, 90 min).

Helpful Hints

High Costs: Thanks to its recent "Celtic Tiger" economic boom, Ireland now rivals Finland as Europe's most expensive country. A pint of beer in a Dublin pub can cost €4. Restaurants and lodging—other than hostels—are more expensive the closer you get to the touristy Temple Bar district (see cheaper options listed in "Sleeping," page 68). Look for pub grub "carvery" lunch or dinner options (usually less than €10), and consider cheap picnics once in a while. If you're staying at a big hotel, don't pay for the expensive optional €10–15 breakfast—you'll likely find a nearby local café that serves breakfast for half that. If you're doing a lot of sightseeing, the Dublin Pass can save money (see "Tourist Information," above).

Tourist Victim Support Service: This thoughtful service can be helpful if you run into any problems (Mon–Sat 10:00–18:00, Sun 12:00–18:00, tel. 01/478-5295).

U.S. Embassy: It's on 42 Elgin Road in the Ballsbridge neighborhood (Mon–Fri 8:30–17:00 for passport concerns, tel. 01/668-7122 or 01/668-8777, www.usembassy.ie).

Internet Access: There are Internet cafés on nearly every street. South of the River Liffey, try Central Cybercafé (Mon–Fri 9:00–22:00, Sat–Sun 10:00–21:00, 6 Grafton Street, tel. 01/677-8298). Global Internet Café is north of the Liffey (Mon–Fri 8:00–23:00, Sat 9:00–23:00, Sun 10:00–23:00, 8 Lower O'Connell Street, tel. 01/878-0295).

Laundry: Capricorn Launderette, a block southwest of Jurys Inn Christ Church on Patrick Street, is full-service only. Allow four hours and about €9 for a load (Mon–Fri 7:30–20:00, Sat 9:00–18:00, closed Sun, tel. 01/473-1779). The All-American Launderette offers self- and full-service options (Mon–Sat 8:30–19:00, Sun 10:00–23:00, 40 South Great George's Street, tel. 01/677-2779).

Car Rental: For Dublin car-rental information, see the appendix.

Festivals: St. Patrick's Day is a five-day extravaganza in Dublin (www.stpatricksday.ie). June 16 is Bloomsday, dedicated to the Irish author James Joyce and featuring the Messenger Bike Rally. On rugby weekends (about 4 per year), hotels raise their prices and are packed. Book ahead during festival times and for any weekend.

Getting Around Dublin

You'll do most of Dublin on foot. Big, green buses are cheap and cover the city thoroughly. Most lines start at the four quays (pron. "keys"), or piers, nearest O'Connell Bridge. If you're away from the center, nearly any bus takes you back downtown. Tell the driver where you're going, and he'll ask for €0.85, €1.25, €1.45, or €1.65, depending on the number of stops. Bring exact change or lose any excess.

Passes: The bus office at 59 Upper O'Connell Street has free "route network" maps and sells Rambler and Short-Hop city-bus passes. The three-day Rambler costs €10 and covers the Airlink airport bus (but not Aircoach buses or DART trains). The three-day Short Hop pass, which costs €15, includes DART trains (but not Airlink or Aircoach buses). Passes are also sold at each TI (bus info tel. 01/873-4222).

DART: Speedy commuter trains run along the coast, connecting Dublin with Dun Laoghaire's ferry terminal and recommended B&Bs. Think of the DART line as a giant "C" that serves coastal suburbs from Bray in the south to Howth in the north (€1.80, 4/hr, 20 min, runs 6:30–23:30, tel. 01/703-3504, www.irishrail.ie).

LUAS: The city's new light rail and subway system has two main lines (red and green) that serve inland suburbs. The more useful line for travelers is the red line, connecting the Connolly and Heuston train stations (€1.30, 6/hr, runs 5:30–00:30, tel. 1-800-676-464, www.luas.ie).

Taxi: Cabbies are honest, plentiful, friendly, and good sources of information (€2.75 minimum fare, €0.50 surcharge per bag, figure €7 or less for most downtown rides, €30 per hour for a guided joyride from most any cab).

TOURS

While the physical treasures of Dublin are mediocre by European standards, the city has a fine story to tell, and people with a natural knack for telling it. It's a good town for walking tours, and the competition is fierce. Pamphlets touting creative walks are posted all over town. There are medieval walks, literary walks, 1916 Easter Rising walks, Georgian Dublin walks, and more. The evening walks are great ways to meet other travelers.

▲▲**Historical Walking Tour**—This is your best introductory walk. A group of hardworking history graduates—many of whom claim

Dublin

* NOT TO SCALE –
O'CONNELL BRIDGE
TO CHRISTCHURCH
ST. STEPHEN'S GREEN,
OR PARNELL SQUARE
IS A 15 MIN. WALK

to have done more than just kiss the Blarney Stone—enliven Dublin's basic historic strip (Trinity College, Old Parliament House, Dublin Castle, and Christ Church Cathedral). You'll get the story of their city, from its Viking origin to the present. Guides speak at length about the roots of Ireland's struggle with Britain. As you listen to your guide's story, you stand in front of buildings that aren't much to see, but are lots to talk about (April–Sept daily at 11:00 and 15:00; Oct–March only Fri, Sat, and Sun at 12:00). From May to September, the same group offers more focused tours (1916 Easter Rising "Terrible Beauty" walks, juicy slice-of-old-life Dublin "Sexual History of Ireland" walks, and gritty "Architecture and Society" walks; call for current schedule). All walks last two hours and cost €10 (but get the €8 "student" discount rate with this book in 2005, depart from front gate of Trinity College, private tours available, tel. 01/878-0227, mobile 087-830-3523, www.historicalinsights.ie).

The 1916 Rebellion company offers, as you might guess, **1916 Rebellion Walks** (€10, €1 discount with this book in 2005, 2 hrs, mid-April–Sept Mon–Sat at 11:30 and 14:30, Sun at 13:00, depart from International Bar at 23 Wicklow Street, mobile 086/858-3847, www.1916rising.com).

▲**Dublin Literary Pub Crawl**—Two actors take 30 or so tourists on a walk, stopping at four pubs. Half the time is spent enjoying their entertaining banter, which introduces the novice to the high *craic* (conversation) of Joyce, O'Casey, and Yeats. The two-hour tour is punctuated with 20-minute pub breaks (free time). While the beer lubricates the social fun, it dilutes the content of the evening (€11, €1 discount with this book in 2005, April–Nov daily at 19:30, plus Sun at noon; Dec–March Thu–Sun only; you can normally just show up, but call ahead in July–Aug, when it can fill up; meet upstairs in Duke Pub, off Grafton on Duke Street, tel. 01/670-5602, www.dublinpubcrawl.com).

▲▲**Traditional Irish-Music Pub Crawl**—This is similar to the Literary Pub Crawl, but features music. You meet upstairs at 19:30 at Gogarty's Pub (Temple Bar area, corner of Fleet and Anglesea) and spend 40 minutes each in the upstairs rooms of three pubs listening to two musicians talk about, play, and sing traditional Irish music. While having only two musicians makes the music a bit thin (Irish music aficionados will tell you you're better off just finding a good session), the evening, though touristy, is not gimmicky. It's an education in traditional Irish music. The musicians demonstrate a few instruments and really enjoy introducing rookies to their art (€11, €1 discount with this book in 2005, beer extra, April–Oct nightly, Nov and Feb–March Fri–Sat only, no tours Dec–Jan, allow 2.5 hrs, expect up to 50 tourists, tel. 01/475-3313, www.musicalpubcrawl.com).

▲**Hop-on, Hop-off Bus Tours**—Two companies (Dublin City Tours and City Sightseeing/Guide Friday) offer hop-on, hop-off bus tours of Dublin, doing virtually identical 90-minute circuits, allowing you to get on or off at your choice of about 19 stops. Buses are mostly topless, with running live commentaries. Both companies go to the Guinness Storehouse, but City Sightseeing/Guide Friday buses stop at Kilmainham Jail (instead of Phoenix Park). Buy your ticket on board. Each company's map, free with your ticket, details various discounts you'll get at Dublin's sights (usually the Guinness Storehouse, Viking Splash tour, Old Jameson Distillery, Dublin Writers' Museum, Dublinia, Christ Church Cathedral, and others). Your ticket is valid for 24 hours from the time you buy it (daily, 4/hr 9:30–17:30, until 18:30 in summer). **Dublin City Tour** runs the green-and-cream buses with drivers that do the narration (€12.50, tel. 01/873-4222). **City Sightseeing** (red buses) and **Guide Friday** (yellow buses) cost more, but come with a guide and a driver, rather than a driver who guides (€14, tel. 01/872-9010).

▲**Viking Splash Tours**—If you'd like to ride in a WWII amphibious vehicle—driven by a Viking-costumed guide who's as liable to spout history as he is to growl—this is for you. The tour starts with a group roar from the Viking within us all. At first, the guide talks as if he were a Viking ("When we came here in 841..."), but soon the patriot emerges as he tags Irish history onto the sights you pass. Near the end of the 75-minute tour (punctuated by occasional group roars at passersby), you don a life jacket for a slow spin up and down a boring canal. Kids who expect a Viking splash may feel they've been trapped in a classroom, but historians will enjoy the talk more than the gimmick (€16, Feb–Nov daily 10:30–17:00, none Dec–Jan, depart about hourly from Bull Alley beside St. Patrick's Cathedral, ticket office at 64–65 Patrick Street, on gray days boat is covered, but still breezy—dress warmly, tel. 01/707-6000, www.vikingsplashtours.com).

SIGHTS

Trinity College

Founded in 1592 by Queen Elizabeth I to establish a Protestant way of thinking about God, Trinity has long been Ireland's most prestigious college. Originally the student body was limited to rich Protestant males. Women were admitted in 1903, and Catholics—though allowed entrance by the school much earlier—were given formal permission to study at Trinity in the 1970s. Today, half of Trinity's 12,500 students are women, and 70 percent are culturally Catholic (although only about 20 percent of Irish youth are churchgoing).

▲▲**Trinity College Tour**—Trinity students organize and lead 30-minute tours of their campus (look for ticket-seller on a

Dublin at a Glance

▲▲▲**National Museum** Interesting collection of Irish treasures from the Stone Age to today. **Hours**: Tue–Sat 10:00–17:00, Sun 14:00–17:00, closed Mon.

▲▲▲**Kilmainham Gaol** Historic jail used by the British as a political prison, today a moving museum honoring the suffering of the Irish people. **Hours**: April–Sept daily 9:30–18:00, Oct–March 9:30–17:00.

▲▲▲**Trinity Old Library** Contains the exquisite illuminated manuscript, the Book of Kells, the most important piece of art from the Dark Ages. **Hours**: June–Sept Mon–Sat 9:30–17:00, Sun 9:30–16:30; Oct–May Mon–Sat 9:30–17:00, Sun 12:00–16:30.

▲▲**Trinity College** Ireland's most famous school, best visited with a 30-minute tour led by one of its students. **Hours**: Late May–Sept daily 10:30–15:30, weather permitting.

▲▲**Dublin Castle** The city's historic 700-year-old castle, featuring ornate English state apartments, tourable only with a guide. **Hours**: Two tours per hour, Mon–Fri 10:00–17:00, Sat–Sun 14:00–17:00.

▲▲**Number Twenty-Nine Georgian House** Restored 18th-century house providing an intimate glimpse of middle-class Georgian life. **Hours**: Tue–Sat 10:00–17:00, Sun 14:00–17:00, closed Mon.

▲▲**Grafton Street** The city's liveliest pedestrian shopping mall. **Hours**: Always open.

▲▲**O'Connell Bridge** Landmark bridge spanning the River Liffey at the center of Dublin. **Hours**: Always open.

stool just inside the gate). You'll get a rundown on the mostly Georgian architecture; a peek at student life, both in the early days and today; and enjoy the company of your guide, a witty Irish college kid (€10, includes €7.50 fee to see Book of Kells, where the tour leaves you; late May–Sept daily 10:30–15:30, departs roughly every 45 min, weather permitting).

▲▲▲**Book of Kells in the Trinity Old Library**—The only Trinity campus interior welcoming tourists (just follow the signs) is the Old Library, with its precious Book of Kells. The first-class *Turning Darkness into Light* exhibit puts the 680-page illuminated manuscript in its historical and cultural context, preparing you to see the original book and other precious manuscripts in the treasury. The

▲▲O'Connell Street Dublin's grandest promenade and main drag, packed with history and ideal for a stroll. **Hours**: Always open.

▲Dublin Experience Decent but overpriced 45-minute slideshow offering a historic introduction to Dublin. **Hours**: June–Sept daily, showings on the hour 10:00–17:00, closed Oct–May.

▲Chester Beatty Library American expatriate's eclectic collection of mostly non-Western artifacts. **Hours**: Mon–Fri 10:00–17:00, Sat 11:00–17:00, Sun 13:00–17:00, Oct–April closed Mon.

▲National Gallery Fine collection of top Irish painters and European masters. **Hours**: Mon–Sat 9:30–17:30, Thu until 20:30, Sun 12:00–17:30.

▲Guinness Storehouse The home of Ireland's national beer, with a museum of beer-making, a gallery of clever ads, and the spectacular Gravity Bar with panoramic city views. **Hours**: Daily 9:30–17:00.

▲Gaelic Athletic Association Museum High-tech museum of traditional Gaelic sports like hurling and Irish football. **Hours**: Mon–Sat 9:30–17:00, Sun 12:00–17:00.

▲St. Stephen's Green Relaxing park surrounded by fine Georgian buildings. **Hours**: Always open.

▲Merrion Square Enjoyable and inviting park with a fun statue of Oscar Wilde. **Hours**: Always open.

▲Temple Bar Dublin's trendiest neighborhood, with shops, cafés, theaters, galleries, pubs, and restaurants—a great spot for live traditional music. **Hours**: Always open.

exhibit is a one-way affair leading to the actual treasury, which shows only four books under glass in one display case. Make a point to spend at least half an hour in the exhibit (before reaching the actual Book of Kells). Especially interesting are the video clips showing the exacting care that went into the monk-uscripts and the ancient art of bookbinding.

Written on vellum (baby calfskin) in the 8th or early 9th century—probably by Irish monks in Iona, Scotland—this enthusiastically decorated copy of the four Gospels was taken to the Irish monastery at Kells in A.D. 806 after a series of Viking raids. Arguably the finest piece of art from what is generally called the Dark Ages, the Book of Kells shows that monastic life in this far fringe of Europe was far from dark. It has been bound into four separate volumes, and at any given time, two of the four gospels are on display. The crowd around the one glass case with the treasures can be off-putting, but hold your own and get up close. You'll see four richly decorated, 1,200-year-old pages—two text and two decorated cover pages. The library treasury also displays two other books—likely the Book of Armagh (A.D. 807) and the Book of Durrow (A.D. 680)—neither of which can be checked out.

Next, a stairway leads upstairs to the 200-foot-long main chamber of the Old Library (from 1732), stacked to its towering ceiling with 200,000 of the library's oldest books. Here, you'll find one of a dozen surviving original copies of the Proclamation of the Irish Republic. Patrick Pearse read these words outside the General Post Office on April 24, 1916, starting the Easter Rising that led to Irish independence. Read the entire thing...imagining that it's yours. Notice the inclusive opening phrase and the seven signatories (each of whom was executed). Another national icon is nearby: the oldest surviving Irish harp, from the 15th century.

Cost and Hours: €7.50; included in €10 Trinity College tour— see above; €10.50 combo-ticket covers *Dublin Experience* movie— see below; June–Sept Mon–Sat 9:30–17:00, Sun 9:30–16:30; Oct–May Mon–Sat 9:30–17:00, Sun 12:00–16:30 (tel. 01/608-2308). A long line often snakes out of the building. Minimize long waiting times by avoiding the midday crunch (roughly 11:30–14:30). For more on the Book of Kells, see page 311 in the Irish History and Culture chapter.

▲**Dublin Experience**—This 45-minute fancy slideshow giving a historic introduction to Dublin is one more tourist movie with the sound turned up. It's good—offering a fine, sweeping introduction to the story of Ireland—but pricey, riding on the coattails of the Book of Kells. Considering that the combo-ticket gets you this for half price, it's not a bad value (€4.50, included in €10.50 combo-ticket with Book of Kells/Old Library, June–Sept daily, showings on the hour 10:00–17:00, closed Oct–May, in modern arts building across from Trinity Old Library).

South of the River Liffey

▲▲**Dublin Castle**—Built on the site of the first Viking fortress, this castle was the seat of British rule in Ireland for 700 years. Located where the Poddle and Liffey Rivers came together, making a black pool (*dubh linn* in Irish), Dublin Castle was the official residence of the viceroy who implemented the will of the British royalty. In this stirring setting, in 1922, the Brits handed power over to Michael

South Dublin

¼ MILE
400 METERS

1 Historical City Walks
2 Trinity College Walks
3 Literary Pub Crawls (Duke Pub)
4 Musical Pub Crawls (Gogarty's Pub)
5 1916 Rebellion Walks
6 Viking Splash Tours
7 City Hall
8 Great George's Arcade
9 Powerscourt Townhouse Shopping Centre

Collins and the Irish. Today, it's used for fancy state and charity functions. The 45-minute tours offer a room-by-room walk through the lavish state apartments of this most English of Irish palaces. The tour finishes with a look at the foundations of the Norman tower and the best remaining chunk of the 13th-century town wall (€5, covered by Heritage Card—see page 4, 2/hr, Mon–Fri 10:00–17:00, Sat–Sun 14:00–17:00, tel. 01/677-7129).

▲**Chester Beatty Library**—Chester Beatty was a rich American mining engineer who retired to Ireland in 1950, later becoming its first honorary citizen. He left his priceless and eclectic collection to his adopted homeland as a public charitable trust.

More an exotic parade of non-Irish treasures than a library, these two floors of rare texts and collectibles sprouted from over 2,000 years of Eastern religions, Islam, and Christianity. You'll see books carved out of jade, ornate snuff bottles, rhino-horn cups, and even the oldest surviving copy of St. Paul's letter to the Romans (A.D. 180). Other highlights include a graceful Burmese book written on palm leaves—bound together to unfold like an accordion—and a densely ornamental sunburst motif from a 500-year-old Iranian Koran (free entry, Mon–Fri 10:00–17:00, Sat 11:00–17:00, Sun 13:00–17:00, Oct–April closed Mon, tel. 01/407-0750, www.cbl.ie). Enter the library via Dublin Castle's pedestrian arch, across Dame Street from the Olympia Theatre; walk straight ahead crossing the courtyard/parking lot, turn right behind the church and castle turret, walk straight for 75 yards, and enter on the left, just past the walled gardens. It's in the modern addition to the Dublin Castle clock tower building.

Dublin City Hall—The first neoclassical building in this very neoclassical city stands proudly overlooking Dame Street, in front of the gate to Dublin Castle. Built in 1779 as the Royal Exchange, it introduced the neoclassical style (then very popular on the Continent) to Ireland. Step inside (it's free) to feel the prosperity and confidence of Dublin in her 18th-century glory days. In 1852, it became the City Hall. Under the grand rotunda, a cycle of heroic paintings tells the city's history. Pay your respects to the 18-foot-tall statue of Daniel O'Connell (the great orator and liberator who won Catholic emancipation in 1829 from the much-depised Protestants over in London). The greeter sits like the Maytag repairman at the information desk, eager to give you more information. Downstairs is a simple *Story of the Capital* exhibition—storyboards and video clips of Dublin's history (€4, covered by Dublin Pass, Mon–Sat 10:00–17:00, Sun 14:00–17:00).

Dublinia—This tries valiantly, but fails, to be a "bridge to Dublin's medieval past." The amateurish look at the medieval town starts with a walk through dim rooms of tableaux, followed by several halls of medieval exhibits, a scale model of old Dublin, and an interesting room devoted to medieval fairs. Then, after piles of stairs, you get a tower-top view of Dublin's skyline of churches and breweries (€6, €8.75 combo-ticket includes Christ Church Cathedral, saving you €3; April–Sept daily 10:00–17:00, Oct–March daily 11:00–16:00, brass rubbing, coffee shop open in summer only, across from Christ Church Cathedral, tel. 01/679-4611).

Christ Church Cathedral—The first church on this spot was built of wood by King Sitric in Viking times (c. 1040). The present structure dates from a mix of periods: Norman and Gothic, but mostly Victorian neo-Gothic (1870s restoration work). The unusually large crypt under the cathedral—actually the oldest building in Dublin—contains stocks, statues, and the cathedral's silver (€5 donation to church, includes downstairs crypt silver exhibition, covered by Dublin Pass, €8.75 combo-ticket includes Dublinia, free brochure with self-guided tour, daily 10:00–17:00). Because of Dublin's British past, neither of its top two churches is Catholic. Christ Church Cathedral and the nearby St. Patrick's Cathedral are both Church of Ireland. In Catholic Ireland, these sights feel hollow. They're more famous than visit-worthy.

Evensong: At Christ Church, a 45-minute evensong service is sung regularly several times a week (Tue–Thu at 18:00, Sat at 17:00, and Sun at 15:30; less regularly during the summer). The 13th-century St. Patrick's Cathedral, where Jonathan Swift (author of *Gulliver's Travels*) was dean in the 18th century, also offers evensong (Sun at 15:15, Mon–Fri at 17:30, but not Wed July–Aug).

▲▲▲National Museum—Showing off the treasures of Ireland from the Stone Age to modern times, this museum is itself a national treasure and wonderfully digestible under one dome. Ireland's Bronze Age gold fills the center. Up four steps, the prehistoric Ireland exhibit rings the gold. In a corner (behind a 2,000-year-old body), you'll find the treasury with the most famous pieces (brooches, chalices, and other examples of Celtic metalwork) and an 18-minute video (played on request), giving an overview of Irish art through the 13th century. The collection's superstars—both dating from the 8th century—are the exquisite silver and bronze Ardagh Chalice and the gold, enamel, and amber Tara Brooch. Jumping way ahead (and to the opposite side of the hall), a special corridor features *The Road to Independence*, with guns, letters, and death masks recalling the fitful birth of the "Terrible Beauty" (1900–1921, with a focus on the 1916 Easter Rising). The best Viking artifacts in town are upstairs with the medieval collection. If you'll be visiting Cong (in Connemara, near Galway), seek out the original Cross of Cong (free entry, Tue–Sat 10:00–17:00, Sun 14:00–17:00, closed Mon, good café, Kildare Street 2, between Trinity College and St. Stephen's Green). Greatest-hits tours are given several times a day (€2, 40 min, tel. 01/677-7444 in morning for schedule). For background information, read "Irish Art" in the Irish History and Culture chapter.

▲**National Gallery**—Along with a hall featuring the work of top Irish painters, this has Ireland's best collection of European masters. It's impressive—although not nearly as extensive as those in London or Paris (free, Mon–Sat 9:30–17:30, Thu until 20:30, Sun 12:00–17:30, call for times of guided tours on weekends, Merrion Square West, tel. 01/661-5133, www.nationalgallery.ie).

▲▲**Grafton Street**—Once filled with noisy traffic, Grafton Street is today Dublin's liveliest pedestrian shopping mall. A five-minute stroll past street musicians takes you from Trinity College up to St. Stephen's Green (and makes you wonder why American merchants are so terrified of a car-free street). Walking by a buxom statue of "sweet" Molly Malone (known by locals as "the tart with the cart"), you'll soon pass two venerable department stores: the Irish Brown Thomas and the English Marks & Spencer. An alley leads to the Powerscourt Townhouse Shopping Centre, which tastefully fills a converted Georgian mansion. The huge, glass-covered St. Stephen's Green Shopping Centre and the peaceful and green Green itself mark the top of Grafton Street.

▲**St. Stephen's Green**—This city park, originally a medieval commons, was enclosed in 1664 and gradually surrounded with fine Georgian buildings. Today, it provides 22 acres of grassy refuge for Dubliners. On a sunny afternoon, it's a wonderful world apart from the big city.

▲▲**Number Twenty-Nine Georgian House**—The carefully restored house at Number 29 Lower Fitzwilliam Street gives an intimate glimpse of middle-class Georgian life—which seems pretty high-class. From the sidewalk, descend the stairs to the basement-level entrance (at the corner of Lower Fitzwilliam and Lower Mount Streets). Start with an interesting 12-minute video (you're welcome to bring in a cup of coffee from the café) before joining your guide, who takes you on a fascinating 35-minute walk through this 1790 Dublin home (€3.50, covered by Dublin Pass, tours leave regularly, Tue–Sat 10:00–17:00, Sun 14:00–17:00, closed Mon, tel. 01/702-6165).

▲**Merrion Square**—Laid out in 1762, this square is ringed by elegant Georgian houses decorated with fine doors—a Dublin trademark—with elegant knobs and knockers. The park, once the exclusive domain of the residents, is now a delightful public escape. More inviting than St. Stephen's Green, it's ideal for a picnic. If you want to know what "snogging" is, walk through the park on a sunny day, when it's full of smooching lovers. Oscar Wilde, lounging wittily on the corner nearest the town center and surrounded by his clever quotes, provides a fun photo op.

▲**Temple Bar**—This was a Georgian center of craftsmen and merchants. As it fell on hard times in the 19th century, the lower rents attracted students and artists, giving the neighborhood a bohemian flair. With recent government tax incentives and lots of development money, the Temple Bar district has become a thriving cultural (and beer-drinking) hotspot. Today, this much-promoted center of trendy shops, cafés, theaters, galleries, pubs with live music, and restaurants feels like the heart of the city. Dublin's "Left Bank"—which, like Paris', is on the south shore of the river—fills the cobbled streets between Dame Street and the River Liffey. ("Bar" means a walkway along the river.) The central **Meeting House Square** (just off Essex Street) hosts free street theater, as well as a lively organic-produce market and a book market (Sat 10:00–18:00). The square is surrounded by interesting cultural centers.

These days, the downsides to Temple Bar are noise and high prices. Crowded summer weekend nights can be a real zoo, with loud "hen" (bachelorette) parties in funky hats promenading the main drag, as drunken party dudes shout from pub doorways to get their attention. Be aware that a pint of beer here is fast approaching €5, at least €1 more than at less glitzy pubs just a couple blocks away (north of the Liffey river or south of Dame Street).

For a listing of events and galleries, visit the **Temple Bar Properties** office and ask for their free annual TASCQ Guide (18 Eustace Street, www.templebar.ie). Rather than follow particular pub or restaurant recommendations (mine are below, under

"Eating"), venture down a few side lanes off the main drag to see what looks good.

The pedestrian-only **Ha' Penny Bridge,** named for the halfpence toll people used to pay to cross it, leads from Temple Bar over the River Liffey to the opposite bank and more sights.

North of the River Liffey

▲▲**O'Connell Bridge**—This bridge spans the River Liffey, which has historically divided the wealthy, cultivated south side from the poorer, cruder north side. While there's plenty of culture north of the river, even today, "the north" is considered rougher and less safe.

From the bridge, look upriver (west) as far upstream as you can. The big concrete building on the left in the distance houses the city planning commission. Maddening to locals, this eyesore is in charge of making sure new buildings in the city are built in good taste. It squats on the still buried precious artifacts of the first Viking settlement established in Dublin in the 9th century.

Across the river stands the Four Courts, today's Supreme Court building, shelled and burned in 1922 during the tragic civil war that followed Irish independence. Irreplaceable birth records were lost as the national archives office burned, making it challenging for those with Irish roots to trace their ancestry today. The closest bridge upstream—the elegant, iron Ha' Penny Bridge—leads

North Dublin

① Daniel O'Connell Statue
② James Larkin Statue
③ Millennium Spire
④ Father Matthew Statue
⑤ C.S. Parnell Statue
⑥ Townhouse of Dublin Hotel
⑦ Jurys Inn Custom House Hotel
⑧ Charles Stewart Budget Accommodations
⑨ Clifden House
⑩ James Joyce Cultural Centre

left into the Temple Bar nightlife district. Just beyond the old-fashioned, 19th-century bridge is Dublin's pedestrian Millennium Bridge, inaugurated in 2000. (Note that buses leave from O'Connell Bridge—specifically, Aston Quay—for the Guinness Storehouse and the Kilmainham Jail.)

Turn 180 degrees and look downstream to see the tall Liberty Hall union headquarters—for now, the tallest building in the Republic (16 stories tall, some say in honor of the 1916 Easter Uprising)—and lots of cranes. Booming Dublin is developing downstream. The Irish (forever clever tax fiddlers) have subsidized and revitalized this formerly dreary quarter with great success. A short walk downstream along the north bank leads to a powerful series of modern statues memorializing the Potato Famine of 1845–1849.

▲▲O'Connell Street Stroll—Dublin's grandest street leads from O'Connell Bridge through the heart of north Dublin. Since the 1740s, it has been a 45-yard-wide promenade. Ever since the first O'Connell Bridge connected it to the Trinity side of town in 1794, it's been

Dublin's main drag. (But it was only named O'Connell after independence was won in 1922.) These days, construction reigns, as the city makes the street more pedestrian-friendly. The street, though lined with fast-food and souvenir shops, echoes with history. Take the following one-hour stroll (you can walk on the tree-lined median strip, which is wide, less crowded, and closer to the statues mentioned below):

Statues and monuments line O'Connell Street, celebrating great figures in Ireland's fight for independence. At the base of the street stands **Daniel O'Connell** (1775–1847), known as "the Liberator" for founding the Catholic Association and demanding Irish Catholic rights in the British Parliament.

Looking a block east down Abbey Street, you can see the famous **Abbey Theatre**—rebuilt after a fire into a nondescript, modern building. It's still the much-loved home of the Irish National Theatre.

The statue of **James Larkin** honors the founder of the Irish Transport Workers' Union. The one monument that didn't wave an Irish flag—a tall column crowned by a statue of the British hero of

Trafalgar, Admiral Nelson—was blown up in 1966...the IRA's contribution to the local celebration of the Easter Rising's 50th anniversary. This spot is now occupied by the 300-foot-tall, stainless steel Millennium Spire that was finally completed in 2003. Dubious Dubliners have nicknamed it "the stiletto in the ghetto."

The **General Post Office** is not just any P.O. It was from here that Patrick Pearse read the Proclamation of Irish Independence in 1916 and kicked off the Easter Rising. The G.P.O. building itself—a kind of Irish Alamo—was the rebel headquarters and the scene of a five-day bloody siege that followed the proclamation. Its pillars remain pockmarked with bullet holes. Step inside and trace the battle by studying the well-described cycle of 10 paintings that circle the main hall (open for business and sightseers Mon–Sat 8:00–20:00, closed Sun).

The busy **Moore Street Market** is nearby (Mon–Sat 8:00–18:00, closed Sun). To get there, detour left two blocks after the Post Office down people-filled Henry Street, then wander to the right into the market. Many of its merchants have staffed the same stalls for 30 years. Start a conversation. It's a great work-a-day scene. You'll see lots of mums with strollers—a reminder that Ireland is Europe's youngest country, with about 40 percent of the population under the age of 25.

Back on O'Connell Street, cross back onto the median strip and continue your walk. The lampposts display the colorful three-castle city seal. The Latin motto below the seal states, "Happy the city where citizens obey." Flames rise from the castles, symbolizing the citizens' zeal to defend Dublin.

St. Mary's Pro-Cathedral, a block east of O'Connell down Cathedral Street, is Dublin's leading Catholic church. But, curiously, it's not a cathedral, even though the pope declared Christ Church one in the 12th century—and later, St. Patrick's. (Stubbornly, the Vatican has chosen to ignore the fact that Christ Church and St. Patrick's haven't been Catholic for centuries.) Completed in 1821, it's done in the style of a Greek temple.

Continuing up O'Connell Street, you'll find a statue of **Father Matthew,** a leader of the temperance movement of the 1830s who, some historians claim, was responsible for enough Irish peasants staying sober to enable Daniel O'Connell to organize them into a political force. (Perhaps understanding this dynamic, the U.S.S.R. was careful to keep the price of vodka affordable.) The fancy Gresham Hotel is a good place for an elegant tea or beer.

Charles Stewart Parnell stands boldly at the top of O'Connell Street. The names of the four ancient provinces of Ireland and all 32 Irish counties (North *and* South, since this was erected before Irish independence) ring the monument, honoring the member of Parliament who nearly won Home Rule for Ireland in the late 1800s. (A sex scandal cost Parnell the support of the Church, which let the air out of any chance for a free Ireland.)

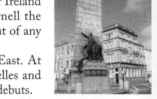

Continue straight up Parnell Square East. At the **Gate Theatre** (on the left), Orson Welles and James Mason got their professional acting debuts.

The **Garden of Remembrance** (past Gate Theater, 1 block up on left, daily 8:30–18:00) honors the victims of the 1916 Rising. The park was dedicated in 1966 on the 50th anniversary of the uprising that ultimately led to Irish independence. The bottom of the cross-shaped pool is a mosaic of Celtic weapons, symbolic of how the early Irish would proclaim peace by throwing their weapons into a lake or river. The Irish flag flies above the park: green for Catholics, orange for Protestants, and white for the hope that they can live together in peace. Across the street...

The **Dublin Writers' Museum** fills a splendidly restored Georgian mansion. No other country so small has produced such a wealth of literature (see page 63). As interesting to fans of Irish literature as it is boring to those who aren't, this three-room museum features the lives and works of Dublin's great writers (€6.50, covered

Dublin's Literary Life

Dublin in the 1700s, grown rich from a lucrative cloth trade, was one of Europe's most cultured and sophisticated cities. The buildings were decorated in the Georgian style still visible today. The city's Protestant elite shuttled between here and London, bridging the Anglo-Irish cultural gap.

Jonathan Swift (1667–1745), the great satirical writer, was also dean of St. Patrick's Cathedral (1713–1745) and one of the city's eminent citizens. His most famous book, *Gulliver's Travels*, poked fun at religious hardliners and the pompous bureaucrats in London who shaped England's misguided Irish policies.

More recently, Dublin around the turn of the 20th century produced some of the world's great modern writers.

Oscar Wilde (1854–1900), born in Dublin and a graduate of Trinity College, wowed London with his quick wit, outrageous clothes, and flamboyant personality. He satirized upper-class Victorian society in comedic plays (like *The Importance of Being Earnest*, 1895) with characters who speak very elegantly about the trivial concerns of the idle rich.

William Butler Yeats (1865–1939), also born and raised in Dublin, captured the passion of the Irish independence movement. His poem "Easter Rising, 1916" contains the refrain that summed up how those events affected Ireland: "All are changed, changed utterly: A terrible beauty is born."

James Joyce (1882–1941) used to wander the back streets of Dublin, observing its seedier side, which he captured in a modern, stream-of-consciousness style. His famous novel *Ulysses*, set in a single day (June 16, 1904), follows turn-of-the-20th-century Dubliners on an odyssey through the city's pubs, hospitals, libraries, and brothels.

And today, Ireland still produces some of the English language's greatest writers. **Seamus Heaney**, a Nobel- and Pulitzer Prize–winning poet, recently published a new translation of the Old English epic, *Beowulf*—wedding the old with the new.

For more on Irish literature, see page 312.

by Dublin Pass, Mon–Sat 10:00–17:00, Sun 11:00–17:00, June–Aug Mon–Fri until 18:00, helpful audioguide available, 18 Parnell Square North, tel. 01/872-2077). With hometown wits such as Swift, Yeats, Joyce, and Shaw, there is a checklist of residences and memorials to see. Aficionados of James Joyce's work may want to hike 400 yards east to visit the **James Joyce Cultural Centre** (Mon–Sat 9:30–17:00, Sun 12:30–17:00, 35 North Great George's Street, tel. 01/878-8547). There's more Joyce memorabilia in Dun Laoghaire at the **James Joyce Museum** (see page 80). Next door to the Dublin Writers' Museum is the...

Charles Stewart Parnell
(1846–1891)

Parnell, who led the Irish movement for Home Rule, did time in Kilmainham Jail. A Cambridge-educated Protestant and Member of Parliament, he had a vision of a modern and free Irish Republic filled mostly with Catholics, but not set up as a religious state. Momentum seemed to be on his side. With the British prime minister of the time, William Gladstone, in favor of a similar form of Home Rule, it looked as if all of Ireland were ripe for independence. Then a sex scandal broke around Parnell and his mistress. The press, egged on by the powerful Catholic bishops (who didn't want a free but secular Irish state), battered away at the scandal until Parnell was finally driven from office. Sadly, after that, Ireland became mired in the Troubles of the 20th century: an awkward independence (1921) featuring a divided island, a bloody civil war, sectarian violence in recent years, and tension ever since. It's said Parnell died of a broken heart. Before he did, this great Irish statesman requested to be buried outside of Ireland.

Hugh Lane Municipal Art Gallery, in a grand neoclassical building, has a fine, bite-sized selection of Pre-Raphaelite, French Impressionist, and 19th- and 20th-century Irish paintings (free, Tue–Thu 9:30–18:00, Fri–Sat 9:30–17:00, Sun 11:00–17:00, closed Mon, tel. 01/874-1903). Sir Hugh went down on the *Lusitania* in 1915; due to an unclear will, his collection is shared by this gallery and the National Gallery in London.

Tucked in the back of the gallery is the **Francis Bacon Studio**, reconstructed here in its original (messy) state from its London location at the time of the artist's death in 1992. Born in Dublin and inspired by Picasso, Bacon reflected his belief that "chaos breeds energy" in his shocking paintings. This compact space contains touch-screen terminals, display cases of personal items, and a few unfinished works. The 10-minute film interview of Bacon may fascinate like-minded viewers...and disquiet others (€7, same hours as rest of gallery).

Your walk is over. Here on the north end of town, it's convenient to visit the Gaelic Athletic Association Museum at Croke Park (described on page 67, a 30-min walk or short taxi ride away). Otherwise, hop on your skateboard and return to the river.

Dublin's Smithfield Village

The neighborhood is worth a look for "Cobblestores" (a redeveloped Duck Lane lined with fancy crafts and gift shops), the Old Jameson Distillery whiskey tour, and a chimney observatory with big Dublin views. The sights are clustered close together, two blocks north of the river behind the Four Courts—the Supreme Court building.

The Old Jameson Distillery—Whiskey fans enjoy visiting the old distillery. You get a 10-minute video, 20-minute tour, and a free shot in the pub. Unfortunately, the "distillery" feels fake and put together for tourists. The Bushmills tour in Northern Ireland (in a working factory, see page 265) and the Midleton tour, near Cork (in the huge, original factory, page 138) are better experiences. If you do take this tour, volunteer energetically when offered the chance to take the "whiskey taste test" at the end (€8.50, covered by Dublin Pass, daily 9:00–18:00, last tour at 17:30, Bow Street, tel. 01/807-2355).

The Chimney—Built in 1895 for the distillery, the chimney is now an observatory. Ride the elevator 175 feet up for a Dublin panorama not quite as exciting as the view from the Guinness Storehouse's Gravity Bar (overpriced at €6, covered by Dublin Pass, Mon–Sat 10:00–17:00, Sun 11:00–17:00, tel. 01/817-3838).

Outer Dublin

The jail and the Guinness Storehouse are the main sights outside of the old center. Combine them in one visit.

▲▲▲**Kilmainham Gaol (Jail)**—Opened in 1796 as the Dublin County Jail and a debtors' prison, and considered a model in its day,

this jail was used frequently as a political prison by the British. Many of those who fought for Irish independence were held or executed here, including leaders of the rebellions of 1798, 1803, 1848, 1867, and 1916. National heroes Robert Emmett and Charles Stewart Parnell each did time here. The last prisoner to be held here was Eamon de Valera, who later became president of Ireland. He was released on July 16, 1924, the day Kilmainham was finally shut down. The buildings, virtually in ruins, were restored in the 1960s. Today, it's a shrine to the Nathan Hales of Ireland.

Start your visit with a guided tour (1 hr, 2/hr, includes 25 min in prison chapel for a rebellion-packed video, spend waiting time in museum). It's touching to tour the cells and places of execution while hearing tales of terrible colonialism and heroic patriotism alongside Irish schoolkids who know these names well. The museum is an excellent exhibit on Victorian prison life and Ireland's fight for independence. Don't miss the museum's dimly lit Last Words 1916 hall upstairs, which displays the stirring last letters patriots sent to loved ones hours before facing the firing squad (€5, covered by Dublin Pass and Heritage Card—see page 4, April–Sept daily 9:30–18:00, Oct–March daily 9:30–17:00, last entry 1 hr before closing; €5 taxi, or bus #51b, #78a, or #79 from Aston Quay or Guinness, tel. 01/453-5984). You could taxi to the jail, then catch the bus from there to Guinness (leaving the prison, take 3 rights, crossing no streets, to the bus stop, and hop bus #51b or #78a). Another option is taking the City Sightseeing/Guide Friday hop-on, hop-off bus, which stops at both the jail and the Guinness Storehouse.

▲**Guinness Storehouse**—A visit to the Guinness Storehouse is, for many, a pilgrimage. Arthur Guinness began brewing the famous stout here in 1759. By 1868, it was the biggest brewery in the world. Today, the sprawling brewery fills several city blocks. Around the world, Guinness brews more than 10 million pints a day. The home of Ireland's national beer welcomes visitors, for a price, with a sprawling new museum (but there are no tours of the actual working brewery). The museum fills the old fermentation plant, used from 1902 through 1988, vacated, and then opened in 2000 as a huge, shrine-like place. Step into the middle of the ground floor and look up. A tall, beer-glass-shaped glass atrium—14 million pints big—leads past four floors of exhibitions and cafés to the skylight. Then look down at Arthur's original 9,000-year lease enshrined under glass in the floor...quite a bargain. Atop the building, the Gravity Bar provides visitors with a commanding 360-degree view of Dublin—with vistas all the way to the sea—and a free beer. The actual exhibit makes brewing seem more grandiose than it is, and treats Arthur like the god of human happiness. Highlights are the cooperage (with old film clips showing the master wood-keg-makers plying their now extinct trade), a display of the brewery's clever ads, and the Gravity Bar, which really is spectacular (€13.50, covered by Dublin Pass, includes a €4 pint, daily 9:30–17:00, enter on Bellevue Street, bus #78a from Aston Quay near O'Connell Bridge, or bus #123 from Dame Street and O'Connell Street, tel. 01/408-4800). Both hop-on, hop-off bus tours stop here.

▲**Gaelic Athletic Association Museum**—The GAA was founded in 1884 as an expression of an Irish cultural awakening. It was created to foster the development of Gaelic sports, specifically Irish football and hurling, and to ban English sports, such as cricket and rugby—but it played an important part in the fight for independence. This museum, at the newly expanded 82,000-seat Croke Park Stadium, offers a high-tech, interactive introduction to Ireland's favorite games. Relive the greatest moments in hurling and Irish-football history. Then get involved. Pick up a stick and try hurling, kick a football, and test your speed and balance. A 15-minute film clarifies the connection between sports and Irish politics (€6, covered by Dublin Pass, Mon–Sat 9:30–17:00, Sun 12:00–17:00; on game Sundays, museum is open 12:00–17:00 to Cusack stand ticket-holders only, as other sections of stands are blocked from museum entry; museum located under the new stand at Croke Park, from O'Connell Street walk 20 min or catch bus #3, #11, #11a, #16, #16a, or #123; tel. 01/819-2323). The €9.50 museum-plus-stadium-tour option is worth it only for rabid fans who yearn to know which locker room is considered the unlucky one (1 hr, tour also covered by Dublin Pass).

Hurling or Irish Football at Croke Park—Actually seeing a match here, surrounded by incredibly spirited Irish fans, is a fun experience. Hurling is like airborne hockey with no injury time-outs, and Irish football looks like a rugged form of soccer. Matches are held on most Sunday afternoons from May to September. Tickets (€20–55) are available at the stadium, except during championships (tel. 01/836-3222, www.gaa.ie).

Greyhound Racing—For an interesting lowbrow look at local life, consider going to the dog races and doing a little gambling (€8, generally Wed, Thu, and Sat at 20:00, Shelbourne Park, tel. 01/668-3502). Greyhounds race on the other days at Harold's Cross Racetrack (€8, Mon, Tue, and Fri at 20:00, tel. 01/497-1081).

Day Trips from Dublin—See the next chapter for information on Newgrange, the Wicklow Mountains, and more.

SHOPPING

Shops are open roughly Monday to Saturday from 9:00 to 18:00, and until 20:00 on Thursday. They have shorter hours on Sunday (if they're open at all). The best shopping area is Grafton, with its neighboring streets and arcades (such as the fun Great George's Arcade between Great George's and Drury Streets), and nearby shopping centers (Powerscourt and St. Stephen's Green). Francis Street creaks with antiques.

For a street market, consider Mother Redcaps (Fri–Sun all day, bric-a-brac, antiques, crafts, Back Lane, Christ Church). For produce, noise, and color, visit Moore Street (Mon–Sat 8:00–18:00, near General Post Office). For raw fish, get a whiff of Michan Street (Tue–Sat 7:00–15:00, behind Four Courts building).

On Saturdays at Temple Bar's Meeting House Square, it's food in the morning (from 9:00) and books in the afternoon (until 18:00). Temple Bar is worth a browse any day for its art, jewelry, new-age paraphernalia, books, music, and gift shops.

ENTERTAINMENT

Ireland has produced some of the finest writers in both English and Irish, and Dublin houses some of Europe's finest theaters. While Handel's *Messiah* was first performed in Dublin (1742), these days Dublin is famous for its rock bands (U2, Thin Lizzy, Sinead O'Connor, and Live Aid founder Bob Geldof's band, the Boomtown Rats, all got started here).

Theater—**Abbey Theatre** is Ireland's national theater, founded by W. B. Yeats in 1904 to preserve Irish culture during British rule (26 Lower Abbey Street, tel. 01/878-7222, www.abbeytheatre.ie). **Gate Theatre** does foreign plays, as well as Irish classics (Cavendish Row, tel. 01/874-4045, www.gate-theatre.ie). The **Gaiety Theatre** offers a wide range of quality productions (King Street South, tel. 01/677-1717, www.gaietytheatre.com). **Point Theatre,** once a railway terminus, is now the country's top live-music venue (East Link Bridge, tel. 01/836-3633, www.thepoint.ie). At the **National Concert Hall,** the National Symphony Orchestra performs most Friday evenings (Earlsfort Terrace, off St. Stephen's Green, tickets €8–22, tel. 01/475-1666, www.nch.ie). Street theater takes the stage in Temple Bar on summer evenings.

Pub Action—Folk music fills the pubs, and street entertainers are everywhere. The Temple Bar area thrives with music—traditional, jazz, and pop. Although it's pricier than the rest of Dublin, it really is *the* comfortable and fun place for tourists and locals (who come here to watch the tourists). **Gogarty's Pub** (corner of Fleet and Anglesea, tel. 01/671-1822) has top-notch sessions upstairs nightly from 21:00. Use this as a kick-off for your Temple Bar evening.

A 10-minute hike up the river west of Temple Bar takes you to a twosome with a local and less touristy ambience. The **Brazen Head**, famous as Dublin's oldest pub, is a hit for an early dinner and late live music (nightly from 21:30, tel. 01/677-9549), with atmospheric rooms and a courtyard made to order for balmy evenings (on Bridge Street). **O'Shea's Merchant Pub**, just across the street, is encrusted in memories and filled with locals taking a break from the grind. They have live traditional music nightly (the front half is a restaurant, the magic is in the back half—enter on Bridge Street, tel. 01/679-3797).

To sample truly traditional Irish song and dance, consider heading to Comhaltas Ceoltoiri Éireann in nearby Dun Laoghaire (see page 80).

SLEEPING

Dublin is popular, and rooms can be tight. Book ahead for weekends any time of year, particularly in summer and during major sporting events. Prices are often discounted on weeknights (Mon–Thu) and from November through February.

Big and practical places (both cheap and moderate) are most central at Christ Church, on the edge of Temple Bar. For classy, older Dublin accommodations, you'll stay a bit farther out (southeast of St. Stephen's Green). The most economical non-hostel lodging is north of the River Liffey (page 73).

For a small-town escape with the best budget values, take the

Sleep Code

(€1 = about $1.20, country code: 353, area code: 01)
S = Single, **D** = Double/Twin, **T** = Triple, **Q** = Quad,
b = bathroom, **s** = shower only. Breakfast is included and credit
cards are accepted unless otherwise noted. To locate hotels, see
map on page 70.

To help you easily sort through these listings, I've divided
the rooms into three categories, based on the price for a standard
double room with bath:

   $$$ **Higher Priced**—Most rooms €130 or more.
    $$ **Moderately Priced**—Most rooms between €70–130.
     $ **Lower Priced**—Most rooms €70 or less.

convenient DART train (at least 3/hr, 20 min) to nearby Dun
Laoghaire (see page 79).

Near Christ Church

These hotels face Christ Church Cathedral, a five-minute walk from
the best evening scene at Temple Bar, and 10 minutes from the
sightseeing center (Trinity College and Grafton Street). The cheap
hostels in this neighborhood have some double rooms. Full Irish
breakfasts, which cost €10–15 at the hotels, are half the price at the
many small cafés nearby; consider Bagel Haven (beside Kinlay
House, hidden on Cow's Lane).

$$ Harding Hotel is a hardwood, 21st-century, Viking-style
place with 53 institutional-yet-hotelesque rooms. The rooms are sim-
pler than Jurys (below), but they're also more intimate (Sb-€64, Db-
€89–106, Tb-€114–131, tell them Rick sent you and get 10 percent
off in 2005, breakfast-€10, Copper Alley, across street from Christ
Church, tel. 01/679-6500, fax 01/679-6504, www.hardinghotel.ie,
harding.hotel@kinlaygroup.ie).

$$ Jurys Christ Church Inn (like its sisters across town, in
Galway, and in Belfast) is central and offers business-class comfort in
all of its 182 identical rooms. This no-nonsense, modern, American-
style hotel chain has a winning keep-it-simple-and-affordable formula. If ye olde is getting old (and you don't mind big tour groups),
there's no better value in town. All rooms cost the same: €108
Sun–Thu (or €117 Fri–Sat) for one, two, or three adults or two adults
and two kids (breakfast extra). Each room has a modern bathroom,
direct-dial telephone, and TV. Two floors are strictly non-smoking.
Request a room far from the noisy elevator (book long in advance for
weekends, parking-€12/day, Christ Church Place, tel. 01/454-0000,
fax 01/454-0012, U.S. tel. 800/423-6953, www.jurysdoyle.com,

Dublin Hotels

1 Harding/Kinlay Hotels
2 Jurys Christ Church Inn
3 Principal Hotel & Temple Bar Hotel
4 To Albany House
5 To Fitzwilliam, Baggot Court & Mespil Hotels
6 To Glenveagh Town House & Roxford Lodge Hotel
7 Four Courts Hostel
8 Avalon House
9 To The Leeson Inn

¼ MILE

400 METERS

info@jurysdoyle.com). Another Jurys is near the Connolly train station (see page 73).

$ Kinlay House, around the corner from Harding Hotel, is the backpackers' equivalent—definitely the place to go for cheap beds in a central location and an all-ages-welcome atmosphere. This huge, red-brick, 19th-century Victorian building has 149 metal, prison-style beds in spartan, non-smoking rooms. There are singles, doubles, and four- to six-bed coed dorms (good for families), as well as a few giant dorms. It fills up most days. Call well in advance, especially for singles, doubles, and summer weekends (S-€44–52, D-€54–64, Db-€58–68, dorm beds-€18–26, includes continental breakfast, kitchen access, launderette-€7.50, Internet access-€4/hr, left luggage, travel desk, TV lounge, small lockers, lots of stairs, Christ Church, 2–12 Lord Edward Street, tel. 01/679-6644, fax 01/679-7437, www.kinlayhouse.ie, kinlay.dublin@kinlaygroup.ie).

$ Four Courts Hostel is a 256-bed hostel beautifully located immediately across the river from the Four Courts, a five-minute walk from Christ Church and Temple Bar. It's bare and institutional (as hostels are), but spacious and well-run, with a focus on security and efficiency (dorm beds-€15–17, S-€45, Sb-€50, bunk D-€60, bunk Db-€66, includes small breakfast, girls' floor and boys' floor, non-smoking, elevator, free Internet access, game room, laundry service, some parking, left luggage room, 15–17 Merchant's Quay, bus #748 from airport, #90 from train or bus station, tel. 01/672-5839, fax 01/672-5862, www.fourcourtshostel.com, info@fourcourtshostel.com).

Between Trinity College and Temple Bar

$$$ Principal Hotel Fleet Street rents 70 decent rooms. For its size, it has an intimate feel with character (Sb-€106–127, Db-€130–169, often midweek deals, breakfast-€13.50, non-smoking rooms, request a quiet room off the street, 19-20 Fleet Street, tel. 01/670-8122, fax 01/670-8103, www.principalhotel.com). Rather than buying the spendy hotel breakfast, walk around the corner to Bewley's on Westmoreland Street.

$$$ Temple Bar Hotel is a 130-room, business-class place, very centrally located midway between Trinity College and the Temple Bar action (Sb-€150, Db-€195, Tb-€255, midweek discounts, non-smoking rooms, Fleet Street, Temple Bar, tel. 01/677-3333, fax 01/677-3088, www.templebarhotel.com, reservations@tbh.ie).

$$ Trinity College turns its 800 student-housing rooms on campus into no-frills, affordable accommodations in the city center each summer (mid-June–Sept, S-€55, Sb-€66, D-€110, Db-€128, all doubles are twins, includes continental breakfast, cooked breakfast-€3 extra, tel. 01/608-1177, fax 01/671-1267, www.tcd.ie /accom, reservations@tcd.ie).

Near St. Stephen's Green

$$$ Albany House's 43 rooms come with classic furniture, high ceilings, Georgian elegance, and some street noise. Book early and request one of the four huge "superior" rooms, which are the same price as standard rooms (Sb-€100–130, Db-€140–180, €120 in slow times, Tb-€170–210, Una promises 10 percent off with this book in 2005, includes breakfast, back rooms are quieter, non-smoking, just 1 block south of St. Stephen's Green at 84 Harcourt Street, tel. 01/475-1092, fax 01/475-1093, http://indigo.ie/~albany, albany@indigo.ie).

$$$ Baggot Court Guest House has 11 fine rooms, but no lounge (Sb-€90–100, Db-€120–165, Tb-€150–210, non-smoking, free parking, 92 Lower Baggot Street, tel. 01/661-2819, fax 01/661-0253, www.baggotcourt.com, baggot@indigo.ie).

$$ The Fitzwilliam has an inviting lounge and rents 13 decent rooms cheaper than the Baggot Court, a block farther away (Sb-€65–75, Db-€100–130, 10 percent discount with cash in 2005, children under 16 sleep free, 41 Upper Fitzwilliam Street, tel. 01/662-5155, fax 01/676-7488, www.fitzwilliamguesthouse.ie, info@fitzwilliamguesthouse.ie).

$ Avalon House, near Grafton Street, rents 281 backpacker beds (dorm beds-€15–30, S-€30–34, Sb-€33–37, twin D-€56–64, twin Db-€60-70, includes continental breakfast, elevator, Ireland bus tickets, Internet access, launderette, a few minutes off Grafton Street at 55 Aungier Street, tel. 01/475-0001, fax 01/475-0303, www.avalon-house.ie).

Away from the Center, East of St. Stephen's Green

$$$ Roxford Lodge Hotel is a memorable splurge in a quiet residential neighborhood a 20-minute walk from Trinity College, with 20 tastefully decorated, whirlpool-tub-laden rooms. The €300 executive suite is honeymoon-worthy (Sb-€90, Db-€140, Tb-€165, Qb-€200, secure parking, 46 Northumberland Road, tel. 01/668-8572, fax 01/668-8158, www.roxfordlodge.ie, roxfordlodge@eircom.net).

$$$ Mespil Hotel is a huge, modern, business-class hotel renting 256 identical three-star rooms (most with a double and single bed, phone, TV, voicemail, and modem hookup) at a good price, with all the comforts. This is a cut above Jurys Inn, for a little more money (Sb, Db, or Tb-€150, breakfast-€15, elevator, non-smoking floors, apartments for week-long stays, 10-min walk southeast of St. Stephen's Green or bus #10, Mespil Road, tel. 01/488-4600, fax 01/667-1244, www.leehotels.com, mespil@leehotels.com).

$$$ The Leeson Inn, with 22 crisply uncluttered rooms, stands proudly Georgian in a great location a five-minute walk south of St. Stephen's Green (Sb-€75–109, Db-€109–149, Tb-€129–169, Qb-€179–189; small first-come, first-served parking lot; 24 Lower Leeson

Street, tel. 01/662-2002, fax 01/662-1567, www.leesoninndowntown .com, info@leesoninndowntown.com).

$$ Glenveagh Town House rents 13 rooms—Victorian upstairs and modern downstairs—southeast of the city center, a 20-minute walk from Trinity College (Sb-€75, Db-€100–130, less in slow times, includes breakfast, parking, 31 Northumberland Road, tel. 01/668-4612, fax 01/668-4559, www.glenveagh.ie, glenveagh@eircom.net). Catch bus #5, #6, #7, #8, or #45 down Northumberland Road into downtown Dublin (every 10 min).

North of the River Liffey
To locate these hotels, see map on page 60.

$$ Townhouse of Dublin, with 80 small, stylish rooms (some with pleasant views into a central garden courtyard), hides behind a brick Georgian facade one block north of the Customs House (Sb-€70, Db-€115, Tb-€130; small first-come, first-served parking lot; 47–48 Lower Gardiner Street, tel. 01/878-8808, fax 01/878-8787, www.townhouseofdublin.com, info@townhouse.com)

$$ Jurys Inn Custom House, on Custom House Quay, offers the same value as the Jurys at Christ Church. Bigger (with 234 rooms) and not quite as well-located (in a boring neighborhood, a 10-min riverside hike from O'Connell Bridge), this Jurys is more likely to have rooms available (Db-€108 Sun–Thu, or €117 Fri–Sat, tel. 01/607-5000, fax 01/829-0400, U.S. tel. 800/423-6953, www .jurysdoyle.com, info@jurysdoyle.com).

$$ Clifden House is a good value, with 15 unpretentious, neatly kept rooms on a gritty Georgian street around the corner from once swanky Mountjoy Square (Sb-€38–60, Db-€70–110, Tb-€90–130, Qb-€90-140, non-smoking, some parking in back, 32 Gardiner Place, tel. 01/874-6364, fax 01/874-6122, www.clifdenhouse.com, bnb@indigo.ie).

$$ Charles Stewart Budget Accommodations is a big, basic place offering lots of forgettable rooms, many long and narrow, with head-to-toe twins, in a great location for a good price (S-€32, Sb-€50–64, D-€60–76, Db-€65–89, Tb-€100–121, Qb-€120–140, frequent midweek discounts, includes cooked breakfast, just beyond top end of O'Connell Street at 5–6 Parnell Square, tel. 01/878-0350, fax 01/878-1387, www.charlesstewart.ie, info@charlesstewart.ie).

EATING

As Dublin does its boom-time jig, fine and creative eateries are popping up all over town. While you can get decent pub grub for €12 on just about any corner, consider saving pub grub for the countryside. And there's no pressing reason to eat Irish in cosmopolitan Dublin. The city's good restaurants are packed from 20:00 on, especially on weekends. Eating early (17:00–19:00) saves time and money (as many better places offer an early-bird special).

Quick and Easy Around Grafton Street

Cornucopia is a small, earth-mama-with-class, proudly vegetarian, self-serve place two blocks off Grafton. It's friendly and youthful, with hearty €8 lunches and €10 dinner specials (Mon–Sat 8:30–20:00, Sun 12:00–19:00, 19 Wicklow Street, tel. 01/677-7583).

O'Neill's offers dependable €10 carvery lunches in a labyrinth of a pub with a central location, across from the main TI (daily 12:00–21:30, Suffolk Street, tel. 01/679-3656).

Graham O'Sullivan Restaurant and Coffee Shop is a cheap, cheery cafeteria serving soup and sandwiches with a salad bar and unpretentious ambience (Mon–Fri 8:00–18:30, Sat 9:00–17:00, Sun 9:00–16:30, 12 Duke Street). Two pubs on the same street—**The Duke** and **Davy Burns**—serve pub lunches. (The nearby Cathach Rare Books shop at 10 Duke Street displays a rare edition of *Ulysses*, among other treasures, in its window.)

Bewley's Café is an old-time local favorite offering light meals from €8 and full meals from €12. Sit on the ground floor among Harry Clarke windows and Art Deco lamps, or upstairs in the bright atrium decorated by local art students (self-service Mon–Sat 7:30–20:00, Sun 8:00–20:00, 78 Grafton Street, tel. 01/635-5470). For a taste of witty Irish lunch theater, check out **Bewley's Café Theatre** upstairs, where you can catch an hour performance with soup and a sandwich for only €12 (daily at 13:00 during a play's run, doors open 12:45, booking info tel. 086-878-4001, best to call ahead to see what's on).

Wagamama Noodle Bar, like its popular sisters in London, is a pan-Asian slurpathon with great and healthy noodle and rice dishes (€10–15) served by walkie-talkie-toting waiters at long communal tables (daily 12:00–23:00, no reservations, often a line, South King Street, underneath St. Stephen's Green Shopping Centre, tel. 01/478-2152).

South Great George's Street is lined with hardworking little eateries. **Juice** keeps vegetarians happy (daily 11:00–22:00, 73 South Great George's Street, tel. 01/475-7856).

Yamamori is a plain, bright, and modern Japanese place serving seas of sushi and noodles (€9 lunches daily 12:30–17:30, €13–18 dinners nightly 17:30–23:00, 71 South Great George's Street, tel. 01/475-5001).

Supermarkets: **Marks & Spencer** department store (on Grafton Street) has a fancy grocery store in the basement with fine takeaway sandwiches and salads (Mon–Fri 9:00–19:00, Thu until 21:00, Sat 9:00–19:00, Sun 12:00–18:30). Locals prefer **Dunne's** department store for its lower prices (same hours, grocery in basement, in St. Stephen's Green Shopping Centre).

Dublin Restaurants

1. Cornucopia Cafeteria
2. O'Neill's Pub
3. Graham O'Sullivan Rest.
4. Davy Burns Pub & The Duke Pub
5. Bewley's Café
6. Wagamama Noodle Bar
7. Juice Vegetarian Café
8. Yamamori Restaurant
9. Marks & Spencer Dept. Store/Grocery
10. Dunne's Dept. Store/Grocery & St. Stephen's Green Shopping Center
11. Bagel Haven
12. Leo Burdock's Fish & Chips
13. Restaurant le Caprice & Trocadero
14. Boulevard Café
15. Gallagher's Boxty House Rest.
16. Bad Ass Café
17. Luigi Malone's Restaurant
18. The Shack Restaurant
19. Gogarty's Pub (Musical Pub Crawl)
20. Brazen Head Pub
21. O'Shea's Merchant Pub

Fast and Cheap near Christ Church

Many of Dublin's **late-night grocery stores** (such as the Spar off the top of Dame Street on Parliament Street) sell cheap salads, microwaved meat pies, and made-to-order sandwiches. A €7 picnic dinner back at the hotel might be a good option after a busy day of sightseeing.

Bagel Haven does fresh bagel sandwiches and healthy fruit salads. Get it to go and enjoy a picnic with a Georgian view in one of Dublin's grassy squares (€3.50–5 breakfasts, €5–8 lunches, Mon–Fri 7:30–16:00, Sat 10:00–17:00, Sun 10:00–16:00, hidden beside Kinlay House on Cow's Lane, tel. 01/675-9900).

Leo Burdocks Fish & Chips is popular with locals (takeout only, daily 12:00–24:00, 2 Werburgh Street, off Christ Church Square).

Classy Restaurants and Cafés

These three restaurants are located within a block of each other, just south of Temple Bar and Dame Street, near the main TI.

Le Caprice is a fine, relaxing Italian place, with a wall of celebrities-who-ate-here photos, a good wine selection, and a friendly staff (€20–26 meals, Tue–Sun 17:30–23:15, closed Mon, 12 St. Andrew Street, tel. 01/679-4050). Consider their €19 early-bird special if your plans will take you elsewhere by 20:00.

Trocadero, across the street, serves beefy European cuisine to locals interested in a slow, romantic meal. The dressy, red-velvet interior is draped with photos of local actors. Come early, or make a reservation. This place is a favorite with Dublin's theatergoers (€18–29 meals, Mon–Sat 17:00–24:00, closed Sun, 3 St. Andrew Street, tel. 01/677-5545). The three-course early-bird special at €20 is a fine value (17:00–19:00, leave by 20:00).

Boulevard Café is mod, local, trendy, and likeable, serving Mediterranean cuisine, heavy on the Italian. They serve salads, pasta, and sandwiches for around €8, three-course lunch specials for €13 (offered Mon–Sat 12:00–16:00), and dinner plates for €13–23 (café open Mon–Sat 12:00–24:00, closed Sun, 27 Exchequer Street, smart to reserve for dinner, tel. 01/679-2131).

At Temple Bar

Gallagher's Boxty House is touristy and traditional, a good, basic value with creaky floorboards and old Dublin ambience. Its specialty is boxties—the generally bland-tasting Irish potato pancake filled and rolled with various meats, veggies, and sauces. The "Gaelic Boxty" is liveliest (€14–20, also serves stews and corned beef, Mon–Fri 9:00–23:00, Sat–Sun 10:00–23:00, 20 Temple Bar, reservations wise, tel. 01/677-2762).

Bad Ass Café is a grunge diner (where Sinead O'Connor was once a waitress) serving cowboy/Mex/veggie/pizzas to old and new hippies. No need to dress up (€8 lunches and €12–18 dinners, kids' specials, daily 11:30–24:00, Crown Alley, just off Meeting House Square, tel. 01/671-2596).

Luigi Malone's, with its fun atmosphere and varied menu of pizza, ribs, pasta, sandwiches, and fajitas, is just the place to take your high-school date (€12–24, daily 12:00–23:00, corner of Cecila and Fownes Streets, tel. 01/679-2723).

The Shack, while a bit pricey and touristy, has a reputation for good quality and serves traditional Irish, chicken, seafood, and steak dishes (€16–26 entrées, daily 11:00–23:00, in the center of Temple Bar, 24 East Essex Street, tel. 01/679-0043).

TRANSPORTATION CONNECTIONS

Within Ireland
From Dublin by bus to: Belfast (6/day, 3 hrs), **Trim** (10/day, 1 hr), **Ennis** (13/day, 4.5 hrs), **Galway** (13/day, 3.5 hrs), **Limerick** (13/day, 3.5 hrs), **Tralee** (7/day, 6 hrs), **Dingle** (4/day, 8 hrs, €23, transfer at Tralee). Bus info: tel. 01/836-6111.

By train from Heuston Station to: Tralee (5/day, 4 hrs, talking timetable tel. 01/805-4266), **Ennis** (2/day, 4 hrs), **Galway** (5/day, 3 hrs, talking timetable tel. 01/805-4222).

By train from Connolly Station to: Rosslare (5/day, 3 hrs), **Portrush** (7/day, 5 hrs, transfer in Belfast), **Belfast** (8/day, 2 hrs, tel. 01/836-3333). The **Dublin–Belfast train** connects the two Irish capitals in two hours at 90 mph on one continuous, welded rail (€33 one-way, €48 round-trip; round-trip the same day only €35 except Fri and Sun). Train info: tel. 01/836-6222. Northern Ireland train info: tel. 048/9089-9400.

Dublin Airport: The airport is well-connected to the city center seven miles away; see "Arrival in Dublin," page 46. Airport info: tel. 01/814-1111, www.dublin-airport.com. For a list of airlines, see page 323.

Ireland and Britain
Spend a few minutes online researching your transportation options across the Irish Sea. Most airline and ferry companies routinely offer discounts (often as much as €10) for tickets purchased from their Web sites.

Dublin and London: The journey by boat plus train or bus takes 7–12 hours, all day or all night (bus: 4/day, €25–42, British tel. 08705-143-219, www.eurolines.co.uk; train: 4/day, €61–118, Dublin train info: tel. 01/836-6222, British train info: 01/703-1884).

If you're going directly to London, flying is your best bet. Check **Ryanair** first (90 min, Irish tel. 01/609-7878, www.ryanair.com). Other options include **British Airways** (toll-free tel. in

Ireland 1-800-62647, in U.S. 800/247-9297, www.britishairways
.com), **Aer Lingus** (tel. 01/886-8888, www.aerlingus.com), and **bmi
british midland** (Irish tel. 01/407-3036, U.S. tel. 800/788-0555,
www.flybmi.com). To get the lowest fares, ask about round-trip
ticket prices and book months in advance (though Ryanair offers
deals nearly all of the time).

Dublin and Liverpool: SeaCat has ferries for car and foot passengers (4 hrs, daily, €28-32 one-way for foot passengers, tel. 800-
805-055, www.steam-packet.com). Car-only ferries are operated by
both P&O Irish Sea Ferries (7.5 hrs, daily, tel. 01/407-3434, www
.poirishsea.com) and Norse Merchant (8 hrs,
Mon–Sat, closed Sun, tel. 01/819-2999, www
.norsemerchant.com). Check in one to two
hours before the sailing time—call to confirm details.

Dublin and Holyhead: Irish Ferries
sails between Dublin and Holyhead in North
Wales (dock is a mile east of O'Connell Bridge, 5/day: 2 slow, 3 fast;
slow boats—3.25 hrs, €30 one-way walk-on fare; fast boats—1.75
hrs, €40; Dublin tel. 01/638-3333, Holyhead tel. 08705-329-129,
www.irishferries.com).

Dun Laoghaire and Holyhead: Stena Line sails between Dun
Laoghaire (near Dublin) and Holyhead in North Wales (3/day, 2 hrs
on HSS *Catamaran*, €30–44 one-way walk-on fare, €4 extra if paying
with credit card, reserve by phone—they book up long in advance on
summer weekends, Dun Laoghaire tel. 01/204-7777, recorded info
tel. 01/204-7799, can book online at www.stenaline.ie).

Ferries to France

Irish Ferries connects Ireland (Rosslare) with France (Cherbourg and
Roscoff) every other day (less often Jan–March). While Cherbourg
has the quickest connection to Paris, your overall time between Ireland
and Paris is about the same (20–25 hrs) regardless of which port is
used on the day you sail. One-way fares range from €50 to €100.
Eurailpass holders go half price. In both directions, departures are
generally between 16:00 and 20:00 and arrive late the next morning.
While passengers can nearly always get on, reservations are wise in
summer and easy by phone. If you anticipate a crowded departure, you
can reserve a seat for €11. Doubles (or singles) start at €54 per person.
The easiest way to get a bed (except during summer) is from the information desk upon boarding. The cafeteria serves bad food at reasonable prices. Upon arrival in France, buses and taxis connect you to your
Paris-bound train (Irish Ferries: Dublin tel. 01/638-3333, recorded
info tel. 01/661-0715, Paris tel. 01 44 94 20 40, www.irishferries.com,
info@irishferries.com; European Ferry Guide: www.youra.com
/ferry/intlferries.html).

Dun Laoghaire

Dun Laoghaire (DUN-leary) is seven miles south of Dublin. This beach resort, with the ferry terminal for Wales and easy connections to downtown Dublin, is a great small-town base for the big city.

For the view, hike out to the lighthouse at the end of the interesting East Pier. The Dun Laoghaire harbor was strategic enough to merit a Martello tower, one in a line built to defend against an expected Napoleonic invasion (the tower now houses a museum, see below). By the mid-19th century, the huge breakwaters—reaching like two muscular arms into the Irish Sea—were completed, protecting a huge harbor. Ships sailed regularly from here to Wales (60 miles away), and the first train line in Ireland connected the terminal with Dublin. While still a busy transportation hub, today the nearly mile-long breakwaters are also popular with strollers, bikers, birders, and fishermen.

Getting to Dun Laoghaire

While buses run between Dublin and Dun Laoghaire, the **DART** commuter train is much faster (4/hr, 20 min, runs Mon–Sat about 6:30–23:30, Sun from 9:00, €1.80 one-way, €3.20 round-trips are good same day only, Eurail valid but uses a flexi-day; for a longer stay, consider the €15 Short Hop 3-day bus-and-rail ticket covering DART and Dublin buses). If you're coming from Dublin, catch a DART train marked "Bray" and get off at the Sandycove or Dun Laoghaire stop, depending on which B&B you choose; if you're leaving Dun Laoghaire, catch a train marked "Howth" to get to Dublin, and get off at the central Tara Street station.

The **taxi** fare from Dun Laoghaire to central Dublin is about €25; to the airport, about €40. Try ABC Taxi service (tel. 01/285-5444). With easy, free parking and DART access into Dublin, this area is ideal for those with **cars** (which cost €20/day to park in Dublin).

ORIENTATION

The Dun Laoghaire **TI** is in the ferry terminal (Mon–Sat 10:00–18:00 year-round, closed Sun). The Net House Café provides a fast **Internet** connection 24 hours a day (€2.50/30 min, 28 Upper George's Street). The Jeeves **laundry** is located in the village of Sandycove (Mon–Sat 8:30–18:00, closed Sun, full-service only, 34 Glasthule Road, next to Daniel's Restaurant and Wine Bar, tel. 01/230-1120).

SIGHTS

James Joyce Museum—The Martello tower at Sandycove is the setting for the opening of the novel *Ulysses*. Literary fans will find memorabilia at the James Joyce Museum in the tower (€6.25, covered by Dublin Pass, ask about discount with DART ticket, Feb–Oct Mon–Sat 10:00–17:00, Sun 14:00–18:00, closed Nov–Jan, tel. 01/280-9265).

ENTERTAINMENT

For an evening of pure Irish music, song, and dance, check out the **Comhaltas Ceoltoiri Éireann**, an association working to preserve this slice of Irish culture. It got started when Elvis and company threatened to steal the musical heart of the new generation. Judging by the pop status of traditional Irish music these days, Comhaltas accomplished its mission. Their "Seisiun" evening is a stage show mixing traditional music, song, and dance (€10, July–Aug Mon–Thu at 21:00, followed by informal music session at 22:30). On Fridays all year long, they have a *ceilidh* (KAY-lee), where everyone does set dances. This style, the forerunner of square dancing, evolved from the French Quadrille dances of 200 years ago, with two couples making up a "set" (€8 includes friendly pointers, 21:30–00:30). At 21:00 on Tuesdays and Wednesdays (free) and Saturdays (€3), there are informal sessions by the fireside. All musicians are welcome. Performances are held in Cuturlann na Éireann, near the Seapoint DART stop, or take bus #7 from Dun Laoghaire, at 32 Belgrave Square, Monkstown (tel. 01/280-0295, www.comhaltas.com). Their bar is free and often filled with music.

SLEEPING

(€1 = about $1.20, country code: 353, area code: 01)

Near the Sandycove DART Station

These listings are within several blocks of the Sandycove DART station and a seven-minute walk to the Dun Laoghaire DART station/ferry landing.

$ **Seaview B&B**, a modern house run by Mrs. Kane, has three big, cheery rooms and a welcoming guests' lounge. While a few blocks farther out than the others, it's worth the walk for its bright and friendly feeling (Db-€70 through 2005 with this book, cash only, strictly non-smoking, just above Rosmeen Gardens at 2 Granite Hall, tel. & fax 01/280-9105, seaviewbedandbreakfast@hotmail.com).

$ **Windsor Lodge** rents four fresh, inviting rooms on a quiet street a block off the harbor and a block from the DART station

Dun Laoghaire

DUBLIN   BAY

WEST PIER

DART TRAIN STATION

TO DUBLIN

CROFTON RD.

FROM HOLYHEAD (N. WALES)

TO COMHALTAS IRISH MUSIC HOUSE

EAST PIER

ERLANA

LOWER MARINE ROAD

QUEENS ROAD

MORAN PARK

PROMENADE PARK

CONVENT RD.

PATRICK ST.

GEORGE'S

POST

MULGRAVE

MELLIFONT PARK ROAD

WINDSOR TERR.

NORTH

CUMBER

CORRIG

UPPER

CLARINDA PARK

TEN. CTS.

GLENAGEARY GARDENS

SUMMERHILL

ROSMEEN GARDENS

ROSMEEN PARK

ISLINGTON

ROAD

TO

SANDYCOVE DART STN.

TO BRAY

TO BRAY

DCH

* NOT TO SCALE - A WALK DOWN TO DOCK FROM GEORGE'S ST. IS ABOUT 5 MIN.

1. Seaview B&B
2. Windsor Lodge
3. Annesgrove B&B
4. Lynden B&B
5. Innisfree B&B
6. Mrs. Howard's B&B
7. Mrs. O'Sullivan's Duncree B&B
8. Provence Restaurant
9. Village Area Restaurants
10. To Martello Tower & James Joyce Museum

(Db-€60–80, Tb-€90, family deals, cash only, non-smoking, 3 Islington Avenue, Sandycove, tel. & fax 01/284-6952, winlodge @eircom.net, Mary O'Farrell).

$ **Annesgrove B&B** has four tidy rooms decorated in beige and brown (S-€50, D-€60, Db-€70, Tb-€90, cash only, parking, close to park and beach, 28 Rosmeen Gardens, tel. 01/280-9801, Anne D'Alton).

Near the Dun Laoghaire DART Station

$ **Lynden B&B,** with a classy, 150-year-old interior hiding behind a somber front, rents four big rooms (S-€40, Sb-€45–50, D-€56, Db-€70, 10 percent discount with this book in 2005, cash only, past

Mulgrave Street to 2 Mulgrave Terrace, tel. 01/280-6404, fax 01/230-2258, lynden@iol.ie, Maria Gavin).

$ Innisfree B&B has a fine lounge and six big, slightly frayed rooms (D-€50, Db-€58, 10 percent discount with this book in 2005, from George's Street, hike up the plain but quiet Northumberland Avenue to #31, tel. 01/280-5598, fax 01/280-3093, innismyth @eircom.net, Brendan and Mary Smyth).

On the same street, you'll find two places renting four big, well-worn rooms each: **$ Mrs. Howard's B&B** (S-€35, Sb-€40, D-€56, Db-€62, cash only, TV lounge, 36 Northumberland Avenue, tel. 01/280-3262, corahoward2003@yahoo.co.uk) and **$ Mrs. O'Sullivan's Duncree B&B** (D-€56, Db-€62, cash only, family room, non-smoking, 16 Northumberland Avenue, tel. 01/280-6118).

EATING

If staying in Dun Laoghaire, I'd definitely eat here and not in Dublin. Glasthule (called simply "the village" locally, just down the street from the Sandycove DART station) has a stunning array of fun, hardworking little restaurants.

Bistro Vino is the rage lately, with cozy, candlelit, Mediterranean ambience and great pasta and seafood (€14–23 meals, €20 early-bird special 17:00–19:00, daily 17:00–23:00, arrive early or have a reservation, 56 Glasthule Road, tel. 01/280-6097).

Reubens serves fish and pasta in a casual setting opposite the Eagle House pub (€11–18 meals, daily 10:00–22:00, 57 Glasthule Road, tel. 01/236-5971).

The big **Eagle House** pub dishes up hearty €9–16 pub meals (until 21:30) in a wonderful atmosphere. This is a super local joint for a late drink. The nearby **Daniel's Restaurant and Wine Bar** is less atmospheric but also good (€18–24 meals, Tue–Sun 18:00–23:00, closed Mon, 34 Glasthule Road, tel. 01/284-1027).

Provence, a classy little French restaurant with occasional live piano music, faces the water and serves fine cuisine (€28–35 main courses, €20 2-course early-bird special before 19:00, Tue–Sat 17:00–22:00, closed Sun–Mon, 1 Martello Terrace, directly down from Sandycove DART station, reservations smart, tel. 01/280-8788).

Walters Public House and Restaurant is a bright, modern place above a pub, offering good food to a dressy crowd (€16–24 meals, €15 early-bird special before 19:00, daily 17:30–22:30, 68 Upper George's Street, tel. 01/280-7442).

George's Street, Dun Laoghaire's main drag three blocks inland, has plenty of eateries and pubs, many with live music. A good bet for families is the kid-friendly **Bits and Pizza** (daily 12:00–24:00, off George's Street at 15 Patrick Street, tel. 01/284-2411).

NEAR DUBLIN

You don't have to go too far from urban Dublin to find the stony skeletons of evocative ruins sprouting from the lush Irish countryside. The story of Irish history is told by ancient burial mounds, early Christian monastic settlements, huge Norman castles, and pampered estate gardens. These sights are separated into regions: North of Dublin (Valley of the Boyne, including Newgrange and the town of Trim) and South of Dublin (Glendalough and the Wicklow Mountains).

North of Dublin:
Valley of the Boyne

The peaceful, green Valley of the Boyne, just 30 miles north of Dublin, has an impressive concentration of historical and spiritual sights. You'll find enigmatic burial mounds at Newgrange older than the Egyptian pyramids; the Hill of Tara (seat of the high kings of Celtic Ireland), where St. Patrick preached his most persuasive sermon; the first Vatican-endorsed monastery in Ireland; and several of Ireland's finest high crosses. You'll see Trim's 13th-century castle—Ireland's biggest—built by Norman invaders. You can wander the site of the historic Battle of the Boyne (1690), in which the Protestants turned the tide against the Catholics and locked in British rule of the Irish.

Planning Your Time
Of these sights, only Newgrange is worth ▲▲▲ (and deserves a good 3 hours). The others, while relatively meager physically, are powerfully evocative to anyone interested in Irish history and culture. Without a car, I'd visit only Newgrange, taking the shuttle bus from Dublin.

The region is a joy by car, because all of the described sights are within a 30-minute drive of each other. If you eat your Weetabix, you could do the entire region in a day. While sights are on tiny roads, they're well-marked with brown, tourist-friendly road signs, and you can manage with your all-Ireland Michelin map. (Note that the Newgrange sights are signposted Brú na Bóinne.)

As you plan your Ireland itinerary, keep in mind that if you're flying into or out of Dublin and want to avoid the intensity and expense of big-city Dublin, you could use Trim as an overnight base (45-min drive from airport, see accommodations listings on page 92) and tour these sights from there.

Getting Around Valley of the Boyne

If you don't have a car, consider one of these round-trip tours from Dublin.

Mary Gibbon's Tours visit both Newgrange (including inside the tomb) and the Hill of Tara in a six-hour trip (€35, €29 if you flash this book in 2005, Mon–Fri only, 10:00 pickup in Dublin at Buswells Hotel on Molesworth Street, 10:15 pickup at Dublin TI on Suffolk Street, 10:30 pickup at Royal Dublin Hotel on O'Connell Street, home by 16:30, book direct rather than through TI, tel. 01/283-9973, www.newgrangetours.com, info@newgrangetours.com).

Over the Top Tours cover everything but Newgrange and Trim. Leaving Dublin at 9:00 and returning by 18:00, they stop at Hill of Tara, the Hill of Slane (free time for lunch), Loughcrew (prehistoric tombs, less famous than Newgrange), the Battle of the Boyne site, and the monasteries of Monasterboice and Mellifont Abbey (€26, daily, departing from Dublin TI on Suffolk Street, 14-seat minibus, reservations required, hold seat by leaving credit card number, toll-free tel. 1-800-424-252, Dublin tel. 01/838-6128, www.overthetoptours.com).

Tír na nÓg Tours (TEER-nuh-ohg) offers two options: Newgrange and the Hill of Tara (Wed and Fri); or Trim Castle, Hill of Tara, Hill of Slane, and Mellifont Abbey (Sat–Sun; €30 for either tour, 9:15 pickup at Gresham Hotel on O'Connell Street, 9:30 pickup at Dublin TI on Suffolk Street, back in Dublin by 17:00, book ahead, tel. 01/836-4684, www.tirnanogtours.com).

SIGHTS

▲▲▲**Newgrange (Brú na Bóinne)**—The famous archaeological site commonly referred to as "Newgrange" (actually one of the tombs) is more properly known as Brú na Bóinne—"dwelling place of the Boyne." The well-organized site centers on a state-of-the-art museum. Visitors are given appointments for shuttle buses that ferry small groups five minutes away to one of two 5,000-year-old passage

Boyne Valley Area

tombs, where a guide gives a 30-minute tour. Newgrange is more famous and allows you inside. Knowth (rhymes with south) opened more recently and is more extensive, but you can't go inside the tomb. At the turnstile, you'll buy a ticket to one or both sights and be given bus departure times (if you plan to see both sights, note that buses depart 90 min apart). Newgrange sells out first and comes with a longer wait. If you opt for Knowth, be sure to see the museum's replica of the Newgrange passage entrance (where a short tour and winter solstice light-show demo often occur upon request); the replica is connected to the video room. Each site is different enough and worthwhile, but for many, seeing just one is adequate. For information on the prehistoric art, see "Irish Art" in the Irish History and Culture chapter.

Newgrange is one single mound, the more restored of the Brú na Bóinne sites. Dating from 3200 B.C., it's 500 years older than the pyramids at Giza. While we know nothing of these people, this most certainly was a sacred spot dealing with some kind of sun-god ritual.

During your tour, you'll squeeze down a narrow passageway to a cross-shaped central chamber under a 20-foot-high, igloo-type stone dome. Bones and ashes were placed here under 200,000 tons of stone and dirt to wait for a special moment. As the sun rose on the shortest day of the year (winter solstice, Dec 21), a ray of light would creep slowly down the 60-foot-long passageway. For 17 minutes, it would light the center of the sacred chamber. Perhaps this was the moment when the souls of the dead would be transported to the afterlife via that mysterious ray of life-giving and life-taking light.

Knowth (the second Brú na Bóinne site) is a necropolis of several grassy mounds around one 85-yard-wide grand tomb. The big mound, covering 1.5 acres, has two passages aligned so that on the spring and fall equinox, rays from the rising and setting sun shine down the passageways to the center chamber. Neither of the passages is open to the public, but you get a glimpse down one when you visit a room cut into the mound to expose the interior construction layers. The Knowth site thrived from 3000 to 2000 B.C. with mysterious burial rituals and sun-tracking ceremonies to please the gods and ensure the regular progression of seasons for crops. The site then evolved into the domain of fairies and myths for the next 2,000 years, and became an Iron Age fortress in the early centuries after Christ. Around A.D. 1000, it was an all-Ireland political center, and, later, a Norman fortress was built atop the mound. You'll see plenty of mysteriously carved stones and new-feeling grassy mounds that you can look down on from atop the grand tomb.

Cost and Hours: Allow an hour for the excellent museum and an hour for each of the tombs you visit. The museum in the Visitors Centre is included in the following prices: Newgrange-€5.50, Knowth-€4.25, both tombs-€9.75, covered by Heritage Card—see page 4 (May–Sept daily 9:00–18:30 or 19:00, slightly shorter hours off-season, Newgrange open year-round, Knowth open April–Oct only, tel. 041/988-0300).

Crowd-Beating Tips: Visits are limited, and on busy summer days, those arriving in the afternoon may not get a spot (no reservations possible). In peak season, try to arrive by 9:30 to avoid a wait. Generally, upon arrival you'll get a bus departure time for one or both of the passage-tomb sites (the last shuttle bus leaves 1.75 hours before closing). Spend your wait visiting the museum, watching the great seven-minute video, and munching lunch in the cheery cafeteria. You can't drive directly to the actual passage tombs.

Getting There: To reach the Visitors Centre from Dublin by **car,** drive north on N1 to Drogheda, where signs direct you to the Brú na Bóinne Visitors Centre.

Without a car, take the Newgrange **shuttle bus** from Dublin directly to the Visitors Centre (€15 round-trip, departs at 8:45 and 11:00 from TI on Suffolk Street or 9:00 and 11:15 from O'Connell Street, return trips depart at 13:00 and 16:00 from the Visitors Centre, run by Over the Top Tours, book by phone, tel. 01/860-0405). More frequent but far less convenient is the Bus Eireann **bus** from Dublin, which drops you in Donore—a 15-minute walk from the Visitors Centre (€15 round-trip, pay driver exact change or buy ticket at Busaras station, buses depart Dublin at 9:00, 10:00, 11:00, 12:00, 13:30, and 14:30 from stop opposite Wynn's Hotel on Lower Abbey Street, just around corner from Busaras central bus station, 90-min trip, transfer in Drogheda, confirm schedule at station and confirm transfer point with driver, tel. 01/836-6111).

▲**Hill of Tara**—This was the most important center of political and religious power in pre-Christian Ireland. While aerial views show plenty of mysterious circles and lines, wandering with the sheep among the well-worn ditches and hills leaves you with more to feel than to actually see. Visits are made meaningful by an excellent 20-minute video presentation and the caring 20-minute guided walk that follows (always available upon request and entirely worthwhile).

You'll see the Mound of Hostages (a Bronze-Age passage grave, c. 2500 B.C.), a couple of ancient sacred stones, a war memorial, and vast views over the Emerald Isle. While ancient Ireland was a pig-pile of minor chieftain-kings scrambling for power, the high king of Tara was king of the mountain. It was at this ancient stockade that St. Patrick directly challenged the power of the high king. When confronted by the pagan high king, Patrick convincingly explained the Holy Trinity using a shamrock: three petals with one stem. He won the right to preach Christianity throughout Ireland, and the country had a new national symbol.

This now desolate hill was also the scene of great modern events. In 1798, passionate young Irish rebels chose Tara for its defensible position, but were routed by better organized (and more sober) British troops. (The cunning British commander had earlier in the day sent three cartloads of whiskey along the nearby road, knowing the rebels would intercept it.) In 1843, the great orator and champion of Irish liberty, Daniel O'Connell, gathered more than 500,000 Irish peasants on this hill for his greatest "monster meeting"—a peaceful show of force demanding the repeal of the Act of Union with Britain.

Stand on the Hill of Tara. Think of the history it's seen, and survey Ireland. It's understandable why this "meeting place of heroes" continues to hold a powerful place in the Irish psyche (€2, covered by Heritage Card—see page 4, includes video and 20-min guided walk, daily 10:00–18:00, last tour 17:15, tel. 046/902-5903). Local guide Jean Thornton, who works on site, brings the lumpy mounds to life—if she's on duty, request her.

Mellifont Abbey—This Cistercian abbey (the first in Ireland) was established by French monks, who came to the country in 1142 to bring the Irish monks more in line with Rome. (Even the abbey's architecture was unusual, marking the first time in Ireland that a formal European-style monastic layout was used.) Cistercians lived isolated, rural lives; lay monks worked the land, allowing the more educated monks to devote all their energy to prayer. After Henry VIII dissolved the abbey in 1539, centuries of locals used it as a handy quarry. Consequently, little survives beyond the octagonal lavabo, where the monks would ceremonially wash their hands before entering the refectory to eat. The lavabo gives a sense of the grandeur that once was. The excellent tours, available upon request and included in your admission, give meaning to the site (€2, covered by Heritage Card—see page 4, May–Oct daily 10:00–18:00, last entry 17:15, no tours Nov–April when site is free, but you can explore on your own, tel. 041/982-6459).

Monasterboice—This ruined monastery is visit-worthy for its round tower and ornately carved high crosses—two of the best such crosses in Ireland. In the Dark Ages, these crosses, illustrated from top to bottom with Bible stories, gave monks a teaching tool as they preached to the illiterate masses. Today, Monasterboice, basically an old graveyard, is always open and free.

The 18-foot-tall Cross of Murdock (Muiredach's Cross, A.D. 923, named after an abbot) is considered the best high cross in Ireland. The circle—which characterizes the Irish high cross—could represent the perfection of God. Or, to help ease pagans into Christianity, it could represent the sun, which was worshipped in pre-Christian Celtic society. Whatever its symbolic purpose, its real function was to support the crossbeam.

Face the cross (with the round tower in the background) and study the carved sandstone. The center panel shows the Last Judgment, with Christ under a dove symbolizing the Holy Spirit. Those going to heaven are on Christ's right, and the damned are being ushered away by devils on his left. Working down, you'll see the Archangel Michael weighing souls, as the Devil tugs demonically at the scales; the adoration of the three—or four—Magi; Moses striking the rock; scenes from the life of David; and, finally, Adam, Eve, and the apple next to Cain slaying Abel. Imagine these carvings with their original colorful paint jobs.

Find the even taller cross nearest the tower. It seems the top section was broken off and buried, while the bottom part remained standing, enduring the Irish weather.

The door to the round tower was originally 15–20 feet above the ground (accessible by ladder). After centuries of burials, the ground level has risen.

Battle of the Boyne Site—One of Europe's great non-sights, this is simply the pastoral riverside site of the pivotal battle in which the

Protestant British broke Catholic resistance, establishing Protestant rule over all Ireland and Britain. Drop into the information center next to the small parking lot and ask for a guided tour (free, May–Sept daily 10:00–18:00, closed Oct–April, tel. 041/988-4343). The attendant will generally take you on a 45-minute historic stroll around the Oldbridge Estate on the south bank of the river.

It was here in 1690 that Protestant King William III, with his English and Dutch army, defeated his father-in-law, Catholic King James II, and his Irish and French army. King William's forces, on the north side of the Boyne, managed to cross the river, and by the end of the day, James was fleeing south in full retreat. He soon departed Ireland, but his forces fought on until their final defeat two years later. James the Second (called "James da Turd" by those who scorn his lack of courage and leadership) never returned and died a bitter ex-monarch in France. King William of Orange's victory, on the other hand, is still celebrated in Northern Ireland every July 12th, with controversial marches by Unionist "Orangemen."

Trim

The sleepy, work-a-day town of Trim, straddling the Boyne River, is marked by the towering ruins of Trim Castle. Trim feels littered with mighty ruins that seem to say, "This little town was big-time...700 years ago." The tall "Yellow Steeple" (over the river from the castle) is all that remains of the 14th-century Augustinian Abbey of St. Mary. A pleasant half-mile walk back toward Dublin takes you to the sprawling ruins of Saints Peter and Paul Cathedral (from 1206), once the largest Gothic church in Ireland. Across the old Norman bridge from the cathedral are the 13th-century ruins of the Hospital of St. John the Baptist.

If you're flying into or out of Dublin's airport and don't want to deal with big-city Dublin, Trim is perfect—an easy 45-minute, 30-mile drive away. You can rent a car at the airport and make Trim your first overnight base (getting used to driving on the other side of the road in easy country traffic), or spend your last night here before returning your car at the airport. Either way, you don't need or want a car in Dublin (where parking is expensive and sightseeing is best on foot, by bus, or by taxi). If you have a car and are going from Trim to Dublin in the middle of your trip, try this compromise: Drive to Dublin's huge Phoenix Park and park there for free. Then grab a Dublin City Tours hop-on, hop-off bus tour to shuttle you through big-city traffic (€12.50, see page 50).

ORIENTATION

Trim's main square is a traffic roundabout, and everything's within a block or two. Most of the shops and eateries are on or near Market Street, as well as banks, a supermarket, and the **launderette** (Mon–Sat 9:00–18:00, closed Sun, Watergate Street, tel. 046/943-7176). The **post office** is tucked in the back of the Spar Market (Mon–Fri 9:00–17:30, Sat 9:00–12:30, closed Sun, Emmet Street).

Tourist Information: The TI is right next to the castle entrance. Drop in for a free map and take a moment to ask them about Mel Gibson's visit to film *Braveheart.* Check out the model of the castle transformed into the movie set (Mon–Sat 10:00–12:30 & 13:30–17:00, Sun 12:00–17:00, shorter hours off-season, Castle Street, tel. 046/943-7227).

SIGHTS

▲▲**Trim Castle**—This is the biggest Norman castle in Ireland. Its mighty keep towers above a very ruined outer wall in a grassy riverside park at the edge of the sleepy town. The current castle was completed in the 1220s and served as a powerful Norman statement to the restless Irish natives. It remains an impressive sight—so impressive, it was used in the 1994 filming of *Braveheart.*

The best-preserved walls ring the castle's southern perimeter and sport a barbican gate that contained two drawbridges. At the base of the castle walls, notice the clever, angled "batter" wall—used by defenders, who hurled down stones that banked off at great velocity into the attacking army.

The massive, 70-foot-high central keep has 20 sides. Offering no place for invaders to hide, it was tough to attack. You can go inside only with the included tour (2/hr, 30 min). In a mostly hollow shell, you'll climb a series of tightly winding original staircases and modern, high catwalks, learn about life in the castle, and end at the top, with great views of the walls and countryside (€1.75 for castle grounds, €3.75 for entrance to keep and required tour, covered by Heritage Card—see page 4, roughly April–Oct daily 10:00–18:00, last entry 17:00, Nov–March Sat–Sun only 10:00–17:00, last entry 16:00, tour spots are limited, so call in peak season to save frustration of arriving to find nothing available, tel. 046/943-8619). Make time to take a 15-minute walk outside, circling the castle walls and stopping at the informative plaques that show the castle from each viewpoint during its gory glory days. Night strollers are treated to views of the castle hauntingly lit in blue-green hues.

Trim

1 Highfield House B&B

2 To Crannmór Guest House
   & Dunderry Lodge Restaurant

3 To Tigh Cathain B&B

4 Brogan's Guesthouse

5 Franzini O'Brien's Restaurant
   & Bennini's Café

6 James Griffin's Pub

7 To David's Lad Pub

8 Marigold Chinese Restaurant

9 Launderette

The Power & Glory—This is a grade-schoolish, 30-minute slide show overview of the personalities and history of the castle, followed by an exhibit on life here in Norman times (€3.25, Mon–Sat 10:00–12:30 & 13:30–17:00, Sun 12:00–17:00, shorter hours off-season, in visitors center building with TI next to castle, Castle Street, tel. 046/943-7227). The show and a free cup of coffee help to pass the time as you wait for your castle tour.

SLEEPING

In and near Trim

$$ **Brogan's Guesthouse** offers 15 rooms divided between its rustic original front guesthouse and its modern annex out back (Sb-€45–55, Db-€72–80, Tb-€108–120, High Street, secure parking, tel. 046/943-1237, fax 046/943-7648, info@brogans.ie).

$$ **Highfield House B&B,** across the street from the castle and a five-minute walk from town, is a stately, 170-year-old former maternity hospital with hardwood floors and seven spacious, high-ceilinged rooms (Sb-€48–50, Db-€72, Tb-€99–110, family-friendly, overlooks roundabout where Dublin Road hits Trim, just before castle at Maudlins Road, tel. 046/943-6386, fax 046/943-8182, www.highfieldguesthouse.com, highfieldhouseaccom@eircom.net, Geraldine Duignan).

$ *Countryside B&Bs:* About a mile outside of Trim in the quiet countryside are these two B&Bs (phone ahead for driving directions). At **Crannmór Guest House**, north of town, Mrs. O'Regan decorates the five rooms with cheery color schemes, and Mr. O'Regan knows all the best fishing holes (Sb-€40–45, Db-€64, Tb-€90, Dunderry Road, tel. 046/943-1635, fax 046/943-8087, www.crannmor.com, cranmor@eircom.net). Southwest of town, Mrs. Keane's **Tigh Cathain B&B** has four rooms with a comfy, rural feel (Db-€62–68, cash only, Longwood Road, tel. 046/943-1996, www.tighcathaintrim.com, mariekeane@esatclear.ie).

EATING

A country market town, Trim offers basic meat-and-potatoes lunch and dinner options. Don't waste time searching for gourmet food. The restaurants and cafés along Market Street are friendly, whole-some, and unpretentious (soup-and-sandwich delis close at 18:00).

Your best cafeteria-style lunch bet is **Bennini's Café,** hidden beside the parking lot to the left of Trim Castle's entry gate (Mon–Fri 9:00–16:30 & 18:00–21:00, Sat–Sun 10:00–16:30 & 18:00–21:00, French's Lane, tel. 046/943-8409).

Franzini O'Brien's, next door, is the only place in town with a fun dinner menu and enough business to make it work. They serve

---

Sleep Code

(€1 = about $1.20, country code: 353, area code: 046)
S = Single, **D** = Double/Twin, **T** = Triple, **Q** = Quad,
b = bathroom, **s** = shower only. Credit cards are accepted, and
breakfast is included unless otherwise noted.

To help you easily sort through these listings, I've divided
the rooms into two categories, based on the price for a standard double room with bath:

    $$ **Moderately Priced**—Most rooms more than €70.
    $ **Lower Priced**—Most rooms €70 or less.

---

pasta, steak, fish, and fajitas in a modern candlelit ambience.
Nothing's Irish but the waiters (€12–25, Mon–Sat 18:30–22:00, Sun
17:00-21:00, French's Lane, tel. 046/943-1002).

If you feel like Chinese food, **Marigold** fits the bill (Mon–Sat
17:30–24:00, Sun 16:00–24:00, Emmet Street, tel. 046/943-8788).

For an expensive (€25–30) but tasty splurge on good, old-fashioned cooking, get driving directions to **Dunderry Lodge,** four miles
north of Trim off the Dunderry Road (Mon–Sat 19:30–21:30, Sun
12:30–14:30 & 18:30–20:30, tel. 046/943-1671).

For an unvarnished pub experience, check out Trim's two best
watering holes. **James Griffin's** (on High Street) is full of local characters, with Mr. Lenihan, who has run the place for 55 years, pre-
siding. **David's Lad** is ideal if you like your beer experience
unfiltered. Rock Hudson dropped by for a pint while filming
Captain Lightfoot (closed Wed, at old Norman Bridge by cathedral
ruins, 20-min walk out of town, but worth it).

Supermarkets: **Super Valu** has everything you need to create a
picnic (Mon–Fri 8:00–21:00, Sat 8:00–21:30, Sun 7:00–18:30,
Haggard Street). The smaller **Spar Market** has fewer choices
(Mon–Sat 8:00–21:00, Sun 9:00–18:00, Emmet Street).

TRANSPORTATION CONNECTIONS

Trim has no train station; the nearest is in Drogheda, on the coast,
but there are no bus connections to Trim from there.

Buses from Trim to **Dublin** (12/day, 1 hr) pick up next to the
castle entry on Castle Street and in front of Tobin's News Shop on
Haggard Street.

South of Dublin:
Glendalough and the Wicklow Mountains

The Wicklow Mountains, while only 10 miles south of Dublin, feel remote—enough so to have provided a handy refuge for opponents to English rule. Rebels who took part in the 1798 Irish uprising hid out here for years. When the frustrated British built a military road in 1800 to help flush out the rebels, the area became more accessible. Today, this same road—now the R115—takes you through the Wicklow area to Glendalough at its south end. While the valley is the darling of Dublin day-trip tour organizers, it doesn't live up to the hype. But two blockbuster sights—Glendalough and the Gardens of Powerscourt—make a visit worth considering.

Getting Around Glendalough and the Wicklow Mountains

By car or tour, it's easy. If you lack wheels, take a tour. It's not worth the trouble on public transport.

By Car: It's a delight. Take the freeway south from Dublin to Enniskerry, the gateway to the Wicklow Mountains. Signs direct you to the gardens and on to Glendalough. From Glendalough, if you're heading west, you can leave the valley (and pick up the highway to the west) over the famous but dull mountain pass called the Wicklow Gap.

By Tour from Dublin: Wild Wicklow Tours cover the region with an entertaining guide packing every minute with information and fun *craic* (conversation). With a gang of 29 packed into tight but comfortable, mountain-gripping buses, the guide kicks into gear from the first pickup in Dublin. Tours cover Dublin's embassy row, Dun Laoghaire, the Bay of Dublin (with the mansions of Ireland's rich and famous), the windy military road over scenic Sally Gap, and the Glendalough monasteries (€28, €25 for students, any of my readers can show this book and pay the student price in 2005, daily year-round, 9:10 pickup at Dublin TI on Suffolk Street, 10:00 pickup at Dun Laoghaire TI, stop for lunch at a pub—cost not included, return through Dun Laoghaire and on to Dublin by 17:30, Dun Laoghaire-ites could stay on the bus to continue into Dublin for the evening, advance booking required, tel. 01/475-3313, www .discoverdublin.ie).

Mary Gibbon's Tours visit both Glendalough and the Gardens of Powerscourt in a six-hour trip (€35, €29 with this book in 2005, 10:00 pickup at Buswells Hotel on Molesworth Street, 10:15 pickup at Dublin TI on Suffolk Street, 10:30 pickup at Royal Dublin Hotel on O'Connell Street, home by 16:30, call ahead to reserve—especially in high season, book direct rather than through TI, tel. 01/283-9973, www.newgrangetours.com, info@newgrangetours.com).

Over the Top Tours bypass mansions and gardens to focus on Wicklow scenery. Stops include Glendalough, the Glenmacnass waterfall, and Blessington lakes (€24, 9:45 pickup at TI on Suffolk Street, return by 17:30, 14-seat minibus, reservations required, hold seat by leaving credit card number, tel. 1-800-424-252, Dublin tel. 01/838-6128, www.overthetoptours.com).

Tír na nÓg Tours visit Glendalough, Sally Gap, Lough Tay, and the Blessington lakes (€30, Tue, Thu, Sat, and Sun, 9:15 pickup at Gresham Hotel on O'Connell Street, 9:30 pickup at TI on Suffolk Steet, back in Dublin by 17:00, book ahead, tel. 01/836-4684, www.tirnanogtours.com).

SIGHTS

▲▲Gardens of Powerscourt—While the mansion's interior, only partially restored after a 1974 fire, isn't much, its meticulously kept aristocratic gardens are Ireland's best. The house was commissioned in the 1730s by Richard Wingfield, first viscount of Powerscourt. The gardens, created during the Victorian era (1858–1875), are

called "the grand finale of Europe's formal gardening tradition...probably the last garden of its size and quality ever to be created." I'll buy that.

Upon entry, you'll get a flier laying out 40-minute and 60-minute walks. The "60-minute" walk takes 30 minutes at a slow amble. With the impressive summit of the Great Sugar Loaf Mountain as a backdrop, and a fine Japanese garden, Italian garden, and goofy pet cemetery along the way, this attraction provides the scenic greenery I hoped to find in the rest of the Wicklow area. The lush movie *Barry Lyndon* was filmed in this well-watered aristocratic fantasy.

The Gardens of Powerscourt, a mile above the village of Enniskerry, cover several thousand acres within the 16,000-acre estate. The dreamy driveway alone is a mile long (€7 March–Oct, €5 Nov–Feb, daily 9:30–17:30, great cafeteria, tel. 01/204-6000, www.powerscourt.ie). Skip the associated waterfall (€4.50, 4 miles away).

▲▲Military Road over Sally Gap—This is only for those with a car. From the Gardens of Powerscourt and Enniskerry, go to Glencree, where you drive the tiny military road over Sally Gap and through the best scenery of the Wicklow Mountains. Look for the German military cemetery, built for U-Boat sailors who washed ashore in World War II. Near Sally Gap, notice the peat bogs and the freshly cut peat bricks drying in the wind. Many locals are nostalgic for the "good old days," when homes were peat-fire heated. At the Sally Gap junction, turn left, where a road winds through the vast Guinness estate. Look down on the glacial lake (Lough Tay) and the Guinness mansion (famous for jet-set parties). Nicknamed "Guinness Lake," the water looks like Ireland's favorite dark-brown stout, and the sand of the beach actually looks like the head of a Guinness beer. From here, the road winds scenically down into the village of Roundwood and on to Glendalough.

▲▲Glendalough—The steep, wooded slopes of Glendalough (GLEN-da-lock, "valley of the two lakes"), at the south end of Wicklow's military road, hide Ireland's most impressive monastic settlement. Founded by St. Kevin in the 6th century, the monastery flourished (despite repeated Viking raids) throughout the "Age of Saints and Scholars," until the English destroyed it in 1398. While it was finally abandoned during the Dissolution of the Monasteries in 1539, pilgrims kept coming, especially on St. Kevin's Day, June 3. (This might have something to do with the fact that a pope said seven visits to Glendalough had the same indulgence value as one visit to Rome.) While much restoration was done in the 1870s, most of the buildings date from the 8th through 12th centuries.

The valley sights are split between the two lakes. The lower lake has the Visitors Centre and the best buildings. The upper lake has scant ruins and feels like a state park, with a grassy lakeside picnic area and school groups. Walkers and hikers will enjoy a choice of nine different trails of varying lengths through the lush Wicklow countryside (longest loop takes 4 hrs).

Planning Your Time: Park free at the Visitors Centre. Visit the center, wander the ruins (free) around the round tower, walk the traffic-free Green Road one mile to the upper lake, and then walk back to your car. Or you can drive to the upper lake (more free parking, except July–Aug, when you'll pay €5). If you're rushed, skip the upper lake. Summer tour-bus crowds are terrible all day on weekends and 11:00–14:00 on weekdays.

Glendalough Visitors Centre: Start your visit here (€2.75, covered by Heritage Card—see page 4, mid-March–mid-Oct daily 9:30–18:00, last entry 17:15, closes earlier off-season, tel. 0404/45325). The 20-minute video provides a good thumbnail background on monastic society in medieval Ireland. While the video is more general than specific to Glendalough, the adjacent museum room features this particular monastic settlement. The model in the center of the room re-creates the fortified village of the year 1050 (although there were no black-and-white Frisian cows in Ireland back then— they would have been red). A browse through the interactive exhibits here shows the contribution these monks made to intellectual life in

South of Dublin

Dark Age Europe (such as illuminated manuscripts and Irish minuscule, a more compact alphabet developed in the 7th century).

From the center, a short and scenic walk along the Green Road takes you to the round tower.

The Monastic Village: Easily the best ruins of Glendalough gather around the famous, 110-foot-tall round tower. Towers like this (usually 60–110 feet tall) were standard features in such settlements, functioning as beacons for pilgrims, bell towers, storage lofts, and last-resort refuges during Viking raids (though, given enough warning, monks were safer hiding in the surrounding forest). They had a high door with a pull-up ladder. Several ruined churches (8th–12th centuries) and a sea of grave markers complete this evocative scene. Markers give short descriptions of the ruined buildings.

In an Ireland without cities, these monastic communities were mainstays of civilization. They were remote outposts where ascetics (with a taste for scenic settings) gathered to commune with God. In the 12th century, with the arrival of grander monastic orders, such as the Franciscans and the Dominicans, and with the growth of cities, these monastic communities were eclipsed. Today, Ireland is dotted with the reminders of this age: illuminated manuscripts, simple churches, carved crosses, and about 100 round towers.

Upper Lake: The Green Road continues one mile farther up the valley to the upper lake. The oldest ruins—scant and hard to find—lie near this lake. If you want a scenic Wicklow walk, begin here.

KILKENNY and the ROCK OF CASHEL

If you're driving from Dublin (on Ireland's east coast) to Dingle (on Ireland's west coast), the best two stops to break the long journey are Kilkenny, often called Ireland's finest medieval town, and the Rock of Cashel, a thought-provoking early Christian site crowning the Tipperary Plain. With a few extra days, there are additional worthwhile destinations along the southeast coast, such as Waterford and County Wexford (described in the next chapter). Folks with even more time can continue on the scenic coastal route west via Cobh, Kinsale, Kenmare, and the Ring of Kerry (covered in Kinsale & Cobh and Kenmare & Ring of Kerry chapters).

Kilkenny

Famous as "Ireland's loveliest inland city," Kilkenny gives you a feel for salt-of-the-earth Ireland. Its castle and cathedral stand like historic bookends on either end of a higgledy-piggledy High Street of colorful shops and medieval facades. It's nicknamed the "Marble City" for its nearby quarry (actually black limestone, not marble), and you can still see the white seashells fossilized within the black stone steps around town. While a small town today (fewer than 10,000 residents), Kilkenny has a big history. It used to be an important center—occasionally even the capital of Ireland in the Middle Ages.

Planning Your Time
Kilkenny is a good overnight for drivers wanting to break the journey from Dublin to Dingle (necessary if you want to spend more time in the Wicklow area and at the Rock of Cashel). A night in Kilkenny comes with plenty of traditional folk music in the pubs (hike over the river and up John Street).

Kilkenny and Cashel

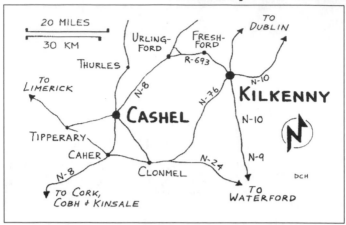

ORIENTATION

(area code: 056)

Tourist Information

The TI, a block off the bridge in the 16th-century Shee Alms poor-house, offers hour-long guided **town walks** (€6, 5/day, first one at 10:30; TI open Mon–Fri 9:00–18:00, Sat 10:00–18:00, closed Sun, Rose Inn Street, tel. 056/775-1500).

Arrival in Kilkenny

The train/bus station is four blocks from John's Bridge, which marks the center of town. The two handiest places to park are in the lot next to the castle (get parking disks at local shops, €1 each, buy 1 for each hour you want to stay, 3 hrs max in one parking space, scratch off your arrival time and leave it on your dash) or in the mul-tistory parking garage on Ormonde Street (€1.30/hr, or just get the 5-day pass for €12 if spending the night).

Helpful Hints

Laundry: Use Hennessy's at 18 Parliament Street (Mon–Sat 8:30–18:00, closed Sun).

Local Guide: Pat Tynan is good (mobile 087-265-1745, fax 056/776-3955, www.tynantours.com).

SIGHTS

▲**Kilkenny Castle**—Dominating the town, this castle is a stony reminder that the Anglo-Norman Butler family controlled the town for 500 years. Tours start with a 12-minute video explaining how the

Kilkenny

TO CASHEL VIA R693 & FRESHFORD

ST. CANICE'S & ROUND TOWER

SMITHWICK'S BREWERY

ROTHE HOUSE

BLACK ABBEY

ST. MARY'S

POST

BUTTER SLIP LANE

TRAIN/BUS STATION

TO DUBLIN

P – PARKING

ST. JOHN'S BRIDGE

RIVER NOIRE

KILKENNY CASTLE

DESIGN CENTRE

DCH

PUDDING LANE

DEAN ST. · IRISHTOWN · ABBEY ST. · PARLIAMENT ST. · BLACKMILL ST. · JAMES ST. · HIGH STREET · ST. KIERNAN'S · FRIARY ST. · PARNELL ST. · ORMONDE ST. · PATRICK ST. · THE PARADE · CASTLE ROAD · MICHAEL ST. · JOHN ST. · MAUDLIN ST. · DUBLIN RD. · NEW ST. · ORMONDE RD.

200 YARDS
200 METERS

1 Club House Hotel
2 Butler Court Hotel
3 Ristorante Rinuccini Rooms
4 Berkeley House Hotel

5 Kilkenny Tourist Hostel
6 Langton's Pub & Restaurant
7 Kyteler's Inn
8 Pennefeather Restaurant
9 Launderette

wooden fort, built here by Strongbow in 1172, evolved into a 17th-century château. Now restored to its later Victorian splendor, the highlight is the beautiful family portrait gallery putting you face-to-face with the wealthy Butler family ghosts. Tours, which start running 30 minutes after the castle opens for the day, are first-come, first-served, fill fast, and can be booked only for the same day (€5, covered by Heritage Card—see page 4, June–Aug daily 9:30–19:00, April–May daily 10:30–17:00, Sept 10:00–18:30, Oct–March 10:30–12:45 & 14:00–17:00, tel. 056/772-1450).

The **Kilkenny Design Centre**, across the street from the castle, is full of local crafts and offers handy cafeteria lunches upstairs (April–Dec Mon–Sat 10:00–19:00, Sun 11:00–19:00; Jan–March Mon–Sat 10:00–19:00, closed Sun; www.kilkennydesign.com).

St. Canice's Cathedral—This 13th-century cathedral is early English Gothic, rich with stained glass, medieval carvings, and floors paved in history. Check out the model of the old walled town in its 1641 heyday (€3, €4 combo-ticket with tower, Mon–Sat 9:00–18:00, Sun 14:00–18:00, tel. 056/776-4971). The 100-foot-tall round tower, built as part of a long-gone, pre-Norman church, recalls the need for a watchtower and refuge. The fun ladder-climb to the top affords a grand view of the countryside (€2, €4 combo-ticket with cathedral, Mon–Sat 10:00–18:00, Sun 14:00-18:00).

Rothe House—This well-preserved Tudor merchant's house expanded around interior courtyards as the prosperous family grew. The museum, which also serves as the County Kilkenny genealogy center, runs a 15-minute video giving a glimpse of life here in Elizabethan times (€3, April–Sept Mon–Sat 10:30–17:00, Sun 15:00–17:00; Oct–March Mon–Sat 13:00–17:00, closed Sun; Parliament Street, tel. 056/772-2893).

SLEEPING

$$$ Club House Hotel is perfectly central. Originally a gentlemen's sporting club, it comes with old-time Georgian elegance; a palatial, well-antlered breakfast room; and 35 large, comfy bedrooms (Sb-€90, Db-€140, 10 percent discount with this book in 2005, Patrick Street, tel. 056/772-1994, fax 056/777-1920, www.clubhousehotel .com, clubhse@iol.ie).

$$ Butler Court, across the street and uphill from the Club House Hotel, offers eight modern rooms behind cheery yellow walls (Sb-€50–70, Db-€100–130, Tb-€160–180, accessible to wheelchair users, Patrick Street, tel. 056/776-1178, fax 056/779-0767, www .butlercourt.com, info@butlercourt.com).

$$ Ristorante Rinuccini, directly opposite the castle, has seven fine rooms off the street above the restaurant (Db-€100–120, Tb-€125–150, cheaper off-season, 1 The Parade, tel. 056/776-1575, fax 056/775-1288, www.rinuccini.com, info@rinuccini.com).

$$ Berkeley House, with 10 rooms across the street and down-hill from Club House Hotel, is smaller, less expensive, and comfort-able (Db-€100–120, Tb-€130–150, 5 Lower Patrick Street, tel. 056/776-4848, fax 056/776-4829, www.berkeleyhousekilkenny.com, berkeleyhouse@eircom.net).

Sleep Code

(€1 = about $1.20, country code: 353, area code: 056)
S = Single, **D** = Double/Twin, **T** = Triple, **Q** = Quad,
b = bathroom, **s** = shower only. All of these places include
breakfast and accept credit cards.

To help you easily sort through these listings, I've divided
the rooms into three categories, based on the price for a standard
double room with bath:

$$$ **Higher Priced**—Most rooms €130 or more.
 $$ **Moderately Priced**—Most rooms between €65–130.
  $ **Lower Priced**—Most rooms €65 or less.

$ Kilkenny Tourist Hostel, filling a fine Georgian townhouse
in the town center, offers cheap beds, a friendly family room, a well-
equipped members' kitchen, and a wealth of local information (dorm
bed-€15, D-€38, Q-€68, cash only, laundry service-€5, 2 blocks
from cathedral at 35 Parliament Street, tel. 056/776-3541, fax
056/772-3397, kilkennyhostel@eircom.net).

EATING

Langton's serves quality Irish dishes (daily 8:00–22:30, 69 John
Street, tel. 056/776-5133), while **Ristorante Rinuccini** provides
your Italian fix (daily 12:00–14:30 & 18:00–22:30, 1 The Parade,
tel. 056/776-1575).

Grab a quick, light lunch at the **Pennefeather Restaurant**
above the Kilkenny Book Centre (Mon–Fri 9:00–17:30, Sat
9:00–17:00, closed Sun, 10 High Street, tel. 056/776-4063).

For basic pub grub in a fun atmosphere, visit the cellar under
Kyteler's Inn, and ask about their witch (daily 12:00–21:30, 27
St. Kieran's Street, tel. 056/772-1064). Try a pint of Smithwick's
in its hometown.

TRANSPORTATION CONNECTIONS

From Kilkenny by train to: Dublin (4/day, 2 hrs), **Waterford**
(4/day, 45 min).

By bus to: Dublin (6/day, 2 hrs), **Waterford** (3/day, 1 hr),
Tralee (3/day, 5 hrs), **Galway** (5/day, 4.5 hrs).

Rock of Cashel

Rising high above the fertile Plain of Tipperary, the Rock of Cashel—worth ▲▲▲—is one of Ireland's most historic and evocative sights. Seat of the ancient kings of Munster (c. A.D. 300–1100), this is the where St. Patrick baptized King Aengus in about A.D. 450. Strategically located and perfect for fortification, the Rock was fought over by local clans for hundreds of years. Finally, in 1101, clever Murtagh O'Brien gave the Rock to the Church. His seemingly benevolent donation increased his influence with the Church, while preventing his rivals, the powerful McCarthy clan, from regaining possession of the Rock. As Cashel evolved into an ecclesiastical center, Iron Age ring forts and thatch dwellings gave way to the majestic stone church buildings enjoyed by tourists today.

Cost and Hours: €5, families-€11, covered by Heritage Card—see page 4, early June–mid-Sept daily 9:00–19:00; mid-March–early June and mid-Sept–mid-Oct daily 9:00–17:30; mid-Oct–mid-March daily 9:00–16:30; last entry 45 minutes before closing. Parking will cost you €2.50 (buy parking ticket at machine inside lot).

Orientation: At the end of the road on top of the Rock, the 15th-century Hall of the Vicars Choral houses the ticket desk, a tiny museum (with St. Patrick's original 12th-century high cross and a few replica artifacts), and a 20-minute video (2/hr, shown in the hall's former dormitory). WCs are next to the parking lot (none up on Rock). You may want to stop by the Bru Boru Cultural Centre (see page 110) to learn more about the Rock before you ascend.

It's a steep, 50-yard walk up to the Rock itself. On this 200-foot-high outcropping of limestone, you'll find a round tower, an early Christian cross, a delightful Romanesque chapel, and a ruined Gothic cathedral, all surrounded by my favorite Celtic-cross graveyard. Bring a coat for the deceptively cool conditions on the high, windy, exposed Rock.

Crowd-Beating Tips: Summer crowds flood the Rock (worst June–Aug 11:00–15:00). Try to plan your visit for early or late in the day. If you're here at a peak time, tour the Rock first and save the movie, museum, and Hall of the Vicars Choral for the end of your visit, when the tourist tide has receded. Otherwise, see the movie and museum first.

Tours: Call ahead to find out the schedule for tours (included in entry price, 45 min, tel. 062/61437). Otherwise, set your own pace with the tour I've outlined below.

Rock of Cashel

SIGHTS

Rock of Cashel

Follow this self-guided tour counter-clockwise around the Rock. To start the tour, climb the stairs opposite the ticket desk.

Hall of the Vicars Choral—This is the youngest building on the Rock (early 1400s). It housed the minor clerics appointed to sing during cathedral services. These vicars—who were granted nearby lands by the archbishop—lived comfortably here, with a large fireplace and white, lime-washed walls (to reflect light and act as a natural disinfectant). Window seats gave the blessedly literate vicars the best light to read by. The furniture is original, but the oak timber roof is a reconstruction, built to medieval specifications using wooden dowels instead of nails. The large wall tapestry, showing King Solomon with the Queen of Sheba, contains intentional errors—to remind viewers that only God can create perfection. The vicars, who formed a sort of corporate body to assist the bishop with local administration, used a special seal to authorize documents, such as land leases. You can see an enlarged wooden copy of the seal (hanging above the fireplace), depicting eight vicars surrounding a seated organist. It was a good system—until some of the greedier vicars duplicated the seal for their own use, forcing the archbishop to curtail its use.

Go outside the hall and find...

St. Patrick's Cross—St. Patrick baptized King Aengus at the Rock of Cashel around A.D. 450. Legend has it that St. Patrick, intensely preoccupied with the holy ceremony, accidentally speared the foot of the king with his crosier staff while administering the baptismal sacrament. But the pagan king stoically held his tongue until the end of the ceremony, thinking this was part of the painful process of becoming a Christian.

This 12th-century cross, a stub of its former glory, was carved to celebrate the handing over of the Rock to the Church 650 years after St. Patrick's visit. Typical Irish high crosses use a ring around the cross' head to support its arms and to symbolize the sun (making Christianity more appealing to the sun-worshipping Celts). But instead, this cross uses the Latin design: The weight of the arms is supported by two vertical beams on each side of the main shaft, representing the two criminals who were crucified beside Christ (today, only one of these supports remains).

On my first visit, 25 years ago, the original cross still stood here. But centuries of wind and rain slowly eroded away important detail, so the cross was moved into the adjacent museum and replaced by this replica.

Turn your back on St. Patrick's Cross and walk about 100 feet slightly uphill along the gravel path beside the cathedral. Roughly opposite the far end of the Hall of the Vicars Choral is the entry to...

Cormac's Chapel—As the wild Celtic Christian church was reined in and reorganized by Rome 850 years ago, new architectural influences from continental Europe began to emerge on the remote Irish landscape. This small chapel—Ireland's first and finest Romanesque church, consecrated in 1134 by King Cormac MacCarthy—reflects this evolution. Travel in your imagination back to the 12th century, when this chapel and the tall round tower (described below) were the only stone structures on the Rock.

The "new" Romanesque style reflected the

ancient Roman basilica floor plan. Its columns and rounded arches created an overall effect of massiveness and strength. Romanesque churches were like dark fortresses with thick walls, squat towers, few windows, and minimal decoration. Irish stone churches of this period (like the one at Glendalough in the Wicklow Mountains, or the Gallarus Oratory near Dingle) were simple rectangular buildings with no ornate stone carving at all.

Tradition says that the chapel's easy-to-cut sandstone was quarried 12 miles away, and the blocks were passed from hand to hand back to the Rock. The two square towers resemble those in Regensburg, Germany, further suggesting that well-traveled medieval Irish monks brought back new ideas from the Continent.

The metal grid chapel door (always unlocked) is a modern addition to keep out nesting birds. Enter the chapel (remembering to close the door behind you) and let your eyes adjust to the low light.

Chapel Interior—Just inside the chapel is an empty stone **sarcophagus**. Nobody knows for sure whose body once lay here (possibly the brother of King Cormac MacCarthy). The damaged front relief is carved in the Scandinavian Urnes style. Vikings raided Ireland, intermarried with the Irish, and were melting into Irish society by the time this chapel was built. Some scholars interpret the relief design (a tangle of snakes and beasts) as a figure eight lying on its side, looping back and forth forever, like the eternity of the afterlife.

With your back to the sarcophagus, let your eyes wander around the chapel interior. You're standing in the **nave**, lit by the three windows (partially blocked by the later cathedral) in the wall behind you. Overhead is a round vaulted ceiling with support ribs. The strong round arches support not only the heavy stone roof, but also the (unseen) second-story scriptorium chamber, where monks once carefully copied manuscripts.

The **chancel arch**, studded with fist-sized heads, framed the altar (now gone). The lower heads are more grotesque, while those nearing the top become serene as they climb closer to God. The arch is off-center in relation to the nave, symbolic of Christ's head drooping to the side as he died on the cross.

Walk into the chancel and look up at the ceiling, examining the faint **frescoes,** a labor of love from 850 years ago. Frescoes are rare in Ireland because of the perpetually moist climate. (Mixing pigments into wet plaster worked better in dry climates, like Italy.) Once vividly colorful, then fading over time, these frescoes were further damaged during the Reformation. Such ornamentation was considered vain by Protestants, who piously whitewashed over them. These surviving frescoes were discovered under multiple whitewash layers during painstaking modern restoration. The rich blue color came from lapis lazuli, an expensive gemstone imported from Asia.

Walk through the other metal grid doorway (don't let the

birds in), opposite the door you used to enter the chapel. You'll find yourself in a…

Forgotten Void—This enclosed space was created when the newer cathedral was wedged between the older chapel and the round tower. Once the main entrance into the chapel, this forgotten doorway is crowned by a finely carved tympanum decorating the arch above it. It's perfectly preserved because the huge cathedral shielded it from the elements. The large lion (symbol of St. Mark's Gospel) is being hunted by a centaur archer (half man, half horse) wearing a Norman helmet (essential conehead attire in the late Middle Ages).

As you exit the chapel (turning left), take a look at the more exposed and weathered tympanum outside, above the south entrance. The carved, bloated "hippo" is actually a bull, part of St. Luke's apocalyptic vision. Tiptoe through the tombstones around the east end of the cathedral to the base of the round tower.

Graveyard and Round Tower—This graveyard still takes permanent guests—but only those put on a waiting list by their ancestors in 1930. A handful of these chosen few are still alive, and once they're gone, the graveyard will be considered full. The 20-foot-tall shaft at the edge of the graveyard, marking the O'Scully family crypt, was once crowned by an elaborately carved Irish high cross—destroyed during a lightning storm in 1976.

Look out over the **Plain of Tipperary**. Called the "Golden Vale," its rich soil makes it Ireland's most prosperous farmland. In St. Patrick's time, it was covered with oak forests. A path leads to the ruined 13th-century Hore Abbey in the fields below (free, always open and peaceful). The abbey is named for the Cistercian monks who wore simple gray robes, roughly the same color as hoarfrost.

Gaze up at the **round tower**, the first stone structure built on the Rock after the Church took over in 1101. The shape of these towers is unique to Ireland. Though you might think towers like this were used as a place to hide in case of invasion, they were used primarily as bell towers and lookout posts. (Enemies could smoke out anyone inside the tower, and with enough warning, monks were better off hiding in the countryside.) The tower stands 92 feet tall, with walls over three feet thick. The doorway, which once had a rope ladder, was built high up not only for security, but also because having it at ground level would have weakened the foundation of the top-heavy structure. The interior once contained wooden floors connected by ladders, and served as safe storage for the monk's precious sacramental treasures. The tower's stability is impressive when you consider its age, the winds it has endured, and the shallowness of its foundation (only 5 feet under present ground level).

Continue walking around the cathedral's north transept, noticing the square holes in the exterior walls. During construction, wooden scaffolding was anchored into these holes. On your way to the cathedral entrance, in the corner where the north transept joins the nave, you'll pass a small **well**. Without this essential water source, the Rock could never have withstood a siege, and would not have been as valuable to clans and clergy. In 1848, a chalice was dredged from the well, likely thrown there by fleeing medieval monks intending to survive a raid. They didn't make it. (If they had, they would have received the chalice.)

Now enter the...

Cathedral—Traditionally, the choir of a church (where the clergy celebrate Mass) faces east, while the nave (where the congregation stands) stretches off to the west. Because this cathedral was squeezed between the preexisting chapel, round tower, and drinking well, the builders were forced to improvise—giving it an extra-long choir and a cramped nave.

Built between 1230 and 1290, the church's pointed arches and high, narrow windows proclaim the Gothic style of the period (and let in more light than earlier Romanesque churches). Walk under the central bell tower and look up at the rib-vaulted **ceiling**. The hole in the middle was for a rope used to ring the church bells. The wooden roof is long gone. When Lord Inchiquin (Oliver Cromwell's general, who was hunting down royalists faithful to the deposed King Charles I) attacked the town of Cashel in 1647, hundreds of townsfolk fled to the sanctuary of this cathedral and held out. Inchiquin packed turf around the exterior and set fire to it, massacring those inside.

Ascend the **terraces** at the choir end of the cathedral, where the main altar once stood. Stand on the gravestones (of the 16th-century rich and famous) with your back to the open east wall (where the narrow windows have crumbled away), and look back down toward the nave. The right wall of the choir is filled with graceful Gothic windows, while the solid left wall hides Cormac's Chapel (which would have blocked any sunlight). The line of stone supports on the left wall once held the long, wooden balcony where the vicars sang. Closer to the altar, high on the same

wall, is a small, rectangular window called the "leper's squint"—which allowed unsightly lepers to view the altar during Mass without offending the congregation.

The grand **wall tomb** on the left contains the remains of archbishop Miler Magrath, the "scoundrel of Cashel," who lived to be 100. From 1570 to 1622, Magrath was the Protestant archbishop of Cashel while simultaneously profiting from his previous position as Catholic bishop of Down. He married twice, had lots of kids, confiscated the ornate tomb lid here from another bishop's grave, and converted back to Catholicism on his deathbed.

Walk back down to the far end of the nave and exit the cathedral on the left, through the porch entrance.

Castle—Back outside, stand beside the huge chunk of wall debris and try to picture where it might have fit in the ruins above. This end of the cathedral was converted into an archbishop's castle in the 1400s (shortening the nave even more). Looking high into the castle's damaged top floors, you can see the bishop's residence chamber and the secret passageways that were once hidden in the thick walls. Lord Inchiquin's cannons weakened the structure during the 1647 massacre, and in 1848, a massive storm (known as "Night of the Big Wind" in Irish lore) flung the huge chunk next to you from the ruins above.

In the mid-1700s, the Anglican Church transferred cathedral status to St. John's in town, and the archbishop abandoned the drafty Rock for a more comfortable residence, leaving the ruins that you see today.

Near the Rock of Cashel

Bru Boru Cultural Centre—Nestled below the Rock of Cashel parking lot, next to the statue of the three blissed-out dancers, this center adds to your understanding of the Rock in its wider historical and cultural context. The highlight of the Sounds of History museum downstairs is the exhibit showing the Rock's gradual evolution from ancient ring fort to grand church ruins— projected down onto a large disc that visitors gather around.

Those headed for Dingle's great traditional music scene will enjoy the surprisingly good, 15-minute film introduction to Irish traditional music in the small museum theater (€5, June–Sept daily 9:00–20:30, Oct–May Mon–Fri 9:00–17:00, closed Sat–Sun, cafeteria, tel. 062/61122).

If you overnight in Cashel, consider taking in a performance of the Bru Boru musical dance troupe in the Centre's large upstairs theater (€15, mid-June–mid-Sept Tue–Sat at 21:00).

Town of Cashel—This huggable town at the base of the Rock affords a good break on the long drive from Dublin to Dingle (**TI** open June–mid-Sept Mon–Sat 9:30–18:00, Sun July–Sept only, closed mid-Sept–May, tel. 062/61333). The Heritage Centre (across hall from TI, tel. 062/62511) handles TI services off-season and presents a modest eight-minute audio explanation of Cashel's history around a walled town model.

SLEEPING

(€1 = about $1.20, country code: 353, area code: 062)
If you spend the night in Cashel, you'll be treated to views of the ruins beautifully illuminated at night.

$$ Legends Townhouse has seven pleasant rooms (most with views of the floodlit ruins) above a friendly restaurant in a convenient location near the base of the Rock (Sb-€50, Db-€110–128, The Kiln, non-smoking, parking, tel. 062/61292, www.legendsguesthouse.com, info@legendsguesthouse.com).

$ Rockville House, with six fine rooms, is close to the Rock (Sb-€39, Db-€50–55, Dominic Street, tel. 062/61760).

$ Abbey House, a bit farther toward town, has five comfortable rooms (Sb-€44, D-€55, Db-€62, Dominic Street, tel. & fax 062/61104, teachnamainstreach@eircom.net).

$ O'Brien's Holiday Lodge is a fun, well-kept hostel behind the rock near Hore Abbey (dorm beds-€16, Db-€45–50, Tb-€60, camping spots-€5 per person, laundry service-€9, Dundrum Road R505, tel. & fax 062/61003, obriensholidayhostel@eircom.net).

EATING

Grab a soup-and-sandwich lunch at tiny **Granny's Kitchen** (next to parking lot at base of Rock) or at snug **King Cormac's** (a block away at base of road up to Rock).

For lunch or dinner, **Pasta Milano's** neon-orange glow is easy to spot above a famine work-project wall (€12–19 meals, daily 12:00–23:00, Ladyswell Street, tel. 062/62729).

For a splurge dinner, consider classy **Chez Hans** (2-course €22 early-bird menu before 19:30, otherwise €25–37 entrées, Tue–Sat 18:00–22:00, closed Sun–Mon, in an old church a block below the Rock, tel. 062/61177). The same folks also run the cheaper **Chez Hans Café** up the street (Tue–Sat 12:00–17:30).

Legends Restaurant offers good dinners with great nighttime views of the lit-up Rock (2-course €24 early-bird menu before 19:30, Tue–Sat 18:30–21:30, closed Sun–Mon, The Kiln, behind hedge beside main parking lot, tel. 062/61292).

TRANSPORTATION CONNECTIONS

Cashel has no train station; the closest one is 13 miles away in the town of Thurles.

From Cashel by bus to: Dublin (6/day, 3 hrs), **Kilkenny** (3/day, 2.5 hrs), **Waterford** (6/day, 2 hrs).

WATERFORD and COUNTY WEXFORD

The best overnight stop in southeast Ireland is the historic Viking and Norman beachhead town of Waterford. From here, you can explore the varied sights of County Wexford.

Waterford

The oldest city in Ireland, Waterford was once more important than Dublin. Today, while tourists associate the town's name with its famous crystal, locals are quick to remind you that the crystal is named after the town, and not vice versa. That said, Waterford is a plain, gray, work-a-day town. Pubs outnumber cafés, freighters offload cargo at the dock, and when radio stations offer dinner at McDonald's as a prize, people actually call in. It's a dose of real Ireland, which was, until a couple of generations ago, one of the poorest countries in Western Europe.

Planning Your Time

A day is more than enough time for Waterford. Visit the crystal factory on the south edge of town on your way in or out—to avoid the midday crowds (the TI at the factory has a free visitor's guide with a town map). In Waterford, your best activity is the historic walk (at 11:45 or 13:45, see "Tours," below), followed by a visit to the Museum of Treasures and Reginald's Tower. To feel the pulse of Waterford, hang out on the town's pedestrian square and stroll through its big, modern shopping mall.

Waterford's History

The Vikings first came in 850 and established Waterford as their base for piracy. Since the spot is located at the gateway to the largest natural navigation system in Ireland, Viking ships could sail 50 miles into Ireland from here. Ireland had no towns at this time, only scattered monastic settlements and small gatherings of clans—perfect for rape, pillage, and plunder. Later, the Vikings decided to "go legal" and do their profiteering from an established trading base they named Vandrafjord ("safe harbor"...eventually Waterford). This became Ireland's first permanent town. It was from this base that the Vikings invaded England in the 10th century.

In the 12th century, a deposed Irish king invited the Normans over from England, hoping to use their muscle to regain his land from a rival clan. The great warrior knight Strongbow came and never left, and that was the beginning of Ireland's long and troublesome relationship with the English.

ORIENTATION

(area code: 051)

Waterford's main drag runs along its ugly harbor, where you'll find the bus station and easy parking lots (€1.40/hr). All sights and recommended accommodations (except the Waterford Crystal factory tour) are within a five-minute walk of the clock tower on the harbor. Both museums and the TI are on the harborfront. The stubby Victorian clock tower marks the middle of the harbor as well as the pedestrian Barronstrand Street that runs a block to the town square.

Tourist Information

The TI is inside the old brick granary warehouse on Merchant's Quay (April–Oct Mon–Fri 9:00–18:00, Sat 10:00–18:00, closed Sun; Nov–March Mon–Sat until 17:00, closed Sun; tel. 051/875-823). As with all Irish TIs, it's basically a shop with a counter where clerks tell you about places that they endorse (i.e., get money from).

City Pass Ticket: If you're visiting all three town sights (Museum of Treasures, Reginald's Tower, and Waterford Crystal), you can save €4.50 on admissions by buying the €10 City Pass Ticket (sold at each sight but not at TI).

Helpful Hints

Post Office: It's on Parade Quay (Mon–Fri 9:00–17:30, Sat 9:00–13:00, closed Sun).

Laundry: Snow White launderette is at 61 Mayor's Walk (Mon–Sat 8:30–18:30, Sun 11:00–18:00, tel. 051/858-905).

Waterford

100 YARDS
100 METERS

P – PARKING
— = OLD CITY WALLS

TRAIN STATION

NEWRATH ROAD

RICE BRIDGE

BUS STATION

R I V E R   S U I R

MUSEUM OF TREASURES

CLOCK TOWER

MEAGHER QUAY

HOLY TRINITY CATHEDRAL

PARADE QUAY

REGINALD'S TOWER

O'CONNELL

GEORGE

BARRON

POST

HIGH

SHOPPING CENTER

NEW

BAILEYS

TO

JAIL

MAYORS WALK

STEPHENS

MICHAEL

BROAD

JOHN

LADY LANE

SPRING GARDENS

PARNELL

THE MALL

CHRIST CHURCH CATHEDRAL

JOHN'S LANE

CASTLE

MANOR

JOHNSTOWN

SOUTH PARADE

TO CRYSTAL FACTORY & CORK

1 The Granville Hotel
2 Dooley's Hotel
3 The Avondale Hotel
4 Brown's Townhouse
5 Mayor's Walk House
6 Beechwood Guesthouse
7 To Quality Hotel
8 Wine Vault Restaurant, Emiliano's Ristorante Italiano & Johnny Fan's Chinese Rest.
9 Sizzlers Restaurant
10 Launderette

Taxi: Consider Street Cabs Ltd. (117 Parade Quay, tel. 051/877-778). Rapid Cabs operate local taxis (tel. 051/858-585) as well as Rapid Express coaches to Dublin airport (tel. 051/872-149).

TOURS

▲▲**Waterford Historic Walking Tour**—Jack Burtchaell and his partners lead informative, hour-long historic town walks that meet at the Waterford Museum of Treasures (behind TI) every day at 11:45 and 13:45 (just show up and pay €5 at the end, mid-March–mid-Oct only, tel. 051/873-711). The tour—really the most enjoyable thing to do in Waterford—is an entertaining walk from the TI to Reginald's Tower, giving you a good handle on the story of Waterford.

SIGHTS

Cathedral of the Holy Trinity—In 1793, the English king granted Ireland the Irish Relief Act, which, among other things, allowed the Irish to build churches and worship publicly. With Catholic France (30 million) threatening Britain (8 million) on one side, and Ireland (6 million) stirring things up on the other, the king needed to take action to lessen Irish resentment.

Granted their new freedom, the Irish built their interesting cathedral in 1796. It's Ireland's first Catholic post-Reformation church, and its only Baroque church. The building was funded by wealthy Irish wine merchants from Cadiz, Spain. Among its treasures are 10 Waterford Crystal chandeliers (free, daily 8:00–19:00).

Nearby: The cathedral faces **Barronstrand Street,** which leads from the clock tower on the harborfront to the pedestrian-friendly **town square.** The street separates the medieval town (on your left when the river is behind you) from the 18th-century city (on your right). A river once flowed here—part of the town's natural defenses just outside the old wall. The huge **shopping center** that dominates the old town was built right on top of the Viking town. In fact, the center is built over a church dating from 1150 that you can see at the bottom of the escalator (next to the kiddie rides).

▲**Reginald's Tower**—This oldest part of the oldest town in Ireland is

named after Regnall, the first Viking leader of Waterford, who built a tower here in A.D. 914 and later founded Jorvik (York, England). The tower you see today dates from 1003 and is supposedly Ireland's oldest intact building, and its first made of mortar. It was the most important corner of the town wall. Inside, you'll see a display of medieval

Thomas Francis Meagher
(1823–1867)

Waterford's favorite son had a short but busy life. Born to a conservative Waterford mayor, Meagher joined Daniel O'Connell's nonviolent movement to repeal the Act of Union with Britain. Impatient with the slow-moving peace process, he joined the radical Young Irelander movement and became an inspiring speaker. He went to France in 1848 and came back with the first Irish tricolor flag—a gift from the French representing the Catholics (green), the Protestants (orange), and peaceful coexistence between them (white). Involved in a failed uprising, Meagher was sentenced to death, but he managed to get his sentence commuted to life in prison in Tasmania. Meagher escaped Tasmania in 1852 and sailed to America, where he studied law and eventually became a lawyer. After he made a trip to Nicaragua to study the feasibility of building a canal across the isthmus, the American Civil War broke out. Meagher was made a general and raised a regiment of Irish immigrants that he famously led into battle for the Union. After the war, he became the first governor of the Montana territory. Then 44-year-old Thomas Francis Meagher fell off a riverboat and drowned.

coins, old city models, a few Viking artifacts, and a short video (€2, covered by City Pass Ticket and Heritage Card—see page 4, includes guided tour any time upon request—ask for the 1-hr version, which adds a historic walk around the block; June–Sept daily 10:00–18:30, Oct–May daily 10:00–17:00, last entry 75 min before closing, tel. 051/304-220).

▲▲**Waterford Museum of Treasures**—This museum presents, with the help of handheld audioguides, a good sweep through the history of Ireland as seen from Waterford. It's housed, along with the TI, in an old stone grain warehouse where the original Waterford Crystal Factory stood (€6, covered by City Pass Ticket; April–Sept Mon–Sat 9:30–18:00, Sun 11:00–18:00; Oct–March Mon–Fri 10:00–17:00, Sat–Sun 11:00–17:00; last entry 1 hour before closing, tel. 051/304-500).

Christ Church Cathedral—This 18th-century, neoclassical Protestant cathedral is the fourth church to stand here (see the exposed Gothic column 6 feet below today's floor level). The macabre tomb of 15th-century mayor James Rice comes with a famous epitaph: "I am what you will be, I was what you are, pray for me." To emphasize the point, he requested that his body be dug up one year after his death (1482) and his partially decomposed remains be used to model his likeness, now seen on the tomb's lid...complete with worms and frogs (€3, generally open 10:00–17:00).

▲▲**Waterford Crystal Factory**—With a tradition dating back to 1783, Waterford is the largest and one of the most respected glassworks in the world. Its fine hour-long tours take visitors through the entire production process and offer a close-up look at many of the plant's 1,600 employees hard at work.

While you ride a bus to one end of the factory, your guide orients you. Then you see a huge furnace—which has been burning nonstop for 30 years—where the dipping, blowing, and shaping take place. (It's powered by natural gas, piped in 90 miles from Kinsale.) Next, you see the etching. Workers, after a five-year apprenticeship, make the art of crystal-blowing and cutting look easy. Each glass piece goes through more than 30 sets of hands before it's ready for sale. Waterford proudly sells no seconds. Due to tiny blemishes detected by quality control, about a third of the pieces are smashed and remelted. (Workers are paid by the successful piece.) The tour finishes with an opportunity to actually meet a cutter, see his diamond-bladed wheel in action, and ask questions. Then you land in the glittering salesroom surrounded by hard-to-pack but easy-to-ship temptations. Before leaving, go upstairs above the gift shop to see the copies of famous sports trophies (they make backups of their most important commissions...just in case).

Cost and Hours: €8, covered by City Pass Ticket, March–Oct daily 8:30–18:00, last tours leave at 16:00 sharp, but shop stays open until 18:00; Nov–Feb Mon–Fri 9:00–15:00, no tours Sat–Sun, but shop is open 9:00–17:00. A handy TI is next to the cafeteria at the back of the reception area.

Tours: Tours are liveliest weekdays before 15:30. Except for a skeleton crew working for the benefit of the tours, the factory is pretty quiet after 16:00 and on weekends. Minimize crowds by coming early and avoiding the afternoon rush. If arriving late, call to confirm tour times (tel. 051/332-500, www.waterfordvisitorcentre.com).

Getting There: The factory is conveniently located on the N25 Cork road about two miles south of the city center. Catch bus #3 from in front of Kelly's department store on Parade Quay (€1.20, 4/hr).

SLEEPING

Waterford is a working-class town. Cheap accommodations are fairly rough. Fancy accommodations are venerable old places facing the water.

$$$ The Granville Hotel is Waterford's top, most historic hotel, grandly overlooking the center of the harborfront. The place is plush,

Sleep Code

(€1 = about $1.20, country code: 353, area code: 051)
S = Single, D = Double/Twin, T = Triple, Q = Quad,
b = bathroom, s = shower only. Unless otherwise noted,
breakfast is included and credit cards are accepted.

To help you easily sort through these listings, I've divided
the rooms into three categories, based on the price for a standard
double room with bath:

$$$ **Higher Priced**—Most rooms €100 or more.
$$ **Moderately Priced**—Most rooms between €65–100.
$ **Lower Priced**—Most rooms €65 or less.

from its Old World lounges to its extravagant rooms (Db-€160–195,
ask about "corporate discounts," Meagher Quay, tel. 051/305-555, fax
051/305-566, www.granville-hotel.ie, stay@granville-hotel.ie).

$$$ **Dooley's Hotel**, a more modern, business-class place with
big motel-style rooms on the harbor, can be less expensive (Db-
€170–190, often discounted much lower, Merchant's Quay, tel. 051/
873-531, fax 051/870-262, www.dooleys-hotel.ie, hotel@dooleys
-hotel.ie).

$$$ **Quality Hotel,** part of the dependable hotel chain, has
large, comfortable rooms and very little personality (Sb-€70–90, Db-
€140–180, Tb-€210–270, Canada Street, parking, tel. 051/856-600,
fax 051/856-605, www.choicehotelsireland.ie, info@waterford
.qualityhotels.ie).

$$ **The Avondale**, facing a noisy street a block inland from
Reginald's Tower, rents six fine rooms (Sb-€45–50, Db-€80–90,
Qb-€140, 2 Parnell Street, tel. 051/852-267, www.staywithus.net,
info@staywithus.net, Margaret and John Fogarty).

$$ **Brown's Townhouse** is a charming, Victorian-style, six-
room place where guests share one big, homey breakfast table. It's
on a quiet residential street a 10-minute walk from the city center
(Sb-€60, Db-€80–100, 29 South Parade, Internet access, parking,
tel. 051/870-594, fax 051/871-923, www.brownstownhouse.com,
info@brownstownhouse.com, Siobhan).

$ **Mayor's Walk House** is a well-worn, grandmotherly place that
takes you right back to the 1950s. Bob and Jane Hovenden rent four
economical yet pleasant rooms (S-€27, D-€48, T-€72, cash only, 12
Mayor's Walk, tel. & fax 051/855-427, mayorswalkbandb@eircom.net).

$ **Beechwood Guesthouse**, sitting quietly next to Christ
Church Cathedral, has three cozy little rooms in a great location (S-
€40, D-€50, cash only, non-smoking, 7 Cathedral Square, tel.
051/876-677, bjoeryan@eircom.net, Mary Ryan).

EATING

For something livelier than tired pub grub, consider three good restaurants (wine bar, Italian, and Chinese) that share a tiny street behind Reginald's Tower. All are small, popular, and serve an early-bird special (2 or 3 courses for around €20 before 19:00). **The Wine Vault**—a cellar wine shop by day—offers decent European cuisine and seafood with a good selection of wines from its 18th-century cellar (lunches Tue–Sat 12:30–14:30, dinners Mon–Sat 17:30–22:30, closed Sun, tel. 051/853-444); you're welcome to climb into the wine cellar below the restaurant. **Emiliano's Ristorante Italiano** (lunches Sat–Sun 12:30–14:30, dinners Tue–Sun 17:00–22:30, closed Mon, tel. 051/820-333) and **Johnny Fan's Chinese Cuisine and Seafood** (Mon–Sat 12:30-14:15 & 17:30–23:30, Sun 13:00–15:00 & 18:00–23:00, tel. 051/879-535) are both next door and lively with locals.

Sizzlers Restaurant serves basic, stick-to-your-ribs meals on the waterfront at reasonable prices (€10–19 meals, Mon–Sat 7:30–23:00, Sun 7:30–22:00, 124 Parade Quay, tel. 051/879-112).

Pub Grub: Waterford's staple food seems to be pub grub. Several typical pubs serve dinner in the city center. For your musical entertainment, just wander around, read the notices, and follow your ears. You'll find plenty of live action on George Street, Barronstrand Street, and Broad Street.

TRANSPORTATION CONNECTIONS

From Waterford by train to: Dublin (4/day, 3 hrs), **Kilkenny** (4/day, 45 min), **Rosslare** (2/day, 1.5 hrs).

By bus to: Cork (13/day, 2.25 hrs), **Kilkenny** (3/day, 1 hr), **Rosslare** (4/day, 1.25 hrs), **Wexford** (7/day, 1 hr).

County Wexford

The southeast corner of Ireland is peppered with pretty views and historic sites easily accessible to drivers as a day trip from Waterford. While most of the sights are mediocre, five (each within an hour's drive of Waterford) are worth considering.

The dramatic Hook Head Lighthouse—capping an intriguing and remote peninsula—comes with lots of history and a great tour. The Kennedy Homestead is a pilgrimage site for Kennedy fans. The *Dunbrody* Famine Ship in New Ross gives a sense of what 50 days on a coffin ship with dreams of "Americay" must have been like. The Irish National Heritage Park in Wexford is a Stone-Age Knott's Berry Farm. And the National 1798 Visitors Centre at Enniscorthy explains the roots of the Irish struggle for liberty.

County Wexford

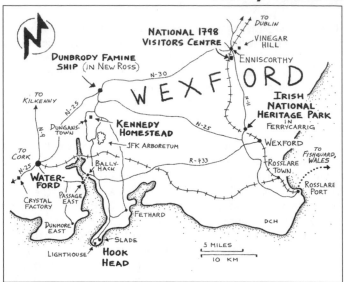

Planning Your Time

New Ross, Enniscorthy, and Wexford are each less than 30 minutes apart, connected by fast highways. The Kennedy Homestead is a 10-minute drive from New Ross, and the lighthouse is a 45-minute trip to the end of the Hook Peninsula. All are well-signposted and easy to find. Connecting Dublin with Waterford, you could visit most of these sights in a best-of-County-Wexford day. On a quick trip, the sights are not worth the trouble by public transit. If you'll be spending the night, Enniscorthy and New Ross are blue-collar towns that provide a good glimpse of working-class Ireland.

If connecting Hook Head and Waterford, use the car-ferry shortcut from Passage East to Ballyhack (€3.50, 5-min crossing, runs continuously, April–Sept daily 7:00–22:00, Oct–March daily 7:00–20:00).

SIGHTS

If you plan on visiting more than one of the following Wexford sights (except the Kennedy Homestead), take advantage of the "Heritage Wexford" discount coupons, which offer 20 percent off each sight (ask for it at the first sight you visit).

▲Hook Head Lighthouse—This is the oldest operating lighthouse in Northern Europe. According to legend, St. Dubhan arrived in the 6th century and discovered the bodies of shipwrecked sailors. Dismayed, he and his followers began tending a fire on the headland to warn future mariners. What you see today is essentially 12th-century, built by the Normans (who first landed 5 miles up the east coast at Baginbun Head in 1169). They established Waterford Harbor as a commercial beachhead to the rich Irish countryside that they intended to conquer. This beacon assured them safe access.

Today's lighthouse is 110 feet tall and looks modern on the outside (it was automated in 1996, and its light can be seen 23 miles out to sea). But it's 800 years old, built on a plan inspired by the lighthouse of Alexandria in Egypt—one of the seven wonders of the ancient world.

Since it's a working lighthouse, it may be toured only with a guide or escort. Fine 30-minute tours leave about hourly. Inside, with its black-stained, ribbed, vaulted ceilings and stout, 10-foot-thick walls, you can almost feel the presence of the Benedictine monks who tended a coal-burning beacon at the top for the Normans. Climbing 115 steps through four levels rewards you with a breezy, salt-air view from the top.

When Oliver Cromwell arrived here to secure the English claim to this area, he considered his two options and declared he'd take strategic Waterford "by Hook or by Crooke." Hook is the long peninsula with the lighthouse. Crooke is a little village on the other side (just south of Passage East).

Cost and Hours: €4.75, March–Oct daily 9:30–17:30, last tour usually at 17:00, Nov–Feb Sat–Sun only 9:30–16:30, tours by request on winter weekdays, call to check tour times before driving out (tel. 051/397-055).

Services: There's a decent cafeteria and a shop with fliers explaining other sights on the peninsula. The ghost story movie about Loftus Hall, shown in the visitors' center, should be saved for rainy days (€3.50, 35 min). Kids-at-heart can't resist climbing out on the rugged rocky tip of the windy Hook Head.

▲**Kennedy Homestead**—Patrick Kennedy, JFK's great-grandfather, left Ireland in 1858. Distant relatives have turned his property into a little museum/shrine for Kennedy pilgrims. Physically, it's not much: A barn and a wing of the modern house survive from 1858. JFK dropped in by helicopter in June of 1963, a few months before he was assassinated. You'll view two short videos: five minutes of Kennedy's actual visit to the farm and a 16-minute newsreel tracing the events of his 1963 trip through Ireland (both fascinating if you like Kennedy stuff). Then Patrick Grennan, a distant Kennedy relative himself, whose grandmother hosted the tea here for JFK, gives you a 15-minute tour. Finally, you're free to peruse the barn, lined with Kennedy-in-Ireland memorabilia and detailing the history of

the Kennedy dynasty. While it's just a private home, anyone interested in the Kennedys will find it worth driving the treacherous
narrow lane to see.

Cost, Hours, Location: €4, July–Aug daily 10:00–17:00,
May–June and Sept 11:30–16:30, by appointment after hours, in
slow times, and Oct–April (no big deal, as it's their home), tel.
051/388-264, www.kennedyhomestead.com. It's four miles south of
New Ross near Dunganstown (look for sign off of R733, long one-
lane road). Don't confuse the Kennedy Homestead with the nearby
JFK Arboretum. The arboretum is lovely, if you like trees and plants.
It's a huge park with 4,500 species of trees and a grand six-county
view—but no Kennedy history.

▲▲Dunbrody Famine Ship—Permanently moored in the tiny port
of New Ross, this was built as a reminder of the countless hungry
Irish who sailed to America on ships like this. The *Dunbrody* is a full-
scale reconstruction of a 19th-century three-masted bark built in
Quebec in 1845. It's typical of the trading vessels that sailed empty to
America to pick up goods, but during the famine
found they could make a little money on the west-
ward voyage. Extended families camped out for 50
days on bunk beds no bigger than a king-size mat-
tress. Often, boats like this would arrive in America
with only 50 percent of their original human
cargo—hence the nickname "coffin ships."

After a 10-minute video about the building of
the ship, you'll follow an excellent guide through
the ship and encounter a couple of grumpy passengers who tell vivid tales about life aboard. Roots-
seekers are welcome to peruse their computerized file of one million
names of immigrants who sailed from 1846 through 1865.

Cost, Hours, Location: €6.50, 45-min tours go 2/hr, April–Oct
daily 9:00–18:00, Nov–March 10:00–17:00, last tour leaves one hour
before closing (tel. 051/425-239, www.dunbrody.com). The
Dunbrody is in New Ross, near the Kennedy Homestead. Parking is
easy and free on Sundays, but during work hours, you'll need to buy a
€1-per-hour disk from the TI desk at the ship's reception.

▲Irish National Heritage Park—This 35-acre wooded park,
which contains an 1857 tower commemorating local boys killed in
the Crimean War, features replicas of buildings from each era of
Irish history. Ireland's countless ancient sights are generally unrec-
ognizable ruins—hard to re-create in your mind. This park is
intended to help out. You'll find buildings and settlements illustrating life in Ireland from the Stone Age through the 12th-century
Norman Age. As a bonus, you'll see animal-skin-clad characters
doing their prehistoric thing—gnawing on meat, weaving, making
arrowheads, and so on.

Your visit begins with a 12-minute video, followed by a 90-minute tour. During 13 stops, your guide explains the various civiliza-tions. The highlight is a monastic settlement from the age when Europe was dark and Ireland was "the island of saints and scholars." While you can wander around on your own, the place is a bit childish (there's nothing actually old here) and only worthwhile if you take the included tour.

Cost, Hours, Location: €7.50, daily 9:30–18:30, until 17:30 in winter, last entry 90 minutes before closing, tours go hourly (tel. 053/20733). It's clearly signposted on the west end of Wexford—you'll hit it before entering town on the N11 Enniscorthy road.

National 1798 Visitors Centre—Located in Enniscorthy, this museum creatively tells the story of the rise of revolutionary thinking in Ireland, which led to the ill-fated rebellion of 1798. Enniscorthy was the crucial Irish battleground of a populist revolution (inspired by the American and French Revolutions) that witnessed the bloodiest days of the doomed 1798 uprising. The material is compelling for anyone intrigued by struggles for liberty, but there's little more here than video clips of reenactments and storyboards on the walls.

Leaving the center, look east across the Slaney River, which divides Enniscorthy, and you'll see a hill with a stumpy tower on it. This is Vinegar Hill, the main battlefield. The tower is the old windmill that once flew the green rebel flag. Drive to the top for the views that the rebels had of the surrounding British forces. The rebels desperately tried to hold the high ground with no shelter from the merciless British artillery fire.

Cost, Hours, Location: €6, April–Oct Mon–Fri 9:30–18:00, Sat–Sun 11:00–18:00, Nov–March until 16:00, last entry one hour before closing (tel. 054/37596, www.iol.ie/~98com). Enniscorthy is 12 miles north of Wexford town. The Visitors Centre is the town's major sight and well signposted.

KINSALE and COBH

County Cork, on Ireland's south coast, is fringed with historic port towns and scenic peninsulas. The typical tour-bus route here includes Blarney Castle and Killarney—places where most tourists wear nametags. A major mistake many tourists make is allowing destinations into their itineraries simply because they're famous (in a song or as part of a relative's big-bus-tour memory). If you have the misfortune to spend the night in Killarney, you'll understand what I mean. The town is a sprawling line of green Holiday Inns littered with pushy shoppers looking for three-leaf clovers.

Rather than kissing the spit-slathered Blarney Stone, spend your time in County Cork enjoying the bustling, historic maritime towns of Kinsale and Cobh.

Kinsale makes a great home base for enjoying the County Cork coast. From Kinsale, you can wade through the salty history of Cobh. Travelers approaching this region from Waterford can easily visit Ardmore and the Old Midleton Whiskey Distillery. Those departing this region for the Ring of Kerry or Dingle can stop by Blarney Castle and Macroom en route.

Kinsale

While nearby Cork is the biggest town in south Ireland, Kinsale (15 miles south) is actually more historic, certainly cuter, and delightful to visit. Thanks to the naturally sheltered bay barbed by a massive 17th-century star fort, you can submerge yourself in maritime history, from the Spanish Armada to Robinson Crusoe to the *Lusitania*. Apart

Kinsale and Cobh Area

from all the history, Kinsale has a laid-back, Sausalito feel with a touch of wine-sipping class.

Planning Your Time

Kinsale is worth two nights and a day. The town's two tiny museums open at 10:00 and will occupy you until the 11:15 town walking tour. After lunch at the Fishy Fishy Café, head out to Charles Fort for great bay views and insights into British military life in colonial Ireland. On the way back, stop for a pint at the Bulman Bar. Finish the day with a gourmet dinner and live music in a pub. Those on the blitz tour can give Kinsale five hours—see the fort, wander the town, and have a nice lunch—before driving on.

ORIENTATION

(area code: 021)

Kinsale, because of its great natural harbor, is older than Cobh (Cork's harbor town). While the town is prettier than the actual harbor, the harbor was its reason for being. Today Kinsale is a wealthy resort of 2,000 residents. The town's long and skinny old center is part modern marina and part pedestrian-friendly medieval town—an easy 15-minute stroll from end to end.

Kinsale's History

Kinsale's remarkable harbor has made this an important port since prehistoric times. The bay's 10-foot tide provided a natural shuttle service for Stone Age hunter-gatherers: They could ride it at two miles per hour, twice a day, the eight miles up and down the River Bandon. In the Bronze Age, when people discovered that it takes tin and copper to make bronze, tin came from Cornwall and copper came from this part of Ireland. From 500 B.C. to A.D. 500, Kinsale was a rich trading center. The result: Lots of Stonehenge-type monuments are nearby (the best is Drombeg Stone Circle, a 1-hour drive west).

Kinsale's importance peaked during the 16th, 17th, and 18th centuries, when sailing ships ruled the waves, turning countries into global powers. Kinsale was Ireland's most perfect natural harbor and the gateway to both Spain and France—potentially providing a base for either of these two powers in cutting off English shipping. Because of this, two pivotal battles were fought here in the 17th century: in 1601 against the Spanish, and in 1690 against the French. Two great forts were built to combat these threats from the Continent. England couldn't rule the waves without ruling Kinsale.

To understand the small town of Kinsale, you need to understand the big picture: Around 1500, the pope gave the world to Spain and Portugal. With the Reformation breaking Rome's lock on Europe, maritime powers, such as England, were ignoring the pope's grant. This was important because trade with the New World and Asia brought huge wealth in spices (necessary for curing meat), gold, and silver. England threatened Spain's New World piñata, and Ireland was Catholic. Spain had an economic and a religious reason to defend the pope and Catholicism. The showdown between Spain and England for mastery of the seas (and control of all that trade) was in Ireland. The excuse: to rescue the dear Catholics of Ireland from the treachery of Protestant England (similar to the claim that democracy, and not oil, was the rationale for the Gulf Wars).

Tourist Information

The TI is as central as can be, at the head of the harbor across from the bus stop (July–Aug Mon–Sat 9:00–19:00, Sun 10:00–17:00; March–June and Sept–Nov Mon–Sat 9:30–17:30, closed Sun; shorter hours Dec–Feb; tel. 021/477-2234). It has a free town map and brochures outlining a world of activities in the vicinity.

Arrival in Kinsale

Since Kinsale doesn't have a train station, you'll arrive by bus (the stop is at Esso gas station on Pier Road at south end of town) or by car. Park your car and enjoy the town on foot. While Kinsale's windy medieval lanes are narrow and congested, parking is fairly easy.

So, the Irish disaster unfolds. The powerful Ulster chieftains Hugh O'Neill and Red Hugh O'Donnell and their clans had been on a roll in their battle against the English. With Spanish aid, they figured they could actually drive the English out of Ireland. In 1601, the Spanish Armada dropped off 5,000 soldiers, who established a beachhead in Kinsale. After the ships left, the Spaniards were pinned down in Kinsale by the English commander (who, breaking with martial etiquette, actually fought in the winter). Virtually the entire Irish fighting force left the north and marched through a harsh winter to the south coast, thinking they could liberate their Spanish allies and win freedom from England.

The numbers seemed reasonable (10,000 Englishmen versus 5,000 Spaniards, as 5,000 Irish clansmen approached). The Irish attacked on Christmas Eve in 1601. But, holding the high ground around fortified and Spanish-occupied Kinsale, a relatively small force of English troops could keep the Spaniards hemmed in, leaving the bulk of the English force to outnumber and rout the fighting Irish. The Irish resistance was broken, and its leaders fled to Europe (the "flight of the Earls"). England made peace with Spain and began the "plantation" of mostly Scottish Protestants in Ireland (the seeds of today's Troubles in Ulster). England ruled the waves, and it ruled Ireland. The lesson: Kinsale is key. England eventually built two huge, star-shaped fortresses to ensure control of the narrow waterway, a strategy it would further develop in later fortifications built at Gibraltar and Singapore.

Kinsale's maritime history continues. Daniel Defoe used the real-life experience of Scottish privateer Alexander Selkirk, who departed from Kinsale in 1703 and was later marooned alone on a desert island, as the basis for his book *Robinson Crusoe*. And it was also just 10 miles offshore from Old Kinsale Head that the passenger liner *Lusitania* was torpedoed by a German submarine in 1915, killing 1,200 and sparking America's entry into World War I.

There's a big lot at the head of the harbor behind the TI (€1.80/hr, €10/day, overnight 18:00–9:00 €7 extra) and a big, safe, free parking lot across the street from St. Multose Church at the top of town, a three-minute walk from most recommended hotels and restaurants. Streetside parking requires a disk (purchase at any newsstand, €0.50/hr, 2-hr maximum 10:30–18:00). The outlying streets, a five-minute stroll from all the action, have wide-open parking.

Helpful Hints

Banking: The two banks in town are Allied Irish Bank on Pearse Street and Bank of Ireland on Emmett Street (both open Mon 10:00–17:00, Tue–Fri 10:00–16:00, closed Sat–Sun).

Internet Access: Kano Computer Services is across the street from the town museum (€6/hr, Mon–Fri 10:00–20:00, Sat 10:00–17:00, closed Sun, Market Square, tel. 021/477-3100).

Post Office: It's on Pearse Street (Mon–Fri 9:00–17:30, Sat 9:00–13:00, closed Sun).

Laundry: The Cullinane launderette washes and dries in a day, but gets my vote for the most expensive laundry in Ireland (€15 minimum per load, no self-service, Mon–Sat 9:00–17:00, closed Sun, Market Street, tel. 021/477-2205). Don't let them take you to the cleaners—if possible, wait to do it in another town.

Bike Rental: The Hire Shop rents bikes (€12/day), plus power tools and fishing gear (Mon–Fri 8:30–18:00, Sat 9:00–18:00, Sun 11:00–17:00, 18 Main Street, tel. 021/477-2875, mobile 086-881-2354).

Taxi: Kinsale Cabs has regular cab service and minibuses available (Market Square, tel. 021/477-2642).

TOURS

▲▲Don Herlihy's Historic Town Walk—To understand the important role Kinsale played in Irish, English, and Spanish history, join Don Herlihy on a fascinating 90-minute walking tour (€7, mid-March–mid-Oct daily at 11:15 from the TI, private tours possible, tel. 021/477-2873). Don is a joy to hear as he creatively brings to life Kinsale's place in history and makes the stony sights more than just buildings. Don collects for the tour at the end, giving anyone disappointed in his talk an easy escape midway through. Don's walk is Kinsale's single best attraction.

Ghost Walk Tour—This is not just any ghost tour—it's more comedy than horror. Two actors weave funny stunts and stories into a loose history of the town, offering a thoroughly entertaining hour (€9, May–Sept Mon–Fri at 21:00, leaves from Tap Tavern, mobile 086/855-5043 or 087/948-0910). This tour doesn't overlap with Don Herlihy's more serious historic town walk (above).

SIGHTS

Kinsale Town Wander—Stroll through the old part of town. The medieval walled town's economy rested on the stocking of ships. The old walls—which followed what is now O'Connell Street and Main Street—defined the original town. The windy Main Street traces the original coastline. Walking this, you'll see tiny lanes leading to today's harbor. These originated as piers—just wide enough to roll a barrel down to an awaiting ship. The wall detoured inland to protect the St. Multose Church, which dates from Norman times (back when worshippers sharpened their swords on the doorway of the

Kinsale

1. Old Presbytery B&B
2. Chart House B&B
3. Gallery B&B
4. Quayside House
5. O'Donovan's B&B
6. Little Skillet Rooms & Restaurant
7. Olde Bakery B&B
8. Sea Gull B&B
9. Guardwell Lodge
10. Gourmet Store & Fishy Fishy Café
11. Patsy's Corner Restaurant
12. Mother Hubbard's Restaurant
13. Hoby's Restaurant
14. Jim Edward's Steak & Seafood
15. Max's Wine Bar & Vintage Rest
16. Muddy Maher's Pub
17. An Seanachai Pub
18. Jean Marc's Chow House
19. Cobra Tandoori Restaurant
20. To Bulman Bar/Restaurant
21. Spaniard Inn Pub
22. Tap Tavern
23. Tierney's Guest House

church—check it out). What seems like part of the old center was actually built later on land reclaimed from the harbor. The town is a kind of quarry, with shale hills ideal for a ready supply of fill.

▲▲**Charles Fort**—Kinsale is protected by what was Britain's biggest star-shaped fort—a state-of-the-art defense when artillery made the traditional castle obsolete. The British occupied it until Irish independence in 1922. Its interior buildings were torched in 1923 by anti-treaty IRA forces to keep it from being used by Free State troops during the Irish Civil War. Guided 45-minute tours (depart on the hour, confirm at entry) engross you in the harsh daily life of the 18th-century British soldier. Before or after your tour, peruse the exhibits in the barracks and walk the walls.

For a coffee, beer, or meal nearby, stop by the Bulman Bar (see page 134) in Summercove, where the road runs low near the water on the way back to town. And to actually see how easily the forts could bottle up this key harbor, stop for the grand harbor view at the high point on the road back into town (above Scilly, just uphill from the Spaniard pub).

Cost, Hours, Location: €3.50, covered by Heritage Card (see page 4), mid-March–Oct daily 10:00–18:00, Nov–mid-March daily 10:00–17:00, last entry 45 min before closing, two miles south of town in Summercove, tel. 021/477-2263.

James Fort—Older, overgrown, and filling a peaceful park, James Fort is Kinsale's other star fort, guarding the bay opposite Charles Fort. Built in the years just after the famous 1601 battle, this fort is more ruined, less interesting, and less visited than Charles Fort. Its satellite blockhouse sat below the fort at the water's edge opposite Summercove and controlled a strong chain that could be raised to block ships from reaching Kinsale's docks.

Easily accessible by car or bike, it's two miles south of town along Pier Road on the west shore of the bay (cross bridge and turn left; you'll dead-end at Castle Park Marina, where you can park or leave your bike). It's up the hill behind the Dock pub.

▲**Desmond Castle**—This 15th-century fortified Norman customs house has had a long and varied history. It was the Spanish armory during their 1601 occupation of Kinsale. Nicknamed "Frenchman's Prison," it served as a British prison and once housed 600 prisoners of the Napoleonic Wars (not to mention earlier American Revolutionary War prisoners captured at sea—who were treated as rebels, not prisoners, and chained to the outside of the building as a warning to any rebellion-minded Irish). In the late 1840s, it was a famine relief center. Today, the evocative little ruin comes with a scant display of its colorful history and the modest, one-room Museum of Wine highlighting Ireland's little-known connection to the international wine trade. In the Middle Ages, Kinsale was renowned for its top-quality wooden casks. Developing strong trade links with Bordeaux, local merchants traded their dependable empty casks for casks full of wine.

Cost, Hours, Location: €2.75, covered by Heritage Card (see page 4), mid-April–Oct daily 10:00–18:00, last entry 17:15, tours given on request, closed Nov–mid-April, Cork Street, tel. 021/477-4855.

▲**Kinsale Regional Museum**—In the center of the old town, traffic circles the old town market, which later became a courthouse and is now the Regional Museum. Drop by at least to read the fun 1788 tax code for all Kinsale commercial transactions (outside at the front door). The modest museum is worth a quick visit for its fun mishmash of domestic and maritime bygones. It also gives a good perspective on the controversial *Lusitania* tragedy. Kinsale had maritime jurisdiction over the waters 10 miles offshore, where the luxury liner was torpedoed in 1915. Hearings were held here in the courthouse shortly afterward to investigate the causes of the disaster—which helped propel America into World War I—and to paint the German Hun as a bloodthirsty villain. Claims by Germany that the *Lusitania* was illegally carrying munitions seem to have been borne out by the huge explosion and rapid sinking of the vessel. But perhaps even more interesting, in the side room, is the boot of the 8-foot, 3-inch Kinsale giant, who lived here in the late 1700s.

Cost, Hours, Location: €2.50, Wed–Sat 10:30–17:30, Sun 14:00–17:30, closed Mon–Tue, Market Square, tel. 021/477-7930.

SLEEPING

Kinsale is a popular place in summer for yachters and golfers (who don't flinch at paying $300 for 18 holes out on the exotic Old Head of Kinsale Golf Course). It's wise to book ahead. I've listed peak-season prices. These places include breakfast, and are all within a five-minute walk of the town center.

$$$ **The Old Presbytery** is a fine, quiet house a block outside of the commercial district, with a goofy floor plan and 10 fine rooms. Well-listed in most guidebooks, it has lots of American guests. The breakfasts are a delight, and Noreen McEvoy runs the place with a passion for excellence (Db-€85–150 depending on room size, family Qb-€160, 2 Qb suites with no breakfast and minimum 3-night stay-€160, private parking, 43 Cork Street, tel. 021/477-2027, fax 021/477-2166, www.oldpres.com, info@oldpres.com).

$$$ **Chart House B&B** is a luxurious Georgian home renting a tidy little single and three grand, sumptuous doubles. It's a block off

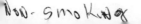
Non-Smoking

Sleep Code

(€1 = about $1.20, country code: 353, area code: 021)
S = Single, D = Double/Twin, T = Triple, Q = Quad,
b = bathroom, s = shower only. Unless otherwise noted,
breakfast is included and credit cards are accepted.

To help you easily sort through these listings, I've divided
the rooms into three categories, based on the price for a standard
double room with bath:

$$$ **Higher Priced**—Most rooms €110 or more.
$$ **Moderately Priced**—Most rooms between €80–110.
$ **Lower Priced**—Most rooms €80 or less.

the harbor at the marina end of the old town. This non-smoking, quiet,
and well-run place is top-end in every respect—high ceilings, chandeliers, and a plush living room (Sb-€40–50, Db-€110–170 depending
on size and season, 6 Dennis Quay, tel. 021/477-4568, fax 021/477-
7907, www.charthouse-kinsale.com, charthouse@eircom.net).

$$ The Gallery, a bright and funky, five-room place with styl-
ish decor, is run by Tom and Carole O'Hare with a fresh
informality—you can have ice cream for breakfast. He's a jazz pianist
and she's an artist (Db-€90–110, family Qb-€140–160, public park-
ing out back, The Glen, tel. 021/477-4558, www.gallerybnb.com,
carole@gallerybnb.com).

$$ Quayside House is a grand, blocky building overlooking a
small park and the bay along Pier Road. Mary Cotter rents six rooms
and offers a warm welcome (Db-€100, €65 in winter, Tb-€135,
family Qb-€160, Pier Road, tel. 021/477-2188, fax 021/477-2664,
www.euroka.com/quayside, quaysidehouse@eircom.net).

$ O'Donovan's B&B is six rooms in a 400-year-old building
made cheery and welcoming by Eileen and Michael O'Donovan.
Right in the charming medieval center, it's handy, but a bit noisy on
Fridays and Saturdays (S-€40, D-€60, Db-€66, non-smoking, 8
Guardwell Street, tel. 021/477-2428, odonovans_bb@iolfree.ie).

$ The Little Skillet is all charm and no grease, with one quaint
room above a wonderful (and equally quaint) restaurant. Narrow stair-
ways lead into a teddy-on-the-beddy world of exposed ceiling timbers
(Db-€60, Main Street, tel. 021/477-4202, www.thelittleskillet.com,
littleskillet@irelandwide.com).

$ The Olde Bakery B&B makes you feel at home, with six quilt-
bedded rooms and a cozy breakfast at the kitchen table, cooked up by
Tom and Chrissie Quigley (D-€60–65, Db-€70–76, non-smoking,
laundry service available, 56 Lower O'Connell Street, tel. 021/477-
3012, www.theoldebakery.com, theoldebakery@oceanfree.net).

$ **Tierney's Guest House** has 10 small rooms with the most central location in town (Sb-€40, Db-€72, Tb-€99, 70 Main Street, tel. 021/477-2205, fax 021/477-4363, www.tierneys-kinsale.com, mtierney@indigo.ie).

$ **The Sea Gull,** perched up the hill right next to Desmond Castle, offers six well-worn rooms run by Mrs. Mary O'Neill, who also runs The Tap Tavern down the hill (S-€35–40, Db-€60–65, Tb-€90, 10 percent discount with this book in 2005, cash only, Cork Street, tel. 021/477-2240, marytap@iol.ie).

$ **Guardwell Lodge** is a big, boxy, new building at the top of the old center, with 64 rooms connected by a prisonlike series of stairways and catwalks in its inner courtyard. While almost a hostel, it has no hostel-type regulations or restrictions. Its stark but modern and comfortable rooms (each with a fine new bathroom) are far and away the best budget beds in this ritzy town. Avoid any room ending in "B," which house a noisy water pump in the closet for the three neighboring rooms (€16–20 beds in 4-bed dorms, Sb-€28–30, Db-€55–60, Tb-€60, no breakfast, all bedding provided, fully equipped self-service kitchen, TV lounge, request quiet room on church side, Guardwell Street, tel. 021/477-4686, fax 021/477-4684, www .guardwelllodge.com, info@guardwelllodge.com).

EATING

As Ireland's self-proclaimed gourmet capital, Kinsale manages to merge friendly, old-fashioned Irish hospitality with quality restaurant options. Local competition is fierce, and restaurants offer creative and tempting menus. You don't have to have a big budget or a cultured palate to enjoy the range of choices available—everything from simple chowder-and-sandwich lunches to memorable fish-and-steak dinner feasts.

Lunch

The Gourmet Store and Fishy Fishy Café is *the* place for a good lunch. It's like eating in a fish market surrounded by the day's catch and a pristine stainless-steel kitchen. Marie and her white-aproned staff hustle wonderful, steaming piles of beautifully presented seafood to eager customers (€20 specials, lunch only, cash only, daily 12:00–15:45, closed Sun off-season, across from church on Guardwell Street, tel. 021/477-4453). Look at the lobster tank and ponder this: A couple of years ago, a soft-hearted, fat-walleted Buddhist tourist bought up the entire day's supply of live lobster (worth over €600) and set them free in the bay. They've refilled the tank since.

For cheap and cheery, try the cramped **Patsy's Corner** or local breakfast hangout, **Mother Hubbard's**. Both are near the Market

Square and serve sandwiches, baguettes, or salads with coffee for under €10.

For a picnic, gather supplies at the **Super Valu** supermarket (Mon–Sat 8:30–21:00, Sun 10:00–21:00, Pearse Street).

Good Dinners in the Old Center

The **Little Skillet** feels intimate, with tasty food and a romantic, rough-stone-and-big-fireplace atmosphere. You'll find all the old-time Irish favorites with traditional Irish music, fresh and seasonal veggies, and absolutely no french fries. You can drop in just for a glass of wine and dessert in the upstairs wine bar. Diners can wait at the bar across the street and are welcome to bring in their own pint (dinners €17–20, 3-course €25 early-bird meal before 19:30, daily 18:00–22:30, Main Street, tel. 021/477-4202).

Hoby's Restaurant, another well-established favorite, offers modern cuisine in a quiet, candlelit room. It's popular with people from Cork coming down for a special night out (3-course €25 dinners, daily 18:00–22:00, Main Street, tel. 021/477-2200).

At **Jim Edward's Steak & Seafood,** one kitchen keeps eaters happy in both the bar and the restaurant. Choose between a noisy maritime ambience in the restaurant (€19–29 meals) or dark and mellow in the bar (€11–17 meals). While cheaper and less gourmet than other Kinsale eateries, it offers decent steaks, seafood, and vegetables (bar daily 12:30–22:00, restaurant daily 18:00–22:00, Market Quay, tel. 021/477-2541).

Several candlelit wine-bar restaurants vie for your attention along the gently curving Main Street. **Max's Wine Bar** has a respected French chef (tel. 021/477-2443). **Vintage** looks like, feels like, and is the most expensive place in town (from 18:30, closed Jan, reservations recommended, near Max's, tel. 021/477-2502).

Pubs with decent kitchens abound, serving casual dinners (€10–17) in a funky atmosphere. Many follow dinner with live music. Consider **Muddy Maher's** (daily 12:30–15:00 & 17:30–21:30, Main Street, tel. 021/477-4602) and **An Seanachai** (daily 12:00–21:00, Market Street, tel. 021/477-7077).

For a break from Irish cooking, **Jean Marc's Chow House** serves up good Asian meals (€14–19 dinners, daily 18:30–22:00, Sept–May closed Tue, Pearse Street, tel. 021/477-7117). Or check out **Cobra Tandoori** for tasty Indian cuisine (€14–18 dinners daily 16:30–23:30, also lunches Sat–Sun 12:00–14:30, 69 Main Street, tel. 021/477-7911).

Fine Food near Charles Fort

The **Bulman Bar and Restaurant** serves seafood with seasonal produce. The mussels are especially tasty; on a balmy day or evening, diners take a bucket and a beer out to the seawall. This is the only real way to eat on the water in Kinsale (€10 lunches, €18–26 meals upstairs in fancy restaurant, daily 12:30–21:30, 200 yards toward Kinsale from Charles Fort in hamlet of Summercove, tel. 021/477-2131). The pub, strewn with fun decor and sporting a big fireplace, is also good for a coffee or beer after your visit to the fort. Without a car (and weather permitting), enjoy Kinsale's best 45-minute stroll back into town, with great harbor views on the Scilly Walk paved pedestrian trail (trailhead marked on left as you climb 100 yards up steep road to town).

NIGHTLIFE

Live Pub Music

Kinsale's pubs are packed with atmosphere and live music (though not always traditional Irish). Rather than target a certain place, simply walk the area between Guardwell, Pearse Street, and the Market Square. Pop into each pub that has live music, and then settle into your favorite. Several of the pubs wind deep into buildings. On a Thursday night, I found six places with live music thriving at 23:00 along this proposed loop. **An Seanachai** (SHAN-ah-key) means "storyteller" in Gaelic, but it's now known for its music (Main Street). **The Tap Tavern** has music on Thursday nights (just below St. Multose Church).

Irish music purists will be rewarded if they take the five-minute taxi ride (€6 one-way) out to the **Bulman Bar,** near the base of Charles Fort. This is Kinsale's best pub for traditional Irish music sessions (Tue–Thu at 21:30, see above). Otherwise, try the tiny **Spaniard Inn,** a 10-minute walk out to the Scilly peninsula across the harbor from town (Wed at 21:30, tel. 021/477-2436).

TRANSPORTATION CONNECTIONS

Like many worthwhile corners of Ireland, Kinsale is not accessible by train. The closest train station is in Cork, 15 miles north. But buses run frequently between Kinsale (stop is at Esso gas station on Pier Road, south end of town) and Cork's train station (11/day, 45 min, €5 one-way, €7 round-trip).

From Cork by bus to: Dublin (6/day), **Galway** (12/day), **Tralee** (8/day), and **Kilkenny** (9/day). Bus info: tel. 021/450-8188.

Cobh

If your ancestry is Irish, chances are this was the last Irish soil your ancestors had under their feet. Cobh (pron. "cove") was the major port of Irish emigration in the 19th century. Of the six million Irish who have emigrated to America, Canada, and Australia since 1815, nearly half left from Cobh.

The first steam-powered ship to make a transatlantic crossing departed from Cobh in 1838—cutting the journey time from 50 days to 18. When Queen Victoria came to Ireland for the first time in 1849, Cobh was the first Irish ground she set foot on. Giddy, the town renamed itself "Queenstown" in her honor. It was still going by that name in 1912, when the *Titanic* made its final fateful stop here before heading out on its maiden (and only) voyage. To celebrate their new independence from British royalty in 1922, locals changed the name back to its original Irish name: Cobh.

ORIENTATION

Cobh sits on a large island in Cork harbor. The town's inviting waterfront is colorful yet salty, with a playful promenade. The butcher's advertisement reads, "always pleased to meet you and always with meat to please you." Stroll past the shops along the water. Ponder the *Lusitania* memorial on Casement Square and the modest *Titanic* memorial nearby on Pearse Square. A hike up the hill to the towering neo-Gothic St. Colman's Cathedral rewards you with a fine view of the port.

Tourist Information
The TI is in the Old Yacht Club on the harbor (Mon–Fri 9:30–17:30, Sat–Sun 13:00–17:00, tel. 021/481-3301, www.cobhharbourchamber.ie).

TOURS

Titanic Trail Tours—Michael Martin leads 90-minute walking tours of Cobh that give you unexpected insights into the tragic *Titanic* voyage, Spike Island (Ireland's Alcatraz), and Cobh's maritime history (€8, daily at 11:00, June–Aug also at 14:00, meet at Commodore Hotel, private tours available, tel. 021/481-5211, www.titanic-trail.com).

SIGHTS

▲**The Queenstown Story**—Cobh's major sightseeing attraction, filling its harborside Victorian train station, is an earnest attempt to make the city's emigration and history interesting. The topics—the famine, Irish emigration, Australia-bound prison ships, the sinking of the *Lusitania,* and the ill-fated voyage of the *Titanic*—are fascinating enough to make this museum a worthwhile stop. But the museum itself, while kid-friendly, is weak on actual historical artifacts. It reminds me of a big, interesting history picture book with the pages expanded and tacked on the wall (€5, May–Oct daily 10:00–18:00, Nov–April 10:00–17:00, last entry 1 hour before closing, tel. 021/481-3591).

Those with Irish roots to trace are welcome to use the Heritage Centre's genealogy search service (www.cobhheritage.com, info @cobhheritage.com).

SLEEPING

(€1 = about $1.20, country code: 353, area code: 021)
The following listings are all centrally located near the harbor, less than a five-minute walk from the Queenstown Story.

Consider $$$ **Waters Edge Hotel**, with a nice harborview restaurant (Sb-€70–90, Db-€110–160, Tb-€130–180, Yacht Club Quay, tel. 021/481-5566, www.watersedgehotel.ie, info@watersedgehotel.ie); $$$ **Commodore Hotel** (Sb-€65–85, Db-€105–130, Tb-€160–195, Westbourne Place, tel. 021/481-1277, commodorehotel@eircom.net); or $ **Ard na Laoi** (Sb-€45–50, Db-€66, Tb-€96, Westbourne Place, tel. 021/481-2742).

TRANSPORTATION CONNECTIONS

By car: Driving to Cobh from Cork or Waterford, leave N25 about eight miles east of Cork, following the little R624 over a bridge, onto the Great Island, and directly into Cobh.

Kinsale to Cobh is 25 miles, takes an hour, and involves catching a small ferry. Leave Kinsale north on R600 toward Cork. Just south of Cork and its airport, go east on R613. You will be following little car-ferry signs, but they ultimately take you to the wrong ferry (Ringaskiddy—to France). After you hit N28, take R610 to Monkstown and then Glenbrook, where a (poorly signposted) shuttle ferry takes you to the Great Island (5 min, €3.50 ride). Once on the island, turn right and drive a mile or two into Cobh. In Cobh, follow the Heritage Centre signs to the Queenstown Story, where you'll find easy parking right at the museum.

By plane: Cork Airport has become an increasingly handy entry point into (or exit point from) Ireland. Located four miles south of Cork city (on the N-27/R600 road to Kinsale, a 20-minute drive away), it offers connecting flights via London Heathrow on Aer Lingus, London Stansted on Ryanair, and Edinburgh on Aer Arann. More distant connections can be made from Frankfurt, Amsterdam, Paris, Prague, and Málaga (tel. 021/431-3131, www.corkairport.com).

County Cork and Nearby

These sights are convenient stops when connecting Kinsale and Cobh with Waterford (to the east) or the Ring of Kerry (to the west).

Between Waterford and Kinsale

If you're driving from Waterford (previous chapter) to Cobh and Kinsale, you can easily visit these sights just off N25 (listed roughly from east to west).

Ardmore—This funky little beach resort, with a famous ruined church and round tower, is a handy stop (just west of Youghal, 3 miles south of N25 between Waterford and Cobh). A couple of buses run daily from Ardmore to Cork and to Waterford.

This humble little port town is just a line of pastel houses that appear frightened by the sea. Its beach claims (very modestly) to be "the most swimmable in Ireland." The beachside **TI**, housed in an alien spacecraft, has a flier laying out a historic walk (June–Aug Mon–Sat 11:00–13:00 & 14:00–17:00, Sun 15:00–17:00, closed Sept–May, tel. 024/94444).

The town's historic claim to fame: Christianity came to Ireland here first (thanks to St. Declan, who arrived in A.D. 416—35 years before St. Patrick). As if to proclaim that feat with an 800-year-old exclamation mark, one of Ireland's finest examples of a round tower stands perfectly intact, 97 feet above an evocative graveyard and a ruined church (noted for the faint remains of some early Christian carvings on its west facade). You can't get into the tower—the entrance is 14 feet off the ground.

Sleeping in Ardmore (area code: 024): **$ Duncrone B&B**, with vividly colorful rooms, is worth considering first (Sb-€38–45, Db-€60, Tb-€90, a half mile outside of town, up past the round tower, tel. 024/94860). **$$ Round Tower Hotel,** more sedate, is in town (Sb-€50, Db-€90, tel. 024/94494). **$ Ardmore Beach Hostel** is a basic stone building located where Main Street hits the Atlantic (€14 beds in 5-bed dorms, €35 family rooms, tel. 024/94166; if no one's home, go next door to Paddy Mac's Pub).

▲**Old Midleton Distillery**—Sometime during your Ireland trip, even if you're a teetotaler, you'll want to tour a whiskey distillery. Of the three major distillery tours (this one, Jameson in Dublin, and Bushmills in Northern Ireland), the Midleton experience is the most interesting. After a 10-minute video, you'll walk with a guide through a great old 18th-century plant on a 45-minute tour; see waterwheel-powered crankshafts and a 31,000-gallon copper still—the largest of its kind in the world; and learn the story of whiskey. Predictably, you finish in a tasting room and enjoy a free not-so-wee glass. The finale is a Scotch/Irish whiskey taste test. Your guide will take two volunteers for this. Don't be shy—raise your hand like an eager little student, and enjoy an opportunity to taste the different brands.

Cost, Hours, Location: Tour-€8, daily 9:00–18:00 year-round, last tour at 17:00, 2/hr in summer, 3/day in winter (tel. 021/461-3594, www.whiskeytours.ie). It's 12 miles east of Cork in Midleton, about a mile off N25, the main Cork–Waterford road. There's easy parking—just drive right into the distillery lot. A cafeteria is onsite.

Between Kinsale and Killarney

If you're driving between Kinsale and the Ring of Kerry (next chapter), you can easily visit these sights (listed from east to west).

Blarney Stone and Castle—The town of Blarney is of no importance, and the 15th-century Blarney Castle is an empty hulk (with no effort at making it meaningful or interesting). It's only famous as the place of tourist pilgrimage, where busloads line up to kiss a stone on its top rampart and get "the gift of gab." The stone's origin is shrouded in myth (it was either brought back from the Holy Land by crusaders, or perhaps was part of Scotland's royal Stone of Scone). The best thing about this lame sight is the opportunity to watch a cranky man lower lemming tourists over the edge, belly up and head back, to kiss the stone while his partner snaps a photo—which will

be waiting for you to purchase back at the parking lot. After a day of tour groups mindlessly climbing up here to perform this ritual, the stone is literally slathered with spit and lipstick.

The tradition goes back to the late 16th century, when Queen Elizabeth I was trying to plant loyal English settlers in Ireland to tighten her grip on the rebellious island. She demanded that the Irish clan chiefs recognize the crown, rather than the clan chiefs, as the legitimate titleholder of all lands. One of those chiefs was Cormac MacCarthy, Lord of Blarney Castle (who was supposedly loyal to the queen). He was smart enough never to disagree with the Queen—instead, he would cleverly avoid acquiescing to her demands by sending a never-ending stream of lengthy and deceptive excuses, disguised with liberal doses of flattery (while subtly maintaining his native Gaelic loyalties). In her frustration, the Queen declared his endless words nothing but "blarney." Walking back, you'll cross a stream littered with American pennies—as if the good-luck fairy can change them into euros.

Cost, Hours, Location: €7, daily 9:00–18:00, later in peak season, shorter hours in winter, free parking lot, helpful TI, tel. 021/438-5252. It's five miles northwest of Cork, the major city in south Ireland.

Macroom—This colorful, inviting market town is a handy stop between Cork and Killarney. The ghostly gateway of its ruined castle (once owned by the father of the William Penn who founded Pennsylvania) overlooks its entertaining main square, where you'll find plenty of parking. This makes for an excellent coffee or lunch stop midway between Cork and Killarney. The Next Door Café, adjacent to the Castle Hotel, serves a good, fast lunch.

KENMARE and the RING OF KERRY

It's no wonder that, since Victorian times, visitors have been attracted to this dramatic chunk of Ireland. Mysterious ancient ring forts stand sentinel on mossy hillsides. A beloved Irish statesman maintained his ancestral estate here, far from 19th-century power politics. And early Christian hermit monks left a lonely imprint of their devotion, in the form of simple stone dwellings atop an isolated rock crag, far from shore...a holy retreat on the edge of the known world.

In this region, the ideal overnight stop is the colorful, tidy town of Kenmare—the best springboard for diving into the famous Ring of Kerry.

Kenmare

Cradled in a lush valley, this charming little town (known as Neidin, or "little nest," in Gaelic) hooks you right away with its rows of vividly colored shop fronts and go-for-a-stroll atmosphere. Its fresh appearance made it Ireland's "Tidy Town" winner in 2000, and the nearby finger of the gentle sea feels more like a large lake (called the Kenmare River, just to confuse things). Far from the assembly-line tourism of Killarney town, Kenmare also makes a great launchpad for enjoying the sights of the Iveragh (eev-er-AH) Peninsula—known to shamrock-lovers everywhere as "The Ring of Kerry."

Planning Your Time
All you need in compact Kenmare is one night and a couple of hours to wander the town. Check out the Heritage Centre (in back rooms of TI) to get an overview of the region's rich history. Visit the Kenmare Lace and Design Centre (above TI, entry next door) to get

a close look at the famously delicate lace. Hands-on access to an ancient stone circle is just a five-minute walk to the edge of town. Finish up by taking a peek inside Holy Cross Church to see the fine ceiling woodwork. Call it an early night to get a jump on the Ring of Kerry in the morning.

ORIENTATION

(area code: 064)
In carefully planned Kenmare, "X" marks the spot. The upper (northern) half of the X contains the town square (flea market Wed and Fri in summer), with an adjacent TI and Heritage Centre, as well as a cozy park.

The lower (southern) half of the X contains three one-way streets, forming a busy triangle of shops, lodging, and restaurants. Use the tall Holy Cross Church spire to get your bearings (next to the northeast parking lot, public WCs across the street).

The two shopping streets in the lower half look alike. If you see the steeple at the end of the street, you're on Henry Street...if not, you're on Main Street. Shelbourne Street is the quiet third leg of the triangle, with a small parking lot.

Tourist Information: The helpful TI is on the town square (May–Oct Mon–Sat 9:00–18:00, Sun 10:00–17:00, closed Nov–April, tel. 064/41233).

Helpful Hints

Banking: Bank of Ireland faces the town square, and Allied Irish Bank takes up the corner of Henry and Main streets (both open Mon 10:00–17:00, Tue–Fri 10:00–16:00, closed Sat–Sun).

Internet Access: Kenmare's dang slow terminals are in the front shop of the post office (see below), with longer hours than the P.O. (€1/10 min, Mon–Fri 8:30–13:00 & 14:00–20:00, Sat 9:30–13:00, closed Sun).

Post Office: It's on Henry Street, at the intersection with Shelbourne Street (Mon–Fri 9:00–13:00 & 14:00–17:30, Sat 10:00–13:00, closed Sun).

Laundry: Try O'Shea's Cleaners and Launderette (Mon–Fri 8:30–18:00, Sat 9:30–18:00, closed Sun, a half mile north of town on N71 in Kenmare Business Park, tel. 064/41394).

Bike Rental: Finnegan's Corner rents bikes for €15 per day and has route maps (July–Aug Mon–Sat 10:00–20:00, Sept–June until 18:00, closed Sun, leave ID for deposit, 38 Henry Street, across from post office, tel. 064/41083).

Parking: The town's two largest public parking lots (free overnight) cling to the two main roads departing town to the north (otherwise street parking is allowed for 2 hours).

Taxi: Try Murnane Cabs (mobile 087-236-4353) or Kenmare Koach and Kab (mobile 087-248-0800).

TOURS

Finnegan's Guided Coach Tours—The company runs a variety of local day tours, departing from the TI at 10:00 and returning by 17:00 (route depends on day: Ring of Kerry on Mon, Wed, and Fri; Ring of Beara on Tue; Glengarrif on Thu; €25 for any tour, reserve 1 day in advance, can book private tours for small groups with enough notice—they may sell out July–Aug, tel. 064/41491, mobile 087-248-0800).

SIGHTS AND ACTIVITIES

Heritage Centre—This museum, in the back rooms of the TI, consists of a series of storyboards and a model of the planned town. A 20-minute visit here explains the nearby ancient stone circle, as well as the history of Kenmare's lacemaking fame and notorious nun (free, May–Oct Mon–Sat 9:00–18:00, Sun 10:00–17:00, closed Nov–April, tel. 064/41233).

Kenmare Lace and Design Centre—A single large room (above the TI) displays the delicate lacework that put Kenmare on the modern map. From the 1860s until World War I, the Poor Clare

convent at Kenmare became the center of excellence for Irish lacemaking. Inspired by antique Venetian lace, but creating their own unique designs, nuns taught needlepoint lacemaking as a trade to girls in a region struggling to get back on its feet in the wake of the catastrophic famine. Queen Victoria commissioned five pieces of lace in 1885, and by the end of the century, tourists began visiting Kenmare on their way to Killarney. Nora Finnegan, who runs the Centre, usually has a work in progress to demonstrate the complexity of fine lacemaking to visitors (free, May–mid-Oct Mon–Sat 10:00–13:00 & 14:00–17:30, closed Sun and mid-Oct–April, tel. 064/42636 or 064/42978).

Druid Stone Circle—Of the 100 stone circles that dot southwest Ireland (counties Cork and Kerry), this is the biggest and most accessible (5-min walk from TI). It's over 3,000 years old, and it may have been used both as a primitive calendar and a focal point for rituals. The circle has a diameter of 50 feet and consists of 15 stones ringing a large center boulder (probably a burial monument). Experts think that

Kenmare's History:
Axes, Xs, Nuns, and Lace

Bronze Age people (2000 B.C.), attracted to this valley for its abundant game and fishing, stashed their prized **axe heads** and daggers in hidden hoards. Nearly 4,000 years later (in 1930), a local farmer from the O'Sullivan clan pried a bothersome boulder from one of his fields and discovered it to be a lid for a collection of rare artifacts that are now on display in the National Museum in Dublin (the "Killaha hoard"). The O'Sullivans (Gaelic for "descendants of the one-eyed") were for generations the dominant local clan, and you'll still see their name on many Kenmare shopfronts.

Oliver Cromwell's bloody Irish campaign (1649) subdued Ireland, but never reached Kenmare. However, his chief surveyor, William Petty, knew good land when he saw it, and took a quarter of what is now County Kerry as payment for his valuable services marking the "lands down" on maps. His heirs, the Lansdownes, created Kenmare as a model 18th-century estate town and developed its distinctive **"X" street plan**. William Petty-Fitzmaurice, the first Marquis of Lansdowne and landlord of Kenmare, became the British Prime Minister and negotiated the peace that ended the American War of Independence in 1783.

Sister Margaret Cusack, a.k.a. Sister Mary Francis Clare, lived in

this stone circle tracked the position of the setting sun to determine the annual solstices, marking the longest and shortest days of the year.

To get to the circle from the city center, face the TI and turn left, walking 200 yards down Market Street as you pass a row of cute 18th-century houses on your right. Beyond the row of houses, veer right through an unmarked modern gate mounted in stone columns, and continue 50 yards down the paved road. You'll see the circle on your left (free, always open).

Holy Cross Church—Finished in 1864, this is Kenmare's grand Catholic church. It's worth visiting to see the ornate wooden ceiling, with 10 larger-than-life angels (carved in Germany's Black Forest). Town lore says that after the church was finished, Father O'Sullivan had the spire topped with a cock to crow over the nearby office of the landlord's agent (who had once denied him the land for a church).

Horseback Riding—Two local stables compete for your spurs. Both offer day treks for all levels of experience through beach and hill scenery (€20/hr). Dromquinna Stables is three miles west of town on N70 to Sneem (tel. 064/41043). Hazelwood Stables is two miles south of town over Our Lady's Bridge on R571 (mobile 087-756-2652, http://homepage.eircom.net/~hazelwood).

Golfing—Another way to experience Ireland's 40 shades of green is to splurge on a scenic day on the links. The Kenmare Golf Club is the town from 1862 to 1881, becoming the famous "**Nun of Kenmare.**" Her controversial religious life began when she decided to become an Anglican nun after her fiancé's sudden death. Five years later, she converted to Catholicism, joined the Poor Clare order as Sister Mary Francis Clare, and moved with the order to Kenmare. She became an outspoken writer who favored women's rights and lambasted the tyranny of the landlords during the famine. She eventually took church funds and attempted to set herself up as abbess of a convent in Knock. Her renegade behavior led to her leaving the Catholic faith, converting back to Protestantism, writing an autobiography, and lecturing about the "sinister influence of the Roman church."

After the devastation of the Great Potato Famine (1845–1849), an industrial school was founded in Kenmare to teach trades to destitute youngsters. The school, run by the Poor Clare sisters, excelled in teaching young girls the art of **lacemaking**. Inspired by lace created earlier in Italy, Kenmare lace caught the eye of Queen Victoria and became much coveted by Victorian society. Examples of it are now on display in the Victoria and Albert Museum (London), the Irish National Museum (Dublin), and the U.S. National Gallery (Washington, D.C.).

right on the edge of town (€45 green fees, on R569 to Cork, tel. 064/41291), or try the Ring of Kerry Golf and Country Club (€70 green fees, 4 miles west of town on N70, pre-booking advisable on weekends, tel. 064/24000, www.ringofkerrygolf.com).

SLEEPING

$$$ **Lansdowne Arms Hotel** is a recently refurbished, centrally located, 200-year-old historical landmark with large, crisp rooms (Fri–Sun: Sb-€100, Db-€150, Tb-€225; Mon–Thu: Sb-€80, Db-€130, Tb-€195; most rooms non-smoking, parking, corner of Main and Shelbourne Streets, tel. 064/41368, fax 064/41114, www .lansdownearms.com, lansdowne@kenmare.com).

$$$ **Sallyport House** is an elegantly quiet house filled with antique furniture that's been in Helen Arthur's family for generations. Ask her to point out the foot-worn doorstep that was salvaged from the local workhouse and built into her stone chimney (Sb-€120, Db-€140–160, Tb-€200–210, closed Nov–mid-March, non-smoking, no kids, parking, 5-min walk south of town before crossing Our Lady's Bridge, tel. 064/42066, fax 064/42067, www.sallyporthouse.com, port@iol.ie).

$$ **Hawthorn House** sports fine woodwork in its eight neat

Kenmare

1. Lansdowne Arms Hotel
2. Sallyport House
3. Hawthorn House & Failte Hostel
4. Willow Lodge
5. Limestone Lodge
6. Waters Edge B&B
7. To Cois Cille B&B
8. Purple Heather & Packies Restaurants
9. Café Mocha
10. Supermarket
11. Lime Tree Rest.
12. Mulcahy's Wine Bar
13. An Leath Phingin Restaurant
14. Horse Shoe Pub & Restaurant
15. Mickey Neds Rest. & Bar
16. P.F. McCarthy's Pub & Rest.
17. Crowley's Pub
18. Foley's Pub
19. Davitt's Pub
20. Finnegans Corner (Bike Rentals)
21. Launderette

Sleep Code

(€1 = about $1.20, country code: 353, area code: 064)
S = Single, D = Double/Twin, T = Triple, Q = Quad,
b = bathroom, s = shower only. Breakfast is included; credit cards
are accepted unless otherwise noted.

To help you easily sort through these listings, I've divided
the rooms into three categories, based on the price for a standard
double room with bath:

$$$ **Higher Priced**—Most rooms €100 or more.
$$ **Moderately Priced**—Most rooms between €65–100.
$ **Lower Priced**—Most rooms €65 or less.

rooms, courtesy of Mr. O'Brien, who's also a carpenter (Db-€80–90, Tb-€100–120, Qb-€100–130, parking, Shelbourne Street, tel. 064/41035, fax 064/41932, www.hawthornhousekenmare.com, info@hawthornhousekenmare.com, Mary and Noel O'Brien).

$$ **Willow Lodge** has seven comfortable rooms, some with whirlpool-equipped bathtubs (Sb-€50–80, Db-€75–85, Tb-€120, non-smoking, parking, just beyond Holy Cross Church, tel. 064/42301, willowlodgekenmare@yahoo.com, Gretta Gleeson-O'Byrne).

$$ **Limestone Lodge** is rock solid, with five homey rooms and a holy well just a stone's throw from the front door. Ask hostess Siobhan Thoma to show off her handmade lace (Sb-€28–35, Db-€60–68, Tb-€84–90, parking, 5-min walk from town over Finnihy Bridge then left beyond parking lot, tel. 064/42541).

$ **Waters Edge B&B** rests on a forest hillside a mile south of town overlooking the estuary. It has four clean, colorful rooms and a kid-friendly backyard (Sb-€35–40, Db-€52–58, Tb-€75–78, non-smoking, parking, tel. 064/41707, mobile 087-413-4235, vnk@gofree .indigo.ie). To get here, drive south over Our Lady's Bridge, stay on the road (bearing left), take the first driveway on the right, go a couple hundred yards up the bumpy paved road, then turn right at the end of the white wall onto the gravel lane a hundred yards to the dead end.

$ **Cois Cille B&B** (koysh kale) is a friendly, old-fashioned place half a mile east of town. It offers three cute rooms and an inviting "grandmother's house" atmosphere (Db-€60, Tb-€90, cash only, non-smoking, parking, 15-min walk from center down Kilgarvan Road next to old church ruin, tel. 064/42683, Sheila Harrington).

$ **Kenmare Failte Hostel** (fawl-chuh) maintains 40 budget beds in a well-kept, centrally located building with more charm than most hostels (dorm beds-€14 in rooms without bath, €4 more in rooms with bath, D-€35, Db-€43, T-€45, Tb-€56, Q-€56, Qb-€68, closed Nov–March, tel. 064/42333, fax 064/42466).

EATING

This friendly little town offers plenty of quality choices, but try to get a table early, as many finer places book up later in the evening during the summer. Pub dinners are a good value and easier on the budget, but might not serve meals as late as restaurants. Soup-and-sandwich lunch options are easy to find.

Lunch
The Purple Heather makes great salads and omelets (€7–18 meals, Mon–Sat 11:00–19:00, closed Sun, Henry Street, tel. 064/41016, run by same people who own classy Packies restaurant, recommended below).

Hey there, bub—**Davitt's** pub does not flub hearty grub (€11–18 meals, daily 8:00–22:00, Henry Street, tel. 064/427-4157).

Café Mocha is a basic €4 sandwich shop where you can flop on a sofa and munch (Mon–Fri 9:00–17:30, Sat 10:00–17:30, Sun 10:00–16:00, tel. 064/42133).

Super Valu supermarket is a good place to stock up for a Ring of Kerry picnic (Mon–Thu 8:00–20:00, Fri 8:00–21:00, Sat 8:00–19:00, Sun 9:00–17:00, Main Street).

Dinner
The **Lime Tree Restaurant** occupies the former Lansdowne Estate office, which gave over 4,000 people free passage to America in the 1840s. These days, it serves delicious, locally caught seafood dishes and has a classy art gallery upstairs (€17–25 meals, April–Oct daily 18:30–22:00, closed Nov–March, reservations smart, Shelbourne Street, tel. 064/41225).

Packies is a popular, expensive bistro with a leafy, low-light interior and few empty seats. Their scallops get rave reviews (€17–29 meals, Mon–Sat 18:00–22:00, closed Sun, reservations smart, Henry Street, tel. 064/41508).

Mulcahy's Wine Bar has a jazz-mellowed ambience and gourmet dishes nurtured by chef Bruce Mulcahy, whose brother Louis is a well-known potter on the Dingle Peninsula (€18–28 meals, daily 18:30–22:00, 36 Henry Street, tel. 064/42383, mobile 087-236-4449).

An Leath Phingin (on LAF fing-in), which means the "half penny," combines rough rock walls with steep, narrow stairs to create a fun, relaxed atmosphere for tasty pasta and pizza (€13–20 meals, Thu–Mon 18:00–22:00, closed Tue–Wed, 35 Main Street, tel. 064/41559).

Horse Shoe Pub and Restaurant, specializing in steak and spare ribs, somehow turns rustic farm-tool decor into a romantic, candlelit sanctuary (€15–25 meals, Mon–Sat 15:00–22:00, Sun 17:00–22:00, Main Street, tel. 064/41553).

Mickey Neds Restaurant and Bar, run by Kerry sports hero Mickey O'Sullivan, goes for a smart, sophisticated look, with dependable pub lunches and filling dinners (€8–11 lunches, €14–23 dinners, Tue–Sat 12:00–22:00, Sun 12:30–18:00, Mon 12:00–15:00, on square where Market Street meets Bridge Street, tel. 064/40200).

P.F. McCarthy's Pub and Restaurant serves salad or sandwich lunches and filling dinner fare (€9–15 meals, Mon–Sat 12:00–20:00, closed Sun, 14 Main Street, tel. 064/41516).

Music in Pubs
Wander Henry Street and stick your head in wherever you hear something you like. Music usually starts at 21:30 and ranges from Irish traditional sessions to sing-along strummers. **Crowley's** is an atmospheric little shoebox of a pub with an unpretentious clientele. **Foley's** jug-stacked window invites you in for a folksy songfest. Across the street, **Davitt's** competes for your ears.

TRANSPORTATION CONNECTIONS

Kenmare has no train station (the nearest is 20 miles away in Killarney). If you leave Kenmare by bus, you'll likely need to transfer in Killarney.

From Kenmare by bus to: Dingle (3/day, 3.25 hrs, change in Tralee or Killarney), **Tralee** (3/day, 2 hrs), **Kinsale** (3/day, 4 hrs), **Dublin** (3/day, 7.5 hrs).

Ring of Kerry

The Ring of Kerry (the Iveragh Peninsula) has been the perennial breadwinner of Irish tourism for decades now. Lassoed by a winding coastal road (the Ring), this mountainous, lake-splattered region is undeniably striking. But as annual flocks of visitors have grown, the area has strained to balance the demand for tourist access with the preservation of the rural charms that everyone has come to see. In towns such as Killarney, the battle has already been lost—what remains there of real Ireland is buried under a pile of postcards and ceramic leprechauns galore.

But fearless motorists, armed with a good map and a reliable alarm clock, can

Ring of Kerry

sidestep the crowds and chow down on the most visit-worthy tid-bits in this feast of Irish sightseeing.

Planning Your Time

More than twice the size of the Dingle Peninsula (see next chapter) and backed by a muscular tourism budget that promotes every sight as a "must-see," the Iveragh Peninsula can seem overwhelming. Be selective, and don't let them pull the turf over your eyes.

By Car: You can drive the Ring (primarily on N70) in one long but satisfying day. Travelers linking overnights in Kinsale and Dingle can insert a night between them in Kenmare (a good base to enjoy the best of the Ring of Kerry).

On a one-day visit to the Ring, I'd budget my time to allow for stops at Staigue Fort (30 min), Derrynane House (1.5 hrs), and the Skellig Experience Centre (1 hr).

Photographers and ambitious early birds may want to take in the adjacent Skellig Ring as well (1 hr). Consider taking along a picnic lunch to be enjoyed from the car at a scenic pullout (the parking lot at Coomakesta Pass has terrific views), or grab a quick pub-grub lunch in a town halfway around. Waterville has plenty of lunch options and a wide beachfront park. If you're considering a boat trip out to the desolate island of Skellig Michael, you'll need to add another day to allow for an overnight in the Portmagee area...and hope for good weather (see page 157).

By Tour: You can take a €25 day-long bus tour of the Ring from Kenmare with Finnegan's Guided Coach Tours (Mon, Wed, and Fri; see page 143). Ring of Kerry tours also go from the super-touristy but well-connected town of Killarney (TI tel. 064/31633).

Driving the Ring of Kerry (Made Less Scary)

Given the fact that every other tourist and his clan seem hell-bent on taking a battering-ram bus tour of this scenic, often narrow-roaded, 120-mile loop, careful pre-planning of your route is time well spent. Study an Ordnance Survey Atlas (€12, sold in most TIs and bookstores in Ireland). The Fir Tree Aerial series makes a useful map that covers both the Iveragh and Dingle Peninsulas, giving you a bird's-eye feel for the terrain (€8, sold in many TIs and bookstores in County Kerry).

Unlike the much shorter Slea Head loop on the neighboring Dingle Peninsula (see next chapter), which can only be driven clockwise, the Ring of Kerry loop can be driven in either direction.

Think of the Ring as a rectangle (with Kenmare in the lower-right corner), and consider the following. Most tour buses depart from Killarney in a virtual convoy and spend the day chugging counter-clockwise around the loop. Rather than getting stuck behind a slow, view-blocking behemoth, drive the loop clockwise (as many locals do).

Since you'll be driving on the left side of the road, the dramatic coastal views (on your left) will never be obstructed by passing vehicles.

If you're approaching the region from Kinsale and Cobh, the best scenario is to visit Muckross House first, giving you a great Killarney lakes experience without wasting time in plastic Killarney town. Then go south on N71 to see some of the Ring's best mountain scenery at Ladies View and Moll's Gap (WCs beside parking lot) before descending into Kenmare to spend the night. Drivers from Kinsale who skip

Blarney and have lunch at Muckross House can be in Kenmare by midafternoon. The flat inland N72 section of the Ring from Killorglin to Killarney (the upper-right corner of the rectangle) is least worthwhile and can be skipped. This leaves you with less of the Ring to tackle the following day. If you depart Kenmare by 9:00 (staying on N70 all the way around to Killorglin), you'll have time to enjoy the Ring and still make it to Dingle town by 19:00. If you don't get an early start, you'll feel rushed and stressed.

Fill up on gas in Kenmare (Esso filling station and Centra market at junction where N70 Sneem road meets N71 Killarney road). Gas is cheaper here than out on the Ring.

The downside of all this is that you'll need to be an alert and courteous driver as you unexpectedly encounter oncoming bus traffic. Buses have the right-of-way. Not all of the Ring road is narrow, but the most challenging stretch is the rugged, curvy coastal section between Derrynane and Waterville (the lower-left corner of the rectangle). There are lots of scenic view pullouts, but it will be up to you to back up to the nearest wide spot in the road to let a less-nimble bus get through a tight curve.

For tips on driving in Ireland, see page 24 in the Introduction.

Muckross House

Perhaps the best Victorian stately home you'll see in Ireland, Muckross House (built in 1843) is magnificently set at the edge of Killarney National Park.

This regular stop on the tour-bus circuit includes several sights in one: the mansion, a set of traditional farms showing rural life in the 1930s, a fine garden idyllically set on a lake, and an information center for the national park. The Victorian period was the 19th-century boom time, when the sun never set on the British Empire and the Industrial Revolution (born in England) was chugging the world into the modern age. Of course, Ireland was a colony back then, with big-shot English landlords. (The English gentry lived very well, while a third of Ireland's population starved in the famine of 1845–1849. Read the Muckross House lord's defense on page 43 of the fine souvenir book.) Be sure to take the 45-minute guided **tour** that gives meaning to the house (included with admission, offered regularly throughout the day).

Muckross House feels lived in—with fine Victorian furniture cluttered around the fireplace under Waterford Crystal chandeliers and lots of antlers. You'll see Queen Victoria's bedroom (ground floor, since she was afraid of house fires; used during her 1861 visit).

The house exit takes you through an **information center** for Killarney National Park, with a relaxing 15-minute video on "Ireland's premier national park," featuring lots of geology, flora, and fauna (free, shown on request).

The **garden** is a hit for those with a green thumb, and a €1.50 guide booklet makes the nature trails interesting. A bright, modern cafeteria (with indoor/outdoor seating) faces the garden. The adjacent crafts shop shows weaving and pottery in action.

Muckross Traditional Farms, designed to give the Muckross stop a little heft, consists of six different farmhouses showing off life in the 1930s. Several farms come with a person ready to feed you a little home-baked bread and reminisce about the old days. If you've yet to see an open-air folk museum, this might be worthwhile— otherwise, it's pretty lightweight. The farms are strung along a mile-long road with an old bus shuttling those who don't want to hike (free, 4/hr).

Cost and Hours: €5.50 for house, €8.25 includes house and old farms, covered by Heritage Card (see page 4). House open daily 9:00–17:30, July–Aug until 19:00, shorter hours in winter; farms open May–Sept only; tel. 064/31440.

Getting There: Muckross House is conveniently located for a break on the long ride from Cork or Cashel to Dingle or Kenmare. From Killarney, follow signs to Kenmare, where you'll find Muckross House three miles south of town. As you approach from Killarney, you'll see a small parking lot two miles before the actual parking lot. This is used by horse-and-buggy bandits to hoodwink tourists into thinking they have to pay to clip-clop to the house. Giddy-up on by, and you'll find a big, safe, and free lot right at the mansion.

Staigue Fort

One of the largest and best-preserved of Ireland's ring forts, Staigue (STAY-ig) is an imposing sight rising out of a desolate high valley. The circular drystone walls were built sometime between 500 B.C. and A.D. 300 without the aid of mortar or cement. About 80 feet across, with walls 12 feet thick at the base and up to 20 feet high, this brutish structure would have taken a hundred men six months to complete. Expert opinion is divided, but most believe that the people who built it would have retreated here at times of tribal war, bringing their valuable cattle inside to protect them from ancient rustlers. Others see the round design as a kind of amphitheater, where local clan chieftains would have gathered for important meetings or rituals. However, the ditch surrounding the outer walls suggest a defensive, rather than ceremonial, function. Without written records, we can only imagine the part this mute ghost played in ancient dramas.

Before you see the fort, pay a visit to the **Staigue Fort Exhibition Centre** to gain an appreciation for the deceptively simple structure. Inside the Exhibition Centre, you'll find a tiny museum, a detailed fort model, and a 10-minute film putting it all into historical context (€3, Easter–Sept daily 10:00–21:00, closed Oct–Easter, tel. 066/947-5127, coffee shop and WCs).

Getting There: The fort is off the main N70 road on the right. Just after passing through the hamlet of Castle Cove, look for signs to "Staigue" on the right, leading up into the interior. You'll find the fort (free and always open) at the top of a 2.5-mile-long rural access road.

Derrynane House

This is the home of Daniel O'Connell, Ireland's most influential preindependence politician, whose tireless nonviolent agitation gained equality for Catholics 175 years ago. The coastal lands of the O'Connell estate that surround Derrynane House are now a national historic park. A visit here is a window onto a man who not only liberated Ireland from the last oppressive anti-Catholic penal laws, but who also first developed the idea of a grassroots movement, organizing on a massive scale to achieve political ends without bloodshed (see sidebar).

The house has a quirky floor plan that can be confusing, so pick up a laminated guide at the front desk. Ask about the next scheduled 20-minute audiovisual show, which fleshes out the highlights of O'Connell's turbulent life and makes the contents of the house more interesting.

In the exhibition room downstairs is a glass case containing the

Daniel O'Connell
(1775–1847)

Born in Cahersiveen and elected in Ennis as the first Catholic member of the British Parliament, O'Connell was the hero of Catholic emancipation in Ireland. Educated in France at a time when the anti-Catholic penal laws limited schooling for Irish Catholics in Ireland, he witnessed the carnage of the French Revolution. Upon his return to Ireland, he saw more bloodshed during the futile Rebellion of 1798. He chose law as his profession, and reluctantly killed a man who challenged him to a duel. Abhorring all this violence, O'Connell dedicated himself to peacefully gaining equal rights for Catholics in an Ireland dominated by a wealthy Protestant minority. He formed the Catholic Association, with a one-penny-per-month membership fee, and quickly gained a huge following (especially among the poor) with his persuasive speaking skills. Although Catholics weren't allowed to hold office, he ran for election to Parliament, anyway, and won a seat in 1828. His unwillingness to take the anti-Catholic Oath of Supremacy initially kept him out of Westminster, but the moral force of his victory caused the government to give in and concede Catholic emancipation the following year. Known as "the Liberator," he was making progress toward his next goal of repealing the Act of Union with Britain when the Potato Famine hit in 1845. O'Connell died two years later in Genoa on his way to Rome, but his ideals lived on: His Catholic Association was the model that taught the fundamentals of political organization to the Irish who later emigrated and rose within American big-city political "green machines."

pistols that were used in O'Connell's famous duel. Beside them are his black gloves, one of which he always wore on his right pistol hand when he went to Mass (out of remorse for the part it played in taking a man's life). The drawing room upstairs is lined with family portraits and contains his ornately carved chair with tiny harp strings and wolfhound collars made of gold. On a wall in the upstairs bedroom is a copy of O'Connell's famous speech imploring the Irish not to riot when he was arrested. Then visit the coach house (out back, beside the tearoom) to see the enormous grand chariot that carried O'Connell through throngs of joyous Dubliners after his release from prison in 1844. He added the small chapel wing to the house in gratitude to God for his prison release.

The grounds of the estate are pleasant enough for a 20-minute stroll to the beach and back, but not at the expense of making you rush through the remainder of your Ring of Kerry day.

Cost and Hours: €2.75, covered by Heritage Card (see page 4),

May–Sept Mon–Sat 9:00–18:00, Sun 11:00–19:00; April and Oct Tue–Sun 13:00–17:00, closed Mon; Nov–March Sat–Sun 13:00–17:00, closed Mon–Fri; last entry 45 min before closing, tel. 066/947-5113.

Getting There: Just outside the town of Derrynane, pick up a handy free map of the estate from the little TI inside the brown Wave Crest market (TI open May–Sept daily 9:00–20:00, closed Oct–April, tel. 066/947-5188; market is an easy place to buy a picnic). One mile after the market, take a left and follow the signs into Derrynane National Historic Park. Visit the ogham stone (below) on your way to the house.

Ogham Stone: On the grounds of Derrynane House is a fine example of an ogham stone. Such pillars were erected by Irish clans around the time of Christ to mark boundaries, or possibly graves of nobility. Ogham (AHG-um) was the first written language of the Irish, inspired by contacts with the Roman alphabet. The notches and diagonal lines carved into the corner of the stone (facing the bay) represent letters of the Irish alphabet. To find the stone as you approach the Derrynane House grounds, watch for a small brown sign next to a rusty little gate on your left, pointing to a stone 25 feet off the road (a mile after turning off N70, just before the Entering National Park sign).

Skellig Ring

This narrow little 20-mile ring road is an unspoiled jewel dangling off the end of the Ring of Kerry necklace. It's a lovely (but time-consuming) bonus for travelers wanting to lose the crowds. The Skellig Ring is bus-free and takes an hour to drive (cars do it in either direction). If you time it right, you'll be out here in the middle of the day—as the worst of the tour-bus traffic goes by on N70. Be ready to pull over to allow occasional oncoming traffic to pass.

Driving the Skellig Ring

Leave the Ring of Kerry (N70) onto R567 about three miles north of Waterville, following the brown "Skellig Ring" signs to Ballinskelligs. The road north from Ballinskelligs to Portmagee is not numbered, but easy to follow, rewarding adventurous motorists with dramatic views of the two Skellig rocks seven miles offshore. A rugged dose of scenic coastal Ireland graces the foreground. St. Finan's Bay lies about halfway around, with a pleasant little picnic-friendly beach (but no WCs). Popping up unexpectedly near the bay is the small Skelligs Chocolate factory, inviting visitors in for a sample and proclaiming their chocolates to be "never boring, always reliably gorgeous, and sometimes a little different—just like the Irish!" (May–Oct Mon–Fri

10:00–16:00, Sat 12:00–16:00, closed Sun and Nov–April, tel. 066/947-9119, www.skelligschocolate.com.)

In 1944, a U.S. Navy PBY seaplane on U-Boat patrol crashed into the summit of Skellig Michael, killing all aboard. A simple memorial can be found a mile down the undulating, dead-end spur road running south along the coast from St. Finan's Bay. The very steep switchback road, climbing north out of St. Finan's Bay, tests your clutch skills (honk at blind hairpin corners to alert oncoming cars) and leads to a spectacular viewpoint on the ridgetop at Coomanaspic Pass. Locals claim this is the highest place you can drive a car in Ireland. The Dingle Peninsula and Blasket Islands are often visible off to the north. From here, put it in low gear and coast down the other side of the ridge, passing a pretty little roadside shrine to the Virgin Mary before arriving in Portmagee. The R565 leads you back to the Ring of Kerry.

Visiting Skellig Michael

If you have more time, consider venturing out to the pointy, secluded island of Skellig Michael. To do it right, visit the Skellig Experience Centre, spend the night in or near Portmagee, and take a boat to the island the next day (book the cruise ahead; see page 159).

Portmagee

Just a short row of snoozy buildings lining the bay, Portmagee is the best harbor for boat excursions out to the Skellig Islands. It's a quiet village with a handful of B&Bs, two pubs, a bakery, a market, and no ATMs. A 100-yard-long bridge connects it to gently rounded Valencia Island, where you'll find the Skellig Experience Centre (on the left at the Valencia end of the bridge; see below). A public parking lot is at the Portmagee end of the bridge, with award-winning WCs (no kidding: Irish Toilet of the Year 2002 runner-up plaque proudly displayed). The first transatlantic cable (for telegraph communication) was laid from Valencia Island in 1866. The tiny post office hides inside O'Connell's Market (Mon–Fri 9:00–17:30, Sat 9:00–13:00, closed Sun).

SLEEPING

(€1 = about $1.20, country code: 353, area code: 066)

$$ **Moorings Guest House** feels like a small hotel, with 14 rooms, a pub and a fine restaurant downstairs, and the most convenient location in town, 50 yards from the end of the pier (Db-€80–90, tel. 066/947-7108, fax 066/947-7220, www.moorings.ie, moorings@iol.ie).

At the homey $ **Island View B&B,** Kathleen O'Donoghue

bakes the daily bread in her antique stove, and can arrange a boat trip out to the Skelligs (S-€30, D-€55, Db-€60, Tb-€80, a half mile south of Portmagee on the road to St. Finan's Bay, tel. 066/947-7188, mobile 087-926-1492, www.islandviewguesthouse.com).

$ Beach Cove B&B offers four comfortable rooms in splendid isolation four miles south, over lofty Coomanaspic ridge from Portmagee, beside the pretty beach at St. Finan's Bay. Charming Bridie O'Connor will arrange a boat trip out to the Skelligs for you. Her adjacent cottage out back has two double rooms and a kitchen, making it ideal for families (Sb-€38, Db-€60, Tb-€80, tel. 066/947-9301, mobile 087-202-1820, www.stayatbeachcove.com, beachcove @eircom.net).

EATING

These options all line the waterfront (between pier and bridge to Valencia Island). **The Moorings** is an expensive restaurant with great seafood caught literally just outside its front door (€18–29 dinners, Tue–Sun 18:00–22:00, closed Mon, reservations smart, 50 yards to the left coming off the pier, tel. 066/947-7108). The **Bridge Bar,** right next door and under the same ownership, does traditional pub grub, but stops serving food a bit early (€12–17 meals, daily 12:00–20:00, live music Fri and Sun nights, tel. 066/947-7108). The **Fisherman's Bar** is less pretentious, with more locals and cheaper prices (€10–16 meals, daily 10:00–21:30, immediately on the right coming off the pier, tel. 066/947-7103). **O'Connell's Market** is the only grocery (100 yards east of the pier; on the left, roughly halfway to the bridge, Mon–Sat 9:00–21:30, Sun 11:00–18:00). **Skellig Mist Bakery** can make basic lunch sandwiches to take on Skellig boat excursions (a couple doors further, toward the bridge, daily 9:30–18:00, tel. 066/947-7250).

Skellig Experience Centre

You'll better appreciate a visit to Skellig Michael if you explore this modest museum first (if you're taking a boat to the island, visit here the afternoon before). Straightforward exhibits explain the unique bird life of the Skellig Islands, as well as the underwater creatures surrounding them. The highlight is the historical coverage of the tenacious early Christian community that somehow sustained itself on these rocks, at the edge of the world, for five centuries. A 15-minute audiovisual show fills in the blanks. Follow it up with a coffee or sandwich in the tearoom, and you've got wind back in your sails. A visit here is also worth considering if a tight schedule or bad weather prevents you from an actual visit to the Skelligs (€4.40, audioguide €0.50 extra, July–Aug daily 10:00–19:00, May–June and Sept daily 10:00–18:00, March–April and Oct daily 10:00–17:00, closed Nov–Feb, call ahead in off-season as hours may vary, on Valencia Island beside bridge linking it to Portmagee, tel. 066/947-6306, www.skelligexperience.com).

Two-hour **boat trips**, circling both Skellig Michael and Little Skellig (but without putting people ashore on them), are available for those who want a close look without the stair climb and vertigo that go with an actual visit to the island (€17, sailing daily about 15:00 and returning by 17:00, weather permitting, depart from Valencia Island pier 50 yards below the Skellig Experience Centre—which you can call for details, see phone number above).

Skellig Michael

A trip to this jagged, isolated pyramid—the Holy Grail of Irish monastic island settlements—rates as a truly memorable experience. After visiting Skellig Michael a hundred years ago, Nobel Prize–winning Irish author George Bernard Shaw called it "the most fantastic and impossible rock in the world."

Rising seven miles offshore, the Skelligs (Gaelic for "splinters") are two gigantic, slate-and-sandstone rocks crouched aggressively on the ocean horizon. The larger of the two, Skellig Michael, is over 700 feet tall and a mile around, with a tiny cluster of abandoned bee-hive huts clinging near its summit like stubborn barnacles. The smaller of the two, Little Skellig, is home to a huge colony of gannets (like a large, graceful seagull with a 4-foot wingspan), protected by law from visitors setting foot on shore.

Skellig Michael (dedicated to the archangel) was first inhabited by ultra-pious, 6th-century Christian monks. Inspired by earlier hermit monks in the Egyptian desert, they sought the purity of isolation to get closer to God. Neither Viking raids nor winter storms could dislodge them as they patiently built a half dozen small, stone, igloo-like dwellings and a couple of tiny oratories. Their remote cliff-terrace perch is still connected to the sea 600 feet below by an amazing series of rock stairs. Viking Olav Trygvasson, who later became King of Norway and introduced Christianity to his country, was baptized here in 956.

Chiseling the most rudimentary life out of solid rock, the monks lived a harsh, lonely, disciplined existence that endured for over 500 years. They collected rainwater in cisterns and lived off fish and birds. To supplement their meager existence, they gathered bird eggs and feathers to trade with passing boats for cereals, candles, and animal hides (used for clothing and for copying scripture). They finally moved their holy community ashore to Ballinskelligs in the early 1100s.

Time—which dragged for medieval monks—flies by for modern visitors to Skellig Michael. Since you'll have only a little more than two hours to explore the island, begin by surmounting the seemingly unending series of stone stairs to the monastic ruins.

Plan on 600 vertical feet of uneven stone stairs with no handrails (with a brief respite at the level saddle between the peaks, 100 feet below the two summits). Save most of your film for the way down. Those who linger too long below risk missing the enlightening, 20-minute free talk among the beehive huts given by Office of Public Works guides (who camp on the island April–Oct) soon after a few boats arrive. Afterward, poke your head into some of the huts and try to imagine the dark, damp, and devoted life of a monk here over 1,000 years ago. After rambling through the ruins, you can give in to photo frenzy as you wander back down the stairs.

When you come back down to the saddle between the two main peaks, gaze at the tallest spire (called the Needle's Eye) and visualize a horizontal natural stone outcrop that once extended from near the summit. A cross was carved into the end of it, and devout pilgrims would crawl out to kiss it as part of their penitential duty. It finally fell 700 feet into the sea in 1977 without loss of life.

The two lighthouses on the far side of the island are now automated, and access to them has been blocked off. There are no WCs or modern shelters of any kind on Skellig Michael—you're roughing it in a remote and magical place for several hours.

If you visit between late April and early August, you'll be surrounded by fearless rainbow-beaked puffins, who nest here in underground burrows. Their bizarre swallowed cooing sounds like a distant chainsaw. These portly little birds live off fish, and divers have reported seeing them 20 feet underwater in pursuit of their prey.

Your return boat journey usually includes a pass near Little Skellig, which looms like an iceberg with a white coat of guano—courtesy of the 20,000 gannets that circle overhead like feathered confetti. You're likely to get a glimpse of gray seals lazing on rocks near the water's edge.

Getting There: To book a boat trip from Portmagee, contact

Murphy's Sea Cruise (€35, office across from O'Connell's Market, tel. 066/947-7156, mobile 087-234-2168, www.esatclear.ie/~skelligsrock, murphyseacruise@esatclear.ie), **Joe Roddy** (tel. 066/947-4268), or **Brendan Casey** (tel. 066/947-2437).

Landing on Skellig Michael is highly weather-dependent. If the seas are too choppy, the boats cannot safely put people ashore on the concrete island pier (a bit like jumping off a trampoline onto an ice rink). Excursions are scheduled to run daily from Easter to late September, but experienced boat captains say they are able to put visitors ashore roughly five days out of seven in an average summer week.

Your best bet is to reserve a room near Portmagee that fits your itinerary, then call a few days in advance to make a boat reservation. Keep your fingers crossed for good weather. Contact the boat operator on the morning of departure to get the final word. If the seas are too rough, he can tell from Portmagee and will make a decision that morning whether or not to go (rather than taking passengers halfway out, then aborting).

Boat trips normally depart Portmagee at 10:30. The crossing takes an hour, and passengers are put ashore from roughly 11:30 until 14:00. That gets people back into Portmagee by 15:00 (with enough time to drive on to Dingle). There is a total fleet of 15 small boats (from Portmagee, Ballinskelligs, Waterville, and Valencia Island) that have permits to land on Skellig Michael. Each boat can carry a dozen passengers. This limits the number of daily visitors and minimizes the impact on the sensitive island ecosystem.

Bring tons of film, a sandwich lunch (easy to buy at Skellig Mist Bakery in Portmagee), water, sunscreen, rain gear, and comfortable hiking shoes for rocky terrain.

DINGLE PENINSULA

Dingle Peninsula, the westernmost tip of Ireland, offers just the right mix of far-and-away beauty, ancient archaeological wonders, and isolated walks or bike rides—all within convenient reach of its main town. Dingle town is just large enough to have all the necessary tourist services and a steady nocturnal beat of Irish folk music.

Although crowded in summer, Dingle still feels like the fish and the farm really matter. Forty fishing boats sail from Dingle, tractor tracks dirty its main drag, and a faint whiff of peat fills its nighttime streets.

For more than 25 years, my Irish dreams have been set here on this sparse but lush peninsula, where locals are fond of saying, "The next parish is Boston." There's a feeling of closeness to the land on Dingle. When I asked a local if he was born here, he thought for a second and said, "No, it was about six miles down the road." When I told him where I was from, a faraway smile filled his eyes, and he looked out to sea and sighed, "Ah, the shores of Americay." I asked his friend if he'd lived here all his life. He said, "Not yet."

Dingle feels so traditionally Irish because it's a *Gaeltacht,* a region where the government subsidizes the survival of the Irish language and culture. While English is always there, the signs, menus, and songs come in Gaelic. Children carry hurling sticks to class, and even the local preschool brags "ALL Gaelic."

Of the peninsula's 10,000 residents, 1,500 live in Dingle town. Its few streets, lined with ramshackle but gaily painted shops and pubs, run up from a rain-stung harbor always busy with fishing boats and yachts. Traditionally, the buildings were drab gray or whitewashed. Thirty years

Dingle Peninsula

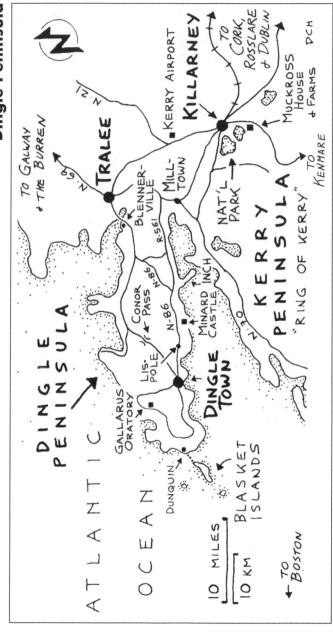

ago, Ireland's "tidy town" competition prompted everyone to paint their buildings in playful pastels.

It's a peaceful town. The courthouse (1832) is open one hour a month. The judge does his best to wrap up business within a half hour. During the day, you'll see teenagers—already working on ruddy beer-glow cheeks—roll kegs up the streets and into the pubs in preparation for another night of music and *craic* (fun conversation and atmosphere).

Dingle Town

Planning Your Time
For the shortest visit, give Dingle two nights and a day. It takes six to eight hours to get there from Dublin, Galway, or the boat dock in Rosslare. By spending two nights, you'll feel more like a local on your second evening in the pubs. You'll need the better part of a day to explore the 30-mile loop around the peninsula by bike, car, or tour bus (see "Dingle Peninsula Circular Tour" on page 179). To do any serious walking or relaxing, you'll need two or three days. It's not uncommon to find Americans slowing way, way down in Dingle town.

ORIENTATION

(area code: 066)
Dingle—extremely comfortable on foot—hangs on a medieval grid of streets between the harborfront (where the Tralee bus stops) and Main Street (3 blocks inland). Nothing in town is more than a five-minute walk away. Street numbers are used only when more than one place is run by a family of the same name. Most locals know most locals, and people on the street are fine sources of information. Remember, locals love their soda bread, and tourism provides the butter. You'll find a warm and sincere welcome.

Tourist Information
The TI is a privately owned, for-profit business—little more than a glorified shop with a green staff who are disinclined to really know the town (July–Aug daily 9:00–19:00, June and Sept–Oct daily 9:30–17:30; Nov–May Mon–Tue and Thu–Sat 10:00–17:00, closed Sun and Wed; on Strand Street by the water, tel. 066/915-1188). For more knowledgeable help, drop by the Mountain Man shop (on Strand Street, see "Dingle Activities," page 166) or talk to your B&B host.

Dingle's History

The wet sod of Dingle is soaked with medieval history. In the darkest depths of the Dark Ages, peace-loving, bookish monks fled the chaos of the Continent and its barbarian raids. They sailed to the drizzly fringe of the known world—places like Dingle. These monks kept literacy alive in Europe. Charlemagne, who ruled much of Europe in the year 800, imported Irish monks to be his scribes.

It was from this peninsula that the semi-mythical explorer/monk, St. Brendan, is said to have set sail in the 6th century in search of a legendary western paradise. Some think he beat Columbus to North America by nearly a thousand years.

Dingle (An Daingean in Gaelic) was a busy seaport in the late Middle Ages. Dingle and Tralee (covered later in this chapter) were the only walled towns in Kerry. Castles stood at the low and high ends of Dingle's Main Street, protecting the Normans from the angry and dispossessed Irish outside. Dingle was a gateway to northern Spain—a three-day sail due south. Many 14th- and 15th-century pilgrims left from the Dingle Peninsula for the revered Spanish church, Santiago de Compostela, thought to house the bones of St. James.

In Dingle's medieval heyday, locals traded cowhides for wine. When Dingle's position as a trading center waned, the town faded in importance. In the 19th century, it was a linen-weaving center. Until 1970, fishing dominated, and the only visitors were scholars and students of old Irish ways. In 1970, the movie *Ryan's Daughter* introduced the world to Dingle. The trickle of Dingle fans has grown to a flood as word of its musical, historical, gastronomical, and scenic charms—not to mention its friendly dolphin—has spread.

Helpful Hints

Before You Go: The local Web site (www.dingle-peninsula.ie) lists festivals and events.

Crowds: Crowds trample Dingle's charm throughout July and August. The absolute craziest times are the Dingle Races (2nd weekend in Aug), Dingle Regatta (3rd weekend in Aug), and the Blessing of the Boats (end of Aug, beginning of Sept). The first Mondays in May, June, and August are bank holidays, giving Ireland's workers three-day weekends—and ample time to fill up Dingle. The town's metabolism (prices, schedules, activities) rises and falls with the tourist crowds, so October through April is sleepy.

Banking: Two banks in town, both on Main Street, offer the same rates (Mon 10:00–17:00, Tue–Fri 10:00–16:00, closed Sat–Sun) and have cash machines. The TI happily changes cash and traveler's checks at mediocre rates. Expect to use cash (rather than credit cards) to pay for most peninsula activities.

Internet Access: Dingle Internet Café is on Main Street (€2.60/30 min, April–Sept Mon–Fri 10:00–22:00, Sat 13:00–20:00, Sun 14:00–20:00, shorter hours Oct–March, tel. 066/915-2478, www.dingleinternetcafe.ie).

Post Office: It's on Main Street near Benners Hotel (Mon–Fri 9:00–17:30, Sat 9:00–13:00, closed Sun).

Laundry: Dingle Cleaners is full-service only—drop off before 10:00 and pick up dried and folded late that afternoon (€8–12 depending on load size, Mon–Sat 9:30–18:00, closed Sun, beside Moran's Market and gas station, tel. 066/915-0680, mobile 087-793-5621).

Bike Rental: Bike rental shops abound. The cheapest is at Kirrary B&B (€8/day, Greys Lane, see "Sleeping," page 173), or try Paddy's Bike Hire (€10/day or €1 more for 24 hrs, €12 for better bikes, daily 9:00–19:00, on Dykegate next to Grapevine Hostel, tel. 066/915-2311). Foxy John's (Main Street), Mountain Man (no helmets), and the Ballintaggert Hostel also rent bikes. If you're biking the peninsula, get a bike with skinny street tires, not slow and fat mountain-bike tires. Plan on leaving €10, plus a driver's license or passport, as a security deposit.

Dingle Activities: The Mountain Man, a hiking shop run by a local guide, Adrian Curran, is a clearinghouse for information on hiking, biking, horseback riding, climbing, peninsula tours, and trips to the Blasket Islands (the shop is the Dingle town contact for the Dunquin–Blasket Islands boats and shuttle-bus rides to the harbor via Moran's taxi service—see "Blasket Islands," page 187). Give them a call a few days ahead of time to see which guided, scenic, mountain day-hikes are scheduled (July–Sept daily 9:00–21:00, Oct–June 9:00–18:00, just off harbor at Strand Street, tel. 066/915-2400, www.themountainmanshop.com).

Travel Agency: Maurice O'Connor at Galvin's Travel Agency can book plane tickets, as well as boat rides to France (Mon–Fri 9:30–18:00, Sat 9:30–17:00, closed Sun, John Street, tel. 066/915-1409).

Farmers Market: On most Saturdays (10:00–14:00), local farmers fill the St. James churchyard on Main Street with their fresh produce and homemade marmalade.

SIGHTS AND ACTIVITIES

▲▲**The Harry Clark Windows of Diseart**—Just behind Dingle's St. Mary Church stands St. Joseph's Convent and Diseart (dee-ZHART), containing a beautiful neo-Gothic chapel built in 1884. The sisters of this order, who came to Dingle in 1829 to educate local girls, worked heroically during the famine. During Mass in the chapel, the Mother Superior would sit in the covered stall in the rear, while the sisters—filling the carved stalls—chanted responsively.

The chapel was graced in 1922 with 12 windows—the work of Ireland's top stained-glass man, Harry Clark. Long appreciated only by the sisters, these special windows—showing six scenes from the life of Christ—are now open to the public. The convent has become a center for sharing Christian Celtic culture and spirituality (free, Mon–Fri 9:30–13:00 & 14:00–17:00, closed Sat–Sun, tel. 066/915-2476, www.diseart.ie).

Enjoy a meditative 15 minutes following the free audioguide that explains the chapel one window at a time. The scenes (clockwise from the back entrance) are: the visit of the Magi, the Baptism of Jesus, "Let the little children come to me," the Sermon on the Mount, the Agony in the Garden, and Jesus appearing to Mary Magdalene. Each face is lively and animated in the imaginative, devout, medieval, and fun-loving art of Harry Clark, whom locals talk about as if he's the kid next door.

▲**Fungie**—In 1983, a dolphin moved into Dingle Harbor and became a local celebrity. Fungie (FOON-gee, with a hard *g*) is now the darling of the town's tourist trade and one reason you'll find so many tour buses parked along the harbor. With a close look at Fungie as bait, tour boats are thriving. The hardy little boats motor seven to 40 passengers out to the mouth of the harbor, where they troll around looking for Fungie. You're virtually assured of seeing the dolphin, but you don't pay unless you do (€12, kids–€6, 1-hr trips depart 10:00–19:00 depending on demand, behind TI at Dolphin Trips office, tel. 066/915-2626). To actually swim with Fungie, rent wetsuits at Bresnan's B&B (Cooleen Street, tel. 066/915-1967) and catch the early-morning 8:00–10:00 trip (€35 includes a wetsuit—unless you've packed your own).

▲**Oceanworld**—The aquarium offers a little peninsula history, 300 different species of local fish in thoughtfully described tanks, and the easiest way to see Fungie the dolphin...on video. Walk through the tunnel while fish swim overhead. The only creatures not local—other than you—are the sharks. The aquarium's mission is to teach, and you're welcome to ask questions. The petting pool is fun. Splashing attracts the rays, which are unplugged (€9, families–€25, daily July–Aug 10:00–20:30, May–June and Sept 10:00–18:00, Oct–April 10:00–17:00, cafeteria, just past harbor on west edge of town, tel. 066/915-2111).

▲**Short Harbor Walk from Dingle**—For an easy stroll along the harbor out of town (and a chance to see Fungie, 90 min round-trip), head east from the roundabout past the Esso station. Just after Bambury's B&B, take a right, following signs to Skelligs Hotel, and go left at the Irish Coast Guard station on the bay. At the beach,

Dingle Hotels and Services

1 Heatons Guesthouse
2 Benners Hotel
3 Greenmount House
4 Captain's House B&B
5 Alpine Guest House
6 Bambury's Guesthouse
7 Barr Na Sraide Inn
8 Coastline Guesthouse
9 Ard Na Greine House B&B
10 Kelliher's Ballyegan House
11 O'Neill's B&B
12 Corner House B&B
13 O Coileain B&B
14 Kirrary B&B (Sciuird Tours)
15 Sraid Eoin House
   & Galvin's Travel Agency
16 Ocean View B&B
17 Grapevine Hostel
18 To Ballintaggart Hostel
19 Milestone House
20 Mainstay Guesthouse
21 Mountain Man Shop & Bike Rental

22 Paddy's Bike Hire
23 Eco-Cruise Office
24 West Kerry Craft Guild
25 Internet Café
26 Super Valu Supermarket
27 World of Leisure

Dingle Area

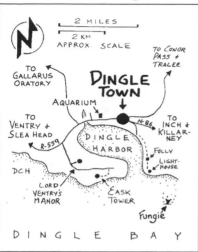

2 MILES

2 KM
APPROX. SCALE

TO CONOR
PASS &
TRALEE

TO
GALLARUS
ORATORY

DINGLE TOWN

AQUARIUM

TO
VENTRY &
SLEA HEAD

R-559

TO
INCH &
KILLAR-
NEY

N-86

DINGLE
HARBOR

FOLLY

LIGHT-
HOUSE

DCH

LORD
VENTRY'S
MANOR

EASK
TOWER

Fungie

D I N G L E   B A Y

climb the steps over the wall and follow the seashore path to the mouth of Dingle Harbor (marked by a tower—some 19th-century fat cat's folly). Ten minutes beyond that is a lighthouse. This is Fungie's neighborhood. If you see tourist boats out, you're likely to see the dolphin. The trail continues to a dramatic cliff.

The Harbor: The harbor was built on land reclaimed (with imported Dutch expertise) in 1992. The string of old stone shops facing the harbor was the loading station for the narrow-gauge railway that hauled the fish from Dingle to Tralee (1891–1953). Make a point to walk out to the end of the breakwater—newly paved, and illuminated at night. The Eask Tower on the distant hill is a marker that was built in 1847 during the famine as a make-work project. In pre-radar days, it helped ships locate Dingle's hidden harbor. The fancy mansion across the harbor is Lord Ventry's 17th-century manor house (see "Dingle Peninsula Circular Tour," page 179).

Sailing—The Dingle Marina Centre offers diving, sailing, traditional currach rowing, and a salty little restaurant. Sailors can join the club for a day to sail (€22, July–Aug, tel. 066/915-1984). Currachs—stacked behind the building—are Ireland's traditional lightweight fishing boats, easy to haul and easy to make. Cover a wooden frame with canvas (originally cowhide) and paint with tar—presto.

Horseback Riding—Dingle Horse Riding takes out beginners (€26/hr for a trail ride) and experienced riders on four-hour (€95) and six-hour (€130) excursions. Bob along beaches or mountains on an English-style ride (closed Nov–Feb, 5-min drive from Dingle, call ahead to book, tel. 066/915-2199, www.dinglehorseriding.com).

Dingle World of Leisure—This is a health club for adults and a good rainy-day option for kids, offering bowling (€18–30/hr depending on time of day), arcade games, a swimming pool, and a children's indoor playground (daily 11:00–23:00, just off John Street, tel. 066/915-0660, www.dingleworldofleisure.com).

Dingle Pitch & Putt—For 18 scenic holes and a driving range, hike 10 minutes past Oceanworld (€5 includes gear, driving range €5 for 100 balls, April–Oct daily 10:00–20:00, closed Nov–March, over bridge take first left and follow signs, Milltown, tel. 066/915-2020).

The Voyage of St. Brendan

It has long been part of Irish lore that St. Brendan the Navigator (A.D. 484–577) and 12 followers sailed from the southwest of Ireland to the "Land of Promise" (what is now North America) in a currach—a wood-frame boat covered with ox hide and tar. According to a 10th-century monk who poetically wrote of the journey, St. Brendan and his crew encountered a paradise of birds, were attacked by a whale, and suffered the smoke of a smelly island in the north before finally reaching their Land of Promise.

The legend and its precisely described locations still fascinate modern readers. A British scholar of navigation, Tim Severin, re-created the entire journey from 1976 to 1977. He and his crew set out from Brendan Creek in County Kerry in a currach. The prevailing winds blew them to the Hebrides, the Faeroe Islands, Iceland, and finally to Newfoundland. While this didn't successfully prove that St. Brendan sailed to North America, it did prove that he could have.

St. Brendan fans have been heartened by an intriguing archaeological find in Connecticut. Called the "Gungywamp," the site includes a double circle of stones and a beehive-like chamber built in the same manner as the stone *clochans* huts on the Dingle Peninsula. The Gungywamp beehive chamber has been carbon-dated to approximately A.D. 600. Outside the chamber, a stone slab is inscribed with a cross that resembles the unique style of the Irish cross.

According to his 10th-century biographer, "St. Brendan sailed from the Land of Promise home to Ireland. And from that time on, Brendan acted as if he did not belong to this world at all. His mind and his joy were in the delight of heaven."

Golf—Located out west, near the tip of the Dingle peninsula in Ballyferriter (9 miles from Dingle town), Ceann Sibeal/Dingle Links offers a round of golf in a hard-to-beat setting (€50–70 green fees, open daily, tel. 066/915-6255, www.dinglelinks.com).

Shopping—Dingle is filled with shops showing off local craftsmanship. The **West Kerry Craft Guild**—a co-op selling the work of 15 local artists—is a delight even if you're just browsing. The prices here are very good, since you're buying directly from the artists (June–Aug daily 10:00–18:00, Sept–May daily 11:00–17:00, 18 Main Street, tel. 066/915-2976). The **Niamh Utsch Jewelry** shop next door is much respected for its unique work. **Lisbeth Mulcahy Weaver**, filled with traditional but stylish woven wear, is also the Dingle sales outlet of the well-known potter from out on Slea Head (Mon–Sat 9:00–18:00, Sun 10:00–18:00, Green Street, tel. 066/915-1688).

East of Dingle Town

▲**Minard Castle**—Seven miles east of Dingle (off Lispole Road) is the largest fortress on the peninsula. Built by the Norman Knights of Kerry in 1551, Minard Castle was destroyed by Cromwell in about

1650. With its corners undermined by Cromwellian explosives, it looks ready to split—it's no longer safe to enter this teetering ruin.

From the outside, look for the faint scallop in the doorway, the symbol of St. James. Medieval pilgrims would stop here before making a seafaring pilgrimage from the Dingle Peninsula to St. James' tomb at Santiago de Compostela in northern Spain. Imagine the floor plan of the castle: ground floor for animals and storage; main floor, with fireplace; then living-quarters floor; and, on top, the defensive level.

The setting is dramatic, with the Ring of Kerry across the way and Storm Beach below. The beach is notable for its sandstone boulders that fell from the nearby cliffs. Grinding against each other in the wave and tidal action, the boulders eroded into cigar-shaped rocks. Pre-Christian Celts would carry them off and carve them into ogham stones to mark clan boundaries (for more on ogham stones, see page 156).

Next to the fortress, look for the "fairy fort," a Stone-Age fort from about 500 B.C.

▲**Puicin Wedge Tomb**—While pretty obscure, this is worth the trouble for its evocative setting. Above the hamlet of Lispole in Doonties, park your car and hike 10 minutes up a ridge. At the summit is a pile of rocks made into a little room with one of the finest views on the peninsula. Beyond the Ring of Kerry, you may just make out the jagged Skellig Rock, noted for its 6th-century monastic settlement (see page 159).

Inch Strand—This four-mile sandy beach, shaped like a half moon, was made famous by the movie *Ryan's Daughter*.

NIGHTLIFE

▲▲▲**Music in Dingle Pubs**—Even if you're not into pubs, take a nap and then give these a whirl. Dingle is renowned among traditional musicians as a place to get work ("€40 a day, tax-free, plus drink"). The town has piles of pubs. There's music every night, and rarely a cover charge. The scene is a decent mix of locals, Americans, and Germans. Music normally starts around 21:30, and the last call for drinks is "half eleven" (23:30), sometimes later on weekends. For a seat near the music, arrive early. If the place is chockablock, power in and find breathing room in the back. By midnight, the door is usually closed, and the chairs are stacked. For more information, see "Traditional Irish Music" on page 36.

While two pubs, the **Small Bridge Bar** (An Droichead Beag) and **O'Flaherty's**, are the most famous for their good beer and folk music, make a point to wander the town and follow your ear. Smaller pubs may feel a bit foreboding to a tourist, but people—locals as well as travelers—are out for the *craic*. Irish culture is very accessible in the pubs; they're like highly interactive museums waiting to be explored. But if you sit at a table, you'll be left alone. Stand or sit at the bar, and you'll be engulfed in conversation with new friends. Have a glass in an empty, no-name pub and chat up the publican. Pubs are no longer smoky, but can be stuffy and hot, so leave your coat at home. The more offbeat pubs are more likely to erupt into leprechaun karaoke.

Pub Crawl—The best pub crawl is along Strand Street to O'Flaherty's (see map on page 168). **Murphy's** is lively, offering rock as well as ballads and traditional music. O'Flaherty's has a high ceiling and is dripping in old-time photos and town memorabilia—it's touristy, but lots of fun, with nightly music in the summer. **John Benny Moriarty's** has dependably good traditional music sessions, with John himself joining in on accordion when he's not pouring pints.

Then head up Green Street. **Dick Mack**, across from the church, is nicknamed "the last pew." This is a tiny leather shop by day, expanding into a pub at night, with several rooms, a fine snug (private booth, originally designed to allow women to drink discreetly), reliably good beer, and strangely fascinating ambience. Notice the Hollywood-type stars on the sidewalk, recalling famous visitors. Established in 1899, this place is now run by the grandson of the original Dick Mack. A painting in the window shows Dick Mack II with the local gang.

Green Street climbs to Main Street, where two more Dick Mack–type places are filled with locals deep in conversation (but without music): **Foxy John's** (a hardware shop by day) and **O Currain's** (across the street, a small clothing shop by day).

A bit higher up Main Street is **McCarthy's Pub**, a smoke-stained relic. It's less touristy and has some fine traditional music sessions and occasional plays on its little stage. Wander downhill to the **Small Bridge Bar** at the bottom. With live music nightly, it's popular for good reason. While the tourists gather around the music, poke around the back and do an end run around the wall, which leads to a window nook actually closest to the musicians. Occasionally, musicians sell CDs of their tunes, which can be a nice keepsake of your time in Ireland.

Off-season: From October through April, the bands play on, though at fewer pubs: Small Bridge Bar (live music nightly), John Benny Moriarty's (Mon, Wed, Thu), McCarthy's (Fri, Sat), and Murphy's (Sat).

Music shops: Danlann Gallery sells musical instruments and woodcrafts (Mon–Fri 10:00–18:00, later in summer, "flexible" on weekends, owner makes violins, Green Street). Siopa an Phiobaire, exclusively a music shop, sells traditional wind instruments (Mon–Fri 10:00–17:00, closed Sat–Sun, Craft Centre, on edge of town a few minutes' walk past Oceanworld, tel. 066/915-1778). Dingle Bodhrans sells homemade traditional goatskin drums and gives lessons (1-hour lesson-€40, Mon–Sat 10:30–18:00, closed Sun, Green Street, enter red iron gate of small alley opposite church, tel. 087-245-7689, Andrea).

Folk concerts—Top local musicians offer a quality evening of live, acoustic, classic Irish music in the fine little St. James Church on Main Street (€10 advance purchase, €12 at the door; Mon, Wed, and Fri at 19:30, May–Sept only; mobile 087/982-9728, see sign on church gate or drop by Murphy's Ice Cream shop for details). If you're not a night owl (music in pubs doesn't begin until 21:30) or prefer not to be packed into a pub with the distractions of conversation, then this is your best opportunity to hear Irish traditional music in a more controlled environment.

Dancing—Some pubs host "set dancing" with live music. Your two best possibilities are the Small Bridge Bar or John Benny Moriarty's pub (see above), but ask at the TI for more suggestions.

Theater—Dingle's great little theater is The Phoenix on Dykegate. Its film club (50–60 locals) meets here Tuesdays year-round at 20:30 for coffee and cookies, followed by a film at 21:00 (€6 for film, anyone is welcome). The leader runs it almost like a religion, with a sermon on the film before he rolls it. The regular film schedule for the week is posted on the door.

SLEEPING

$$$ **Heaton's Guesthouse**, big, peaceful, and American in its comforts, is on the water just west of town, at the end of Dingle Bay—a five-minute walk past Oceanworld on The Wood. The 16 thoughtfully appointed rooms come with all the amenities (Db-€86–128, suite Db-€130–180, creative breakfasts, parking, The Wood, tel. 066/915-2288, fax 066/915-2324, www.heatonsdingle.com, heatons @iol.ie, Cameron and Nuala Heaton).

$$$ **Benners Hotel** was the only place in town a hundred years ago. It stands bewildered by the modern world on Main Street, with sprawling public spaces and 52 abundant, overpriced rooms (Db-€200 July–Aug, €160 May–June, €150 Sept–May, discounts on Web site,

Sleep Code

(€1 = about $1.20, country code: 353, area code: 066)
S = Single, D = Double/Twin, T = Triple, Q = Quad,
b = bathroom, s = shower only. Prices vary with the season, with
winter cheap and August tops. Breakfast is included and credit
cards are accepted unless otherwise noted.

To help you easily sort through these listings, I've divided
the rooms into three categories, based on the price for a standard
double room with bath:

$$$ **Higher Priced**—Most rooms €100 or more.
$$ **Moderately Priced**—Most rooms between €60–100.
$ **Lower Priced**—Most rooms €60 or less.

tel. 066/915-1638, fax 066/915-1412, www.dinglebenners.com,
info@dinglebenners.com).

$$ Greenmount House sits among chilly palm trees in the
countryside at the top of town. A five-minute hike up from the town
center, this guesthouse commands a fine view of the bay and moun-
tains. John and Mary Curran run one of Ireland's best B&Bs, with
five superb rooms (Db-€75–95—top price through the summer) and
seven sprawling suites (Db-€100–150) in a modern building with
lavish public areas and breakfast in a solarium (reserve in advance, no
children under 8, most rooms at ground level, parking, top of John
Street, tel. 066/915-1414, fax 066/915-1974, www.greenmount
-house.com, info@greenmount-house.com).

$$ Captain's House B&B is a shipshape place in the town
center, fit for an admiral, with eight classy rooms, peat-fire lounges,
a stay-awhile garden, and a magnificent breakfast in the conserva-
tory. Mary, whose mother ran a guest house before Dingle was discovered, loves her work and is very good at it (Sb-€50–60,
Db-€80–100, great suite-€140–160, The Mall, tel. 066/915-1531,
fax 066/915-1079, captigh@eircom.net, Jim and Mary Milhench).

$$ Alpine Guest House looks like a Monopoly hotel, but that
means it's comfortable and efficient. Its 13 spacious, bright, and fresh
rooms come with wonderful sheep-and-harbor views, a cozy lounge,
a great breakfast, and friendly owners (Db-€70–95, Tb-€85–130,
prices vary with room size and season, 10 percent discount with this
book through 2005, no smoking, parking, Mail Road, tel. 066/915-
1250, fax 066/915-1966, www.alpineguesthouse.com, alpinedingle
@eircom.net, Paul). Driving into town from Tralee, you'll see this a
block uphill from the Dingle roundabout and Esso station.

$$ Bambury's Guesthouse, big and modern, with views of grazing sheep and the harbor, rents 12 airy, comfy rooms (Db-€70–110,

prices depend on size and season, family deals; coming in from Tralee, it's on your left on Mail Road, 2 blocks before Esso station; tel. 066/915-1244, fax 066/915-1786, http://bamburysguesthouse.com, info@bamburysguesthouse.com).

$$ **Milestone House** is a 15-minute walk out of town (at mile 0.8 on the "Dingle Peninsula Circular Tour" in this chapter—see page 179). It has warmly decorated rooms, great views of Dingle harbor, and an ancient boundary stone in the front yard. Friendly Barbara Carroll is a font of sightseeing tips (Sb-€40–45, Db-€60–70, Tb-€90–105, Qb-€110–120, parking, tel. & fax 066/915-1831, www.iol.ie/~milstone, milestonedingle@eircom.net).

$$ **Mainstay Guesthouse** is smack-dab in the center of town, with 14 modest rooms, a cheery breakfast area, and an inviting back garden (Sb-€48–58, Db-€76–96, Tb-€114–144, non-smoking, tel. 066/915-1598, fax 066/915-2376, www.mainstaydingle.com, info @mainstaydingle.com, Gus and Ruth Cero).

$$ **Barr Na Sraide Inn**, central and hotelesque, has 22 comfortable rooms (Db-€70–100, family deals, self-service laundry, bar, parking, past McCarthy's pub, Upper Main Street, tel. 066/915-1331, fax 066/915-1446, www.barrnasraide.com, barrnasraide@eircom.net).

$$ **Coastline Guesthouse**, on the water next to Heaton's Guesthouse (listed above), is a modern, sterile place with seven bright, spacious rooms (Db-€70–90, Tb-€100–140, 10 percent discount with the 2005 edition of this book—except in July and Aug, non-smoking, parking, The Wood, tel. 066/915-2494, fax 066/915-2493, www.coastlinedingle.com, coastlinedingle@eircom.net, Vivienne O'Shea).

$$ **Ard Na Greine House B&B** is a charming, windblown, modern house on the edge of town. Mrs. Mary Houlihan rents four well-equipped, comfortable rooms (with fridges) to non-smokers only (Sb-€52, Db-€70, Tb-€80, parking, 8-min walk up Spa Road, 3 doors beyond Hillgrove Hotel, tel. 066/915-1113).

$$ **Kelliher's Ballyegan House** is a big, plain building with six fresh, comfortable rooms on the edge of town, and great harbor views (Db-€70, Tb-€100, cash only, non-smoking, parking, Upper John Street, tel. 066/915-1702, Hannah and James Kelliher).

$$ **O'Neill's B&B** is a homey, friendly place with six decent rooms on a quiet street at the top of town (Db-€70 with the 2005 edition of this book, family deals, cash only, strictly non-smoking, parking, John Street, tel. 066/915-1639, Mary O'Neill).

$$ **Corner House B&B** is my longtime Dingle home. It's a simple, traditional place with five large, uncluttered rooms, run with a twinkle and a grandmotherly smile by Kathleen Farrell (S-€40, D-€75, T-€90, plenty of plumbing, but it's down the hall, cash only, reserve with a phone call and reconfirm a day or 2 ahead, central as can be on Dykegate Street, tel. 066/915-1516). Mrs. Farrell, one of

the original three B&B hostesses in a town now filled with them, is a great storyteller.

$$ Collins B&Bs: The following two B&Bs, which take up a quiet corner in the town center, are run by the same Collins—Coileain in Gaelic—family that does archaeological tours of the peninsula (see "Sciuird Archaeology Tours," page 186). Both offer fine rooms (O Coileain's are a bit bigger), cheap bike rental (€8/day), identical prices (Db-€70–74), and a homey friendliness. **O Coileain B&B** is run by a young family—Rachel, Michael, and their two cute little girls (tel. 066/915-1937, archeo@eircom.net). **Kirrary B&B**, just over the fence, is grandma's place, with a homey charm (good place to rent bikes, tel. 066/915-1606, collinskirrary@eircom.net, Eileen Collins).

$$ Sraid Eoin House offers four modest but pleasant, top-floor rooms above Galvin's Travel Agency (Db-€65–70, Tb-€90–100, 10 percent discount with cash and the 2005 edition of this book, John Street, tel. 066/915-1409, fax 066/915-2156, sraideoinhouse@hotmail .com, friendly Kathleen and Maurice O'Connor).

$ Ocean View B&B rents three tidy rooms (2 with views) in a humble little waterfront row house overlooking the bay (S-€28, D-€46, welcome treat on arrival, 5-min walk from center, 100 yards past Oceanworld at 133 The Wood, tel. 066/915-1659, thewood @gofree.indigo.ie, Mrs. Brosnan).

Hostels: **$ Grapevine Hostel** is clean and friendly, quietly yet very centrally located, with a cozy fireplace lounge and a fine members' kitchen. Each four- to eight-bed dorm has its own bathroom. Dorms are coed, but there's a female-only room (26 beds, €15–17 per person, Db-€40, laundry-€5, open all day, Dykegate Lane, tel. 066/915-1434, www.grapevinedingle.com, hostel@grapevinedingle .com, run by Siobhan—sheh-vahn).

$ Ballintaggart Hostel, a backpackers' complex, is housed in a stylish old manor house used by Protestants during the famine as a soup kitchen (for those hungry enough to renounce Catholicism). It comes complete with laundry service (€6), a classy study, a family room with a fireplace, and a resident ghost (130 beds, €14 in 10-bed dorms, €18 beds in Qb, Db-€50, no breakfast, but there's a kitchen, a mile east of town on Tralee Road, tel. 066/915-1454, fax 066/915-2207, www.dingleaccommodation.com, info@dingleaccommodation .com). Ask the Tralee bus to drop you here before arriving in Dingle.

EATING

For a rustic little village, Dingle is swimming in good food.

Budget Tips: The Super Valu supermarket/department store, at the base of town, has everything and stays open late (Mon–Sat 8:00–21:00, Sun 8:00–19:00, daily until 22:00 in June–Aug). Smaller groceries are scattered throughout the town, such as Centra on Main Street (Mon–Sat 8:00–21:00, Sun 8:00–18:00). Consider a grand view picnic out on the end of the newer pier (as you face the harbor, it's the pleasure-boat pier on your right).

Fancy restaurants serve early-bird specials from 18:00 to 19:00. Many "cheap and cheery" places close at 18:00, and pubs do good €12 dinners all over town. Most pubs stop serving food around 21:00 (to make room for their beer drinkers).

James G. Ashe Pub and Restaurant, an old-fashioned joint, is popular with locals for traditional Irish food at great prices. Try their beef-and-Guinness stew (€10 lunches, €15–22 dinners, lunch 12:00–16:00, dinner 18:00–21:00, Main Street, tel. 066/915-0989).

The Old Smokehouse, serving happy locals in a rustic, woody setting, offers the best moderate-value meals in town, with fresh Dingle Bay fish and good vegetables (€16–24 dinner plates, daily 18:00–22:00, corner of Main Street and The Mall, tel. 066/915-1061).

John Benny Moriarty's is a waterfront pub dishing up traditional Irish fare (food daily 12:30–21:30, music after 21:30, The Pier). **Paudie Brosnan's** pub, a few doors down, has fresh mussels.

An Café Litearta, a likeable eatery hidden behind an inviting bookstore, serves tasty soup and sandwiches to a good-natured crowd of Gaelic-speakers (Mon–Sat 10:00–18:00, closed Sun, tel. 066/915-2204, Dykegate Street).

At the **Global Village Restaurant,** Martin Bealin concocts his favorite dishes, gleaned from his travels around the world. It's an eclectic, healthy, meat-eater's place popular with locals for its interesting cuisine (€18–24 dinners, good salads and great Thai curry, daily 17:00–21:30, top of Main Street, tel. 066/915-2325 or 087/917-7700).

Fenton's is a good place for seafood meals with a memorable apple-and-berry-crumble dessert (€18–27 main courses, 3-course meals-€27, early-bird specials before 19:00, Tue–Sun 18:00–21:30, closed Mon, reservations smart, on Green Street down the hill below the church, tel. 066/915-2172 or 087/248-2487).

The **Stone House Restaurant**, on the Slea Head loop, offers good meals in a great atmosphere. It's a worthy choice for those looking for an out-of-the-way dinner and a 20-minute scenic drive. It's right across the road from the Dunbeg fort, at mile 7.7 on the "Dingle Peninsula Circular Tour"—see page 182 (open Wed–Mon 12:30–15:30 for €8–12 lunches and 18:30–22:00 for €17–23 dinners, closed Tue, dinner reservations essential, tel. 066/915-9970).

Dingle's Five Fancy Restaurants

Chart House Restaurant serves contemporary cuisine with a menu dictated by what's fresh and seasonal. Settle back into the sharp, clean, lantern-lit, harborside ambience (€28 dinners, June–Sept daily

Dingle Restaurants

1. James G. Ashe Pub/Restaurant
2. Old Smokehouse Restaurant
3. John Benny Moriarty's Pub
4. Paudie Brosnan's Pub
5. An Café Liteartá
6. Global Village Restaurant
7. Fenton's Restaurant
8. Chart House Restaurant
9. Beginish Restaurant
10. Doyle's Seafood Bar
11. Half Door Restaurant
12. Small Bridge Bar
13. O'Flaherty's Pub
14. Murphy's Pub
15. Dick Mack Pub
16. Foxy John's Pub
17. O Currain's Pub
18. McCarthy's Pub
19. Wild Banks Restaurant

18:30–22:00, Oct–May closed Tue, at roundabout at base of town, tel. 066/915-2255).

Beginish Restaurant, serving modern European fare with a fish forte in an elegant Georgian setting, is probably your best dressy splurge meal in town (€21–29 plates, Wed–Sun 18:00–21:30, closed Mon–Tue, you'll be glad you reserved ahead, Green Street, tel. 066/915-1588).

Wild Banks Restaurant is named for nearby fishing grounds, and Chef Laura Walker does a great job preparing the local catch. There's a nice wine selection, and the white-chocolate crème brûlée dessert gets raves (€25–29 dinners, €24 early-bird 3-course meals before 20:00, Tue–Sun 18:00-21:30, closed Mon, halfway down Main Street, tel. 066/915-2888).

Two of Dingle's long-established top-notch restaurants—**Doyle's Seafood Bar** (more famous, with excellent seafood and service, tel. 066/915-1174) and **The Half Door** (heartier portions, also open for lunch Mon–Sat 12:30–14:00, tel. 066/915-1600)—are neighbors on John Street. They're in the guidebooks for good reason, and therefore filled with tourists. Both have the same dinner hours (Mon–Sat 18:00–21:30, closed Sun), offer an early-bird special (3-course meal-€36, 18:00–19:00), and take reservations (wise).

TRANSPORTATION CONNECTIONS

The nearest train station is in Tralee, 30 miles away.

From Dingle by bus to: Galway (5/day, 6.5 hrs), **Dublin** (5/day, 8 hrs), **Rosslare** (2/day, 9 hrs), **Tralee** (6/day, 75 min, €9); fewer departures on Sundays. Most bus trips out of Dingle require at least one or two (easy) transfers. Dingle has no bus station and only one bus stop, on the waterfront behind the Super Valu supermarket (bus info tel. 01/830-2222, or call Tralee station at 066/712-3566). For more information, see "Transportation Connections" in Tralee, page 191.

By car: Drivers choose two roads into town: the easy southern route or the much more dramatic, scenic, and treacherous Conor Pass (see "Transportation Connections" in Tralee, page 191). It's 30 miles from Tralee either way.

Dingle Peninsula Circular Tour

A sight worth ▲▲▲, the Dingle Peninsula loop trip is about 30 miles long (must go in clockwise direction). It's easy by car, or it's a demanding three hours by bike—if you don't stop.

While you can take the basic guided tour of the peninsula (see "Tours," page 186), the self-guided route below makes it unnecessary. A fancy map is also unnecessary, if you follow my instructions.

Self-Guided Tour by Bike or Car

I've keyed in mileage to help locate points of interest. If you're driving, as you leave Dingle, reset your odometer at Oceanworld. Even if you get off track or are biking, derive distances between points from my mileage key. To get the most out of your circle trip, read through this entire section before departing. Then go step by step (staying on R559 and following The Slea Head Drive signs). Roads are very congested in August.

The Dingle Peninsula is 10 miles wide and runs 40 miles from Tralee to Slea Head. The top of its mountainous spine is Mount Brandon—at 3,130 feet, the second-tallest mountain in Ireland. While only tiny villages lie west of Dingle town, the peninsula is home to 500,000 sheep.

Leave Dingle town west along the waterfront (0.0 miles at Oceanworld). There's an eight-foot tide here. The seaweed was used to make formerly worthless land arable. (Seaweed is a natural source of potash—organic farming before it was trendy.) Across the water, the fancy Milltown House B&B (with flags) was Robert Mitchum's home for a year during the filming of *Ryan's Daughter*. Look for the narrow mouth of this blind harbor (where Fungie frolics) and the Ring of Kerry beyond that. Dingle Bay is so hidden, ships needed the tower (1847) on the hill to find its mouth.

0.4 miles: At the roundabout, turn left over the bridge. The hardware store building on the right was a corn-grinding mill in the 18th century.

0.8 miles: The Milestone B&B is named for the stone pillar (*gallaun* in Gaelic) in its front yard. This may have been a prehistoric grave or a boundary marker between two tribes. The stone goes down as far as it sticks up. The peninsula, literally an open-air museum, is dotted with more than 2,000 such monuments dating from the Neolithic Age (4000 B.C.) through early Christian times. Another stone pillar stands in the field across the street in the direction of the yellow manor house of Lord Ventry (in the distance).

Lord Ventry, whose family came to Dingle as post–Cromwell War landlords in 1666, built this mansion in about 1750. Today, it houses an all-Gaelic boarding school for 140 high-school girls.

As you drive past the Ventry estate, you'll pass palms, magnolias, and exotic flora introduced to Dingle by Lord Ventry. The Gulf Stream causes the mild climate (it never snows), which supports subtropical plants. Consequently, fuchsias—imported from Chile and spreading like weeds—line the roads all over the peninsula and redden the countryside from June to September. And over 100 inches of rain a year give this area its "40 shades of green."

Ten yards past the Tobair Michael B&B (on left) a tiny white wall with a blue marker marks the St. Michael's Well. A

Dingle Peninsula Circular Tour

Christianized Celtic holy well, it's still the site of a Mass on St. Martin's day. St. Martin was the Christian antidote to pagan holy places. Generally, when you see something dedicated to him, it sits upon something that pre-Christian people worshipped.

3 miles: Stay off the "soft margin" as you enjoy views of Ventry Bay, its four-mile-long beach (to your right as you face the water), and distant Skellig Michael, which you'll see all along this part of the route. Skellig Michael—jutting up like France's Mont St. Michel—contains the rocky remains of an 6th-century monastic settlement (see page 159). Next to it is a smaller island, Little Skellig—a breeding ground for gannets (seagull-like birds with 6-foot wingspans). In 1866, the first transatlantic cable was laid from nearby Valentia Island to Newfoundland. It was in use until 1965. Mount Eagle (1,660 feet), rising across the bay, marks the end of Ireland. In the village of Ventry, Gaelic is the first language. The large hall at the end of the village is used as a classroom, where big-city students come on field trips to be immersed in the Gaelic language.

4.7 miles: The rushes on either side of the road are the kind used to make the local thatched roofs. Thatching, which nearly died out because of the fire danger, is more popular now that anti-flame treatments are available. Black-and-white magpies fly.

5.3 miles: The Irish football star Paidi O Se (Paddy O'Shea) is a household name in Ireland. He now trains the Kerry team and runs the pub on the left. (Easy beach access from here.)

5.6 miles: The blue house hiding in the trees 100 yards off the road on the left (view through the white gate) was kept cozy by Tom Cruise and Nicole Kidman during the filming of *Far and Away*.

6.6 miles: *Taisteal go Mall* means "go slowly"; there's a red-colored, two-room schoolhouse on the right (20 students, 2 teachers). On the left is the small Celtic and Prehistoric Museum, a strange private collection of prehistoric artifacts with no real connection to Dingle (overpriced at €5, daily 10:00–17:00).

6.9 miles: The circular mound on the right is a late-Stone Age ring fort. In 500 B.C., it was a petty Celtic chieftain's headquarters, a stone-and-earth stockade filled with little stone houses. These survived untouched through the centuries because of superstitious beliefs that they were "fairy forts." While this is unexcavated, recent digging has shown that people have lived on this peninsula since 4000 B.C.

7.3 miles: Look ahead up Mount Eagle at the patchwork of stone-fenced fields.

7.7 miles: Dunbeg Fort, a series of defensive ramparts and ditches around a central *clochan,* though ready to fall into the sea, is open to tourists. There are no carvings to be seen, but the small *(beg)* fort *(dun)* is dramatic (€2, daily 9:30–20:00, descriptive handout). Forts like this are the most important relics left from Ireland's Iron Age (500 B.C. to A.D. 500). Since erosion will someday take this fort, it has been excavated.

Along the road, you'll see a new stone-roofed house built to blend in with the landscape and the region's ancient rock-slab architecture (A.D. 2000). It's the Stone House Restaurant, serving good lunches (daily 12:30–15:30, tel. 066/915-9970).

7.8 miles: Just 50 yards up the hill is a cottage abandoned by a family named Kavanaugh 150 years ago, during the famine. It still contains their original furniture. Gabriel Kavanaugh proudly displays his Kerry livestock in an adjacent pen, including some local red deer—once plentiful, but now rare (€3, tel. 066/915-6241).

8.2 miles: A group of beehive huts, or *clochans,* is a short walk uphill (€2, daily 9:30–19:00, WC). These mysterious stone igloos, which cluster together within a circular wall, are a better sight than the similar group of beehive huts a mile down the road. Look over the water for more Skellig views.

Farther on, you'll ford a stream. There has never been a bridge here; this bit of road—nicknamed the "upside-down bridge"—was designed as a ford.

9.2 miles: Pull off to the left at this second group of beehive huts. Look downhill at the scant remains of the scant home that was burned as the movie equivalent of Lord Ventry tried to evict the tenants in *Far and Away*. Even without Hollywood, this is a bleak and godforsaken land. Look above at the patches of land slowly made into farmland by the inhabitants of this westernmost piece of Europe. Rocks were cleared and piled into fences. Sand and seaweed were laid on the clay, and in time, it was good for grass. The created land, if at all tillable, was generally used for growing potatoes; otherwise, it was only good for grazing. Much has fallen out of use now. Look behind at the Ring of Kerry in the distance, and ahead at the Blasket Islands.

9.9 miles: At Slea Head, marked by a crucifix, a pullout, and great views of the Blasket Islands (described on page 187), you turn the corner on this tour. On stormy days, the waves are "racing in like white horses."

10.4 miles: Pull into the little parking lot (at Dunchaoin sign) to view the Blaskets and Dunmore Head (the westernmost point in Europe) and review the roadside map (which traces your route) posted in the parking lot. The scattered village of Dunquin has many ruined rock homes abandoned during the famine. Some are fixed up, as this is a popular place these days for summer homes. You can see more good examples of land reclamation, patch by patch, climbing up the hillside. Mount Eagle was the first bit of land Charles Lindberg saw after crossing the Atlantic on his way to Paris in 1927. Villagers here were as excited as he was—they had never seen anything so big in the air. Ahead, down a road on the left, a plaque celebrates the 30th anniversary of the filming of *Ryan's Daughter*.

11.9 miles: The Blasket Islanders had no church or cemetery on the island. This was their cemetery. The famous Blasket story-teller Peig Sayers (1873–1958) is buried in the center. At the next intersection, drive down the little lane that leads left (100 yards) to a small stone marker commemorating the 1588 shipwreck of the *Santa Maria de la Rosa* of the Spanish Armada. Below that is the often tempestuous Dunquin Harbor, from which the Blasket ferry departs. Island farmers—who, on a calm day, could row across in 20 minutes—would dock here and hike 12 miles into Dingle to sell their produce. When transporting sheep, farmers would lash the sheep's pointy little hoofs together and place them carefully upside down in the currach—so they wouldn't puncture the frail little craft's canvas skin.

12 miles: Back on the main road, follow signs to the Great Blasket Centre.

13.5 miles: Leave the Slea Head Road left for the Great Blasket Centre (described on page 188).

13.7 miles: Back at the turnoff, head left (sign to Louis Mulcahy Pottery).

14.5 miles: Passing land that was never reclaimed, think of the work it took to pick out the stones, pile them into fences, and bring up sand and seaweed to nourish the clay and make soil for growing potatoes. Look over the water to the island aptly named the "Sleeping Giant"—see his hand resting happily on his beer belly.

15.1 miles: The view is spectacular. Ahead, on the right, study the top fields, untouched since the planting of 1845, when the potatoes didn't grow, but rotted in the ground. The faint vertical ridges of the potato beds can still be seen—a reminder of the famine (easier to see a bit later). Before the famine, 40,000 people lived on this peninsula. After the famine, the population was so small that there was never again a need to farm so high up. Today, only 10,000 live on the peninsula. Coast downhill. The distant hills are crowned by lookout forts built back when Britain expected Napoleon to invade.

18.3 miles: Ballyferriter (Baile an Fheirtearaigh), established by a Norman family in the 12th century, is the largest town on this side of Dingle. The pubs serve grub, and the old schoolhouse is a museum (€2, Easter–Sept daily 10:00–16:30, closed off-season). The early-Christian cross next to the schoolhouse looks real. Tap it...it's fiberglass—a prop from *Ryan's Daughter.*

19.1 miles: At the T junction, signs direct you to Dingle ("An Daingean, 11 km") either way. Go left, via Gallarus (and still following Slea Head Way). Take a right over the bridge, still following signs to Gallarus.

19.5 miles: Just beyond the bridge, you'll pass the Tigh Bhric pub and market (great pub-grub lunches, tel. 066/915-6325). Just a few yards before the sign to Mainistir Riaise (Reasc monastic enclosure), detour right up the lane. After 0.2 miles (the unsigned turnout on your right), you'll find the scant remains of the walled Reasc Monastery (dating from the 6th–12th centuries). The inner wall divided the community into sections for prayer and business (cottage industries helped support the monastery). In 1975, only the stone pillar was visible, as the entire site was buried. The layer of black felt marks where the original rocks stop and the excavators' reconstruction begins. The stone pillar is Celtic (c. 500 B.C.). When the Christians arrived in the 5th century, they didn't throw out the Celtic society. Instead, they carved a Maltese-type cross over the Celtic scrollwork. The square building was an oratory (church—you'll see an intact oratory at the next stop). The round buildings would have been *clochans*—those stone, igloo-type dwellings. The monastery ran cottage industries with a double-duty kiln. Just outside the wall (opposite the oratory, past the duplex *clochan*, at the bottom end), find a stone hole with a passage facing the southwest wind. This was the kiln—fanned by the wind, it was used for cooking and drying grain. Locals would bring their grain to be dried and ground, and the monks would keep a tithe. With the arrival of the Normans in the 12th century, these small religious communities were replaced by relatively big-time state and church governments.

20 miles: Return to the main road, continue to the right.

21.1 miles: At the big hotel (Smerwick Harbor), turn left, following the sign to Gallarus Oratory.

21.8 miles: At the big building (with camping sign), go right and follow the sign for the oratory where you'll find a small tourist center—with a shop, WC, and video theater. For €3, you get a 17-minute video overview of Dingle Peninsula's historic sights.

The Gallarus Oratory, built about 1,300 years ago, is one of Ireland's best-preserved early-Christian churches. Shaped like an upturned boat, its finely fitted drystone walls are still waterproof. Notice the holes once used to secure covering at the door and the fine alternating stonework on the corners.

From the oratory, the little lane leads directly up and over the hill, home to Dingle. To complete this tour, however, you should return to the main road and continue (following sign to An Mhuirioch).

22.9 miles: Turn right at the fork and immediately take a right (at the blue shop sign) at the next fork. Pass a 19th-century church.

24.2 miles: The ruined Kilmalkedar church was the Norman center of worship for this end of the peninsula. It was built when England replaced the old monastic settlements in an attempt to centralize their rule. The 12th-century Irish Romanesque church is surrounded by a densely populated graveyard (which, over the centuries, has risen noticeably above the surrounding fields). In front of the church, you'll find the oldest medieval tombs, a stately early-Christian cross (substantially buried by the rising graveyard and therefore oddly proportioned), and a much older ogham stone. This stone, which had already stood here 900 years when the church was built, is notched with the mysterious, Morse-code-type ogham script used from the 3rd to 7th centuries. It marked a grave, indicating this was a pre-Christian holy spot. The hole was drilled through here centuries ago as a place where people would come to seal a deal—standing on the graves of their ancestors and in front of the house of God, they'd "swear to God" by touching fingers through this stone. You can still use this to renew your marriage vows (free, B.Y.O.

spouse). The church fell into ruin during
the Reformation. As Catholic worship
went underground until the early 19th
century, Kilmalkedar was never rebuilt.

24.6 miles: Continue uphill, overlooking the water. You'll pass another
"fairy fort" (Ciher Dorgan) dating back to
1000 B.C. (free, go through the rusty
"kissing gate").

25.5 miles: At the crest of the hill, enjoy a three-mile coast back
into Dingle town (in the direction of the Eask Tower).

28.3 miles: *Tog Bog E* means "take it easy." At the T junction,
turn left. Then turn right at the roundabout.

29 miles: You're back into Dingle town. Well done.

TOURS

▲▲Sciuird Archaeology Tours—Sciuird (SCREW-id; Irish for
"excursion") tours are offered by a father-son team with Dingle history—and a knack for sharing it—in their blood. Tim Collins, who's
a retired Dingle police officer, and his son Michael give serious, 2.5-
hour minibus tours (€20, departing at 10:30 and 14:00, depending
upon demand). Drop by the Kirrary B&B (at Dykegate and Grey's
Lane) or call 066/915-1606 to put your name on the list. Call early.
Tours fill quickly in summer. Off-season (Oct–April), you may have
to call back to see if the necessary five people signed up to make a
bus go. While skipping the folk legends and the famous sights (such
as Slea Head), your guide will drive down tiny farm roads (the Gaelic
word for road literally means "cow path"), over hedges, and up ridges
to hidden Celtic forts, mysterious stone tombs, and forgotten castles
with sweeping seaside views. The running commentary gives an intimate peek into the history of Dingle. Sit as close to the driver as possible to get all the information. They do two completely different
tours: west (Gallarus Oratory) and east (Minard Castle and a wedge
tomb). I enjoyed both. Dress for the weather. In a gale storm with
horizontal winds, Tim kept saying, "You'll survive it."

More Minibus Tours—**Moran's Tour,** which does a quickie minibus
tour around the peninsula, offers meager narration and a short stop at
the Gallarus Oratory (€17 to Slea Head, normally May–Sept at 10:00
and 14:00 from Dingle TI, 2.5 hrs; Moran's is at Esso station at
roundabout, tel. 066/915-1155 or mobile 087-275-3333). There are
usually enough seats, though it's best to book a day ahead. But if no
one shows up, consider a private Moran taxi trip around the peninsula
(€70 for 4 people, cabbie narrates 2.5-hour ride).

Eco-Cruises—Dingle Marine Eco Tours offers a 2.5-hour, birds-
and-rocks boat tour of the peninsula. The guided tour sails either

east toward Minard Castle or west toward the Blasket Islands (€25, April–Sept, departs 16:00, weather permitting, office around corner from TI, tel. 066/915-0768).

Blasket Islands

This rugged group of six islands off the tip of Dingle Peninsula seems particularly close to the soul of Ireland. The population of Great Blasket Island, as many as 160 people, dwindled until the government moved the last handful of residents to the mainland in 1953. Life here was hard. Each family had a cow, a few sheep, and a plot of potatoes. They cut their peat from the high ridge and harvested fish from the sea. There was no priest, pub, or doctor. These

people formed the most traditional Irish community of the 20th century— the symbol of antique Gaelic culture.

A special closeness to an island— combined with a knack for vivid storytelling—is inspirational. From this primitive but proud fishing/farming community came three writers of inter-

national repute, whose Gaelic work—basically tales of life on Great Blasket—has been translated into many languages. You'll find *Peig* (by Peig Sayers), *Twenty Years a-Growing* (Maurice O'Sullivan), and *The Islander* (Thomas Ó'Crohan) in shops everywhere.

In the summer, there's a café and hostel (open May–Sept, mobile 086-852-2321) on Great Blasket Island, but it's little more than a ghost town overrun with rabbits on a peaceful, grassy, three-mile-long poem.

Getting to the Blasket Islands

The 40-passenger Blasket ferry runs hourly, and in summer, every half hour, depending on weather and demand (€20 round-trip, April–mid-Oct 10:00–18:00, no boats mid-Oct–March). There may be a bus from Dingle town to Dunquin—leaving in the morning and picking up in the late afternoon—coordinated with the ferry schedule (also €17 taxi service by Moran, tel. 066/915-1155; Dunquin ferry tel. 066/915-6422). Dunquin has a fine hostel (tel. 066/915-6121).

In summer, a fast, 12-passenger boat called the *Peig Sayers* runs between Dingle town and the Blaskets. The ride (which may include a quick look at Fungie) traces the spectacular coastline all the way to Slea Head, in a boat designed to slice expertly through the ocean chop. Because of the tricky landing at Great Blasket's primitive and tiny boat ramp, any substantial swell can make actually going ashore impossible (€30 same-day round-trip, departs from the sailing pier in Dingle at 9:00, 11:00, 13:00, and 15:00, includes 40-min ride with free time to explore island; or €70 overnight trip, includes dinner, a bed in the island's hostel, and breakfast; for info, call Mary at 066/915-1344 or mobile 087-672-6100).

SIGHTS

▲▲Great Blasket Centre—This state-of-the-art Blasket and Gaelic heritage center gives visitors the best look possible at the language, literature, and way of life of the Blasket Islanders. See the fine 20-minute video (shows on the half hour), hear the sounds, read the poems, browse through old photos, and then gaze out the big windows at those rugged islands, and imagine. Even if you never got past limericks, the poetry of these people—so pure and close to each other and nature—will have you dipping your pen into the cry of the birds (€3.50, covered by Heritage Card—see page 4, Easter–Oct daily 10:00–18:00, July–Aug until 19:00, closed Nov–Easter, cafeteria, on the mainland facing the islands, well-signposted, tel. 066/915-6444). Visit this center before visiting the islands.

Tralee

While Killarney is the tour-bus capital of County Kerry, Tralee is its true leading city. Except for the tourist complex around the TI and during a few festivals, Tralee feels like a bustling Irish town. A little outdoor market combusts on The Square (Thu–Sat).

Tralee's famous Rose of Tralee International Festival, usually held in mid-August (likely Aug 19–23 in 2005), is a celebration of arts and music, culminating in the election of the Rose of Tralee—the most beautiful woman at the festival. While the rose garden in the Castle Gardens surrounding the TI is in bloom from summer through October, Tralee's finest roses are going about their lives in the busy streets of this workaday town.

ORIENTATION

(area code: 066)

For the tourist, the heart of Tralee is Ashe Memorial Hall, housing the TI and the Kerry the Kingdom museum, located near the rose garden and surrounded by the city park. Beyond the park is the Aqua Dome and steam railway that, if you were here 50 years ago, would chug-chug you to Dingle. Today, it goes only to the touristy windmill.

Tourist Information

The TI is hidden under the east end of Ashe Memorial Hall, which also houses the Kerry the Kingdom museum (TI open July–Aug daily 9:00–19:00, May–June daily 9:00–18:00, Sept–April daily 9:00–17:00, Jan–Feb closed Sat–Sun, tel. 066/712-1288). The **post office** is on Edward Street (Mon–Fri 9:00–17:30, Sat 9:00–13:00, closed Sun).

Arrival in Tralee

From the train and bus station (both located in the same building, with bike rental available), the Ashe Memorial Hall is a 10-minute walk through the center of town. Exit the station right, take a near-immediate left on Edward Street, then turn right on Castle Street and left on Denny. The Hall is at the end of Denny. Drivers should knock around the town center until they find a sign to the TI. Parking on the street requires a disk (€1.20/hr, sold at TI and newsstands—have them date it for you—or from exact-change machines on the street).

SIGHTS AND ACTIVITIES

▲▲**Kerry the Kingdom**—This is the place to learn about life in Kerry. The museum has three parts: Kerry slide show, museum, and medieval-town walk. Get in the mood by relaxing for 15 minutes through the Enya-style, continuous slideshow of Kerry's spectacular scenery, then wander through 7,000 years of Kerry history in the museum (well-described, no need for free headphones). The Irish say that when a particularly stupid guy moved from Cork to Kerry, he raised the average IQ in both counties—but this museum is pretty well-done. It starts with good background on the archaeological sites of Dingle, and goes right up to a video showing highlights of the Kerry football team (a fun look at Irish football). I liked the displays on the Antarctic adventures of Kerryman Tom Crean on three Scott/Shackleton expeditions. The lame finale is a stroll back in time on a 1450 re-creation of Tralee's Main Street (€8, March–Dec daily 9:30–17:30, closed Jan–Feb, tel. 066/712-7777, www.kerrymuseum.ie). The Café Park Gate makes a handy basic lunch stop (under Ashe Memorial Hall, beside TI, same hours). Before leaving, horticulture enthusiasts will want to ramble through the rose garden in the adjacent park.

Blennerville Windmill—On the edge of Tralee, just off the Dingle road, spins a restored mill originally built in 1800. Its eight-minute video tells the story of the windmill, which ground grain to feed Britain as the country steamed into the Industrial Age (€5 gets you a 1-room emigration exhibit, the video, and a peek at the spartan interior of the working windmill, April–Oct daily 9:30–17:30, closed Nov–March, tel. 066/712-1064).

A restored narrow-gauge steam railway runs hourly between Tralee's Ballyard Station (near the Aqua Dome swim center) and the windmill (€5 round-trip, 15 min each way, tel. 066/712-1064). In the 19th century, Blennerville was a major port for America-bound emigrants. It was also the home port where the *Jeannie Johnston* was built. This modern-day replica of a 19th-century ship is now sailing the world, explaining the Irish emigrant experience.

Siamsa Tire Theatre—The National Folk Theater of Ireland, Siamsa Tire (shee-EM-sah TEE-rah), stages two-hour dance and theater performances based on Gaelic folk traditions. The songs are in Irish, but there's no dialogue (€18, April–Oct Mon–Sat at 20:30, next to Kingdom of Kerry building in park, tel. 066/712-3055, siamsatire@eircom.net).

Swimming—The Aqua Dome is a modern-yet-fortified swim center—the largest indoor water world in Ireland—at the Dingle end of town, near the Ashe Memorial Hall. Families enjoy the huge slide, wave pool, and other wet amusements (adults-€10, kids-€9, locker-€1, bring your own towels, July–Aug daily 10:00–22:00, less off-season, tel. 066/712-8899 or 066/712-9150).

Music and Other Distractions—Tralee has several fine pubs within a few blocks of each other (on Castle Street and Rock Street), offering live traditional music most evenings. There's greyhound racing (Fri and Sat year-round plus Tue in summer, 20:00–22:15, 10 30-second races every 15 min, 10-min walk from station or town center, tel. 066/718-0008). Entry to the track costs €7—plus whatever you lose gambling. At just about any time of day, you can drop into a betting office to check out the local gambling scene.

SLEEPING

(€1 = about $1.20, country code: 353, area code: 066)
The Comfort, Ashe, and Finnegan's accommodations are central. Meadowlands and Dowling's Leeside B&B are across the street from each other, a 10-minute walk from the train station (take Oakpark Road) or a €4 cab ride.

$$$ **Meadowlands** is a classy 58-room guest house with a bar that serves great pub meals. If you want to splurge in Tralee, do it here (Db-€160–200, suites-€250–300, parking, Oakpark Road, tel. 066/718-0444, fax 066/718-0964, www.meadowlands-hotel.com, info@meadowlands-hotel.com).

$$ **Comfort Inn** has 45 predictable, quality rooms in the center of town. They charge by the room, making triples and family quads a good deal (April–Sept Db/Tb/Qb-€69–99, a bit more on festival

or holiday dates, cheaper off-season rates, full Irish breakfast-€8.50, continental breakfast-€4.50, some parking, Castle Street, tel. 066/712-1877, fax 066/712-2273, www.comfortinns.ie, info@tralee-comfortinns.ie).

$$ Ashe TownHouse, built in 1826, is a solid Georgian relic, sporting 12 brightly restored rooms in the heart of town (Sb-€40, Db-€70, Tb-€75–90, Qb-€100–120, 15 Denny Street, tel. & fax 066/712-1003, www.accommodation-kerry.com, theashetownhouse @eircom.net).

$ Dowling's Leeside B&B is a tidy, modest house hosted by charming Maura and Seamus Dowling, with four comfy rooms that feel surrounded by trees, even though they're on a busy street (tiny Sb-€30, Db-€54–56, Tb-€70, private parking, Oakpark Road, tel. 066/712-6475, dowlingsbandb@hotmail.com).

$ Finnegan's Hostel, in a stately Georgian house, is a block from TI at 17 Denny Street (€16 beds in 3-bed dorms, Sb-€20, Db-€40, tel. 066/712-7610, www.finneganshostel.com, finneganshostel @eircom.net).

EATING

The Cookery is good (€10 lunches Tue–Sat 12:30–17:30, €15–24 dinners Tue–Sat 18:00 22:00, closed Sun–Mon, a block off The Square, 16 Abbey Street, tel. 066/712-8833). Or try **Finnegans Cellar** (daily 17:30–22:00, €14–20 dinners, 17 Denny Street, tel. 066/718-1400). Shop for a picnic at **Tesco,** the big grocery off The Square (Mon–Sat 8:00–22:00, Sun 10:00-20:00).

TRANSPORTATION CONNECTIONS

Day-trippers, beware: The station has lockers, but not enough.

From Tralee by train to: Dublin (4/day, 3/day on Sun, 4 hrs, €52), **Rosslare** (1/day except Sun, 5 hrs, €51). Train info: tel. 066/712-3522.

By bus to: Dingle (6/day, less off-season and on Sun, 75 min, €9 one-way, €14 round-trip), **Galway** (8/day, 4 hrs), **Limerick** (9/day, 2 hrs), **Doolin/Cliffs of Moher** (2/day, 5 hrs), **Ennis** (8/day, 3 hrs, change in Limerick), **Rosslare** (2/day, 7 hrs, €21.50), **Shannon** (8/day, 2.5 hrs). Tralee's bus station is at the train station. Bus info: tel. 066/712-3566.

Car rental: Duggan's Garage Practical Car Hire rents Fiat Puntos (€111/48 hrs, includes everything but gas, must be 25 years old, 2 blocks from train station on Ashe Street, tel. 066/712-1124, fax 066/712-7527).

Airports

Kerry Airport, a 45-minute drive from Dingle town (just off the main road from Killarney to Tralee), offers connecting flights via **Dublin** on Aer Arann, **London Stansted** on Ryanair (www.ryanair .com), and even **Frankfurt-Hahn** on Ryanair (tel. 066/976-4644, www.kerryairport.ie).

Shannon Airport, the major airport in Western Ireland, has direct flights to **Dublin** (2–3/day, 30 min) and **London** (6/day, 1 hr). Ryanair and Aer Lingus (www.aerlingus.ie) fly out of Shannon. Airport info: tel. 061/471-444. Shannon Airport TI: tel. 061/471-664 (daily 6:30–18:00, June–Sept until 19:00). Shannon Airport also has easy bus connections to **Limerick** (nearly hrly, 1 hr, can continue to Tralee—2 hrs, and Dingle—1.25 hrs more), **Ennis** (nearly hrly, 45 min), and **Galway** (every 2 hrs, 2 hrs). Bus info: tel. 061/313-333, www.buseireann.ie.

Route Tips for Drivers

From Tralee to Dingle: Drivers choose between the narrow, but very exciting, Conor Pass road or the faster, easier, but still narrow N86 through Lougher and Anascaul. On a clear day, Conor Pass comes with incredible views over Tralee Bay and Brandon Bay, the Blasket Islands, and the open Atlantic. Pull over at the summit viewpoint to look down on Dingle town and harbor. While in Kerry, listen to Radio Kerry FM 97. To practice your Gaelic, tune in to FM 94.4.

Between Tralee and Galway/Burren/Doolin: The Killimer–Tarbert ferry connection allows those heading north for the Cliffs of Moher (or south for Dingle) to avoid the 80-mile detour around the Shannon River. If you're going to Galway, the Limerick route is faster, but the ferry route is more scenic (1 trip/hr, 20 min, €13/carload, leaves on the half hour going north and on the hour going south, until 21:00 April–Sept, until 19:00 Oct–March, no need to reserve, tel. 065/905-3124, www.shannonferries.com).

GALWAY

Galway feels like a boomtown—rare in Western Ireland. With 65,000 people, it's the county's main city, a lively university town, and the region's industrial and adminstrative center. Amid the traditional regions of Connemara and the Aran Islands, it's also a Gaelic cultural preserve.

Galway offers tourists plenty of traditional music, easy bus connections to Dublin (1/hr, 3.5 hrs, €15), and a convenient jumping-off point for a visit to the Aran Islands.

While Galway has a long and interesting history, its British overlords (who ruled until 1921) had little use for anything important to the Irish heritage. Consequently, precious little from old Galway survives. What does remain has the interesting disadvantage of being built in the local limestone, which, even if medieval, looks like modern stone construction. The city's quincentennial celebration in 1984 prompted a spirit of preservation.

What Galway lacks in sights, it makes up for in ambience. Spend an afternoon just wandering its medieval streets, with their delightful mix of colorful facades, labyrinthine pubs, weather-resistant street musicians, and steamy eateries.

Blustery Galway heats up after dark, with fine theaters and a pub scene that attracts even Dubliners. Visitors mix with old-timers and students, as the traditional music goes round and round.

If you hear a strange language on the streets and wonder where those people are from...it's Irish, and so are they.

Planning Your Time

Galway's sights are little more than pins on which to hang the old town. The joy of Galway is its street scene. You can see its sights in three hours, but without an evening in town, you've missed the best. Many spend three nights and two days: one for the town and

Galway's History

The medieval fishing village of Galway went big-time when the
Normans captured the territory from the O'Flaherty family in
1234. Making the town a base, the Normans invited in their
Anglo friends, built a wall (1270), and kicked out the Irish.
Galway's Celtic name (Gaillimh) comes from an old Irish word,
gall, which means "foreigner." Except for a small section in the
Eyre Square Shopping Centre and a chunk at the Spanish Arch,
that Norman wall is gone.

In the 14th century, 14 merchant families, or tribes, controlled Galway's commercial traffic, including the lucrative wine
trade with Spain and France. These English families constantly
clashed with the local Irish. Although the wall was built to "keep
out the O's and the Macs," it didn't always work. A common
prayer at the time was, "From the fury of the O'Flahertys, good
Lord deliver us."

Galway's support of the English king helped it prosper. But
with the rise of Oliver Cromwell, Galway paid for that prosperity.
After sieges in 1651 by Cromwell's troops and in 1691 by the
Protestant King William of Orange, Galway declined. It wasn't
until the last half of the 20th century that it regained some of its
importance and wealth.

another for a side-trip to the Burren, the Aran Islands, or Connemara (see next chapter). Tour companies make day trips to all three
regions cheap and easy.

ORIENTATION

(area code: 091)

The center of Galway is Eyre Square. Within two blocks of the
square, you'll find the TI, Aran boat offices, a bike rental shop, a
tour pickup point, the best cheap beds, and the train station. The
train and bus station butt up against the Great Southern Hotel, a
huge gray railroad hotel that overlooks and dominates Eyre Square.
The lively old town lies between Eyre Square and the river. From
Eyre Square, Williamsgate Street leads right through the old town
(changing names several times) to Wolfe Tone Bridge. Nearly everything you'll see and do is within a few minutes' walk of this spine.

Tourist Information

The TI, located a block from the bus/train station in the ground floor
of the Forster Court Hotel, has a bookshop and many booking services (June–Sept daily 9:00–17:45, Oct–May Mon–Fri 9:00–17:45,
Sat 9:00–12:45, closed Sun, tel. 091/537-700, www.irelandwest.ie).

Pick up the TI's *Galway Magazine* (€3, persistent readers will find several maps and walking tours amid the ads).

Arrival in Galway

Trains and most buses share the same station, virtually on Eyre Square (which has the nearest ATMs). To get to the TI, go left on Station Road as you exit the station (toward Eyre Square), then turn right on Forster Street. Some buses from Dublin and Dublin's airport use the Forster Street Bus Park, next to the TI.

For drivers, the most central and handiest parking garage is under Jurys Inn in the town center. To park nearby for free, try across the bridge along the Claddagh Quay or by the Siamsa Theatre.

Helpful Hints

Crowd Control: Expect huge crowds—and higher prices—during the Galway Arts Festival (last half of July), Galway Oyster Festival (4 days near end of Sept), and the three sets of Galway Races (a week in late July/early Aug, 3 days in mid-Sept, and 3 days in late Oct).

Internet Access: The e-2008 Internet Café is located next to the Park House Hotel (€2.10 per 30 min, daily 9:00–24:00, Forster Street). There are also several good places along High Street near Jurys Inn.

Laundry: These two launderettes are both centrally located: Launderland is close to the recommended B&Bs on College Road (Mon–Fri 8:30–18:30, Sat 9:00–18:00, closed Sun, €8 dropoff, Bothar Ui Eithir, 2-min walk up hill from TI, tel. 091/568-393). Prospect Hill Launderette is 100 yards off Eyre Square (Mon–Fri 8:30–18:00, Sat 8:30–17:00, closed Sun, €6.50 self-serve, €8–10 dropoff, 44 Prospect Hill, tel. 091/568-343).

Bike Rental: Celtic Rent-a-Bike has good bikes and long hours (€20/day, daily 8:00–20:00, on Queen Street, a block past Kinlay House, 2 blocks off Eyre Square, if no one's there buzz the Celtic Tourist Hostel upstairs, tel. 091/566-606).

Markets: On Saturday, a fun market clusters around St. Nicholas' Church (all day, but best 9:00–12:00). An antique market clinks and clanks daily at the base of the medieval wall in the Eyre Square Shopping Centre (best Thu–Sat).

TOURS

▲**Walking Tours**—Kay Davis enjoys taking small groups on grand-motherly two-hour walks through old Galway. Starting at the TI, she covers Eyre Square, the cathedral, and the old town, and then finishes up at the Spanish Arch (€8, tickets at TI, late June–Sept Mon, Wed, Fri at 11:30; Kay also does private walks, tel. 091/792-431).

Galway

1. Park House Hotel
2. Skeffington Arms Hotel
3. Great Southern Hotel
   & O'Flaherty's Pub
4. Jurys Galway Inn
5. Kinlay House Hostel
6. Garvey's Inn
7. River God Restaurant
8. Kirwan's Lane Creative Cuisine
9. Busker Brownes Restaurant & Pub
10. McDonagh's Fish & Chips
11. Nimmo's Wine Bar Bistro
12. Golden Roof Restaurant
13. Galway Bakery Company (GBC)
14. Monroe's Pub
15. Taaffe's Pub
16. The Quays Pub
17. Pucan Pub

▲**Hop-on, Hop-off City Bus Tours**—Several companies run

guided, 60-minute, hop-on, hop-off double-decker buses from the TI or Eyre Square, making six stops—including the cathedral, Salthill, and the Spanish Arch. You're allowed to get off and explore and hop back on later (€10, daily 10:30–16:30, 4/day, buses usually depart every 90 min from TI on Forster Street).

SIGHTS

Medieval Galway's "Latin Quarter"

From the top of Eyre Square, Williamsgate Street (named for the old main gate of the Norman town wall that once stood here) is the spine of medieval Galway, leading downhill straight to the Corrib River. While the road changes names several times (William, Shop, High, and Quay Streets), it leads generally downhill and straight past these sights:

Lynch's Castle—Now the Allied Irish Bank, Galway's best 16th-century fortified townhouse was once the home of the Lynch family—the most powerful of the town's 14 tribes. More than 60 Lynch mayors ruled Galway in the 16th and 17th centuries.

Collegiate Church of St. Nicholas—This church, located a half block off the main street on the right, is the finest surviving medieval building in town (1320) and is dedicated to St. Nicholas of Myra, the patron saint of sailors. Columbus is said to have worshipped here in 1477, undoubtedly while contemplating a scary voyage. Its interior is littered with obscure town history (€3 donation for admission). On Saturday, a wonderful market surrounds the church.

The Quay Pub—The pub, once owned by "Humanity Dick," an 18th-century Member of Parliament who was the original animal-rights activist, is worth a peek inside for its lively interior. The lane just before it leads to the...

Druid Theatre—This 100-seat theater offers top-notch contemporary Irish theater. Drop by to see if anything's playing tonight (€15–18 tickets, Chapel Lane, tel. 091/568-660, www.druidtheatre.com).

Spanish Arch and City Museum—Overlooking the Corrib River, these make up the best surviving chunk of the old city wall. The Spanish Arch (1584), the place where Spanish ships would unload their cargo, is a reminder of Galway's former importance in trade. Fragments of old Galway are kept in the tiny museum, which was closed for renovation in 2004. An expanded and improved museum is due to reopen at the same location in 2005 (€3, May–Sept daily 10:00–13:00 & 14:00–17:00, Oct–April Wed–Sun 11:00–13:00 & 14:00–17:00, closed Mon–Tue, call to verify price and hours, tel. 091/567-641).

Corrib River Sights—At the Corrib River, you'll find a riverside park perfect for a picnic (or get takeout from the town's best chippie, McDonagh's, across the street). Over the river (southeast of the bridge) is the modern housing project that, in the 1930s, replaced the original Claddagh. Claddagh (CLA-dah) was a picturesque, Gaelic-speaking fishing village with a strong tradition of independence—and open sewers. This gaggle of thatched cottages actually functioned as an independent community, with its own "king," until the early 1900s.

The old Claddagh village has since disappeared, but the tradition of its popular ring (sold all over town) lives on. The Claddagh ring shows two hands holding a heart that wears a crown. The heart represents love, the crown is loyalty, and the hands are friendship. If the ring is worn with the tip of the heart pointing toward the wrist, it signifies that the wearer is married or otherwise taken. However, if the tip of the heart points toward the fingertip, it means the wearer is available.

Look at the monument (just before the bridge) given to Galway by the people of Genoa, celebrating Columbus' visit here in 1477. (That acknowledgment, from a town known in Italy for its stinginess, helps to substantiate the murky visit.) From the bridge, look up the river. The green copper dome marks the city's Cathedral of St. Nicholas (described below). Down the river is a tiny harbor with a few of Galway's famous square-rigged "hooker" fishing ships tied up and on display. Called "hookers" for their hook-and-line fishing, these sturdy yet graceful boats were later used for transporting turf from Connemara until improved roads and electricity made them obsolete. Beyond that, a huge park of reclaimed land is popular with the local kids for Irish football and hurling. From there, the promenade leads to the resort town of Salthill.

Central Galway

▲**Eyre Square**—In the Middle Ages, this was a field just outside the town wall. The square is named for the mayor who gave the land to the city in 1710. While still called Eyre Square, it now contains John F. Kennedy Park—established in memory of the Irish-American president's visit in 1963, a few months before he was assassinated. (Though Kennedy is celebrated as America's first Irish-Catholic president, there have been several presidents who are descendants of Protestant Ulster stock.) On a sunny day, grassy Eyre Square is a popular hangout. Walk to the rust-colored Quincentennial Fountain (built in 1984 to celebrate the 500th anniversary of the incorporation of the city). The sails represent Galway's square-rigged fishing ships, the vessels that made Galway a trading center so long ago. The Browne Doorway, from a 1627 fortified townhouse, is a reminder of the 14 family tribes that once ruled the town. Each had a town castle—much like the towers that characterize the towns of Tuscany, with their feuding noble families. So little survives of medieval Galway that the town makes a huge deal of any surviving window or crest. The cannons are from the Crimean War (1854). The statue is of Patrick O'Connor, Galway's favorite Gaelic poet, who'd sit on a limestone wall, as sculpted, recording the local life.

The Eyre Square Shopping Centre—a busy, modern shopping mall (see the arcaded entry from the square)—leads to a surviving piece of the old town wall that includes two reconstructed towers (and an antiques market).

▲▲Cathedral of St. Nicholas—Opened by American Cardinal Cushing in 1965, this is one of the last great stone churches built in Europe. The interior is a treat—mahogany pews set on green Connemara marble floors under a Canadian cedar ceiling. The acoustically correct cedar enhances the church's fine pipe organ. Two thousand worshippers sit in the round facing the central altar. A

Dublin woman carved 14 larger-than-life Stations of the Cross. The carving above the chapel (left of entry) is from the old St. Nicholas church. Explore the modern stained glass. Find the Irish holy family— with Mary knitting and Jesus offering Joseph a cup of tea. The window depicting the Last Supper is particularly creative—find the 12 apostles.

Next, poke your head into the side chapel with a mosaic of Christ's resurrection (if you're standing in the nave facing the main altar, it's on the left and closest to the front). Take a closer look at the profiled face to the right of Christ—the one looking up while praying with clasped hands. It's JFK, nearly a saint in Irish eyes at the time this cathedral was built.

Church bulletins at the doorway tell of upcoming Masses and concerts (located across Salmon Weir Bridge on outskirts of town, tel. 091/563-577).

Salmon Weir Bridge—This bridge was the local "bridge of sighs." It led from the courthouse (opposite the church) to the prison (torn down to build the church—unlikely in the United States). Today, the bridge provides a fun view of the fishing action. Salmon run up this river most of the summer (look for them). Fishermen, who wear waders and carry walking sticks to withstand the strong current, book long in advance to get half-day appointments for a casting spot.

Canals multiplied in this city (sometimes called the Venice of Ireland) to power more water mills.

Galway Legends

Because of the dearth of physical old stuff, the town milks its legends. Here are a few you'll encounter repeatedly:

- In the 15th century, the mayor, one of the Lynch tribe, condemned his son to death for the murder of a Spaniard. When no one in town could be found to hang the popular boy, the dad—who loved justice more than his son—did it himself.
- Columbus is said to have stopped in Galway in 1477. He may have been inspired by tales of the voyage of St. Brendan, the Irish monk who is thought by some (mostly Irish) folks to have beaten Columbus to the New World by nearly a thousand years.
- On the main drag, you'll find a pub called the King's Head. It was originally given to the man who chopped off the head of King Charles I in 1649. For his safety, he settled in Galway—about as far from London as an Englishman could get back then.

Outer Galway

▲Galway Irish Crystal Heritage Center—This is an impressive-sounding name for a sight in a grand building made to order for big bus groups. Still, this cheap tour (handy for drivers) is the place to see the making of Irish crystal. Tours go every half hour. After a guided tour through the museum and a quick look at craftsmen cutting crystal (Mon–Fri only), you sit for 10 minutes while a video subliminally sells you crystal and wows you with Galway sights. The museum, more interesting than Galway's City Museum, gives you a good rundown on Claddagh village and a chance to see a large hooker named *Fiona* (€4, Mon–Fri 9:00–17:30, Sat 10:00–17:30, Sun 11:00–17:00, good cafeteria, 5 min out of Galway on Dublin road N6, or take Merlin Park bus—every 20 min—from Eyre Square, tel. 091/757-311, www.galwaycrystal.ie).

▲Salthill—This small resort packs pubs, discos, a splashy water park, amusement centers, and a fairground up against a fine mile-long beach promenade. At the Atlantaquaria aquarium, which features solely Irish water life, kids can help feed the fish at 15:00 (€7.50, daily 10:00–17:00, touch tanks, The Promenade, tel. 091/585-100). For beach time, a relaxing sunset stroll, late-night traditional music, or later-night disco action, Salthill hops. To get to Salthill, catch bus #1 from Eyre Square in front of the IAB bank, next to the Great Southern Hotel (€1.20, runs 7:00–23:00).

Dog Racing—Join the locals and cheer on the greyhounds on Thursday, Friday, and Saturday evenings from 20:00 to 22:00 (€8, barking distance from my recommended B&Bs, a 10-min walk from Eyre Square, tel. 091/562-273).

NIGHTLIFE

Folk Theater—Galway's folk theater, **Siamsa**, features Irish music, folk drama, singing, and dancing, including the step dancing popularized by *Riverdance* (€20, late June–Aug Mon–Fri at 20:45, Claddagh Hall, Nimmo's Pier, tel. 091/755-479, http://homepage.eircom.net/~siamsa).

▲**Traditional Irish Music in Pubs**—Galway, like Dingle and Doolin, is a mecca for good Irish music (nightly 21:30–23:30). But unlike Dingle and Doolin, this is a university town (enrollment: 12,000), and many pubs are often overrun with noisy students. Still, the chances of landing a seat close to a churning band surrounded by new Irish friends are good any evening of the year. Touristy and student pubs are found and filled along the main drag down from Eyre Square to the Spanish Arch, and across Wolfe Tone Bridge along William Street West and Dominick Street. Across the bridge, start at **Monroe's,** with its vast, music-filled interior (live music nightly, set dancing Tue, Dominick Street, tel. 091/583-397). Several other pubs within earshot also feature almost-nightly traditional music.

Pubs known for Irish music along the main drag include **Taaffe's** (nightly music sessions at 17:00 and 21:30, Shop Street, across from St. Nicholas Church, tel. 091/564-066) and **The Quays** (traditional music Mon–Thu at 21:30, Fri–Sun at 17:00, young scene, Quay Street, tel. 091/568-347).

Pucan Pub, a cauldron of music and beer-drinking with an older crowd—including lots of tourists—is worth a look (music nightly at 22:00, sometimes traditional, just off Eyre Square on Forster Street, tel. 091/561-528).

SLEEPING

There are three price tiers for most beds in Galway: high season (Easter–October), off-season, and charge-what-you-like festivals and race weekends (see "Crowd Control," page 195). I've listed high-season rates. B&Bs simply play the market. If you're on a tight budget, call around and see what the prices are. All B&Bs include a full fried breakfast.

Hotels

For a fancy hotel, Park House Hotel offers the best value. For a budget hotel, go to Jurys. For cheap beds, hit the hostel.

$$$ **Park House Hotel,** a plush, business-class place, is ideally located a block from the train station and Eyre Square. Its 68 spacious rooms come with all the comforts you'd expect (Db-€150–185 is the "corporate rate" you should get most of the year, ask if there's a discount, Sun night is slow and rooms can rent for Db-€125,

Sleep Code

(€1 = about $1.20, country code: 353, area code: 091)
S = Single, D = Double/Twin, T = Triple, Q = Quad,
b = bathroom, s = shower only. All of these places accept
credit cards.

To help you easily sort through these listings, I've divided
the rooms into three categories, based on the price for a standard
double room with bath:

$$$ **Higher Priced**—Most rooms €100 or more.
$$ **Moderately Priced**—Most rooms between €60–100.
$ **Lower Priced**—Most rooms €60 or less.

good restaurant, elevator, free garage, helpful staff, Forster Street,
tel. 091/564-924, fax 091/569-219, www.parkhousehotel.ie,
parkhousehotel@eircom.net).

$$$ **Skeffington Arms Hotel,** which feels more Irish (and a bit
smokier) than the Park House or Jurys, escapes most of the tour-
group scene because it has only 23 rooms. Centrally located on Eyre
Square, it's furnished in a dark-wood, Victorian style (Db-
€118–150, pub downstairs, Eyre Square, tel. 091/563-173, fax
091/561-679, www.skeffington.ie, info@skeffington.ie).

$$$ **Great Southern Hotel,** filled with palatial Old World ele-
gance and 90 rooms, marks the end of the Dublin–Galway train line
and the beginning of Galway. Since 1845, it has been Galway's landmark hotel (Db-€280, some discounts during slow times, breakfast-
€15 extra, sauna, stuffy staff, at the head of Eyre Square, tel.
091/564-041, fax 091/566-704, www.gshotels.com, res@galway
-gsh.com).

$$ **Garvey's Inn,** with 18 comfortable but occasionally smoky
rooms, offers the best price on Eyre Square. Mrs. Garvey adds a per-
sonal touch that bigger places can't offer (Sb-€55–65, Db-€90–130,
above a great pub, tel. 091/562-224, fax 091/562-526, www
.garveysinn.com, info@garveysinn.com).

$$ **Jurys Galway Inn** has 130 American-style rooms in a
modern hotel, centrally located where the old town hits the river.
The big, bright rooms have two double beds and huge modern bath-
rooms. You'll pay the same per room whether it's for a single, a
couple, three adults, or a family of four (€72–103 Sun–Thu,
€99–115 Fri–Sat depending on season, continental breakfast-€7.50
extra per person, full Irish breakfast-€10, elevator, lots of tour
groups, non-smoking floor, parking-€9, Quay Street, tel. 091/566-
444, fax 091/568-415, U.S. tel. 800/423-6953, www.jurysdoyle.com,
jurysinngalway@jurysdoyle.com).

Hostel: $ **Kinlay House** is a no-nonsense place just 100 yards from the train station, with 220 beds (1–8 beds per room) in bare, clean, and simple rooms, including 15 doubles/twins. Easygoing people of any age feel welcome here, but if you want a double, book well ahead—several months in advance for weekends (dorm bed-€16–20, Db-€52, elevator, self-service kitchen, Internet access, launderette, baggage storage, on Merchants Road, just off Eyre Square, tel. 091/565-244, fax 091/565-245, www.kinlayhouse.ie, kinlay.galway@usit.ie).

B&Bs

Drivers following city-center signs into Galway pass right by a string of B&Bs just after the greyhound-racing stadium. These are about an eight-minute walk from Eyre Square (from the station, walk up Forster Street, which turns into College Road). All of the listings are on College Road, except for the lowest-priced listing (Flanagan's). The College Crest Guest House and the Petra House are the best values. For locations, see the map on page 204.

$$$ **Ardawn House** is a classy B&B with nine comfortable rooms (Sb-€70, Db-€80–140, Qb-€160, College Road, near stadium on right, tel. 091/568-833, fax 091/563-454, www.galway.net /pages/ardawn-house, ardawn@iol.ie).

$$ **College Crest Guest House** is a proud establishment with 12 big, fresh rooms and a cushy lounge (Sb-€60–70, Db-€80–90, Tb-€120, non-smoking, parking, closest to town at 5 College Road, tel. & fax 091/564-744, www.collegecrest.com, info@collegecrest.com). Marion Fitzgerald enjoys her work and runs this place with care and flair.

$$ **Petra House**, a peaceful-feeling brick building, rents six great rooms, including a family room. The owners, Joan and Frank Maher, keep everything lovingly maintained (Sb-€50–60, Db-€76–89, elegant sitting room, next door to Ardawn House—listed above, 29 College Road, tel. & fax 091/566-580, www.galway.net /pages/petra-house, petrahouse@eircom.net).

$$ **Four Seasons B&B** is well-kept, with seven inviting rooms hosted by Eddie and Helen Fitzgerald (Sb-€50–60, Db-€75–89, Tb-€100–130, Qb-€110–150, parking, 23 College Road, tel. 091/564-078, fax 091/569-765, www.galway.net/pages/fourseasons, 4season@gofree.indigo.ie).

$$ **Asgard Guest House** offers eight restful rooms and an appealing glass atrium breakfast room (Sb-€40–60, Db-€70–80, Tb-€90–105, 21 College Road, tel. & fax 091/566-855, www.galway.net /pages/asgard, asgard@eircom.net, Geraldine Lohan).

$$ **Balcony House B&B** rents nine pleasant rooms (Db-€70–100, Tb-€105–140, Qb-€140–160, 27 College Road, tel. & fax 091/563-438, www.aaabalconyhouse.com, Michael and Teresa Coyne).

$ *On Prospect Hill Road:* This road (leaving Eyre Square from Richardson's Bar on Prospect Hill Road) is lined with small row

Galway B&Bs

TO SLIGO & DONEGAL

TO THE BURREN, CRYSTAL CENTRE & DUBLIN

R 336

R 339

HILL ROAD

COLLEGE PARK ROAD

THE GREEN

❶ Ardawn House B&B
❷ Petra House B&B
❸ Balcony House B&B
❹ Four Seasons B&B
❺ Asgard Guest House
❻ College Crest Guest House
❼ Mrs. Bridie Flanagan's B&B
❽ Prospect Hill Launderette
❾ Launderland

PROSPECT

BOTHAR

FORSTER ST.

UI EITHIR

LOUGH
ATALIA

EYRE

KENNEDY PARK

SQUARE

STATION RD.

WILLIAM

SQUARE

TRAIN + BUS STATION

DCH

↓ TO OLD TOWN

100 YARDS
100 METERS

★NOTE: UPPER PORTION OF MAP NOT TO SCALE

houses, many of which do B&B. **Mrs. Bridie Flanagan's B&B** is a humble, friendly, old home with a welcoming living room and four bedrooms—two big and two cramped (tiny D-€50, fine Db-€60, T-€70, 85 Prospect Hill, tel. 091/561-515).

In Salthill

$$ **Carraig Beag B&B**, the classiest, friendliest, and most peaceful of all, is a big brick home on a residential street a block off the beach, just beyond the resort town of Salthill. Catherine Lydon, with the help of her husband, Paddy, rents six big, bright, fresh, and comfy rooms with a welcoming living room and a communal breakfast table (Sb-€40–65, Db-€60–80, family room-€75–120; 8-min drive from Galway, follow the beach past Salthill, take second right after golf course on Knocknacarra Road and go 2 blocks to 1 Burren View

Heights, tel. 091/521-696, thelydons@eircom.net, www.dirl.com /galway/salthill/carraig-beag.htm). The #2 bus (€1.20, 3/hr) goes from Eyre Square (picks up in front of Skeffington Arms pub) to the Knocknacarra stop at the B&B's doorstep. Catherine can arrange for day-tour pickups at her place.

EATING

This college town is filled with colorful, inexpensive eateries. People everywhere seem to be enjoying their food. Each of these places is at the bottom of the old town, within a block or two of Jurys Inn.

River God is a bistro/restaurant passionately run by Patric Juillet, who cooks fine "world French" cuisine. He slices, dices, and prices as if his bottom line were filling people with very good food (€12 2-course lunch deals, €20 3-course dinners, daily 12:30–23:00, reservations recommended, above Bunch of Grapes pub at 2 High Street, tel. 091/565-811).

Kirwan's Lane Creative Cuisine, considered Galway's best restaurant, is a dressy place where reservations are required (€20 lunches, €22–30 dinners, daily 18:00–22:30, open for lunch 12:30–14:30, on Kirwan's Lane a block from Jurys, tel. 091/568-266).

Busker Brownes has three eateries in a sprawling place popular for its good, cheap food. Enter on Cross Street for the restaurant (and walk to the back for better seating), or enter on Kirwan's Lane for the ground-floor pub; upstairs from the pub is the third section (€9–20 meals, daily 11:00–21:00, "Sunday morning jazz session" at 13:00, Cross Street and Kirwan's Lane, tel. 091/563-377).

McDonagh's Fish & Chips is a favorite "chipper." It has a fast, cheap section and a classier restaurant. If you're determined to try Galway oysters, remember that they're in season September through April only. At other times, you'll eat Pacific oysters—which doesn't make much sense to me (€9 cheap lunch, €13–20 in restaurant, Mon–Sat 12:00–15:00 & 17:00–22:00, 22 Quay Street, tel. 091/565-001).

Nimmo's Wine Bar Bistro lurks peacefully in an old stone warehouse behind the Spanish Arch and has terrific €6 fish soup and a diverse wine list. The candlelit ambience is great even for a cup of coffee (€14–25 meals, Tue–Sun 18:00–22:00, Fri & Sat 12:30–15:00, closed Mon, Long Walk Street, tel. 091/561-114).

Golden Roof Restaurant serves hearty Chinese food and is closest to my College Road B&B listings and the TI (€8–12 meals, Mon–Fri lunch 12:30–14:30, Mon–Sun dinner 17:00–23:30, about 50 yards up Bothar Street off Forster, tel. 091/561-992).

O'Flaherty's Pub has a sports-bar feel and affordable pub grub (€10–18 meals, daily 12:30–21:30, under Great Southern Hotel on Eyre Square, tel. 091/509-621).

The **Galway Bakery Company (GBC)** is a popular and basic place for a quick Irish meal (€8–12 meals in ground-floor cafeteria, pricier restaurant upstairs, daily 8:00–21:00, 7 Williamsgate Street, near Eyre Square, tel. 091/563-087).

Supermarkets: A **Super Valu** is in Eyre Square Shopping Centre (Mon–Sat 9:00–18:30, Thu–Fri until 21:00, closed Sun), and **Dunne's** is just moments away, accessed through the Eyre Square Shopping Centre or around the corner at tiny Castle Street, off the pedestrian street called Williamsgate (Mon–Sat 9:00–18:30, Thu–Fri until 21:00, Sun 12:00–18:00, supermarket in basement). Lots of smaller grocery shops are scattered throughout town.

Medieval Banquet: If you have a car, consider a **Dunguaire Castle medieval banquet** in Kinvarra, a 30-minute drive south of Galway (for more information, see page 216). The 17:30 banquet can be done very efficiently as you're driving into or out of Galway (B&Bs accommodate late arrivals if you call).

TRANSPORTATION CONNECTIONS

From Galway by train to: Dublin (6/day, 3 hrs). For **Belfast, Tralee,** and **Rosslare,** you'll change in or near Dublin. Train info: tel. 091/561-444.

By bus to: Ennis (14/day, 1.25 hr), **Doolin/Cliffs of Moher** (4/day, 2 hrs), **Limerick** (14/day, 2 hrs), **Rosslare** (2/day, 6.5 hrs), **Belfast** (4/day, 7 hrs), **Dublin** (15/day, 3.5 hrs, €15; also see Citylink, below). Bus info: tel. 091/562-000.

Citylink (tel. 091/564-164, www.citylink.ie) runs cheap and fast bus service from Galway's Forster Street Bus Park to **Dublin** (Tara Street DART Station, 7/day, 3 hrs, €12), **Dublin Airport** (7/day, 3.5 hrs, €17), or **Shannon Airport** (4/day, 1.5 hrs, €13).

By car: For ideas on driving from Galway to Derry or Portrush in Northern Ireland, see "Between Derry and Galway" on page 236).

NEAR GALWAY

In three different directions, Galway has interesting sights: County Clare and the Burren to the south, the Aran Islands to the west, and the Connemara region to the north.

To see the Burren by car, visit it en route between Galway and Dingle (or take a tour from Galway). The Aran Islands (use public transportation) and Connemara (easy by car or tour) each take a day.

Bus Tours of the Burren and Connemara

Two Galway companies—Lally and O'Neachtain—run all-day, €25 tours of nearby regions. Tours of the Burren do a loop south of Galway, covering Kinvarra, Aillwee Cave, Poulnabrone Dolmen, and the Cliffs of Moher. Tours of Connemara include the *Quiet Man* Cottage, Kylemore Abbey, Clifden, and the "Famine Village." Tours go most days from about 10:00 to 17:30 (depart near Galway's TI, call to confirm exact itinerary: Lally tel. 091/562-905, www.lallytours.com; O'Neachtain tel. 091/553-188, www.oneachtaintours.com). Drivers take cash only; to pay with a credit card, book at the TI.

County Clare and the Burren

Those connecting Dingle in the south with Galway in the north can entertain themselves along the way by joyriding through the fascinating landscape and tidy villages of County Clare. Ennis, the major city of the county, with a medieval history and a market bustle, is a work-a-day Irish town ideal for anyone tired of the tourist crowds. The dramatic Cliffs of Moher, overlooking the Atlantic, offer tenderfeet a thrilling hike. The Burren is a unique, windblown limestone wasteland that hides an abundance of flora, fauna, caves, and history. For your evening entertainment, you can join a tour-bus

County Clare and the Burren

group in a castle for a medieval banquet at Kinvarra, or meet up with traditional Irish music enthusiasts from around Europe for tin-whistling in Doolin.

Planning Your Time

By **train** and **bus**, your gateways to this region are Ennis from the south and Galway from the north (consider a tour from Galway; see "Bus Tours," above).

By **car**, the region can be an enjoyable daylong drive-through or a destination in itself. None of the sights has to take much time. But do get out and walk a bit.

If you're driving from Dingle to Galway, I'd recommend this day plan, rather than the main road via Limerick: Drive north from Tralee via Listowel to catch the Tarbert–Killimer car ferry (avoiding Limerick traffic and the 80-mile drive around the Shannon estuary; see "Route Tips" at the end of Dingle chapter), then drive the coastal route to the Cliffs of

Moher for an hour break. The scenic drive through the Burren, with a couple of stops and a tour of the caves, takes about two hours. There's a 17:30 medieval banquet at Dunguaire Castle near Kinvarra (just 30 min south of Galway, see "Kinvarra" on page 216).

Skip the **Bunratty Castle and Folk Museum**. I'd leave this most commercial and least lively of all European open-air folk museums to the jet-lagged, big-bus, American tour groups (located just a potty stop from the Shannon Airport, past Limerick on the road to Ennis).

Cliffs of Moher

A visit to the Cliffs of Moher (pron. "more"), a ▲▲▲ sight, is one of Ireland's great natural thrills. For five miles, the dramatic cliffs soar as high as 650 feet above the Atlantic.

You can get here by bus from Galway (2/day in summer, 1.5 hrs, €15 round-trip). Drivers park at the lot for €4. You'll find a vis-

itors center–type complex with a shop, cafeteria, and a TI (April–Oct daily 9:30–17:30, closed Nov–March, tel. 065/708-1171). Walk 200 yards to the cliff's edge, past harpists and accordion players, and along a low wall of the local Liscannor slate. Notice the squiggles made by worms, eels, and snails long ago, when the slate was still mud on the sea floor. O'Brien's Tower, built in 1853, marks the highest point of the cliffs (€1 tower entry not worth it).

For the best thrill, read the warning, consider the risk (wind gusts can be sudden, strong, and fatal), then step over the slate barrier and down onto the stone platform. Here, there are no crowds. If you're a risk-taking fool, belly out and take a peek over the ledge. You'll find yourself in a dramatic world where the only sounds are the waves, the wind, the gulls, and your stomach signaling frantically for help. There's a particularly peaceful corner of the platform over on the far right. On the far left, watch the birds play in the updrafts. In the distance, on windy days, the Aran Islands can be seen wearing their white necklace.

Before leaving the area, drivers could take 10 minutes to check out the holy well of St. Bridget, located beside the tall column about two miles south of the cliffs on the main road to Liscannor. In the short hall leading into the hillside spring, you'll find a treasure of personal and religious memorabilia left behind by devoted visitors seeking cures and blessings. The simple gray column outside was a folly erected 150 years ago by a local land-lord with money and ego to burn.

To get a different perspective of the cliffs (up instead of down), you can cruise along their base between Doolin and Liscannor. **Cliffs of Moher Cruises** makes the 75-minute voyage past sea stacks and crag-perched birds. Boats depart from the main pier in Doolin (same dock as Aran Islands boat) or from Liscannor (in Liscannor, find the dock by following signs for Cliffs of Moher cruises near Vaughan's pub). A free shuttle bus takes you back to whichever port you departed from (€20, Easter–Sept daily, 1/day from Liscannor, 3/day from Doolin, weather and tides permitting, call or go online to check sailing schedule and to reserve, tel. 065/708-6060, mobile 087/245-3239, www.mohercruises.com).

Doolin

(area code: 065)
This town is a strange phenomenon. Tourists go directly from Paris or Munich to Doolin. It's on the tourist map for its three pubs that feature Irish folk music. A few years ago, this was a mecca for Irish musicians. They came together here to jam before a few lucky afi-cionados. But now the crowds and the foreigners are overwhelming the musicians, and the quality of music is not as reliable. Still, as Irish and European music-lovers alike crowd the pubs, the *bodhrán* beat goes on. The Michael Russell Heritage Centre may eventually become a museum of traditional music. For now, some *ceilidh* dances are held here. Ask at a pub if anything's scheduled.

Doolin has plenty of accommodations and a Greek-island-with-out-the-sun ambience. The "town" is just a few homes and shops strung out along a valley road from the tiny harbor. There are several good restaurants, and each pub serves decent dinners before the music starts. Nearest the harbor, the Lower Village (Fisherstreet) has **O'Connor's Pub** (tel. 065/707-4168) and is the closest thing to a com-mercial center. A mile farther up the road, the Upper Village (Roadford) straddles a bridge with the other two destination pubs, **McGann's** (tel. 065/707-4133) and **McDermott's** (tel. 065/707-4328). The **Lazy Lobster** is a casual restaurant serving tasty seafood, just across from McDermott's (€19–25 meals, Tue–Sun 18:30–21:30, closed Mon, tel. 065/707-4085). Music starts in the pubs around 21:30 and finishes around midnight. Get there before 21:00 if you want a place to sit, or pop in later and plan on standing. On my last trip, I hit Doolin on a mediocre music night. The *craic* is fine regardless.

Dial-A-Cab is a handy service for folks without wheels wanting to link a night of fun in Doolin with a bed in Lisdoonvarna (tel. 086/812-7049 or 087/290-2060).

From Doolin, you can hike or bike (rentals in town) up Burren Way for three miles to the Cliffs of Moher. (Get advice locally on the trail condition and safety).

Ferries: The boats from Doolin to the Aran Islands (described below) can be handy, but are often canceled. Even a balmy day can

be too windy (or the tide can be too low) to allow for a sailing from Doolin's crude little port. If you're traveling by car and have time limits, don't risk sailing from Doolin. Without a car, you can travel from the Aran Islands to Galway by the bigger boats, so Doolin might work for you. But it's a longer trip to Inishmore (some sailings make a stop at Inisheer en route), so consider an overnight stay on the islands (to Inishmore: €20 one-way, €32 same-day round-trip, 2/day, 2.5 hrs, leaves at 9:30 and 13:00, depending on season, returns at 11:30 and 16:00; to Inisheer: €15 one-way, €25 same-day round-trip, 5/day, 30 min, leaves roughly every 90 min, 10:00–17:30; tel. 065/707-4455 to see what's sailing). Doolin also offers boat cruises along the Cliffs of Moher (see "Cliffs of Moher," page 209).

Sleeping in Doolin: **Harbour View B&B** is a fine modern house with six rooms, a mile from the Doolin fiddles, overlooking the valley. Mrs. Cullinan keeps the guests' living room stocked with books and games (Sb-€45, Db-€60, Tb-€80, larger family-room deals, includes classy breakfast, on main road halfway between Lisdoonvarna and the Cliffs of Moher, next to Statoil gas station, tel. 065/707-4154, fax 065/707-4935, www.harbourviewdoolin.com, clarebb@eircom.net). **Doolin Hostel**, right in Doolin's Lower Village, caters creatively to the needs of backpackers in town for the music (dorm bed-€13.50, Db-€38, Qb-€68, Lower Village, tel. or fax 065/707-4421, www .kingsway.ie/doolinhostel, doolinhostel@iol.net).

Lisdoonvarna

(area code: 065)
This town of 1,000 was known for centuries for its spa and its matchmakers. Today, except for a couple of September weeks during its Matchmaking Festival, it's pretty sleepy. (The bank is only open one day a week.) Still, it's more of a town than Doolin (5 miles away) and, apart from festival time, less touristy. Lisdoonvarna has good traditional music in its pubs. I'd stay here, rather than in Doolin, and commute.

Sleeping in Lisdoonvarna: **Ballinsheen House** perches on a hill with five tastefully-decorated rooms and a pleasant glassed-in break-fast terrace (Sb-€33–40, Db-€54–64, Tb-€75–96, Qb-€100–120, parking, 5-min walk north of town on N67 Galway Road, tel. 065/707-4806, mobile 087/656-9434, fax 065/707-4859, Mary Gardiner). **Marchmont B&B** rents two large twin/family rooms and two small doubles in a fine old house (Db-€55, on N67 Galway Road near main square, just past post office, tel. 065/707-4050, Eileen Barrett). **St. Enda's B&B** is an old-fashioned, whitewashed place, with four modest rooms, run for the last 50 years by proper proprietress Mary Finn (Sb-€30–37, Db-€54–60, non-smoking, parking, 2-min walk north of town on N67 Galway Road, tel. 065/707-4066).

The Burren

Literally "the rocky place," the Burren is just that. The 10-square-mile limestone plateau, a ▲▲ sight, is so barren that a disappointed Crom-wellian surveyor of the 1650s described it as "a savage land, yielding neither water enough to drown a man, nor a tree to hang him, nor soil enough to bury him." But he wasn't much of a botanist, because the Burren is a unique ecosys-tem, with flora that have managed to adapt since the last Ice Age, 10,000 years ago. It's also rich in prehistoric and early-Christian sites. The first human inhabitants of the Burren came about 6,000 years ago, began cutting down trees, and are partially responsible for the stark land-scape we see today. This limestone land is littered with more than 2,000 historic sites, including about 500 Iron Age stone forts.

SIGHTS

Sightseeing the Burren
The drive from Kilfenora to Ballyvaughan offers the best quick swing through the historic Burren.

Kilfenora (5 miles southeast of Lisdoonvarna) is a good start-ing point. Its hardworking, community-run **Burren Centre** shows an intense 18-minute video explaining the geology and botany of the region, and then ushers you into its enlightening new museum exhibits (€5.75, mid-March–May and Sept daily 10:00–17:00, June–Aug daily 9:30–18:00, closed Nov–mid-March, tel. 065/708-8030, www.theburrencentre.ie). You'll see copies of a fine 8th-century golden collar and 9th-century silver brooch (originals now

The Burren

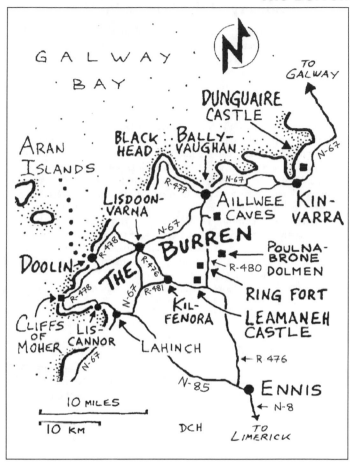

in Dublin's National Museum). The ruined church next door has a couple of 12th-century crosses, but isn't much to see. Mass is still held in the church, which claims the pope as its bishop. Kilfenora, as the smallest and poorest diocese in Ireland, was almost unable to function after the famine, so in 1866 Pope Pius the IX supported the town as best he could—by personally declaring himself its bishop.

For lunch in Kilfenora, consider the cheap and cheery **Burren Centre Tea Room** (daily 9:30–17:30) or the more atmospheric **Vaughan's Pub.** If you're spending the night in County Clare, make an effort to join the locals at the fun set-dancing get-togethers run by the Vaughans in the Barn Pub adjacent to their regular pub (€4, Thu and Sun at 21:30, tel. 065/708-8004, www.vaughanspub.com).

Botany of the Burren in Brief

The Burren is a story of water, rock, geological force, and time. It supports the greatest diversity of plants in Ireland. Like nowhere else, Mediterranean and Arctic wildflowers bloom side by side in the Burren. It's an orgy of cross-pollination that attracts more insects than Doolin does music-lovers—even beetles help out. Limestone, created from layers of coral, seashells, and mud, is the foundation of the Burren. (This same basic slab resurfaces 10 miles or so out to sea to form the Aran Islands.) The earth's crust heaved it up, and the glaciers swept it bare—dropping boulders as they receded. Rain, reacting naturally with the limestone to create a mild but determined acid, slowly drilled potholes into the surface. Rainwater cut through weak parts in the limestone, leaving crevices on the surface and Europe's most extensive system of caves below. These puddles grew algae, which dried into a powder. That, combined with bug parts and rabbit turds (bunnies abound in the Burren), created a very special soil. Plants and flowers fill the cracks in the limestone. Grasses and shrubs don't do well here, and wild goats eat any trees that try to grow, giving tender little flowers a chance to enjoy the sun. Different flowers appear in different months, sharing space rather than competing. The flowers are best in June and July.

Leamaneh Castle, a ruined shell of a fortified house, is not open to anyone these days. From the outside, you can see how the 15th-century fortified tower house (the right quarter of the remaining ruin) was expanded 150 years later (the left three-quarters of the ruin). The castle evolved from a refuge into a manor, and windows became wider to allow for better views, as defense became less of a priority. From the castle, turn north on R480 (direction: Ballyvaughan). After about five miles, you'll hit the start of the real barren Burren.

The **Caherconnell (Cahercommaun) ring fort** (one of 500 or so in the area) can be seen to the left on the crest of a hill just off the road. You can park in the gravel lot and wander up for a quick look at the fort and a 10-minute film in the modest Visitors Center (€3 for fort only, €5 with film, Easter–June and Sept–Oct 10:00–17:00, July–Aug 9:30–18:00, closed Nov–Easter, tel. 065/708-9999, www.burrenforts.ie).

The stretch from the ring fort north to Ballyvaughan offers the starkest scenery. Soon you'll see a 10-foot-high stone table a hundred yards off the road to the right (east, toward an ugly gray metal barn). This is the **Poulnabrone Dolmen,** a portal tomb that looks like a stone table. Two hundred years ago, locals called this a "druid's altar." Four thousand years ago, it was a grave chamber within a cairn of stacked stones that have since been eroded or carried away.

Wander over for a look. (It's crowded with tour buses in midday, but it's all yours early or late.)

Be a geologist. Wander for some quiet time with the wildflowers. You're walking across a former tropical seabed, laid down at an unimaginable time, when Ireland was at the equator (before continental drift nudged it north). Look for fossils: White smudges were coral. Scratches on rocks were ground by other rocks embedded in the belly of an advancing glacier. The rounded boulders came from Connemara, carried on a giant conveyor belt of ice, then left behind by the melting glaciers. V-shaped valleys were carved by the swift glacial runoff.

The **Aillwee Caves** are touted as "Ireland's premier show-caves." I couldn't resist a look. While fairly touristy and not worth the time or money if you've seen a lot of caves, they offer your easiest look at the massive system of caves that underlie the Burren. Your guide walks you 300 yards into the plain but impressive cave, giving a serious, 40-minute geology lesson. During the Ice Age, underground rivers carved countless caves such as these. Brown bears, which became extinct in Ireland a thousand years ago, found this cave great for hibernating. But the caves are a constant 50 degrees, and I needed my sweater (€9, €22 family ticket, open daily at 10:00, last tour at 18:30 July–Aug, otherwise 17:30, Dec–Feb call ahead for limited tours, clearly signposted just south of Ballyvaughan, tel. 065/707-7036).

Ballyvaughan

(area code: 065)

Really just a crossroads, Ballyvaughan is the closest town to the Burren and an ideal rural oasis for those intending to really explore the region.

If you're entering the Burren from Galway, the **Burren Exposure** is your best first stop in Ballyvaughan. Located in a modern little building overlooking Galway Bay, at the edge of the bleakness,

its excellent three-part audiovisual presentation tells the geological, human, and floral story of this unique chunk of Ireland (€6, March–Nov 9:00–18:00, shows every 12 min, closed Dec–Feb, plush sea-view cafeteria, tel. 065/707-7277).

Shane Connolly leads in-depth, three-hour guided walks through the

Burren, explaining the diverse flora, geology, history, and man's role in shaping this landscape. Wear comfortable shoes for wet, rocky fields, and prepare to meet a proud farmer who really knows his stuff (€15, daily at 10:00, call to book and find out meeting point in Ballyvaughan, tel. 065/707-7168, http://homepage.eircom.net /~burrenhillwalks).

Sleeping and Eating in Ballyvaughan: **Rusheen Lodge**, near the fringe of the Burren, offers nine prim rooms and a great breakfast (Sb-€52–68, Db-€76–96, tel. 065/707-7092, fax 065/707-7152, www .rusheenlodge.com, rusheen@iol.ie).

Your best bet for a memorable meal is the seemingly out-of-place **Holywell Italian Café**, hidden a mile inland from Bally-vaughan. This is a great deal, with a limited menu of surprisingly good pasta and pizza dinners at reasonable prices (€8–12, daily 11:00–23:00, off N67 near Newtown Castle, call for directions, tel. 065/707-7322).

Kinvarra

(area code: 091)
This tiny town, between Ballyvaughan and Galway (30 min from each), is waiting for something to happen in its minuscule harbor. It faces Dunguaire Castle, a four-story tower house from 1520 that stands a few yards out in the bay.

The **Dunguaire Castle medieval banquet** is Kinvarra's most tourist-worthy sight. The 500-year-old Dunguaire Castle hosts a touristy but fun medieval banquet (€48, April–Oct almost nightly at 17:30 and 20:30, closed Nov-March, reservations tel. 061/360-788, castle tel. 091/637-108). The evening is as intimate as 55 tourists gathered under one time-stained, barrel-vaulted ceiling can be. You get a decent four-course meal with wine (or mead if you ask sweetly), served amid an entertaining evening of Irish tales and folk songs. Remember that in medi-eval times, it was considered polite to flirt with wenches. It's a small and multitalented cast: One harpist and three singer/actors who serve the "lords and ladies" between tunes. The highlight is the 40-minute stage show—featuring songs and poems by local writers—that comes with dessert.

Sleeping in Kinvarra: **Cois Cuain B&B** is a small but stately house with a garden, overlooking the square and harbor of the most charming village setting you'll find. Mary Walsh rents three super-homey rooms for non-smokers (Db-€68, cash only, The Quay, tel. & fax 091/637-119).

Ennis

This bustling market town (pop. 20,000), the main town of County Clare, provides those relying on public transit with a handy transportation hub (good connections to Limerick, Dublin, and Galway; see "Transportation Connections," page 219). Ennis is less than 15 miles from Shannon Airport (www.shannonairport.com) and makes a good first or last night base in Ireland for travelers not locked into Dublin flights. It also offers a chance to wander around a work-a-day Irish town that does not rely on the tourist dollar (but doesn't shun it either).

The **TI** is just off O'Connell Street Square (June–Sept daily 9:30–17:30, Sat–Sun closed 13:00–14:00, Oct–May closed Sun, tel. 065/682-8366). The White Knights self-service **launderette** is on Old Barrack Street (Mon–Sat 9:00–18:00, closed Sun).

SIGHTS

Clare Museum—This worthwhile museum, housed in the large TI building, has eclectic displays on ancient ax heads, submarine development, and local boys who made good—from 10th-century High King Brian Boru to 20th-century statesman Eamon DeValera (free, June–Sept daily 9:30–13:00 & 14:00–17:30, Sun 14:00–17:00, Oct–May closed Mon, tel. 065/682-3382, www.clarelibrary.ie /eolas/claremuseum).

Ennis Friary—The Franciscan monks arrived here in the 13th century, and the town grew up around their friary (like a monastery). Today, it's still worth a look, with some fine limestone carvings in its ruined walls (€1.50, sometimes includes tour, covered by Heritage Card—see page 4, April–Oct daily 10:00–17:00, closed Nov–March, tel. 065/682-9100). Ask the guide to fully explain the crucifixion symbolism in the 15th-century *Ecce Homo* carving.

Glór Irish Music Centre—The town's modern theater center (*glór* is Irish for "sound") connects you with Irish culture. It's worth considering for traditional music, dance, or storytelling performances (€8–20, April–Sept usually at 20:00, 5-min walk behind TI, Friar's Walk, tel. 065/684-3103, www.glor.ie).

Traditional Music—Live music begins in the pubs around 21:30. The best is **Cruise's** on Abbey Street, with music nightly year-round, and good food (bar is cheaper than restaurant, tel. 065/682-8963). Other pubs offering traditional music are **Quinn's** on Lower Market Street (Sat year-round, tel. 065/682-8148); the rough-and-tumble **Kelly's** on Carmody Street at the intersection with Dumbiggle Road (Sat, tel. 065/682-8155); and **May Kearney's,** across the bridge from the friary, 100 yards up Newbridge Road (Thu–Sat, also Sun at 18:00, tel. 065/682-4888). The **Old Ground Hotel**

Sleep Code

(€1 = about $1.20, country code: 353, area code: 065)
S = Single, D = Double/Twin, T = Triple, Q = Quad,
b = bathroom, s = shower only. Breakfast is included, and credit
cards are accepted unless otherwise noted.

    To help you easily sort through these listings, I've divided
the rooms into categories, based on the price for a standard
double room with bath:

  $$$ **Higher Priced**—Most rooms €70 or more.
   $$ **Moderately Priced**—Most rooms between €50–70.
    $ **Lower Priced**—Most rooms €50 or less.

hosts live music year-round at its pub (Thu–Sun, open to anyone);
though tour groups stay at the hotel, the pub is low-key and feels
real, not staged.

SLEEPING

Hotels

These are both fancy places that you'll share with tour groups. The
stately, ivy-covered, 18th-century $$$ **Old Ground Hotel** has 114
rooms with a family feel (Sb-€80–110, Db-€105–140, suite-
€130–190, rates vary with season, 2-night weekend stays include a
dinner, at intersection of Station Road and O'Connell Street, a few
blocks from station, tel. 065/682-8127, fax 065/682-8112, www
.flynnhotels.com, oghotel@iol.ie). The $$$ **Temple Gate Hotel** is
more modern and less personal (Db-€150–180, rates lower off-season,
non-smoking floor, O'Connell Street Square, in courtyard with TI,
tel. 065/682-3300, fax 065/682-3322, www.templegatehotel.com,
info@templegatehotel.com).

B&Bs

The first two places are on Station Road, a block or two toward the
town center from the train/bus station. $$ **Grey Gables B&B** is
upscale and has eight rooms (Sb-€40, Db-€65, parking, tel.
065/682-4487, www.bed-n-breakfast-ireland.com, marykeane.ennis
@eircom.net, Mary Keane). $ **Rockfield B&B,** a little nearer to
town, has four decent, simple rooms (S-€25–35, Db-€50, Tb-€75,
cash only, parking, tel. 065/682-4749, Pauline O'Driscoll).

    $$ **Stonehaven B&B** is a kid-friendly place with three comfortable rooms (Sb-€40–42, Db-€60–64, Tb-€85–90, cash only, 10-
min walk from town on N68 Kilrush road, tel. 065/684-1775, www
.stonehavenclare.com).

EATING

Get some **pub grub** at one of the places mentioned under "Traditional Music," page 217. Or, for an easy, pub-free dinner, try the simple **Numero Uno Pizzeria** (Tue–Fri 12:00–23:30, Sun–Mon 17:00–23:30, tel. 065/684-1740, on Old Barrack Street off Market Place).

TRANSPORTATION CONNECTIONS

From Ennis by train to: Limerick (8/day, 40 min), **Dublin** (6/day, 3 hrs). Train info: tel. 065/684-0444.

By bus to: Galway (14/day, 1 hr), **Dublin** (11/day, 4 hrs), **Rosslare** (5/day, 5 hrs), **Limerick** (15/day, 60 min), **Doolin/Lisdoonvarna** (3/day, 60–90 min), **Tralee** (6/day, 3 hrs). Bus info: tel. 065/682-4177.

Aran Islands

The Aran Islands consist of three limestone islands: Inishmore, Inishmaan, and Inisheer. The largest, Inishmore (9 miles by 2 miles), is by far the most populated, interesting, and visited. The landscape of all three islands is harsh: steep, rugged cliffs and windswept, rocky fields divided by stone walls. During the winter, severe gales sweep the islands; because of this, most of the settlements on Inishmore are found on its more peaceful eastern side.

There's a stark beauty about these islands and the simple lives its inhabitants eke out of six inches of topsoil and a mean sea. Precious little of the land is productive. In the past, people made a precarious living from fishing and farming. The layers of limestone rock meant that there was little natural soil. Farming soil has been built up by the islanders—the result of centuries of layering seaweed with sand. The fields are small, divided by several thousand miles of drystone wall. Most of these are built in the Aran "gap" style, in which angled upright stones are filled with smaller stones. This allows a farmer who wants to move stock to dismantle and rebuild the walls easily. Nowadays, tourism boosts the local economy.

The islands are a *Gaeltacht* area. While the islanders speak Irish among themselves, they happily speak English with their visitors. Many of them have direct, personal connections with America and will ask you if you know their cousin Paddy in Boston.

Today, the 800 people of Inishmore (literally "the big island") greet as many as 2,000 visitors a day. The vast majority of these are day-trippers. They'll hop on a minibus at the dock for a 2.5-hour tour to Dún Aenghus, then spend an hour or two browsing through the few shops or sitting at a picnic table outside a pub with a pint of Guinness.

The other islands, Inishmaan and Inisheer, are smaller, much less populated, and less touristy. While extremely quiet, they do have B&Bs, daily flights, and ferry service. For most, the big island is quiet enough.

On Inishmore Island: Kilronan

By far the Aran Islands' largest town, Kilronan is still just a village. Groups of backpackers wash ashore with the landing of each ferry. Minibuses, bike shops, and a few men in pony carts sop up the tourists. There are around a dozen shops and B&Bs, and about half as many restaurants. Most of Kilronan huddles around the pier. A few blocks inland up the high road, you'll find the **Heritage Centre** (primitive Internet access upstairs, €2.50/15 min, €4/30 min, daily 10:00–17:00), the best folk-music pub, a **post office** (Mon–Fri 9:00–13:00 & 14:00–17:30, Sat 9:00–13:00, closed Sun), and a tiny **bank** across from the roofless Anglican church ruins (open only on Wed 10:00–12:30 & 13:30–15:00, plus Thu June–Aug). The huge SPAR **supermarket,** two blocks inland from the harbor, seems too big for the tiny community and has the island's only ATM

Inishmore Island

(Mon–Sat 9:00–20:00, Sun 10:00–17:00). Bring cash: Some B&Bs and other businesses don't accept credit cards. A couple of huts near the pier rent bikes (€10/day, plus €10 deposit).

ORIENTATION

Tourist Information
The TI is helpful, but don't rely on it for accommodations. The B&B owners who work with the TI are out of town and desperate (daily 10:00–17:00, June–Aug until 18:30, shorter winter hours, faces the harbor, tel. 099/61263). Ask the TI for a map of the island (if your ferry operator didn't already give you one). This map is all the average day-tripper or leisure biker will need to navigate. But serious hikers who plan on scampering out to the island's craggy fringes will want to invest in the detailed, black-and-white *Oileain Aran* map by Tim Robinson (€7, sold in Kilronan TI and many mainland bookstores). Public WCs are 100 yards beyond the TI on the harbor road.

Getting Around Inishmore Island
Just about anything on wheels functions as a taxi. A trip from Kilronan to Dún Aenghus to the Seven Churches and back to Kilronan costs €10 per person in a shared minibus. Flag them down and don't hesitate to bargain. Pony carts cost about €40 for two people (€60 for 4) for a trip to the west end of the island. Biking is great though hilly, with occasional headwinds (30 min to start of trailhead up to Dún Aenghus). Bikers should take the high road over and the low road back—fewer hills, scenic shoreline, and, at low tide, 50 seals basking in the sun. Keep a sharp lookout along the roads for handy modern stone signposts (with distances in kilometers) that point the way to important sites. They're in Irish, but you'll be clued in by the small metal depictions of the site embedded within them.

TOURS

▲**Island Minibus Tours**—There can't be more than 100 vehicles on the island, and the majority of them seem to be minibuses. A line of buses awaits the arrival of each ferry, offering 2.5-hour, €10 island tours. Chat with several to find a driver who likes to talk. I learned that 800 islanders live in 14 villages, with three elementary schools and three churches. Most own a small, detached field where they keep a couple of cows (sheep are too much trouble). When pressed for more information, my guide explained that there are 400 different

flowers and 19 different types of bees
on the island. The tour, a convenient
time-saver, zips you to the end of the
island for a quick stroll in the desolate
fields, gives you 10 minutes to wander
through the historic but visually
unimpressive "Seven Churches," and
then drops you for two hours at Dún
Aenghus (30 min to hike up, 30 min at the fort, 20 min hike back
down, 40 min in café for lunch or shops at dropoff point) before running you back to Kilronan. Ask your driver to take you back along the
smaller coastal road (scenic beaches and sunbathing seals at low tide).

SIGHTS

▲**Aran's Heritage Centre**—This little museum, while nothing
impressive, offers a worthwhile introduction to the island's traditional lifestyle, geology, and archaeological wonders (€3.50 for
museum only, €5.50 combo-ticket includes *Man of Aran* movie,
July–Aug daily 10:00–19:00, April–June and Sept–Oct daily 10:00–
17:00, closed Nov–March, tel. 099/61355).

Man of Aran: This 1934 silent movie, giving a good look at traditional island life with an all local cast, is shown at the Heritage
Centre (included in €5.50 ticket to Heritage Centre, 1 hr, 6
shows/day in summer, 3 shows/day off-season). The movie features
currachs (canoe-like boats) in a storm, shark fishing with hand-held
harpoons, cultivation of the fields from bare rock, and life in the
early 1900s, when you couldn't rent bikes.

▲▲▲**Dún Aenghus**—This is the island's blockbuster sight. The
stone fortress hangs spectacularly and precariously on the edge of a
cliff, 300 feet above the Atlantic. The crashing waves seem to say,
"You've come to the end of the world." Little is known about this
2,000-year-old Celtic fort. Its concentric walls are 13 feet thick and

10 feet high. As an added
defense, the fort is ringed with
a commotion of spiky stones,
sticking up like lances, called a
chevaux-de-frise (literally, "Frisian
horses," named for the Frisian
soldiers who used pikes like
these to stop charging cavalry).

Slowly, as the cliff erodes, hunks of the fort fall into the sea. Dún
Aenghus doesn't get crowded until after 11:00. I enjoyed a half hour
completely alone at 10:00 in the tourist season. If you can, get there
early or late—you can slip through the fence anytime (€2, covered
by Heritage Card—see page 4, April–Oct daily 10:00–18:00,

Nov–March daily 10:00–16:00, guides at fort June–Aug answer questions and can sometimes give free tours if you call ahead, 5.5 miles from Kilronan, tel. 099/61008). A small museum displays findings from recent digs and tells the story of the fort. Advice from rangers: Wear walking shoes, and watch your kids closely; there's no fence between you and a 200-foot cliff overlooking the sea.

Seven Churches (Na Seacht Teampaill)—Close to the western tip of the island, this gathering of ruined chapels, monastic houses, and fragments of a high cross dates from the 8th–11th centuries. The island is dotted with reminders that Christianity was brought to the islands in the 5th century by St. Enda, who established a monastery here. Many great monks studied under Enda. Among these "Irish apostles," who started Ireland's "Age of Saints and Scholars" (A.D. 500–900), was Columba, the founder of a monastery on the island of Iona in Scotland.

Kilmurvey—The island's second village sits below Dún Aenghus. With a gaggle of homes, a B&B, a great sheltered beach, and a pub, this is the place for peaceful solitude (except for the folk music in the pub).

Ancient Sites near Killeany—The quiet eastern end of Inishmore offers three ancient sites in evocative settings for overnight visitors with more time, or for those seeking rocky hikes devoid of crowds. First, get a good hiking map from the Kilronan TI. Then consider a soup-and-sandwich lunch at Tigh Fitz pub to fuel up either before or after a half day spent exploring these sights on foot. Ask the folks at the pub for directions (almost always a memorable experience in Ireland).

Closest to the road, amid the dunes one mile past Tigh Fitz pub and just south of the airport, is the 8th-century **St. Enda's Church** (Teaghlach Einne). Protected from wave erosion by a stubborn breakwater, it sits half-submerged in a sandy graveyard, surrounded by a sea of sawgrass and peppered with tombstones. St. Enda is said to be buried here, along with 125 other saints who flocked to Inishmore in the 5th century to learn from him.

St. Benen's Church (Teampall Bheanáin) perches high on a desolate ridge opposite Tigh Fitz pub. Walk up the stone-walled

lane, passing a holy well and the stubby remains of a round-tower base. Then take another visual fix on the church's silhouette on the horizon and zigzag up the stone terraces to the top. The 20-minute hike from Tigh Fitz pub pays off with a great view. Dedicated to St. Benen, a young disciple of St. Patrick himself, this tiny 6th-century oratory is aligned north–south (instead of the usual east–west) to protect the doorway from prevailing winds.

Hidden on a remote, ragged headland an hour's walk from Kilronan to the south side of the island, you'll find the **Black Fort** (Dún Duchathair). Next to Dún Aenghus, this is Inishmore's most dramatic fortification. Built on a promontory with cliffs on three sides, its defenders would have held out behind drystone ramparts, facing the island's interior attackers. Watch your step on the uneven ground, be ready to course-correct as you go, and chances are you'll have this windswept ruin all to yourself.

Ragus—Irish for "desire," this is a riveting hour of quality Irish song-and-dance performed in the small Halla Ronain community center in Kilronan. Ten energetic young Irish

adults give you an opportunity to see Irish step dancing up close, accompanied by a small group of musicians earnestly playing traditional Irish instruments. The center is a five-minute walk from the boat dock and offers day-trippers a mid-afternoon performance you can plan as your last stop before catching the late-afternoon boat back to the mainland. Buy tickets at the Aran Fisherman Restaurant in Kilronan or at the door (€15, Sun–Fri at 14:30 and 20:30, mid-June–Aug, tel. 099/61515, mobile 087-237-1642).

Pub Music—Kilronan's four pubs sporadically offer music on summer nights. Nothing is regularly scheduled, so ask at your B&B or look for posted notices on the front of the Spar supermarket or post office. Joe Watty's Pub, on the high road 100 yards past the post office, sometimes has good Irish folk music. Tigh Fitz, one mile down the airport road, often has folk music and dancing on Fridays, Saturdays, and Sundays. The more central Joe Mac's Pub (next to the hostel) and American Bar (next to the high cross at the base of the high road) are also possibilities.

The Halla Ronain community center becomes a dance hall on some Saturday and Sunday nights, when from midnight to 2:00 locals have a *ceilidh* (KAY-lee), the Irish equivalent of a hoedown. Ask at the TI to see if it's on during your stay.

SLEEPING

(€1 = about $1.20, country code: 353, area code: 099)
Remember, this is a poor island. Most rooms are plain, with sparse plumbing. Only The Pier House takes credit cards.

$$$ **The Pier House** stands solidly a hundred yards beyond the pier, offering 12 decent rooms, a good restaurant downstairs, a dramatic setting, and sea views from most of its rooms (Sb-€45–55, Db-€70–90, tel. 099/61417, fax 099/61122, pierh@iol.ie).

Kilronan

TO DÚN AENGHUS
(MAIN HIGH ROAD)

ARAN'S
HERITAGE
CENTRE

TO LOW
COAST
ROAD

200 YDS.

200 M

HALLA RONAIN
COMM. CTR.
(RAGUS)

TO
AIRPORT
(KILLEANY
ROAD)

BOATS TO
ROSSAVEEL, GALWAY,
INISHMAAN & DOOLIN

1 The Pier House B&B
2 Clai Ban B&B
3 Costello's B&B
4 St. Brendan's B&B

5 Seacrest B&B
6 Hostel
  & Joe Macs Pub
7 Sein Ceibh Café
8 Aran Fisherman Rest.

9 Joe Watty's Pub
10 American Bar
11 SPAR Supermarket
   Lios Aengus Café

$$$ **Man of Aran B&B**, as classy as a thatched cottage can be, is in the peaceful countryside outside of touristy Kilronan. Rooms are quiet and rustic, with fireplaces. The restaurant uses all-organic, homegrown vegetables and herbs (€25–30 meals). The setting is pristine—this is where the movie of the same name was filmed over 70 years ago (S-€45, D-€70, Db-€74, cash only, reserve well in advance, bear right just 100 yards after passing Kilmurvey beach before Dún Aenghus turnoff, 4 miles from Kilronan, tel. 099/61301, fax 099/61324, manofaran@eircom.net).

$$ **Clai Ban**, about the only really cheery place in town, is worth the 10-minute walk from the pier. You might be lucky enough to hear the sounds of the Hernon youngsters practicing traditional music (Sb-€40–60, Db-€55–70, Tb-€80–100, cash only, walk past bank out of town and down lane on left, tel. 099/61111, fax 099/61423, Marion Hernon).

$$ **Costello's B&B** has four plain rooms in a plain home in a fine garden setting (D-€53, Db-€60, cash only, with your back to the

SPAR supermarket's entrance, take little alley at one o'clock—ahead slightly to right—to last house, tel. 099/61241, Sally Costello).

$$ Seacrest B&B offers six uncluttered rooms in a central location next to the Aran Fisherman restaurant. Geraldine Faherty manages the rooms, while Tom Faherty keeps the ferries afloat (Sb-€38, Db-€50–60, Tb-€66, cash only, non-smoking, tel. 099/61292, mobile 087/617-9911).

$ St. Brendan's B&B, hiding a cozy living room behind ivy-covered walls and a windblown garden, rents eight well-worn and basic rooms (Sb-€40, D-€46–50, Db-€50–55, cash only, about €2 less per person off-season, save €2 if you have the continental breakfast, from TI, walk uphill and go left when road forks, tel. 099/61149).

$ Kilronan Hostel, overlooking the harbor near the TI, is cheap but noisy, above Joe Mac's Pub (€14–16 beds in 4- to 6-bed rooms, cash only, includes breakfast, self-service kitchen, tel. 099/61255, www.kilronanhostel.com, kilronanhostel@ireland.com).

EATING

Kilronan's cafés dish up soup, soda bread, sandwiches, and tea. **Lios Aengus**, next door to the SPAR market, does simple lunches (daily 9:30–17:00, June–Aug until 18:00, tel. 099/61030).

Sein Ceibh ("Old Pier"), which seems to slam out more meals than the rest of the town combined, is popular for its fish-and-chips and great clam chowder (eat in or take out, April–mid-Oct daily 11:00–20:00, closed mid-Oct–March, tel. 099/61228).

Aran Fisherman serves a good dinner (daily 12:30–16:00 & 17:00–22:00, arrive before 19:00 to avoid a wait, tel. 099/61104).

The **Pier House** operates a dependable restaurant below its guesthouse (€8–14 lunches, €18–26 dinners, daily 11:00–22:00, tel. 099/61811).

The **SPAR supermarket** has all the groceries you'll need (Mon–Sat 9:00–20:00, Sun 10:00–17:00).

TRANSPORTATION CONNECTIONS

By ferry from Rossaveel and Galway: Two companies sail to the Aran Islands; the first one listed, Island Ferries, sells tickets from a small counter in the Galway TI and runs a shuttle bus from Galway for the 45-minute drive to the docks from Rossaveel (see below for details). O'Brien Shipping sails from Galway.

Island Ferries sails to Inishmore from Rossaveel, a port 20 miles west of Galway (3/day April–Oct, 2/day Nov–March, 40-min crossing; if you're coming from Galway, allow 2 hrs one-way including

45-min bus ride, €19 round-trip boat crossing plus €6 round-trip for Galway–Rossaveel shuttle bus; ask about high-season discount for pre-booking, which can drop boat trip to €15 and shuttle bus to €5). Shuttle buses depart Galway (from Merchants Road in front of Kinlay House) 60 minutes before the sailing, and return to Galway immediately after each boat arrives. Ferry schedule for April–Oct: from Rossaveel at 10:30, 13:30, and 18:30; from Inishmore at 9:00, 12:00, and 17:00 (plus 19:30 June–Aug, WCs on board). Island Ferries has two offices, one at the Galway TI, and the other across from Kinlay House on Merchants Road (tel. 091/568-903, www .aranislandferries.com).

Drivers should go straight to the ferry landing in Rossaveel, passing several ticket agencies and pay parking lots. At the boat dock, you'll find a convenient €4-per-day lot and a small office selling tickets for Island Ferries. Check to see what's going when and for how much.

O'Brien Shipping operates smaller, slower boats departing once a day between 8:30 and 10:30 from Galway (not Rossaveel) and stopping at all three Aran Islands (€15, June–Aug Tue, Thu, Fri, Sat; Sept–May Tue, Thu, Sat, New Docks Road, tel. 091/567-676). Boats carry cargo as well, so they go in anything less than a gale—only a couple departures a year are canceled, but call to confirm schedule. For drivers, there's a €5 parking lot at the dock.

By ferry from Doolin: This ferry is handy if you're in Doolin, but it's notorious for being canceled because of wind or tides (for specifics, see "Doolin," page 210).

By plane: Aer Arann, a friendly and flexible little airline, flies three planes a day (every hour during peak season) and stops at all three islands (€44 round-trip, groups of 4 or more €37 each, 10-min flight). These flights get booked up—reserve a day or two in advance with a credit card. Their nine-seat planes take off from the Connemara Regional Airport (not the Galway airport), 20 miles west of Galway. A minibus shuttle—€6 round-trip—runs from Kinlay House on Merchants Road an hour before each flight. The Kilronan airport is small (baggage is transported from the plane to the "gate" in a shopping cart). A minibus shuttle to and from Kilronan costs €5 round-trip (2 miles from the airport).

For reservations and seat availability, contact the airline (tel. 091/593-034, fax 091/593-238, www.aerarannislands.ie). Ask for a 10 percent discount—they distribute lots of coupons.

Connemara

If you have a car, consider spending a day exploring the wild western Irish fringe known as Connemara. Gaze up at the peak of Croagh Patrick, the mountain from which St. Patrick supposedly banished the snakes from Ireland. Pass through the desolate Doo Lough valley on a road stained with tragic famine history. Bounce on a springy peat bog, and drop in at a Westport pub owned by a member of the Chieftains (a well-known traditional Irish music group). This beautiful area also claims a couple of towns—Cong and Leenane—where classic Irish movies were filmed, as well as photogenic Kylemore Abbey.

Connemara makes an easy day trip by car from Galway. Without a car, you can take a tour from Galway (see "Bus Tours of the Burren and Connemara," at the beginning of the chapter) or at least get to Westport by bus (see "Westport," page 231). Public transportation in this region is patchy, and some areas are not served at all. Trains connect Galway and Westport to Dublin, but not to each other.

SIGHTS

Connemara Loop Trip

This is a full day of driving (about 150 miles, using Galway as your base). With an early start, your day will be less rushed. Those wanting to slow down and linger can sleep in Westport. These country roads, punctuated by blind curves and surprise bumps, are shared by trucks, tractors, and sheep. Drive sanely, and bring rain gear and your sense of humor. This is the real Ireland.

Take along a good map (Michelin's maps are widely sold in Ireland) and study a loop connecting these points before you start: Galway, Cong, Westport, Louisburgh, Leenane, Kylemore Abbey, and back to Galway.

Route Summary: Take N84 north out of Galway. At Cross, take R346 into Cong and R345 back out again. At Neale, go north on R334 and pick up N84 again from Ballinrobe to Partry. Take R330 from Partry to Westport. After lunch in Westport, go west on R335 through Louisburgh and south through Doo Lough Valley all the way to Leenane. Pick up N59 in Leenane and take it as far past Kylemore Abbey to Letterfrack and Connemara National Park. Double back from Letterfrack and take R344 south to the junction with N59. The N59 will take you back via Maam Cross and Oughterard to Galway.

The Tour Begins: From Galway's Eyre Square, drive north out of town on Prospect Hill Road. Follow the signs at each roundabout

Connemara

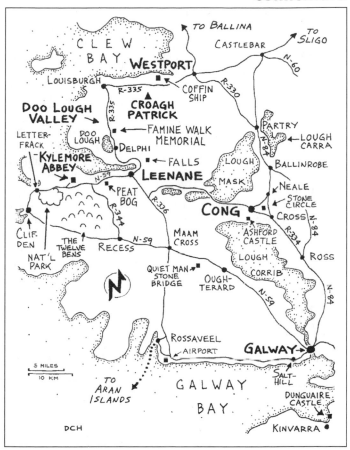

in the direction of Castlebar onto N84. You'll soon be out of Galway's suburbs and crossing miles of flat bogland laced with simple rock walls. You may notice the flags on the phone poles changing colors: from burgundy and white to green and red. These are the colors of the local hurling and football teams. You've crossed the border from County Galway into County Mayo. At Cross, take R346 into Cong. You'll pass the grand, gray gateway of Ashford Castle (on left) as you approach the town.

Cong—Plan to spend an hour in Cong. Cross the small bridge and park in front of the abbey. Drop into the **TI** across from the abbey entrance for a map (March–Nov daily 10:00–18:00, July–Aug until 19:00, closed Dec–Feb, tel. 094/954-6542). Public WCs are 50 yards down the street across from the *Quiet Man* **cottage.** That's right, pilgrim, this town is where John Wayne and Maureen O'Hara made the famous John Ford film *The Quiet Man* 50 years ago. The cottage's modest historical exhibits (upstairs) and film props (downstairs) are really only worth it for diehard fans of the Duke (€3.80, mid-March–Oct daily 10:00–17:00, closed Nov–mid-March, tel. 094/954-6089). Fuel up with a cup of coffee and a homemade dessert at the **Hungry Monk Café** (July–Aug daily 10:00–18:00, mid-March–June and Sept–Oct Tue–Sun 10:00–18:00, closed Mon, closed Nov–mid-March, Internet access, on Abbey Street between WCs and TI, tel. 094/954-6866).

We're here for the ruins of **Cong Abbey** (free and always open). The abbey was built in the late 1100s, when Romanesque was going out of style, and Gothic was coming in; you'll see the mixture of rounded Romanesque and pointy Gothic arch styles in the doorway. The famous Cross of Cong (an Irish art treasure now on display in Dublin's National Museum), which held a holy relic of what was supposedly a splinter of the True Cross, was held aloft at the front of processions of Augustinian monks during High Masses in this church. Rory O'Connor, the last Irish high king, died in this abbey in 1198. After O'Connor realized he could never outfight the superior Norman armies, he retreated to Cong and spent his last years here in monastic isolation.

Take a walk through the cloister and down the path behind the abbey. The forested grounds are lush, and the stream water is incredibly clear. Cong's salmon hatchery contributes to western Ireland's reputation for great fishing. The monks fished for more than sinners. They built the modest **Monk's Fishing Hut** (just over the footbridge) right on the bank so that the river flowed underneath. They lowered a net

though the floor and attached a bell to the rope; whenever a fish was netted, the bell would ring.

Next stop is **Ashford Castle**. To reach the castle from the abbey, face the Romanesque/Gothic main entrance and go left around the corner of the abbey, walking 15 minutes down the pleasant forested lane onto the grounds of the castle, which is hidden behind the trees.

Garden-lovers happily pay the stiff €5 entry fee (in effect during peak bloom June–Aug, usually free rest of year) to a kid patrolling the bridge, so they can stroll the lakeside paradise once owned by the Guinness beer family. The renovated Victorian castle rents some of the finest rooms in all of Ireland. President Reagan stayed here in 1984, and actor Pierce Brosnan chose these grounds for his wedding reception in 2001.

From Cong to Neale: Cong (from *conga,* Irish for "isthmus") lies between two large lakes. Departing Cong over the same bridge by which you entered, look down through the thick vegetation to see a dry canal. Built between 1848 and 1854, this canal was a famine work project that stoked only appetites. The canal, complete with locks, would have linked Lough Mask to the north with Lough Corrib to the south. But the limestone bedrock was too porous, and the canal wouldn't hold water.

Take R345 out of Cong. Heading north, you'll pass through the tiny hamlet of...

Neale—About 120 years ago, a retired army captain named Boycott was hired to manage the nearby estate of Lord Erne. But the strict captain harshly treated the tenants who worked his lands, so they united to ostracize him by deserting their jobs and isolating his estate. Over time, the agitation worked, and eventually "boycotting" became a popular tactic in labor conflicts.

From Neale to Westport: At Neale, go north on R334, then take N84 from Ballinrobe to Partry. At Partry, turn left off N84 onto R330 in the direction of Westport (the easy-to-miss turnoff is immediately after you pass the thatch-roofed Village Inn). Just over 200 years ago, in the countryside a few miles to your right, a French invasion force supported by locals dealt the British an embarrassing loss in the **Battle of Castlebar.** The surprised British forces were routed, and their rapid retreat is slyly remembered in Irish rebel lore as the "Castlebar races." Unfortunately for the rebels, this proved to be the last glimmer of hope for Irish victory in the uprising of 1798. The British reorganized, and within weeks defeated the small force of 1,300 Frenchmen and the ill-equipped Irish rebels. The captured French soldiers were treated as prisoners of war, while the Irish rebels were executed.

Westport—On arrival in Westport, park along the Mall under the trees that line the canal-like river. This is a planned town, built in the Georgian style in the late 1700s to support the adjacent estate of Westport House (skip it for better manors at Powerscourt and Muckross). The town once thrived on the linen industry created by local Irish handlooms. But after the Act of Union with Britain in 1801, the town was unable to compete with the industrialized British linen-makers, and fell into decline. The town is still pretty and a good place for a relaxed lunch and some exploration on foot.

The **TI** is on James Street (Mon–Sat 9:00–17:00, closed Sun, July–Aug daily until 18:00, tel. 098/25711). The **Westport Heritage Centre** gives a good overview of town history and the nearby Croagh Patrick pilgrimage tradition (€3, downstairs beneath the TI). On

Ireland's Misunderstood Nomads

When you see a small cluster of trailers at the side of an Irish road, you're looking at a dying way of life. These are Travellers, a nomadic throwback to the days when wandering craftsmen, musicians, and evicted unfortunates crowded rural Ireland. Often mislabeled as Gypsies, they have no ethnic ties to those Eastern European nomads, but instead have Irish heritage going back centuries.

There were once many more Travellers, living in tents and using horse-drawn carts as they wandered the countryside in search of work. Before the famine, when Irish hospitality was a given, Travellers filled a niche in Irish society. They would do odd jobs, such as repairing furniture, sweeping chimneys, and selling horses. Skilled tinsmiths, they mended pots, pans, and stills for *poitín*—Irish moonshine. (Travellers used to be called "tinkers," but they now consider this label derogatory.) Post-famine rural depopulation and the gradual urbanization of the countryside forced this nomadic group to adapt to an almost sedentary existence on the fringes of towns.

Today, the 30,000 remaining Travellers are outsiders, usually treated with suspicion by the traditionally conservative Irish. Locals often complain that petty thefts go up when Travellers set up camp in a nearby "halting site," and that they leave their refuse behind when they depart. Travellers tend to keep to themselves, marry young, have large families, and speak their own Gaelic-based language (called Shelta, Gammon, or Cant). Attempts to settle Travellers in government housing and integrate their children into schools have met with mixed success.

Tuesday and Thursday nights in July and August, 90-minute **town walks** depart at 20:00 from the clock tower at the top of Bridge Street (€5, tel. 098/26852). **Laundry** can be dropped off early at Gills and picked up late the same day (€8.50, Mon–Sat 9:00–18:30, closed Sun, tel. 098/25819).

Eating in Westport: Most of your best bets are clustered on Bridge Street. For a quick and easy lunch, try **O'Cee's Coffeeshop** (cafeteria-style lunches €8, Mon–Sat 8:30–19:00, Sun 10:00–16:00, Shop Street, tel. 098/27000) or the **Stuffed Sandwich Company** (Mon–Sat 9:30–18:00, Bridge Street, tel. 098/27611). A good dinner choice is **J.J. O'Malleys** (€16–24 meals, daily 17:00–22:00, Bridge Street, tel. 098/27307). Irish music fans will seek out **Matt Molloy's pub** (Bridge Street, tel. 098/26655). Matt Molloy isn't just the owner of the pub—he's also flautist for the Chieftains, the group credited with much of the resurgence of interest in Irish music worldwide over the past 30 years.

Sleeping in Westport (area code: 098): For those wanting extra time to explore, Westport is the best place along this route to spend a night. All of the following listings are centrally located. Prices vary quite a bit depending on the season. **Westport Inn** has a fresh, woody feel, with 34 comfortable rooms and convenient, free underground parking (Sb-€49–90, Db-€90–160, Mill Street, tel. 098/29200, fax 098/29250, www.westportinn.ie). The **Clew Bay Hotel** is a couple of doors down from the TI, with 28 large modern rooms (Sb-€60–90, Db-€80–160, James Street, tel. 098/28088, fax 098/25783, www .clewbayhotel.com). Right on the leafy Mall is the **Olde Railway Hotel**, with a "retire to the study to drink port and smoke your pipe" kind of feel (Db-€160 July–Sept, less off-season, The Mall, parking, tel. 098/25166, fax 098/25090, www.theolderailwayhotel.com). The homey **Teallach an Ghabha B&B** has four comfy, modest rooms (S-€45, Db-€70, cash only, Altamount Street, tel. 098/25704).

Transportation Connections: If you want to visit Westport, but lack wheels, here are your options. You can take a bus to/from **Galway** (7/day, 2 hrs), **Derry** (4/day, 5.5 hrs, change in Sligo), or **Dublin** (5/day, 5 hrs). You can also reach Dublin by train (3/day, 4 hrs).

From Westport to Murrisk by car: Leave Westport heading west on R335. After about five miles, as you're driving along scenic Clew Bay, you'll reach a wide spot in the road called Murrisk. Stop here. In the field on your right (opposite Campbell's Pub) is the...

Coffin Ship—This bronze ship sculpture is one of the most powerful famine memorials you'll see in Ireland. It's a "coffin ship," like those

of the 1840s that carried the sick and starving famine survivors across the ocean in hope of a new life. Unfortunately, many of the ships contracted to take the desperate immigrants were barely seaworthy and no longer fit for dependable commerce. The poor were weak from starvation and vulnerable to "famine fever," which they then spread to others in the putrid, cramped holds of these awful ships. Many who lived through the six- to eight-week journey died shortly after reaching their new country. Pause a moment to look at the silent skeletons swirling around the ship's masts. Now contemplate the fact that famine exists today. And before judging the lack of effective relief intervention by the British government of that time, consider the rich world's ability to ignore similar suffering today.

Across the road from the coffin ship is...

Croagh Patrick—This small mountain rises 2,500 feet above the bay. In the 5th century, St. Patrick is said to have fasted on its summit for 40 days. It's from here that he supposedly rang his bell, driving all the snakes out of Ireland. The snakes never existed, of course, but they represent the pagan beliefs that Patrick's newly arrived Christianity replaced. Every year on the last Sunday of July,

"Reek Sunday" (a "reek" is a mountain peak), more than 50,000 pilgrims hike two hours up the rocky trail to the summit in honor of St. Patrick. The most penitent hike barefoot. On that Sunday, Mass is celebrated throughout the day in a modest chapel on the top.

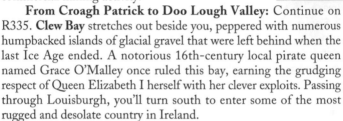

A few years ago, valuable gold deposits were discovered within Croagh Patrick. Luckily, public sentiment has kept the sacred mountain free of any commercial mining activity.

From Croagh Patrick to Doo Lough Valley: Continue on R335. **Clew Bay** stretches out beside you, peppered with numerous humpbacked islands of glacial gravel that were left behind when the last Ice Age ended. A notorious 16th-century local pirate queen named Grace O'Malley once ruled this bay, earning the grudging respect of Queen Elizabeth I herself with her clever exploits. Passing through Louisburgh, you'll turn south to enter some of the most rugged and desolate country in Ireland.

Doo Lough Valley—Signs of human habitation vanish from the bogland, and ghosts begin to appear beside the road. About eight miles beyond Louisburgh, stop at the simple, gray stone cross on the left. The lake ahead is Doo Lough (Irish for Black Lake), and this is the

site of one of the saddest famine tales.

In the early 1800s, County Mayo's rural folk were almost exclusively dependent on the potato for food. They were the hardest hit when the Potato Famine came in 1845. In the winter of 1849, about 600 starving Irish walked 12 miles from Louisburgh to Delphi Lodge. They hoped to get food from their landlord, but were turned away. On the walk back, almost 400 of them died along the side of this road. Today, the road still seems to echo with the despair of those hungry souls, and inspires an annual walk that commemorates the tragedy. Archbishop Desmond Tutu made the walk in 1991, shortly before South Africa ended its apartheid system.

From Doo Lough Valley to Leenane: Continue south on R335. You'll get a fine view of **Aasleagh Falls** on the left. In late May, the banks below the falls explode with lush, wild rhododendron blossoms. Cross the bridge after the falls and turn right onto N59 toward Leenane. You'll drive along Killary Harbor, Ireland's version of a fjord. This long, narrow body of water was carved by an advancing glacier.

Leenane—This town is a good place for a break. The 1990 movie *The Field,* starring Limerick-born Richard Harris, was filmed here.

Take a glance at the newspaper clippings about the making of the movie on the wall of Hamilton's Pub. While you're there, find the old photo of the British battleships that filled Killary Harbor when the king of England visited a century ago. Drop into the **Leenane Cultural Centre** (on the left as you enter town) to see an interesting wool-spinning and weaving demonstration (€2.50, April–Sept).

From Leenane to a Peat Bog: As you continue west on N59, notice the rows of blue floats in Killary Harbor. They're there to mark mussel farms growing in the cold seawater. Climbing out of the fjord valley about five miles past Leenane, you'll pass some good areas to get a close look at a turf cut in a peat bog.

A Slog on the Bog—Walk a few yards onto the spongy green carpet. Watch your step on wet days to avoid squishing into a couple of inches of water. Find a dry spot, and jump up and down to get a feel for it. Have your companion jump; you'll feel the vibrations 10 feet away.

These bogs once covered almost 20 percent of Ireland. As the climate got warmer at the end of the last Ice Age, plants began growing along the sides of the many shallow lakes and ponds. When the plants died in these waterlogged areas, there wasn't enough oxygen for them to fully decompose. The moss built up, layer after dead layer, over the centuries. In World War I, this sphagnum moss was collected to use in bandages to soak up blood (it absorbs many times its weight in fluids).

It's this wet, oxygen-starved ecosystem that preserved ancient artifacts so well, many of which can be seen in Dublin's National

Museum. Even forgotten containers of butter, churned centuries ago and buried to keep cool, have been discovered. Since these acidic bogs contain few nutrients, unique species of carnivorous plants have adapted themselves to life here by trapping and digesting insects. The tiny pink Sundew (about 2 inches tall) has delicate spikes glistening with insect-attracting fluid. Take a moment to find a mossy area and look closely at the variety of tiny plants. In summer, you'll see white tufts of bog cotton growing in marshy areas.

People have been cutting, drying, and burning peat as a fuel source for over a thousand years. The cutting usually begins in April or May when drier weather approaches. You'll probably see stacks of "turf" piled up to dry along recent cuts. Pick up a brick and fondle it. Dried peat is surprisingly light and stiff. In central Ireland, there are even industrial peat cuts that were begun after World War II to fuel power stations. But in the past decade, recognition of the rare habitat that the bogs provide has encouraged conservation efforts, and the smell of burning peat is becoming increasingly rare.

From Peat Bog to Kylemore Abbey: Continue west on N59 and pass the junction with R344 (direction: Recess) on the left; you'll come back to this junction on your way back to Galway. The road soon crosses a shallow lake, with a great view of Kylemore Abbey to the right. But you'll get a better photo from the parking lot a couple of hundred yards ahead, so don't stop here. Pull into the lot and take a few minutes to enjoy the view.

Kylemore Abbey—This neo-Gothic country house was built by the wealthy English businessman Mitchell Henry in the 1860s, after he and his wife had honeymooned in the area. Now they are both buried on the grounds. During World War I, refugee Benedictine nuns from Belgium took it over, and today, it's an exclusive girls' boarding school. The best thing about the abbey is the view of it from the lakeshore. Tours inside are a letdown, so just enjoy its setting. WCs are in the gift shop next to the parking lot (€7 combo-ticket for abbey and gardens, daily 9:00–17:30, tel. 095/41146, www.kylemoreabbey.com).

Connemara National Park—Less than five miles west of the abbey, just after passing through the town of Letterfrack (go left off N59), the park encompasses almost 5,000 acres of wild bog and mountain scenery. The visitors center displays worthwhile exhibits of local biology, fauna, and flora, which are well explained in the 15-minute *Man and the Landscape* film that runs every half hour. Nature-lovers may want to reverse the direction of my driving loop (and skimp on sightseeing time at other stops) in order to enjoy a two-hour walking tour with a park naturalist, departing the visitors center Monday–Friday at 10:30 in July and August. Bring rain gear and hiking shoes (visitors center-€2.75, covered by Heritage Card—see page 4, mid-March–Oct daily 10:00–17:30, June–Aug until 18:30, last admission 45 min before closing, tel. 095/41054, www.heritageireland.ie).

Returning to Galway: Drive back the way you came. Turn right on the R344 (direction: Recess). Off to the right is Connemara's Twelve Bens mountains—but it's late, and we're headed for home. At the junction with the N59, turn left and follow the signs back to Galway.

Between Galway and Derry

Travelers continuing on to Northern Ireland (or County Donegal) should get an early start. Allow a long day for the drive from Galway to Derry (or Portrush), with these interesting stops along the way. Knock is right on the N17 heading north out of Galway, while Strokestown is further east in County Roscommon.

Knock—In this tiny town in 1879, locals saw the Virgin Mary and

Joseph appear against the south gable of the church. Word of miraculous healings turned the trickle of pilgrims into a flood, and put Knock solidly on the pilgrimage map. Today, you can visit the shrine. At the edge of the site, a small but interesting folk museum shows "evidence" of the healings, photos of a papal visit, and interesting slices of traditional life.

▲▲**Strokestown Park National Famine Museum**—The Great Potato Famine of 1845–1849 was the bleakest period in Irish history—so traumatic that it halved the Irish population, sent desperate Irish peasants across the globe, and crystallized Irish-nationalist hatred of British rule. The National Famine Museum fills a mansion (on the former estate of the Mahon family, mentioned below) in the market town of Strokestown, 60 miles northeast of Galway. Visitors can absorb the thoughtfully done exhibits explaining how three million Irish peasants survived on a surprisingly nutritious pre-famine diet of buttermilk and potatoes (12 lbs per day per average male laborer).

Major Mahon, the ill-fated landlord during the famine, found it cheaper to fill three "coffin ships" bound for America with his evicted, starving tenants than pay the taxes for their upkeep in the local workhouse. When almost half died at sea of "famine fever," he was assassinated. After visiting the museum, take a tour of the musty "Big House" to learn about the gulf that divided the Protestant ascendancy and their Catholic house servants. Afterward, find the servants' tunnel—built to avoid disturbing the Mahon family's views—connecting the kitchen to the stable (€8.50 for museum and house, €5 for museum or house, mid-March–Oct daily 10:30–17:30, tel. 078/33013, www.strokestownpark.ie).

Drivers connecting Westport or Galway to either Dublin or Northern Ireland can stop here en route and grab lunch at the museum café.

NORTHERN IRELAND

All of Ireland was once a colony of Great Britain. Unlike its Celtic cousins, Scotland and Wales, Ireland has always been distant from London—due more to its Catholicism than to the Irish Sea.

Protestant settlers from England and Scotland were "planted" in Catholic Ireland to help assimilate the island into the British economy. These settlers established their own cultural toehold on the island, but the Catholic Irish held strong to their Gaelic culture.

Over the centuries, British rule has not been easy. By the beginning of the 20th century, the sparse Protestant population could no longer control the entire island. When Ireland won its independence in 1921 (after a bloody guerilla war against British rule), 26 of the island's 32 counties became the Irish Free State, ruled from Dublin with dominion status in the British Commonwealth—like Canada. In 1949, they left the Commonwealth and became the Republic of Ireland, removing all political ties with Britain.

Meanwhile, the six remaining northeastern counties (the only ones with a Protestant majority), which had voted not to join the Irish Free State in 1922, remained part of the United Kingdom.

In this new political entity called Northern Ireland, the long-established Orange Order and the military muscle of the newly mobilized Ulster Volunteer Force (UVF) worked to defend the union with Britain—so their political philosophy was "Unionist." This was countered on the Catholic side by the Irish Republican Army (IRA). The IRA wanted all 32 of Ireland's counties to be united in one Irish nation—so their political goals were "Nationalist."

In World War II, the Republic stayed neutral, while the North enthusiastically supported the Allied cause—winning a spot close to London's heart. After the war, the split between North and South seemed permanent, and Britain invested heavily in Northern Ireland to bring it solidly into the United Kingdom fold.

Northern Ireland

As 94 percent of the Republic of Ireland (the South) was Catholic and only 6 percent was Protestant, there was no question as to which group was dominant. But in the North, the Catholics, although a minority, were a sizable 35 percent and demanded attention. Discrimination was considered necessary to maintain the Protestant status quo in the North, leading to the Troubles that have filled headlines since the late 1960s.

This isn't a fight over Protestant and Catholic religious differences—it's about whether Northern Ireland will stay part of the United Kingdom or become part of the Republic of Ireland. The indigenous Irish of Northern Ireland, who generally want to unite with Ireland, happen to be Catholic. The descendants of Scottish and English settlers, who generally want to remain part of Britain, happen to be Protestant.

Partly inspired by the Civil Rights movement in America in the 1960s, the Catholic minority in Northern Ireland claimed they were discriminated against in gaining better jobs and housing. Extremists polarized issues, and demonstrations became violent. Unionists were afraid that if the island became one nation, the relatively poor Republic of Ireland would drag down the North, and the high percentage of Catholics could mean repression of the Protestants. As Protestants and Catholics clashed in 1969, the British Army entered

How Big, How Many, How Much

- Northern Ireland is 5,222 square miles, a little bigger than Connecticut.
- Population is 1.7 million (about 325 per square mile, 55 percent Protestant, 45 percent Catholic).
- £1 (pound sterling) = about $1.70

the fray. They've been there ever since. In 1972, a watershed year, combatants moved from petrol bombs to guns, and a new, more violent IRA emerged. In this most recent 30-year chapter in the struggle for an independent and united Ireland, more than 3,000 people have been killed.

A 1985 agreement granted Dublin a consulting role in the Northern Ireland government. Unionists bucked this idea, and violence escalated. That same year, Belfast City Hall draped a huge, defiant banner under its dome, proclaiming, "Belfast Says No."

In 1994, the banner came down. In the 1990s—with Ireland's membership in the European Union, the growth of its economy, and the weakening of the Catholic Church's influence—the consequences of a united Ireland were less threatening to the Unionists. Also in 1994, the IRA declared a cease-fire, and the Protestant UVF followed suit. Talks are still underway, interrupted by sporadic hostilities.

The Nationalists want British troops out of Ireland, while the Unionists want the IRA to turn in its arms. Optimists hailed the signing, in 1998, of a breakthrough peace plan called the "Good Friday Accord" by Nationalists and the "Belfast Agreement" by Unionists. This led to the emotional release of prisoners on both sides in 2000. Major hurdles to a lasting peace persist, but the downtown checkpoints are history, and "bomb damage clearance sales" are over. And today, more tourists than ever are venturing to Belfast and Derry.

Terminology

Ulster (one of Ireland's 4 ancient provinces) consists of nine counties in the northern part of the island of Ireland. Six of these make up Northern Ireland (pronounced "Norn Iron" by locals), while three counties remain part of the Republic.

Unionists—and the more hard-line Loyalists—want the North to remain in the United Kingdom. The Ulster Unionist Party (UUP), led by Nobel Peace Prize co-winner David Trimble, is the political party representing moderate Unionist views. The Democratic Unionist Party (DUP), led by Reverend Ian Paisley, chooses to take a harder stance in defense of Unionism. The Ulster Volunteer Force (UVF), the Ulster Freedom Fighters (UFF), and the **Ulster Defense Association (UDA)** are the Loyalist paramilitary organizations mentioned most frequently in newspapers and on spray-painted walls.

Nationalists—and the more hard-line **Republicans**—want a united and independent Ireland ruled by Dublin. The **Social Democratic Labor Party (SDLP),** founded by Nobel Peace Prize co-winner John Hume and led by Mark Durkan, is the moderate political party representing Nationalist views. **Sinn Fein** (shin fayn), led by Gerry Adams, takes a harder stance in defense of Nationalism. The **Irish Republican Army (IRA)** is the Nationalist paramilitary organization (linked with Sinn Fein) mentioned most often in the press and in graffiti.

Orange and the red, white, and blue of the Union Jack are the favored colors of the Unionists. Green is the color of the Republicans. To gain more insight into the complexity of the Troubles, see the University of Ulster's Conflict Archive at http://cain.ulst.ac.uk.

Safety
Tourists in Northern Ireland are no longer considered courageous (or reckless). A United Nations study conducted in 2003 found that Northern Ireland was statistically the second safest country in the developed world (after Japan). You're safer in Northern Ireland than in any other part of the United Kingdom—and far safer than in most major U.S. cities. You have to look for trouble to find it here. Just don't seek out spit-and-sawdust pubs in working-class Protestant neighborhoods and sing Catholic songs. Tourists notice the tension mainly during the "marching season" (peaking in early July). July 12 is traditionally the most confrontational day of the year in the North, when proud Protestant Unionist Orangemen march to celebrate their Britishness and their separate identity from the Republic of Ireland (often through staunchly Nationalist Catholic neighborhoods). Lay low if you stumble onto any big Orange parades.

Northern Ireland is a Different Country
When you leave the Republic of Ireland and enter Northern Ireland, you are crossing an international border. Although you don't have to flash your passport, you do change stamps, phone cards, and money—and your Eurailpass is no longer valid. Instead of using euros, as in the Republic of Ireland, you need to switch to the British pound sterling (£). Northern Ireland issues its own Ulster pound and also uses English pounds. Like the Scottish pound, Ulster pounds are interchangeable with English pounds. But if you're heading to England next, it's best to change your Ulster pounds into English ones (free at any bank in Northern Ireland, England, Wales, or Scotland).

BELFAST

Belfast was only a village in the 17th century. With the influx, or "plantation," of English and (more often) Scottish settlers, the character of the place changed. After the plantation—and subjugation of the native Irish—Belfast boomed, spurred by the success of the local linen, ropemaking, and shipbuilding industries. The Industrial Revolution took root with a vengeance. While the rest of Ireland remained rural and agricultural, Belfast earned its nickname ("Old Smoke") during the time when many of the brick buildings you'll see today were built. The year 1888 marked the birth of modern Belfast. After Queen Victoria granted city status to this boomtown of 300,000, its citizens built the city's centerpiece, City Hall.

Belfast is the birthplace of the *Titanic* (and many ships that didn't sink). The two huge, mustard-colored cranes (the biggest in the world, nicknamed Samson and Goliath) rise like skyscrapers above the harbor. They stand idle now, but serve as a reminder of this town's former shipbuilding might.

It feels like a new morning in Belfast. It's hard to believe that the bright and bustling pedestrian zone was once a subdued, traffic-free security zone. Now there's no hint of security checks, once a tiresome daily routine. On my last visit, the children dancing in the street were both Catholics and Protestants. They were part of a community summer-camp program giving kids from both communities reasons to live together, rather than apart.

Still, it's a fragile peace and a tenuous hope. Mean-spirited murals, hateful bonfires built a month before they're actually burned, and pubs with security gates are reminders that the island is split—and almost a million Protestant Unionists prefer it that way.

Planning Your Time

Big Belfast is thin on sights. For most, one day of sightseeing is plenty.

Day Trip from Dublin: On the handy, two-hour Dublin–Belfast train (and its cheap £25 day-return tickets, £33 on Fri or Sun), you could make Belfast a day trip: 7:35–Catch the early-morning train from Dublin; 11:00–City Hall tour (Mon–Fri), browse the pedestrian zone, lunch, ride a shared cab up the Falls Road; 15:00–Visit Ulster Museum or side-trip to the Ulster Folk and Transport Museum; Evening–Return to Dublin (last train Mon–Sat at 20:10, Sun at 18:10). Confirm train times at local stations. Note that the TI offers Town Walks at 14:00 on Wednesday, Friday, Saturday, and Sunday. On Saturday, there's a morning market (at St. George's) and only one City Hall tour (at 14:30).

Staying Overnight: Belfast makes a pleasant overnight stop, with plenty of cheap hostels, reasonable B&Bs, hotel deals (on Fri–Sun), and a resort neighborhood full of B&Bs 30 minutes away in Bangor.

Two Days in Belfast: Splice in the Living History bus tour, Ulster Museum, and Botanic Gardens, or take a day trip to the Antrim Coast.

Four Days in Northern Ireland: On the first day, catch the train from Dublin to Derry (9:00–15:00). Spend the second day touring Derry, then take a late afternoon train to Portrush (16:00–17:00). On the third day, visit the Antrim Coast sights, returning to Portrush to sleep. On Day Four, catch the morning train to Belfast (8:00–10:00), visit Belfast (following the "Day Trip Plan from Dublin," above), and return to Dublin by train (19:00–21:00).

Coming from Scotland: With good ferry connections (from Stranraer or Troon in Scotland, or Liverpool in England; see "Transportation Connections," page 258), it's easy to begin your exploration of the Emerald Isle in Belfast, then head south to Dublin and the Republic.

ORIENTATION

(area code: 028)

For the first-time visitor in town for a quick look, Belfast is pretty simple. There are three zones of interest: **central** (Donegall Square, City Hall, pedestrian shopping, TI), **southern** (Ulster Museum, Botanic Gardens, university), and **western** (working-class sectarian neighborhoods west of the freeway). Belfast's "Golden Mile"—stretching from Hotel Europa to the university district—connects the central and southern zones, with many of the best dinner and entertainment spots.

Greater Belfast

Tourist Information

The modern TI (look for Welcome Center signs) has fine, free city maps and an enjoyable bookshop with Internet access (June–Aug Mon–Sat 9:00–19:00, Sun 12:00–17:00; Sept–May Mon-Sat 9:00–17:30, closed Sun, 47 Donegall Place, 1 block north of City Hall, tel. 028/9024-6609, www.gotobelfast.com). For the latest on evening fun, get *The List* free at the TI or *That's Entertainment* at newsstands (50p).

Arrival in Belfast

Arriving by fast train, you'll go directly to Central Station (with ATMs and free city maps at ticket counter). From the station, a free Centerlink bus loops to Donegall Square, with stops near Shaftesbury Square (recommended hostels), the bus station (some recommended hotels), and the TI (free with any train or bus ticket, 4/hr, never on Sun, during morning rush hour bus runs only between station and Donegall Square). Allow about £3 for a taxi from Central Station to Donegall Square.

Slower trains arc through Belfast, stopping at several downtown stations, including Central Station, Great Victoria Station (most central, near Donegall Square and most hotels), Botanic (close to the university, Botanic Gardens, and some recommended hostels), and Adelaide (near several recommended B&Bs). It's easy and cheap to connect stations by train (75p).

Helpful Hints

Phone Tips: To call the Republic of Ireland from Northern Ireland, dial 00-353, then the area code without its initial 0, then the local number. To call Northern Ireland from the Republic of Ireland, dial 048, then the local eight-digit number.

Irish Tourist Board: Traveling on to the Republic of Ireland, are ye? If it's information you'll be wanting, pop on in (Mon–Fri 9:00–17:00, plus June–Sept Sat 9:00–12:30, Oct–May closed weekends, 53 Castle Street, off Donegall Place, tel. 028/9026-5500).

U.S. Embassy: It's at Danesfort House (Mon–Fri 8:30–17:00, closed Sat–Sun, 233 Stranmillis Road, www.usembassy.org.uk).

Internet Access: Revelations Internet Café is at 27 Shaftesbury Square, near the City Hostel (£4/hr, Mon–Fri 10:00–22:00, Sat 10:00–18:00, Sun 11:00–19:00, tel. 028/9032-0337).

Post Office: The main P.O., with lots of fun postcards, is at the intersection of Castle Place and Donegall Place (Mon–Sat 9:00–17:30, closed Sun, 2 long blocks north of Donegall Square).

Laundry: Globe Launderers is at 37 Botanic Avenue (£4.50-self-serve, £7-dropoff, Mon–Fri 8:00–21:00, Sat 8:00–18:00, Sun 12:00–18:00, tel. 028/9024-3956). For the B&B neighborhood south of town, the closest is Whistle Laundry (£6-dropoff, Mon–Fri 9:00–18:00, Sat 9:00–17:30, closed Sun, 160 Lisburne Road, at intersection with Eglantine Avenue, tel. 028/9038-1297).

Bike Rental: McConvey Cycles is at 183 Ormeau Road (£10/24 hrs, Mon–Sat 9:00–18:00, closed Sun, tel. 028/9033-0322).

Market: On Friday and Saturday mornings, St. George's Market is a commotion of clothes, produce, and seafood (at corner of Oxford and East Bridge Streets, 5 blocks east of Donegall Square).

Getting Around Belfast

If you line up your sightseeing logically, you can do most of the town on foot.

If you're here in July and August, you can take advantage of "Day Tracker" tickets that give individuals one day of unlimited train travel anywhere in Northern Ireland for £6.50 (making it easy to side-trip to Bangor, the Ulster Folk and Transport Museum in Cultra, or Carrickfergus Castle). Families (up to 2 adults and 2 kids under 16) visiting in July and August get an even better deal: the £15 one-day Family Pass, valid for train and bus travel. Buy your pass at any train station in the city.

Belfast

For information on trains and buses in Belfast, contact Translink (tel. 028/9066-6630, www.translink.co.uk).

By Bus: Buses go from Donegall Square East to Malone Road and my recommended B&Bs (#70 and #71, 3/hr, £1.20, all-day pass-£3.20).

By Taxi: Taxis are reasonable and should be considered. Rather than use their meters, many cabs charge a flat £3 rate for any ride up to two miles. It's £1 per mile after that. Ride a shared cab if you're going up the Falls Road (explained below).

TOURS

▲**Walking Tour**—A Town Walk takes you through the historic core of town (£5, 90 min; departs from TI at 14:00 on Wed, Fri, Sat, and Sun; sometimes more tours added—check with TI, tel. 028/9024-6609).

▲**Big Bus Tours**—**City Sightseeing** offers the Living History Tour, the best introduction to the city's recent and complicated political and social history. You'll cruise the Catholic and Protestant working-class neighborhoods, with a commentary explaining the political murals and places of interest—mostly dealing with the Troubles of the last 25 years. You see things from the bus and get out for photos only (£8, May–Sept daily on the hour 10:00–16:00, fewer tours in winter—call first, 1.5 hrs, depart from corner of Royal Avenue and Castle Place across from McDonald's, 2 blocks north of Donegall Square; pay cash at kiosk or on bus, or book by phone with credit card; tel. 028/9062-6888, www.city-sightseeing.com).

Minibus Tours—The **Mini-Coach** tour company offers a Belfast City Tour, covering the troubled areas in depth, with time for photo stops (£8, 2 hrs, daily at 10:30, Mon–Fri also at 12:30, leaves from Belfast International City Hostel, book in advance, tel. 028/9031-5333, www.minicoachni.co.uk). Their Antrim Coast tour visits the Giant's Causeway, Dunluce Castle (photos only), the Carrick-a-Rede rope bridge (March–Sept), and Old Bushmills Distillery—£4 admission not included (£16, daily 9:30–17:45 depending on demand, book through and depart from hostel listed above). They also have private guides.

Or consider **Alternative Tours** (£8, 2 hrs with small group "walkabouts" of 7 people or less, will pick up on request, mobile 0787-926-8153, alternative_tours@hotmail.com).

Boat Tours—The Lagan Boat Company shows you shipyards on a 75-minute **Titanic Tour** cruise, narrated by a member of the Belfast Titanic Society (£5, daily departures at 12:30, 14:00, 15:30 from Lagan Lookout on Donegall Quay, tel. 028/9033-0844, www.laganboatcompany.com).

Bailey's Historical Belfast Pub Walk—Mixing drinks and history, you'll start at the Crown Dining Room pub and end six pubs later (£6, drinks not included, May–Oct Thu at 19:00, Sat at 16:00, 2 hrs, book in advance, pub above Crown Liquor Saloon on 46 Great Victoria Street, across from Hotel Europa, tel. 028/9268-3665, Judy Crawford).

SIGHTS

Catholic and Protestant Neighborhoods

It will be a happy day when the sectarian neighborhoods of Belfast have nothing to be sectarian about. For a look at a couple of the original home bases of the Troubles, explore the working-class neighborhoods of the Catholic Falls Road and the Protestant Shankill Road or Sandy Row.

You can get tours of Falls Road or Shankill Road (see listings below), but rarely are both combined in one tour. Ken Harper is part of a new breed of Belfast taxi drivers who will give you an insightful private tour of both (£25 minimum or £7.50 per person for a 90-min tour, tel. 028/9074-2711, mobile 0771-175-7178).

▲▲**Falls Road**—At the intersection of Castle and King Streets, you'll find the Castle Junction Car Park. This multistory parking garage's basement (entrance on King Street) is filled with old black

cabs—and the only Irish-language signs in downtown Belfast. These shared black cabs efficiently shuttle residents from outlying neighborhoods up and down the Falls Road and to the city center. This service originated more than 30 years ago at the beginning of the Troubles, when locals would hijack

city buses and use them as barricades in the street fighting. When bus service was discontinued, local paramilitary groups established the shared taxi service. Any cab goes up the Falls Road, past Sinn Fein headquarters and lots of murals, to the Milltown Cemetery (£2, sit in front and talk to the cabbie). Hop in and out. Easy-to-flag-down cabs run every minute or so in each direction on the Falls Road. Twenty trained cabbies do one-hour tours (£22.50/1–3 people, £25/4–6 people, £10 per additional hour, cheap for a small group of up to 6 riders, tel. 028/9031-5777, www.wbta.net).

The Sinn Fein office and bookstore are near the bottom of Falls Road. The bookstore is worth a look. Page through books featuring color photos of the political murals that decorate the buildings. Money raised here supports families of imprisoned IRA members.

A sad, corrugated structure called the Peace Wall runs a block or so north of Falls Road, separating the Catholics from the Protestants in the Shankill Road area.

At the Milltown Cemetery, walk past all the Gaelic crosses down to the far right-hand corner (closest to the highway), where the IRA Roll of Honor is set apart from the thousands of other graves by little green railings. They are treated like fallen soldiers. Notice the memorial to Bobby Sands and nine other hunger strikers. They starved themselves to death in the nearby Maze prison in 1981, protesting for political prisoner status as opposed to terrorist criminal treatment. The prison closed in the fall of 2000.

Shankill Road and Sandy Row—You can ride a shared black cab through the Protestant Shankill Road area (departing from intersection of Peters Hill and Gardiner Street, not well-marked, but watch where cabs circle and pick up locals; 1-hour tour-£20/1–2 people, £30/3–6 people, tel. 028/9032-8775).

An easier (and cheaper) way to get a dose of the Unionist side is to walk Sandy Row. From Hotel Europa, walk a block down Glengall Street, then turn left for a 10-minute walk along a working-class Protestant street. A stop in the Unionist memorabilia shop, a pub, or one of the many cheap eateries here may give you an opportunity to talk to a local. You'll see murals filled with Unionist symbolism. The mural of William of Orange's victory over the Catholic King James II (Battle of the Boyne, 1690) thrills Unionist hearts. (From the south end of Sandy Row, it's a 10-min walk to the Ulster Museum, below.)

More Sights in Belfast

▲▲**City Hall**—This grand structure, with its 173-foot-tall copper dome, dominates the town center. Built between 1898 and 1906, with its statue of Queen Victoria scowling down Belfast's main drag, and the Union Jack flapping behind her, it's a stirring sight. In the garden, you'll find memorials to the *Titanic* and the landing of the U.S. Expeditionary Force in 1942—the first stop en route to Berlin. Take the free 45-minute tour (June–Sept usually Mon–Fri at 11:00, 14:00, and 15:00, Sat only at 14:30; Oct–May Mon–Sat 14:30 only; never on Sun; for Sat

tours, enter back of building—south side, otherwise enter front; call to check schedule and to reserve, tel. 028/9027-0456). The tour gives you a rundown on city government and an explanation of the decor that makes this an Ulster political hall of fame. Queen Victoria and King Edward VII look down on city council meetings. The 1613 original charter of Belfast granted by James I is on display. Its

Central Belfast

(T) - Taxi Stand

❶ Hotel Europa
❷ Jurys Inn
❸ Granada Travelodge
❹ Morning Star Pub & Restaurant
❺ Kelly's Cellars Pub
❻ Crown Liquor Saloon & Dining Room
❼ Bewley's
❽ Caffè Metz
❾ Marks & Spencer
❿ Tesco Supermarket
⓫ Falls Road Taxi Garage
⓬ Shankill Road Taxi Queue

Great Hall—bombed by the Germans in 1941—looks as great as it did the day it was made.

If you can't manage a tour, at least step inside, admire the marble swirl staircase, and drop into the "What's On in Belfast" room, just inside the front door.

Linen Hall Library—Across the street from City Hall, the 200-year-old Linen Hall Library welcomes guests. It has a fine, hardbound ambience, a coffee shop, and a royal newspaper reading room.

Described as "Ulster's attic," the library takes pride in being a neutral space, where anyone trying to make sense of the sectarian conflict can view the Troubled Images, a historical collection of engrossing political posters (Mon–Fri 9:30–17:30, Sat 9:30–16:00, closed Sun, get free visitor's pass at entrance on Fountain Street, 17 Donegall Square North, tel. 028/9032-1707, www.linenhall.com).

Golden Mile—This is the overstated nickname of Belfast's liveliest dining and entertainment district, which stretches from the Opera House (Great Victoria Street) to the university (University Road).

The **Grand Opera House**, originally built in 1895, bombed and rebuilt in 1991, and bombed and rebuilt again in 1993, is extravagantly Victorian and *the* place to take in a concert, play, or opera (closed to sightseers, ticket office across street open Mon–Fri 8:30–21:00, Sat 8:30–18:00, closed Sun, tel. 028/9024-1919, www.goh.co.uk). **Hotel Europa**, next door, while considered the most bombed hotel in the world, feels pretty casual (listed under "Sleeping," page 256).

Across the street is the museumlike **Crown Liquor Saloon**. Built in 1849, it's now a part of the National Trust. A wander through its mahogany, glass, and marble interior is a trip back into the day of Queen Victoria (although the privacy provided by the snugs—booths—allows for un-Victorian behavior; Mon–Sat 11:30–24:00, Sun 12:30–23:00; consider a lunch stop, see "Eating," page 257). Upstairs, the Crown Dining Room serves pub grub, is decorated with historic photos, and is the starting point for a pub walk (see "Tours," page 247).

Lagan Lookout Visitors Centre—This center shows off the fruits of the city's £800 million investment in its harbor. The tides of the River Lagan left the town with unsightly mud flats daily. The weir, built in 1994, controls the tides, stabilizing the depth of the harbor. It also doubles as a free pedestrian bridge over the river, affording walkers a fine view of the harbor area, including the big cranes and the new convention center. The visitors center, while mildly entertaining and enthusiastically "interactive," is not worth the £1.50 entry fee (Mon–Fri 11:00–17:00, Sat 12:00–17:00, Sun 14:00–17:00, in winter shorter hours and closed Mon, 5-min walk from TI, just past tipsy 4-feet-off-center Albert Clock Tower, tel. 028/9031-5444).

▲**Ulster Museum**—While mediocre by European standards, this is Belfast's one major museum. It's free and pretty painless: Ride the elevator to the top floor and follow the spiraling exhibits downhill; there's a cheery café halfway down. You'll find an interesting *Made* *in Belfast* exhibit just before an arch that proclaims, "Trade is the golden girdle of the globe." The delicately worded history section is given an interesting British slant (such as the implication that the Great Famine of 1845 was caused by the Irish population doubling in 40 years—without a mention of various English contributions to the suffering). After a wander through the *Early Medieval Ireland* exhibit and a peek at a pretty good mummy, top things off with the *Girona* treasure. Soggy bits of gold, silver, leather, and wood were salvaged from the Spanish Armada's shipwrecked *Girona*—lost off the Antrim Coast north of Belfast in 1588 (free, Mon–Fri 10:00–17:00, Sat 13:00–17:00, Sun 14:00–17:00, in Botanic Gardens on Stranhills Road, south of downtown, tel. 028/9038-3048, www.magni.org.uk).

▲**Botanic Gardens**—This is the backyard of Queen's University. On a sunny day, you couldn't imagine a more relaxing park setting. On a cold day, step into the Tropical Ravine for a jungle of heat and humidity. Take a quick walk through the Palm House, reminiscent of the one in London's Kew Gardens, but smaller (free, Mon–Fri 10:00–12:00 & 13:00–17:00, Sat–Sun 13:00–17:00, less in winter, tel. 028/9032-4902). The Ulster Museum is on the grounds.

The Odyssey—This huge millennium project complex offers a food pavilion (with a Hard Rock Café) and **W5**, a science center with stimulating, interactive exhibits for youngsters (adults-£6, kids-£4, Mon–Sat 10:00–18:00, Sun 12:00–18:00; W5 stands for who, what, when, where, why; tel. 028/9046-7833, www.w5online.co.uk). There's also a 12-screen cinema (with IMAX) and a 10,000-seat arena, where the Belfast Giants professional hockey team plays (2 Queen's Quay, 10-min walk from Central Station, tel. 028/9045-1055, www.theodyssey.co.uk).

Near Belfast

▲▲**Ulster Folk and Transport Museum**—This 180-acre, two-museum complex straddles the road and rail at Cultra, midway between Bangor and Belfast (8 miles east of town).

The Folk Museum, an open-air collection of 34 reconstructed buildings from all over the nine counties of Ulster, showcases the region's traditional lifestyles. After wandering through the old-town site (church, print shop, schoolhouse, humble Belfast row house, and so on), you'll head off into the country to nip into cottages, farmhouses, and mills. Most houses are warmed by a wonderful peat fire and a friendly attendant. It can be dull or vibrant, depending on when you visit and your ability to chat with the attendants. Drop a peat brick on the fire.

The Transport Museum (downhill, over the road from the folk section) consists of three buildings. Start at the bottom and trace the evolution of transportation from 7,500 years ago—when people first decided to load an ox—to modern times. The lowest building holds an intriguing section on the sinking of the Belfast-made *Titanic.* In the next two buildings, you roll through the history of bikes, cars, and trains. The car section rumbles from the first car in Ireland (an 1898 Benz), through the "Cortina Culture" of the 1960s, to the local adventures of John DeLorean and a 1981 model of his car.

Cost, Hours, Location: £5 for Folk Museum, £5 for Transport Museum, £6.50 combo-ticket for both, £18 for families; July–Sept Mon–Sat 10:00–18:00, Sun 11:00–18:00; March–June Mon–Fri 10:00–17:00, Sat 10:00–18:00, Sun 11:00–18:00; Oct–Feb closes daily at 16:00. Check the schedule for special events that day (tel. 028/9042-8428, www.magni.org.uk). Allow 3 hours for your visit. Expect lots of walking. Those with a car can drive from one section to the next.

From Belfast, reach **Cultra** by taxi (£10), bus #1 or #2 (2/hr, 30 min from Laganside Bus Centre), or train (£3.70 round-trip, 2/hr, 15 min, from any Belfast train station or from Bangor). Trains and buses stop right in the park, but train service is more dependable. Public transport schedules get skimpy on Saturday and Sunday.

Carrickfergus Castle—Built during the Norman invasion of the late 1100s, this historic castle stands sentry on the shore of Belfast Lough. William of Orange landed here in 1690, when he began his Irish campaign against deposed King James II. These days, the castle feels a bit sanitized and geared toward kids, but it's an easy excursion if you're seeking a castle experience near the city (£3; April–Sept Mon–Sat 10:00– 18:00, Sun 14:00–18:00; Oct– March Mon–Sat 10:00–16:00, Sun 14:00–16:00; last entry 30 min before closing, 20-min train ride from Belfast on line to Larne costs £4.20 round-trip, tel. 028/9335-1273).

SLEEPING

South Belfast

Many of Belfast's best budget beds cluster in a comfortable area just south of the Ulster Museum and the university. Two train stations (Botanic and Adelaide) are nearby, and buses zip down Malone Road every 20 minutes. Any bus on Malone Road goes to Donegall Square East. Taxis, cheap in Belfast, take you downtown for about £3 (your host can call one).

$$$ **Malone Lodge Hotel**, by far the classiest listing in this neighborhood, provides slick, business-class comfort and spacious

South Belfast

TO BELFAST CENTER

200 YARDS
200 METERS

SHAFTESBURY SQUARE

Post

DONEGALL PASS

BOTANIC STATION

DONEGALL ROAD

TO M-1 FREEWAY

CITY HOSPITAL STATION

CROMWELL ROAD

UNIVERSITY STREET

CLARE
CAMDEN
FITZWILLIAM
ELMWOOD
COLLEGE GDNS.
WELLESLEY
WELLINGTON PARK
EGLANTINE AVE.
MALONE AVE.
WINDSOR

QUEEN'S UNIVERSITY

PALM HOUSE

BOTANIC

ULSTER MUSEUM

GARDENS

RIVER LAGAN

TO ④ & ⑪   DCH

❶ Benedicts Hotel
❷ Holiday Inn Express
❸ Malone Lodge Hotel
❹ Malone Guest House
❺ Camera Guest House
❻ Eglantine Guest House
❼ Botanic Lodge B&B

❽ The George B&B
❾ Marine House B&B
❿ Windermere Guest House
⓫ Queen's Elms Halls of Residence
⓬ Belfast Intl. Youth Hostel

⓭ The Ark Hostel
⓮ Cayenne Restaurant
⓯ Maggie May's Rest.
⓰ Bishop's Fish & Chips
⓱ Villa Italia Rest.
⓲ Globe Launderette
⓳ Whistle Launderette

rooms in a charming environment on a quiet, leafy street (Sb-£60–95, Db-£80–100, superior Db-£95–115, weekend deals, elevator, 60 Eglantine Avenue, tel. 028/9038-8000, fax 028/9038-8088, www.malonelodgehotel.com, info@malonelodgehotel.com).

$$ **Camera Guest House** rents nine smoke-free rooms and comes with an airy, hardwood feeling throughout (S-£32–42, Sb-£45–48, Db-£54–60, 44 Wellington Park, tel. 028/9066-0026, fax 028/9066-7856, malonedrumm@hotmail.com, Paul Drumm).

Sleep Code

(£1 = about $1.70; country code: 44, area code: 028)
(To call Belfast from the Republic of Ireland, dial 048 before the local 8-digit number.)
S = Single, **D** = Double/Twin, **T** = Triple, **Q** = Quad, **b** = bathroom, **s** = shower only. Unless otherwise noted, breakfast is included and credit cards are accepted.

To help you easily sort through these listings, I've divided the rooms into three categories, based on the price for a double room with bath:

$$$ **Higher Priced**—Most rooms £80 or more.
$$ **Moderately Priced**—Most rooms between £50–80.
$ **Lower Priced**—Most rooms £50 or less.

$$ Malone Guest House is a classy, stand-alone, Victorian house fronting the busy Malone Road. It's homey and well-run by Mrs. Millar, who rents 13 prim rooms (Sb-£35, Db-£55, Tb-£65, 79 Malone Road, at intersection with Adelaide Park and bus stop, tel. 028/9037-5090, fax 028/9022-3020, maloneguesthouse @maloneroad.fsnet.co.uk).

$ Windermere Guest House has 11 rooms, including several small but pleasant singles, in a large Victorian house (S-£24, Sb-£35, very small D £34, D-£46, Db-£50, T-£54, 60 Wellington Park, tel. 028/9066-2693, fax 028/9068-2218, www.windermereguesthouse .co.uk, hilary-w@ntlworld.com).

$ *Eglantine Avenue B&Bs:* On the same quiet street (Eglantine Avenue), you'll find these three budget choices: **The George B&B** (6 fine, smallish rooms, S-£25, Sb-£35, Db-£45, at #9, tel. & fax 028/9068-3212), **Eglantine Guest House** (8 pleasant rooms, S-£25, D-£44, T-£60, cash only, at #21, tel. 028/9066-7585, fax 028/9066-7585), and the grand old **Marine House B&B** (10 high-ceilinged rooms, Sb-£40, Db-£50, Tb-£75, Qb-£80, at #30, tel. & fax 028/9066-2828, www.marineguesthouse3star.com, marine30@utvinternet.co.uk).

$ Botanic Lodge rents 16 decent rooms on a lively but stylish street, with lots of fun eateries nearby (S-£25, Sb-£35, D-£40, Db-£45, 87 Botanic Avenue, 10-min walk to City Hall, tel. & fax 028/9032-7682).

Hotels

Belfast is more of a business town than a tourist town, so business-class room rates are lower or soft on weekends.

$$$ **Hotel Europa** is Belfast's landmark hotel—fancy, comfortable, and central—with four stars and good weekend rates. Modern yet elegant, this place was former President Clinton's choice when he visited (Db-£100–160 plus £12 breakfast Mon–Thu, Db-£80–110 Fri–Sun—includes breakfast, President Clinton's suite-£395, 5 non-smoking floors, Great Victoria Street, tel. 028/9027-1066, fax 028/9032-7800, www.hastingshotels.com).

$$ **Jurys Inn,** an American-style place that rents its 190 identical modern rooms for one simple price, is perfectly located two blocks from City Hall (up to 3 adults or 2 adults and 2 kids for £78, breakfast-£8 extra per person, 3 non-smoking floors, Fisherwick Place, tel. 028/9053-3500, fax 028/9053-3511, U.S. tel. 800/423-6953, www.jurysdoyle.com, jurysinnbelfast@jurysdoyle.com).

$$ **Granada Travelodge,** quiet and extremely central, is a basic, Jurys-style business hotel with 90 cookie-cutter rooms high on value, low on character (Db-£45–55, continental breakfast-£5, Irish breakfast-£7, a block from Hotel Europa and City Hall at 15 Brunswick Street, tel. 08700-850-950 or 028/9033-3555, fax 028/9023-2999, www.travelodge.co.uk).

$$ **Belfast Holiday Inn Express,** not as central as the above hotels, offers the same basic formula (Db-£59–69, kids free, includes continental breakfast, non-smoking floors, elevator, 106A University Street, by Botanic Station, tel. 028/9031-1909, fax 028/9031-1910, exhi-belfast.com, mail@exhi-belfast.com).

$$ **Benedicts Hotel** has a local feel in a good location at the northern fringe of the Queen's University district, with a popular bar that's a maze of polished wood (Sb-£50–60, Db-£60–70, Tb-£95–100, elevator, 7-21 Bradbury Place, tel. 028/9059-1999, fax 028/9059-1990, www.benedictshotel.co.uk, info@benedictshotel.co.uk).

Hostels and Dorms

$ **Belfast International City Hostel**, providing the best value among Belfast's hostels, is big and creatively run, offering single and double rooms, along with dorms. It's located near the Botanic train station, in the heart of the lively university district and close to the center. Features include free lockers, left luggage, Internet access, videos, kitchen, self-serve laundry (£3), cheap breakfast-only cafeteria, elevator, 24-hour reception, and no curfew (beds in 6-bed dorm-£8.50, beds in quad-£10, S-£17, D-£26, 22-32 Donegall Road, tel. 028/9031-5435, fax 028/9043-9699, www.hini.org.uk, info@hini .org.uk). Paul, the manager of the hostel, is a veritable TI, with a passion for his work. The hostel is the starting point for Mini-Coach Tours (see "Tours," page 247).

$ **The Ark**, a smaller, hipper, more youthful and easygoing hostel, is in the university district near the Botanic train station (beds in 4-bed dorms: Sun–Thu-£9.50, Fri–Sat-£10; D-£36, T-£42, laundry-£3, kitchen, 18 University Street, tel. 028/9032-9626, fax 028/9032-9647, www.arkhostel.com, info@arkhostel.com).

$ Queen's Elms Halls of Residence is a big, brick Queen's University dorm renting 300 basic, institutional rooms (mainly singles) to travelers during summer break. Singles should book in advance and ask for a "self-catering room" to snare a spot in the newer building (mid-June–early Sept only, S-£13.50, Sb-£18.50, D-£23, cheaper for students, coin-op laundry, self-serve kitchen; reception building is 50 yards down entry street, marked Elms Village on low brick wall, 78 Malone Road; tel. 028/9097-4525, fax 028/9097-4524, www.qub.ac.uk, qehor@qub.ac.uk).

EATING

Downtown

If it's £6 pub grub you want, consider these places. The **Morning Star** is woody and elegant (daily 12:00–22:00, restaurant upstairs, 17 Pottinger's Entry, tel. 028/9023-5986). The very Irish **Kelly's Cellars** is 300 years old and hard to find, but worth it (Mon–Wed 11:30–20:00, Thu–Sat 11:30–24:00, closed Sun, live traditional music Fri–Sat nights and Sat at 15:30, restaurant upstairs Mon–Sat 12:00–18:00, 32 Bank Street, behind Tesco supermarket, tel. 028/9024-2628). The small, antique **Crown Liquor Saloon** (see page 247) has a mesmerizing mishmash of mosaics and shareable snugs—booths—topped with a smoky tin ceiling (Mon–Sat lunch only 12:00–15:00, closed Sun, 46 Great Victoria Street, across from Hotel Europa, tel. 028/9027-9901). The **Crown Dining Room** upstairs offers dependable £7–13 meals (Mon–Sat 12:00–21:00, closed Sun, tel. 028/9027-9901, use entry on Amelia Street when the Crown is closed).

For cafés, choose among the many popular eateries in the streets north of Donegall Square. **Bewley's**, popular in Ireland, offers a good-value cafeteria, with seating under a conservatory-style roof (Mon–Sat 8:00–17:30, Thu until 19:00, closed Sun, north end of Donegall's Arcade); to save money, skip the coffee house with table service and choose the cafeteria section instead. **Caffè Metz** has a sleek, light-wood design and £6 meals, including salads (Mon–Sat 9:00–17:00, closed Sun, 12 Queen Street, at intersection with College Street, next door to U.S. Embassy, tel. 028/9024-9484).

Marks & Spencer has a coffee shop serving skinny lattes, and a supermarket in its basement (Mon–Sat 8:30–18:00, Thu until 21:00, Sun 13:00–18:00, WCs on 2nd floor, Donegall Place, a block north of Donegall Square). **Tesco**, another supermarket, is a block north of M&S and two blocks north of Donegall Square (Mon–Sat 8:00–19:00, Thu until 21:00, Sun 13:00–17:00, Royal Avenue and Bank Street). Picnic on the City Hall green.

Near Shaftesbury Square and Botanic Station

Cayenne is a trendy yet friendly restaurant refuge hiding behind Belfast's most understated exterior. It's your best bet for gourmet food—innovative global cuisine—without a snobby attitude (£12–22 meals, Mon–Fri 12:00–14:30 & 18:00–22:00, Sat 18:00–23:00, Sun 17:00–21:00, reservations a good idea on weekends, Shaftesbury Square at 7 Ascot House, look for plain, gray, blocky slab front, tel. 028/9033-1532).

Maggie May's serves hearty, simple, cheap meals (£4–8, Mon–Sat 8:00–22:30, Sun 10:00–22:30, 50 Botanic Avenue, 1 block south of Botanic Station, tel. 028/9032-2662).

Bishop's is the locals' choice for fish-and-chips (daily 12:00–22:00, pasta and veggie options, classier side has table service, Bradbury Place, just south of Shaftesbury Square, tel. 028/9043-9070).

Villa Italia packs in crowds hungry for linguini and *bistecca*. With its checkered tablecloths and a wood-beamed ceiling draped with grape leaves, it's a little bit of Italy in Belfast (£9–14, Mon–Sat 17:00–23:30, Sun 16:00–22:30, 39 University Road, 3 long blocks south of Shaftesbury Square, at intersection with University Street, tel. 028/9032-8356).

TRANSPORTATION CONNECTIONS

For updated schedules and prices for both trains and buses in Northern Ireland, check with Translink (tel. 028/9066-6630, www.translink.co.uk).

From Belfast by train to: Dublin (8/day, 2 hrs), **Derry** (9/day, 2 hrs), **Larne** (hrly, 1 hr), **Portrush** (9/day, 1.75 hrs). Service is less frequent on Sundays. Train info: tel. 028/9066-6630. In July and August, consider a £6.50 "Day Tracker" ticket, good for all-day train use in Northern Ireland (see page 245).

By bus to: Portrush (5/day, 2 hrs, £8), **Glasgow** (2/day, 5 hrs, £20), **Edinburgh** (2/day, 6 hrs, £25), **London** (2/day, 12 hrs, £46). The Europa Bus Centre is behind Hotel Europa (Ulsterbus tel. 028/9033-7003 for destinations in Scotland and London, tel. 028/9066-6630 for destinations in Northern Ireland).

By plane: Belfast has two airports. Belfast City Airport (www.belfastcityairport.com) is a five-minute taxi ride from town (near the docks), while Belfast International Airport (www.bial.co.uk) is 18 miles west of town, connected by buses from the Europa Bus Centre behind the Europa Hotel. British Airways flies to **Glasgow** (3/day, 45 min, as low as £60 round-trip, British Airways' Belfast office tel. 0845-606-0747, central booking tel. 0345-222-111), and bmi british midland flies to **London's** Heathrow Airport (12/day, £35, tel. 0870-6070-555).

By ferry to Scotland: There are a number of options, ports, and companies. You can sail between Belfast and **Stranraer** on Stena Line ferry (5/day, 1.75-hr crossing, Mon–Thu £17, Fri–Sun £22, tel. 028/9074-7747, www.stenaline

.co.uk), or between Belfast and **Troon** on Seacat (3/day, 2.5-hr crossing, £15–20, also takes cars for £100–150, Troon–Glasgow trains 2/hr, 30 min; easy connections from Glasgow to most anywhere in Britain, British tel. 0870-552-3523, www.seacat.co.uk). P&O Ferry (tel. 0870-2424-777, www.poirishsea.com) goes from **Larne** (20 miles north of Belfast, 1 train/hr, TI tel. 028/2826-0088) to **Cairnryan** (11/day, 1 hr, £25) or to **Troon** (2/day, 2 hrs, £28).

By ferry to England: You can sail overnight from Belfast to **Birkenhead** (10 min from Liverpool)—with dinner and break-fast—for £35 (plus £40 for a cabin that sleeps 4) on North Merchant Ferries (8 hrs, nightly at 22:00, tel. 0870-600-4321, www.norsemerchant.com).

Bangor

(£1 = about $1.70, country code: 44, area code: 028)
To stay in a laid-back seaside hometown—with more comfort per pound—sleep 30 minutes east of Belfast in Bangor (BANG-grr). Formerly a slick Belfast seaside escape, Bangor now has a sleepy and almost residential feeling. But with elegant old homes facing its newly spruced-up harbor, and the lack of even a hint of big-city Belfast, Bangor has appeal. The harbor is a five-minute walk from the train station. Bangor's TI is at 34 Quay Street (July–Aug Mon–Fri 9:00–18:00, Sat 10:00–17:00, Sun 13:00–17:00, June and Sept closes at 17:00 Mon–Fri, Oct–May closed Sun, tel. 028/9127-0069).

Getting to Bangor

Catch the train from Belfast Central to Bangor (2/hr, 30 min, £3.50, go to the end of the line; don't get off at Bangor West), stopping en route at Cultra (Ulster Folk and Transport Museum). The journey gives you a good close-up look at the giant Belfast harbor cranes.

If day-tripping into Belfast from Bangor, get off at Belfast Central (which has a free Rail-Link shuttle bus to the town center, 4/hr, not Sun) or stay on until the Botanic Station for the Ulster Museum, the Golden Mile, and Sandy Row.

SLEEPING AND EATING

$$ Royal Hotel is a fine old place right on the harbor, with good weekend rates for its 50 rooms (Db-£75 weekdays, £65 weekends, view rooms are £10 pricier, 26 Quay Street, tel. 028/9127-1866, fax 028/9146-7810, www.royalhotelbangor.com, info@royalhotelbangor .com). **$ Pierview House B&B** is a chandeliered winner, with three of its five spacious rooms overlooking the sea (Sb-£22.50, D-£35, grand Db-£45, family room, 28 Seacliff Road, tel. 028/9146-3381, osborne1948@aol.com, Andrew Osborne).

For good £7–11 meals, try **Lord Nelson Bistro** (daily 12:00–21:30, in the Marine Court Hotel facing harbor, 18–20 Quay Street). The bar next door at the **Royal Hotel** serves £7 lunches and £8–12 dinners (daily 12:00–14:30 & 17:00–21:00). Consider **Ganges** for Indian food (daily 12:00–14:00 & 17:30–22:30, 9 Bingham Street, tel. 028/9145-3030).

ANTRIM COAST and PORTRUSH

The Antrim Coast—the north of Northern Ireland— is one of the most interesting and scenic coastlines in Ireland. Within a few miles of the Portrush train terminal, you can visit some evocative castle ruins, tour the world's oldest whiskey distillery, risk your life on a bouncy rope bridge, and hike along the famous Giant's Causeway.

The homey seaside resort of Portrush used to be known as "the Brighton of the North." While it's seen its best days, it retains the atmosphere and architecture of a genteel, middle-class seaside resort. Portrush fills its peninsula with family-oriented amusements, fun eateries, and B&Bs. Summertime fun-seekers promenade along the tiny harbor and tumble down to the sandy beaches, which extend in sweeping white crescents on either side.

Superficially, it has the appearance of any small British seaside resort, but its history and large population of young people (students from the University of Ulster at Coleraine) give Portrush a little more personality. Along with the usual arcade amusements, there are nightclubs, restaurants, summer theater in the town hall, and convivial pubs that attract customers all the way from Belfast. At the end of the train line and just a few miles from several important sights, it's an ideal base for exploring the highlights of the Antrim Coast.

Planning Your Time
You need a full day to explore the Antrim Coast, so allow two nights in Portrush. An ideal day might lace together Dunluce Castle, Old Bushmills Distillery, and the Giant's Causeway, followed by nine holes on the Portrush pitch-and-putt course.

ORIENTATION

(area code: 028)

Portrush's pleasant and easily walkable town center features sea views in every direction. On one side are the harbor and restaurants, and on the other are Victorian townhouses and vast, salty views. The tip of the peninsula is marked by a lighthouse and a park filled with tennis courts, lawn-bowling greens, and putting greens.

The town is busy with students during the school year. July and August are beach-resort boom time. June and September are laid-back and lazy. Families pack Portrush on Saturdays, and revelers from Belfast crowd its hotels on Saturday nights.

Tourist Information

The TI, more generous and helpful than those in the Republic, is in the big, modern Dunluce Centre (July–Aug daily 9:00–19:00, otherwise Mon–Fri 9:00–17:00, Sat–Sun 12:00–17:00, closed Nov–Feb, tel. 028/7082-3333). Get the North Ireland driving map (£3.50), the free *Stop & Visit* brochure, and a free Belfast map if you're Belfast-bound.

Arrival in Portrush

The train tracks stop at the base of the tiny peninsula that Portrush fills (no baggage check at station). The TI is three long blocks from the train station (follow signs down Eglinton Street and turn left at fire station). All listed B&Bs are within a 10-minute walk of the train station (see "Sleeping," page 269). The bus stop is two blocks from the train station.

Getting Around the Antrim Coast

By Bus: In July and August, a couple of all-day bus passes are available (but one doesn't include Portrush). The bus pass to buy is the £4.20 **Bushmills Open Topper**, connecting Portrush, Old Bushmills Distillery, and the Giant's Causeway every two hours. The £3.50 **Causeway Rambler**—which links Old Bushmills Distillery, the Giant's Causeway Visitors Centre, and the Carrick-a-Rede Rope Bridge hourly—is less convenient, because it doesn't include Portrush in its circuit (to get from Portrush to Bushmills, take a £7 taxi, or those who want to see the Rope Bridge—along with the other sights—could even consider getting both passes). For either pass, pick up a schedule at the TI and buy the ticket from the driver (in Portrush, the Bushmills Open Topper bus stops at Dunluce

Avenue, next to public WC, a 2-min walk from TI). For more info, call Translink (tel. 028/9066-6630, www.translink.co.uk).

By Car: Distances are short, and parking is easy. Don't miss the treacherous yet scenic coastal route down to the Glens of Antrim.

By Bike: The Antrim Coast can be enjoyed by bike, and **MacCool's Hostel** rents them for £5 per day, even if you're not staying at the hostel (see "Sleeping," page 270).

By Taxi: Groups (up to 4) go reasonably by taxi, which costs only £9 from Portrush to the Giant's Causeway. A couple of companies to try are **Causeway Coast Taxi** (tel. 028/7082-3421) and **North West Taxi** (tel. 028/7082-4446).

TOURS

Awakin Causeway Quest Tour—This 90-minute bus tour takes you to viewpoints for Antrim Coast sights (Giant's Causeway, Carrick-a-Rede Rope Bridge, Dunseverick Castle, Fair Head, Whitepark Bay, and Ballycastle), but without time to explore them. Interactive onboard audio-visual displays flesh out the local history, making this a quick rainy option for non-hikers (£15, June–Aug departs Portrush TI once per day at 9:15; otherwise most tours depart from Giant's Causeway: 10:00, 12:00, 14:00, 16:00; you can take a taxi between Causeway and Portrush; book tour in advance, tel. 028/2073-0364, www.causewayquest.com).

SIGHTS AND ACTIVITIES

Portrush
Barry's Old Time Amusement Arcade—This is a fine chance to see Northern Ireland at play (open weekends and summer only). Just below the train station on the harbor, it's filled with candy floss (cotton candy) and little kids learning the art of one-armed bandits, 2p at a time. Get £1 worth of 2p coins from the machine, and go wild (July–Aug daily 13:00–22:30, May–June Sat–Sun 10:00–18:00).

Pitch-and-Putt at the Royal Portrush Golf Course—Irish courses, like those in Scotland, are highly sought after for their lush but dry greens in glorious settings. While serious golfers can get a tee time at the Royal Portrush (green fees Mon–Fri-£90, Sat–Sun-£110), rookies can get a smaller dose of this wonderful golf setting at the neighboring Skerry 9 Hole Links pitch-and-putt range. You get two clubs and balls for £4.50, and they don't care if you go around twice (daily 8:30–19:30, 10-min walk from station, tel. 028/7082-2311).

Portrush Recreation Grounds—For some easygoing exercise right in town, this well-organized park offers lawn-bowling greens (£3.20/hr with gear), putting greens, tennis courts, a great kids' play

Portrush

1. Peninsula Hotel
2. Comfort Hotel/Counties Café
3. Harbour Heights & Ardenlee B&Bs
4. Belvedere Town House
5. MacCool's Hostel
6. Anvershiel B&B
7. Glenkeen Guest House
8. Pierview B&B
9. Don Giovanni's Restaurant
10. Ramore Wine Bar, Coast Pizza Pasta Bar, Harbour Bistro/Bar & Waterworld
11. Scullery Sandwich Shop
12. Bus Stop

park, and a café (tennis shoes, balls, and rackets can all be rented for a small price; Easter–Sept Mon–Sat 10:00–dusk, Sun 13:00–19:00, tel. 028/7082-4441).

Other major Portrush amusements include the **Dunluce Centre** (kid-oriented fun zone) and **Waterworld** (£4.50, daily 10:00–19:00 Easter–Aug, Sept only 10:00–18:00 on weekends, pool, waterslides, bowling, wedged between Harbour Bistro/Bar and Ramore Wine Bar, tel. 028/7082-2001).

Antrim Coast

▲Dunluce Castle—These romantic ruins, perched dramatically on the edge of a rocky headland, pay testimony to this region's turbulent past. During the Middle Ages, the castle resisted several sieges. But on a stormy night in 1639, dinner was interrupted as half of the kitchen fell into the sea, taking the servants with it. That was the last straw for the lady of the castle. The

countess of Antrim packed up and moved inland, and the castle "began its slow submission to the forces of nature." While it's one of the largest castles in Northern Ireland and is beautifully situated, there's precious little to see among its broken walls.

The 16th-century expansion of the castle was financed by the salvaging of a shipwreck. In 1588, the Spanish Armada's *Girona* sank on her way home after an aborted mission against England, laden with sailors and the valuables of three abandoned sister ships. More than 1,300 drowned, and only five washed ashore. (The shipwreck was excavated in 1967, and a bounty of golden odds and silver ends wound up in Belfast's Ulster Museum—see page 251.)

Castle admission includes an impromptu guided tour of the ruins that's interesting for its effort to defend the notion of "Ulster, a place apart—facing Scotland, cut off from the rest of Ireland by dense forests and mountains..." (£2; April–Sept Mon–Sat 10:00–18:00, Sun 14:00–18:00; winter Mon–Sat 10:00–16:00, shorter hours Sun; last entry 30 minutes before closing, tel. 028/2073-1938).

▲▲Old Bushmills Distillery—Bushmills claims to be the world's oldest distillery. Though King James I (of Bible fame) only granted its license to distill "Aqua Vitae" in 1608, whiskey has been made here since the 13th century. Distillery tours waft you through the process, making it clear that Irish whiskey is triple distilled—and therefore smoother than Scotch whisky (distilled merely twice and minus the "e"). The 45-minute tour starts with the mash pit, which is filled with a porridge that eventually becomes whiskey. (The leftovers of that porridge are fed to the county's particularly happy cows.) You'll see thousands of oak casks—the kind used for Spanish sherry—filled with aging whiskey. The finale, of course, is the tasting in the 1608 Bar—the former malt barn. When your guide asks for a tasting volunteer, raise your hand quick and strong. Four volunteers per tour get to taste test eight different whiskeys (Irish versus Scotch and bourbon). Everyone else gets a single glass of his or her choice. Non-whiskey enthusiasts might enjoy a cinnamon-and-cloves hot toddy. To see the distillery at its lively best, visit when the

Antrim Coast

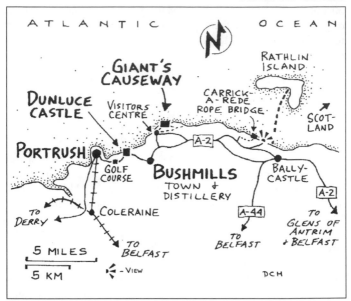

100 workers are manning the machinery—Monday morning through Friday noon (weekend tours see a still still). Tours are limited to 35 people and book up. In summer, call in your name to get a tour time before you arrive (£5, April–Oct daily, tours are on the half hour from 9:30, last tour at 16:00, Sun from 12:00; Nov–March daily at 10:30, 11:30, 13:30, 14:30, and 15:30; tel. 028/2073-1521). You can get a decent lunch in the tasting room after your tour. The distillery is signposted a quarter mile from Bushmills town center.

For an overnight, consider **Valley View Farm B&B** (Sb-£25–28, Db-£40–44, 6a Ballyclough Road, 4 miles south of Bushmills, tel. 028/2074-1608, fax 028/2074-2739, www.valleyviewbushmills.com, valerie.mcfall@btinternet.com).

▲▲**Giant's Causeway**—This four-mile-long stretch of coastline is famous for its bizarre basalt columns. The shore is covered with hexagonal pillars that stick up at various heights. It's as if the earth were offering God his choice of 37,000 six-sided cigarettes.

Geologists claim the Giant's Causeway was formed by volcanic eruptions 60 million years ago. As the lava surface cooled, it contracted and cracked into hexagonal shapes. As the layer of hardened but alligatored rock settled, it broke into its many stair-like steps.

In actuality, the Giant's Causeway was made by a giant Ulster warrior named Finn MacCool, who wanted to reach his love on the Scottish island of Staffa. Way back then, the causeway stretched to Scotland, connecting the two lands. Today, while the foundation has settled, the formation still extends undersea to Staffa, just off the Scottish coast. Finn's causeway was ruined (into today's "remnant of chaos") by a rival giant. As the rival fled from ferocious Finn back to his Scottish homeland, he ripped up the causeway so Finn couldn't chase him.

For cute variations on the Finn story, as well as details on the ridiculous theories of modern geologists, start your visit in the Visitors Centre. The real information is on the walls of the exhibition, while a video gives a worthwhile history of the Giant's Causeway, with a regional overview (£1, 4/hr, 12 min). A gift shop and cafeteria are standing by.

A minibus (70p each way, 4/hr) zips tired tourists a half mile directly to the Grand Causeway, the highlight of the entire coast.

For a better dose of the Causeway, consider this plan. Follow the high cliff-top trail from the Visitors Centre 10 minutes to a great viewpoint, then five minutes farther to reach the Shepherd's Stairway. Zigzag down to the coast; at the T junction, go 100 yards right to the towering pipes of "the Organ." Then retrace your steps and continue left to the "Giant's Boot" for some photo fun and the dramatic point where the stairs step into the sea. Just beyond that, at the asphalt turnaround, you'll see the bus stop for a lift back to the Visitors Centre. You could walk the entire five-mile Giant's Causeway. The 75p hiking guide points out the highlights named by 18th-century guides (Camel's Back, Giant's Eye, and so on). The causeway is free and always open (Visitors Centre open daily 10:00–17:00, July–Aug until 18:00, £5 to park, tel. 028/2073-1855).

A quaint, narrow, gauge-steam locomotive now connects the Causeway to Bushmills on a two-mile, 15-minute journey. Departures from the Bushmills station (on Ballaghmore Road, 15-min walk from distillery) are on the half hour from 11:30 to 17:30; return trips leave from the Causeway station on the hour, starting from 11:00 to 17:00 (£5 round-trip, £3.50 one-way, runs daily June–Sept, sporadic weekends rest of year, tel. 028/2073-2844 or 028/2073-2594 recorded info, www.giantscausewayrailway.org).

▲▲Carrick-a-Rede Rope Bridge—For 200 years, fishermen have strung a narrow, 80-foot-high bridge (planks strung between wires) across a 65-foot-wide chasm between the mainland and a tiny island.

The Scottish Connection

The Romans called the Irish the "Scoti." When the Scoti crossed the narrow channel and invaded the land of the Picts 1,500 years ago, that region became known as Scotland. Ireland and Scotland were never conquered by the Romans and retained similar clannish Celtic traits. Both share the same Gaelic branch of the linguistic tree.

On clear summer days from Carrick-a-Rede, the island of Mull in Scotland is visible, only 17 miles away. Much closer on the horizon is the boomerang-shaped Rathlin Island, part of Northern Ireland. Rathlin is where Scottish Robert the Bruce (of *Braveheart* fame) retreated in 1307 after defeat at the hands of the English. Legend has it that he hid in a cave on the island, where he observed a spider patiently rebuilding its web each time a breeze knocked it down. Inspired by the spider's perseverance, he gathered his Scottish forces once more and finally defeated the English at the decisive battle of Bannockburn.

Flush with confidence from his victory, Robert the Bruce decided to open up a second front against the English...in Ireland. In 1315, he sent his brother Edward over to enlist their Celtic Irish cousins in an effort to thwart the English. After securing Ireland, Edward hoped to move on and enlist the Welsh, thus cornering

The bridge (not the original) still gives access to the salmon nets that are set during the summer months to catch the fish turning the coast's corner. (The complicated system is described at the gateway.) A pleasant one-mile walk takes 20 minutes from the parking lot to the rope bridge, and the island affords fine views and great seabird-watching, especially during nesting season (£2 trail and bridge fee, pay at hut beside parking lot, April–Sept daily 10:00–18:00, July–Aug until 19:30, gone in winter, parking, tel. 028/2076-9839, www.ntni.org.uk).

If you have a car and a picnic lunch, don't miss the terrific coastal viewpoint rest area one mile steeply uphill and east of Carrick-a-Rede (on B-15 road to Ballycastle). The grassy area, with tables, offers one of the best picnic spots in Northern Ireland (but no WCs). Feast on bird's-eye views of the rope bridge, nearby Rathlin Island, and the not-so-distant Island of Mull in Scotland.

▲Antrim Mountains and Glens—Not particularly high (never more than 1,500 feet), the Antrim Mountains are cut by a series of large glens running northeast to the sea. Glenariff, with its waterfalls (especially the "Mare's Tail"), is the most beautiful of the nine glens.

England with their pan-Celtic nation. But Edward's timing was bad—Ireland was in the midst of a famine. His Scottish troops had to live off the land and began to take food and supplies from the starving Irish. He might also have been trying to destroy Ireland's crops to keep them from being used as a colonial "breadbasket" to feed English troops. The Scots quickly wore out their welcome, and Edward the Bruce was eventually killed in battle near Dundalk in 1318.

This was the first time in history that Ireland was used as a pawn by England's enemies. Ireland was seen as the English Achilles' heel by Spain and France, who later attempted Irish invasions. The English Tudor and Stewart royalty countered these threats in the 15th and 16th centuries by starting the "plantation" of loyal subjects in Ireland. The only successful long-term settlement by the English was here in Northern Ireland, which remains part of the United Kingdom today.

What if Ireland and Scotland had been permanently welded together as a nation 700 years ago? You'll notice the strong Scottish influence in this part of Ireland today when you ask a local a question and he answers, "Aye, a wee bit." The Irish joke that the Scots are just the Irish who couldn't swim.

SLEEPING

Portrush has decent hotels, but its B&Bs seem well-worn. August and Saturday nights can be tight. Otherwise, it's a "you take half a loaf when you can get it" town. Rates vary with the view and season—probe for softness. Each listing faces the sea, though sea views are worth paying for only if you get a bay window. Ask for a big room (some doubles can be very small; twins are bigger). Lounges are invariably grand and have bay-window views. All places listed have lots of stairs, but most are perfectly central and within a few minutes' walk of the train station. Parking is easy.

$$$ **Comfort Hotel**, in the middle of town, is a glitzy, modern, 50-room establishment with a good restaurant (Db-£75–100, breakfast-£7 per person, elevator, 73 Main Street, tel. 028/7082-6100, fax 028/7082-6160, www.comforthotelportrush.com, info@comforthotelportrush.com).

$$ **Peninsula Hotel** is a big place right in the town center, with huge, fresh rooms, modern decor, and comforts. Ask for a room far from its disco, which can be a problem on party nights (Sb-£40–50, Db-£60–80, Tb-£90–105, elevator, 15 Eglinton Street, tel. 028/7082-2293, fax 028/7082-4315, www.peninsulahotel.co.uk, reservations@peninsulahotel.co.uk).

Sleep Code

(£1 = about $1.70, country code: 44, area code: 028)
S = Single, **D** = Double/Twin, **T** = Triple, **Q** = Quad,
b = bathroom, **s** = shower only. Breakfast is included, and credit
cards are accepted unless otherwise noted.

To help you easily sort through these listings, I've divided
the rooms into three categories, based on the price for a standard
double room with bath:

$$$ **Higher Priced**—Most rooms £70 or more.
  $$ **Moderately Priced**—Most rooms between £50–70.
    $ **Lower Priced**—Most rooms £50 or less.

$$ Harbour Heights B&B rents 11 cozy, non-smoking rooms,
some with scenic harbor views (Sb-£35, Db-£60–70, Tb-£80–90,
10 percent discount with cash and this book, 17 Kerr Street, tel.
028/7082-2765, fax 028/7082-2558, www.harbourheightsportrush
.com, info@harbourheightsportrush.com, Ann Rossborough).

$ Pierview B&B, close to the best restaurants, has four com-
fortable, non-smoking rooms with the best breakfast atrium views
in town, overlooking the quaint harbor (Sb-£25–30, Db-£40–45,
Tb-£55–60, cash only, parking, 53 Kerr Street, tel. 028/7082-3234,
Adeline Chambers).

$ Belvedere Town House, a stately place on the quiet side of
town, with 14 spacious, relatively well-appointed rooms, is the best
value in town (S-£20–25, Db-£40–50, 5 percent extra if you
pay with a credit card, farthest from station but with easy parking—
ideal for drivers, at 15 Lansdowne Crescent, tel. 028/7082-2771,
belvederetownhouse@hotmail.com, Thomas Burns).

$ Ardenlee B&B has six bigger-than-average rooms and a fine
location near the train station (Db-£45–50, Tb-£60–75, Qb-
£85–90, cash only, 10 percent discount with this book through 2005,
19 Kerr Street, tel. 028/7082-2639, www.ardenleehouse.co.uk,
Rosy Turnbull).

$ MacCool's Portrush Independent Hostel is a friendly and
laid-back place enthusiastically run by Ailish Laughlin, with 18 beds
in four rooms (6- and 8-bed dorm rooms, £10 per bed, D-£24, cash
only, one all-female room, lockers, guests' kitchen, game-stocked
lounge, non-smoking, Internet access-£1.50/30 min, handy laundry
service-£3/load, bike hire-£5/day, surfing lessons-£20/2 hrs, 35
Causeway Street, tel. 028/7082-4845, www.portrush-hostel.com,
portrushhostel@hotmail.com).

$ Anvershiel B&B, with six non-smoking rooms, is a five-
minute walk from the train station (Sb-£30, Db-£45, Tb-£67.50, £5

discount per room for 2-night stays and cash, 10 percent discount with cash and this book through 2005, easy parking, 16 Coleraine Road, tel. 028/7082-3861, www.anvershiel.co.uk, enquiries@anvershiel .co.uk, Victor and Erna Bow). Down the same road is **$ Glenkeen Guest House** (10 rooms, Sb-£32, Db-£50, Tb-£57, some smoke-free rooms, plenty of parking, 59 Coleraine Road, 10-min walk from station, tel. & fax 028/7082-2279, www.glenkeenguesthouse.co.uk, glenkeen@btinternet.com, Mrs. Little).

EATING

Being close to a university town (Coleraine) and a get-away-from-Belfast town, Portrush has more than enough chip joints. Eglinton Street is lined with cheap and cheery eateries. **The Scullery** makes £2 sandwiches and healthy wraps to take away and enjoy by the beach—or on an Antrim Coast picnic (July–Aug daily 8:30–20:30, Sept–May until 17:00, 4 Eglinton Lane, tel. 028/7082-1000).

Counties Café serves dependable meals at reasonable prices (£8–14 meals, daily 7:30–21:00, on ground floor of Comfort Hotel, tel. 028/7082-6100).

For Italian food, try candlelit **Don Giovanni's** (£7–13 pasta dishes, daily 17:30–23:00, tel. 028/7082-5516).

The following four restaurants, located within 50 yards of each other (all under the same ownership and overlooking the harbor on Harbour Road), get just about everyone's vote for the best food values in town.

Sharing a building with the Coast Pizza Pasta Bar, the salty, modern, and much loved **Ramore Wine Bar** is upstairs, bursting with happy eaters. They're enjoying the most inviting menu I've seen in Ireland, featuring huge £7–14 meals ranging from steaks to vegetarian food. Share a decadent Banofee (banana toffee) pie with a friend for dessert (daily 12:15–14:15 & 17:00–22:00, tel. 028/7082-4313). Downstairs is the energetic **Coast Pizza Pasta Bar,** with good red wine (from £2/glass) as a welcome break after all the Guinness. Come early for a table, or sit at the bar (July–Aug Mon–Thu 17:00–22:00, Fri–Sat 16:00–22:30, Sun 15:00–21:30, Sept–June closed Mon–Tue, tel. 028/7082-3311).

The **Harbour Bistro** (run by the Ramore folks, with the same winning formula) offers a more subdued, darker, bistro ambience than the wine bar and meals for a few pounds more (£6 lunches Fri–Sun 12:30–14:30, £8–15 dinners daily 17:00–22:00, tel. 028/7082-2430).

The adjoining **Harbour Bar** has an old-fashioned pub downstairs and a plush, overstuffed lounge with a toasty fire and grand views upstairs—a great place to enjoy a drink.

TRANSPORTATION CONNECTIONS

From Portrush by train to: Coleraine (2/hr, 12 min, sparse on Sunday morning), **Belfast** (9/day, 4/Sun, 2 hrs, transfer in Coleraine), **Dublin** (7/day, 2/Sun, 5 hrs, transfer in Coleraine). In July and August, consider a £6.50 "Day Tracker" ticket, good for all-day train use in Northern Ireland (see page 245).

By bus to: Belfast (along scenic coast, 7/day, 2.5 hrs), **Dublin** (1/day, 5.5 hrs).

Useful updated schedules and prices for both trains and buses in Northern Ireland can be obtained from **Translink** (tel. 028/9066-6630, www.translink.co.uk).

DERRY and COUNTY DONEGAL

The town of Derry (or Londonderry to Unionists) is the mecca of Ulster Unionism. When Ireland was divvied up, the Foyle River was the logical border between the North and the Republic. But, for sentimental and economic reasons, the North kept Derry, which is on the Republic's side of the river. Consequently, this predominantly Catholic city has been much contested throughout the Troubles, though the conflict is only one dimension of Derry.

County Donegal, to the west of Derry, is about as far-flung as Ireland gets. A forgotten economic backwater (part of the Republic but riding piggyback on the North), it lacks blockbuster museums or sights. But a visit here is more about the journey, and adventurous drivers—a car is a must—will be rewarded with a time-capsule peek into old Irish ways and uncompromisingly beautiful scenery.

Planning Your Time

Travelers heading north from Westport or Galway should get an early start (the town of Donegal makes a good lunch stop), so they can spend a couple of hours in Derry and see the essentials. In Derry, visit the Tower Museum and catch some views from the town wall before continuing on to Portrush for the night.

With more time, spend the night in Derry, so you can see the powerful murals of the Bogside and take a walking tour around the walls to gain an appreciation of this underrated city. With two nights in Derry, consider heading back over the border into the Republic to enjoy a scenic driving loop through part of remote County Donegal (see page 290).

Derry

This pivotal city has a more diverse history and a prettier setting than Belfast. And with a quarter the population, it feels more manageable to visitors.

ORIENTATION

(area code: 028)

The Foyle River flows north, slicing Derry into eastern and western chunks. The old town walls and worthwhile sights are all on the west side. Waterloo Place and the adjacent Guildhall Square, just outside the north corner of the old city walls, are the pedestrian hubs of city activity. The Strand Road area extending north from Waterloo Place makes a comfortable home base, with the majority of lodging and restaurant suggestions within a block or two on either side. The Diamond and its War Memorial statue mark the heart of the old city within the walls.

Tourist Information

The TI sits on the riverfront and has a room-finding service, books walking tours, and gives out free city maps (Mon–Fri 9:00–19:00, Sat 10:00–18:00, Sun 10:00–17:00, 44 Foyle Street, tel. 028/7126-7284, www.derryvisitor.com).

Arrival in Derry

Derry's little end-of-the-line train station is next to the river on the east side of town (15-min walk across Craigavon Bridge from the TI or £3 taxi ride to Guildhall Square), with service to Portrush, Belfast, and Dublin. The Ulsterbus station is a couple of minutes' walk south of Guildhall Square.

Derry is compact enough to see on foot, so drivers stopping for a few hours can park at the Foyleside parking garage, across from the TI (£0.80/hr, £2.20/4 hrs, Mon–Tue 8:00–19:00, Wed–Fri 8:00–22:00, Sat 8:00–20:00, Sun 12:00–19:00, tel. 028/7137-7575). Drivers staying overnight can ask about parking at their B&B, or try the Quayside parking garage behind the Travelodge (£0.60/hr, £2/4 hrs, £1/hr after first 6 hours, Mon–Fri 8:00–21:30, Sat 8:00–20:30, Sun 12:30–18:30).

Helpful Hints

Phone Tips: To call the Republic of Ireland from Northern Ireland, dial 00-353, then the area code without its initial 0, then the local number. To call Northern Ireland from the Republic of Ireland, dial 048, then the local eight-digit number.

Banking: Northern Bank, First Trust Bank, Ulster Bank, and Bank of Ireland cluster around Waterloo Place and Guildhall Square (all Mon–Fri 9:30–16:30).

Internet Access: Bean-there.com Internet Café is on the Diamond, in the center of the old walled city (£2.50/30 min, Mon–Fri 8:30–17:30, Sat 10:00–17:30, Sun 10:00–17:00, tel. 028/7128-1303).

Post Office: The main post office is just off Waterloo Place behind the Guild Hall (Mon–Fri 9:00–17:30, Sat 9:00–12:30, closed Sun, Custom House Street).

Laundry: City Clean can do a load of laundry for £6 (drop off in morning to pick up later that day, Mon–Sat 9:00–17:30, closed Sun, Waterloo Place, tel. 028/7136-1962).

Taxi: Try Maiden City Taxi (tel. 028/7126-1666) or Sackville Taxi (tel. 028/7135-4442).

TOURS

Walking Tours—You have several options for tours, each including a section of the Derry Walls. The TI runs solid 90-minute tours with different focuses on certain afternoons: Monday-Siege, Wednesday-Emigration, and Friday-Living History of the Troubles (£4, July–Aug Mon–Fri 11:15 and 15:15, Sept–June Mon–Fri at 14:30 only, tel. 028/7126-7284).

Martin McCrossan and his staff lead 60-minute tours of the city, departing from 11 Carlisle Road just below Ferryquay Gate (£4, Mon–Sat 10:00, 12:00, 14:00; call to confirm schedule, tel. 028/7127-1996 or mobile 077-1293-7997, www.irishtourguides.com).

Stephen McPhilemy leads private tours of his hometown, Belfast, and the North Coast—when he's not on the road guiding tours for Rick Steves several months a year (tel. 028/7130-9051, mobile 078-0101-1027, nirelandtours@btinternet.com).

The **Bogside Artists**, famous for their dramatic wall mural painting, do informal hour-long walks in the Bogside, explaining the inspiration for their memorable works (£3, check with TI or call for current schedule, walks depart from their studio behind Bogside Inn pub, tel. 028/7137-3842, www.bogsideartists.com).

Bus Tours—The double-decker bus tours by **City Sightseeing** are especially good on a rainy day. You'll be driven around the city in an hour-long loop that covers the Guild Hall, city walls, political wall murals (both Bogside and Waterside), cathedrals, and shirt factories. Unlike many hop-on, hop-off bus tours in other cities, with City Sightseeing, your ticket is only good for one lap around the loop, and you're not allowed to get on and off en route (£6—pay driver, May–Sept daily at 10:00, 12:00, 14:00, 16:00; departs from in front of TI or beside the Guild Hall; mobile 078-0895-7330 or 078-1218-8607).

Derry

1 Travelodge
2 Tower Hotel
3 Merchant's House B&B
4 Saddler's House B&B
5 Palace Hostel
6 Mandarin Palace Restaurant
7 Exchange Restaurant & Wine Bar
8 Fitzroy's Restaurant
9 Mange 2 Restaurant
10 Leprechaun Restaurant & Bakery
11 Austins Department Store Café
12 Peadar O'Donnell's Pub
13 Internet Café
14 Verbal Arts Centre
15 Craft Village
16 Bogside Inn Pub

SELF-GUIDED WALKS

Though calm today, Derry is marked by years of tumultuous conflict. These two walks will increase your understanding of the town's history. The first walk, starting at the old city walls and ending at the Anglican Cathedral, focuses on Derry's early days. The second tour (page 280) helps you easily find the city's compelling murals, which document the time of the Troubles. These tours can be done separately or linked, depending on your time.

Walk the Walls

Squatting determinedly in the city center, the old city walls of Derry (built 1613–1618 and still intact, except for wider gates to handle modern vehicles) hold an almost mythic place in Irish history.

It was here in 1688 that a group of brave apprentice boys, many of whom had been shipped to Londonderry as orphans after the great fire of London in 1666, took their stand. They slammed the city gates shut in the face of the approaching Catholic forces of deposed King James II. With this act, the boys galvanized the city's indecisive Protestant defenders inside the walls.

Months of negotiations and a grinding 105-day siege followed, during which a third of the 20,000 refugees and defenders crammed into the city perished. The siege was finally broken in 1689, when supply ships broke through a boom stretched across the Foyle River. The sacrifice and defiant survival of the city turned the tide in favor of newly crowned Protestant King William of Orange, who arrived in Ireland soon after and defeated James at the pivotal Battle of the Boyne.

To fully appreciate the walls, take a walk on top of them (free and open from dawn to dusk). Almost 20 feet high and at least as thick, the walls form a mile-long oval loop that you can cover in less than an hour. But the most interesting section is the half circuit facing away from the river, starting at Magazine Gate (stairs face the Tower Museum inside the walls) and finishing at Bishop's Gate.

From Magazine Gate, walk the wall as it heads uphill, snaking along the earth's contours like a mini–Great Wall of China. In the row of buildings on the left (just before crossing over Castle Gate), you'll see an arch entry into the **Craft Village**, an alley lined with a cluster of cute shops that showcase the recent economic rejuvenation of Derry (Mon–Sat 9:30–17:30, closed Sun).

After crossing over Butcher Gate, you'll pass a large, square pedestal on the right that once supported a column in honor of Governor George Walker, the commander of the defenders during

Derry's History

Once an island in the Foyle River, Derry (from *daire,* Irish for "oak grove") was chosen by St. Colmcille around A.D. 546 for a monastic settlement. He later banished himself to the island of Iona in Scotland out of remorse for sparking a bloody battle over the rights to a holy manuscript he had secretly copied.

A thousand years later, after defeating the last powerful Ulster-based Gaelic chieftains in the battle of Kinsale in 1601, the English took advantage of the power vacuum to begin the "plantation" of Ulster with loyal Protestant subjects imported from Scotland and England. The native Irish were displaced to less desirable rocky or boggy lands (sowing the seeds of the modern-day Troubles). A dozen wealthy London guilds took on Derry as an investment, and changed its name to Londonderry. They built the last great walled city in Ireland to protect their investment from the surrounding hostile Irish locals. The walls proved their worth in 1688–1689, when the town's Protestant defenders, loyal to King William of Orange, withstood a prolonged siege by the forces of Catholic King James II. "No surrender" is still a passionate rallying cry among Ulster Unionists determined to remain part of the United Kingdom.

The town became a major port of emigration to the New World in the early 1800s. Then, when the Industrial Revolution provided a steam-powered sewing factory, the city developed a thriving shirtmaking industry, employing mostly Catholic women who had honed their skills in rural County Donegal in what was initially a cottage industry. Although Belfast grew larger and wealthier, Unionists cherished Londonderry, and, in 1921, insisted

the famous siege. In 1973, the IRA blew up the column, which had 105 steps to the top (one for each day of the siege).

Ahead on the left at the corner of Society Street is the **Apprentice Boys Memorial Hall** (built 1873), which houses the private lodge and meeting rooms of this all-male, Protestant organization dedicated to the memory of the original 13 apprentice boys. The end of the siege is celebrated each year with a controversial march atop the walls by the modern-day Apprentice Boys Society on the Saturday closest to the August 12 anniversary date. These walls are considered sacred ground for devout Unionists, who claim that many who died during the famous siege were buried within the battered walls for lack of space. A few more steps take you past the small Anglican **St. Augustine Chapel**, set in a pretty graveyard, where some believe the original 6th-century monastery of St. Colmcille stood.

As you walk ahead, it's hard to miss the British Army surveillance tower on the left. It's situated here for the bird's-eye view it that it be included in Northern Ireland when it was partitioned from the new Irish Free State (later to become the Republic of Ireland). A bit of gerrymandering ensured that the Unionist Protestant minority maintained control of the city, despite the Nationalist Catholic majority.

Londonderry was a key escort base for U.S. convoys headed for Britain in World War II, and dozens of German U-boats were instructed to surrender here at the end of the war. Poor Catholics unable to find housing took over the abandoned military barracks, with multiple families living in each dwelling. Only homeowners were allowed to vote, and the Unionist minority controlling city government was not eager to build more housing that would tip the voting balance away from them. Sectarian pressures built over years until 1972, when the ugly events of Bloody Sunday brought worldwide attention to the Troubles (see "The Murals of the Bogside," page 280).

Today, life has stabilized in Derry, and the population has increased by 25 percent in the last 30 years to about 105,000. The modern Foyleside Shopping Centre, bankrolled by investors from Boston, was completed in 1995. The 1998 Good Friday Peace Accord has provided a two-steps-forward, one-step-back progress, and the British Army has become less visible. With a population that is 70 percent Catholic, the city has agreed to alternate Nationalist and Unionist mayors. There is a feeling of cautious optimism as Derry, the scene of bombs and bloody conflicts in the 1960s and 1970s, now boasts a history museum that airs all viewpoints.

affords of the once turbulent Catholic **Bogside** district below. Stop at the Double Bastion fortified platform that occupies this corner of the city walls. The old cannon is nicknamed "Roaring Meg" for the fury of its firing during the siege.

From here, you can see across the Bogside to the not-so-far-away hills of County Donegal in the Republic. Derry was once an island, but as the river gradually changed its course, the area below began to drain. Over time, and especially after the Potato Famine (1845–1849), Catholic peasants from rural Donegal began to move into Derry to find work and settled on this least desirable land...on the bog side of the city.

Directly below and to the right are Free Derry Corner and Rossville Street, where the tragic events of Bloody Sunday took place in 1972 (see "The Murals of the Bogside," below). Down on the left is the 18th-century Long Tower Catholic church, named after the medieval round tower that once stood in the area (see "Long Tower Church," below). The building behind you (next to the army tower) is a former Presbyterian school that now houses the **Verbal Arts Centre**, which promotes the development of local literary arts in the form of poetry, drama, writing, and storytelling. Drop in for a cup of coffee in their coffeehouse and see what performances might be on during your visit (entry next to army tower on Bishop Street, tel. 028/7126-6946, www.verbalartscentre.co.uk).

Continuing another 50 yards around the corner, you'll reach Bishop's Gate, from which you can look down Bishop Street Without (outside the walls) and Bishop Street Within (inside the walls), while another, shorter British Army surveillance tower peeks over your shoulder. Take a moment to look at the wall, topped by a high mesh fence, running along the left side of Bishop Street Without. This is a **Peace Wall**, built to ensure the security of the Protestant enclave living behind it in the Fountain neighborhood. When the Troubles reignited 30 years ago, there were 20,000 Protestants living on this side of the river. Sadly, today this small housing estate of 1,500 people is all that remains of that proud community. The rest have chosen to move across the river to the Waterside district. The old brick tower halfway down the peace wall was part of the old jail that briefly held doomed rebel Wolfe Tone, after the 1798 revolt against the English.

From Bishop's Gate, those short on time can descend from the walls and walk 15 minutes directly back through the heart of the old city, along Bishop Street Within and Shipquay Street to Guildhall Square. With more time, consider visiting St. Columb's Anglican Cathedral, the Long Tower Catholic church, and the murals of the Bogside (all described below).

The Murals of the Bogside

The Catholic Bogside area was the tinderbox of the modern Troubles in Northern Ireland. A terrible confrontation 33 years ago sparked a sectarian inferno, and the ashes have not yet fully cooled. Today, the murals of the Bogside give visitors an accessible glimpse of this community's passionate perception of those events.

Inspired by civil rights marches in America in the mid-1960s and the 1968 Prague Spring uprising, civil rights groups began to protest in Northern Ireland. Initially their goals were to gain better housing, secure fair voting rights, and end employment discrimination for Catholics in the North. Tensions mounted, and clashes with the predominantly Protestant Royal Ulster Constabulary police force became frequent. Eventually, the British Army was called in to keep the peace. On January 30, 1972, a group protesting internment without trial held an illegal march through the Bogside neighborhood.

The Murals of the Bogside

1 Peace
2 The Hunger Strikers
3 The Rioter
4 Civil Rights
5 Operation Motorman
6 Bloody Sunday
7 Bernadette
8 Petrol Bomber
9 Death of Innocence
10 Bloody Sunday Commemoration

They were fired upon by members of a British regiment, who claimed that snipers had fired on them first. The tragic result of the clash, now remembered as **Bloody Sunday**, caused the death of 14 civilians and led to a flood of fresh IRA volunteers.

These events are memorialized in 10 murals painted on the ends of residential flats along a 300-yard stretch of Rossville Street and Lecky Road, where the march took place. You can reach them from Waterloo Place via William Street, from the old city walls at Butcher's Gate via the long set of stairs extending below Fahan Street on the grassy hillside, or by the stairs leading down from the Long

Political Murals

The dramatic and emotional murals you'll encounter in Northern Ireland will likely be one of the enduring travel memories you'll take home with you. They evolved from the colorful annual displays of flags and streamers that were hung each July in Protestant neighborhoods during the 19th century to commemorate the victory of King William III at the Battle of the Boyne. With the advent of industrial paints, these temporary seasonal displays became permanent territorial statements. These Unionist murals were created during the extended political debate that eventually led to the partitioning of the island in 1921 and the creation of Northern Ireland. Murals expressing opposing views in Nationalist Catholic neighborhoods were outlawed. The ban remained until the eruption of the modern Troubles, when staunchly Republican Catholic communities isolated themselves behind barricades, eluding state control and gaining freedom to express their pent-up passions.

In Derry, this form of symbolic, cultural, and ideological resistance first appeared in 1969, with the simple "You are now entering Free Derry" message that you'll still see painted on the surviving gable wall at Free Derry corner.

Found mostly in working-class neighborhoods of Belfast and Derry, today's political murals have become a dynamic form of popular culture, blurring the line between art and propaganda, and giving visitors a striking glimpse of each community's history, identity, and values.

Tower Church. These days, this neighborhood is quiet and safe.

The murals were begun in 1994 by two brothers and their childhood friend, all of whom grew up in the Bogside during the tragic events. One of the brothers, Tom Kelly, gained a reputation as a "heritage mural" painter, specializing in scenes of life in the old days. In a surprising and hopeful development, Kelly was invited into Derry's Protestant Fountain neighborhood to work with a youth club there to paint three proud heritage murals to cover over paramilitary graffiti.

The Bogside murals face different directions (and some are partially hidden by buildings), so they're not all visible from a single viewpoint. Plan on walking about three long blocks along Rossville Street (which becomes Lecky Road) to see them all. Locals are used to visitors and don't mind if you photograph the murals.

The best place to start is from Williams Street, walking south along the right side of Rossville Street toward Free Derry Corner (described below). The murals will all be on your right.

The first mural you'll walk past is the most recently painted one.

Finished in the summer of 2004, the colorful collage of *Peace* was inspired by a campaign of write-in suggestions for positive peace-time images from this generation of Derry city schoolchildren.

Next, *The Hunger Strikers* features two long-haired men wearing blankets. This mural represents the IRA prisoners who refused to wear the uniforms of common criminals in an attempt to force the British to treat them instead as legitimate political prisoners (who were allowed to wear their own clothes).

Now look for *The Rioter,* which depicts an outgunned but undaunted local youth behind a screen shield. He holds a stone, while a British armored vehicle approaches (echoing the famous Tiananmen Square photo of the lone man facing the tank).

Nearby is *Civil Rights,* showing a marching Derry crowd carrying an anti-sectarian banner. It dates from the days when Martin Luther King, Jr.'s successful nonviolent protest marches were having a dramatic global ripple effect. Civil rights marches—inspired into action using the same methods to combat a similar set of grievances—gave this long-suffering community a powerful new voice.

Now cross over to the other side of Rossville street to see the **Bloody Sunday Monument**. This small, fenced-off stone obelisk lists the names of those who died that day, most within 50 yards of

this spot. Take a look at the map pedestal by the monument, which shows how a rubble barricade was erected to block the street. An eight-story housing project called Rossville Flats stood here in those days. When peaceful protests failed and Republican youths became more aggressive, British troops feared being hit by Molotov cocktails thrown from the roof.

Cross again, this time over to the grassy median strip that runs down the middle of Rossville Street. At one end stands a granite letter H inscribed with the names of the 10 IRA hunger strikers who died in H-block of the Maze prison in 1981. From here, you get a good view of the *Operation Motorman* mural (at the corner of Fahan Street). In it, a soldier wields a sledgehammer, depicting the massive push by the British Army to open up the Bogside's barricaded "no-go" areas, which the IRA had controlled for three years.

Walk down to the other end of the median strip, where the white wall of **Free Derry Corner** announces, "You are now entering

Free Derry" (imitating a similarly defiant slogan of the time in once-isolated West Berlin). This was the gable end of a string of houses that stood here over 30 years ago.

Cross back to the right side of the street (now Lecky Road) to see *Bloody Sunday*, in which a small group of men are carrying a body from the ill-fated march. It's taken from a famous photo of Father Daly waving a white handkerchief to request safe passage. The blood-stained civil rights banner was inserted under the soldier's feet for extra emphasis.

Beside it is a mural called *Bernadette*. The woman with the megaphone is Bernadette Devlin McAliskey, an outspoken civil rights leader who became the youngest elected member of Parliament. Behind her kneels a woman supporter, banging a trashcan lid against the street in a traditional expression of protest in Republican neighborhoods. Trash can lids were also used to warn neighbors of the approach of British patrols.

Petrol Bomber, showing a teen wearing an army surplus gas mask, captures the Battle of the Bogside, when locals barricaded off their community, effectively shutting out British rule. The British army attempted to use tear gas and supposedly non-lethal rubber bullets to disperse hostile crowds.

In *The Death of Innocence*, a young girl stands in front of bomb wreckage. She is Annette McGavigan, a 14-year-old who was killed

by crossfire in the Bogside in 1971. She was the 100th fatality of the Troubles, which eventually took over 3,000 lives. The gun beside her points to the ground, signifying that it's no longer being wielded. The large butterfly above her shoulder symbolizes the hope for peace. The artists have said they will return to add a rising sun within the butterfly when they feel confident that the peace process has succeeded.

Finally, around the corner, you'll see a circle of male faces. This mural, painted in 1997 to observe the 25th anniversary of the tragedy, is called *Bloody Sunday Commemoration* and shows the 14 victims. They are surrounded by a ring of 14 oak leaves—the symbol of Derry.

Take a few moments to walk into the **Bogside Inn** pub (facing this last mural across Westland Street) and order a beverage. This pub has been here through it all. Spend a little time examining the black-and-white news photos of Bloody Sunday and bomb damage around the city taken during the darkest days of Derry.

Former Nationalist leader John Hume (Nobel Peace Prize co-winner in 1998 with Unionist leader David Trimble) still has a house in the Bogside. He once borrowed an old quote to explain his nonviolent approach to the peace process when he said: "An eye for an eye leaves everyone blind."

SIGHTS

▲▲**Tower Museum Derry**—Housed in a modern reconstruction of a fortified medieval tower house belonging to the local O'Doherty clan, this well-organized museum provides an excellent introduction to the city and sorts out some of the tangled historical roots of Northern Ireland's Troubles. Combining modern audiovisuals with historical artifacts, the displays tell the story of the city from a skillfully unbiased viewpoint. Starting with the city's monastic origins 1,500 years ago and moving through pivotal events, such as the 1688–1689 siege and unexpected blips like Amelia Earhart's emergency landing, they'll give you a better handle on what makes this unique city tick. Catch the thought-provoking, 14-minute film in the small theater, which gives an evenhanded local perspective on the tragic events of the sectarian conflict. As you exit the small theater, scan the displays of paramilitary paraphernalia in the hallway lined with colored curb stones—red, white, and blue Union Jack colors for Loyalists; and green, white, and orange Irish tricolor for Republicans. There, you'll find tiny notes written by IRA hunger-striker Bobby Sands, which were smuggled out of the Maze prison. The recently opened tower section holds the Spanish Armada exhibits, filled with items taken from a galleon that sank offshore in 1588 (£5, July–Aug Mon–Sat 10:00–17:00, Sun 14:00–17:00, Sept–June Tue–Sat 10:00–17:00, closed Sun–Mon, Union Hall Place, tel. 028/7137-2411).

Guild Hall—This neo-Gothic building, complete with clock tower, is the ceremonial seat of city government. It first opened in 1890 on reclaimed lands that were once the mudflats of the Foyle River. Destroyed by fire and rebuilt in 1913, it was massively damaged by IRA bombs in 1972. In an ironic twist, Gerry Doherty, one of those convicted of the bombings, was elected as a member of the City Council a dozen years later. Inside are the Council Chamber, party offices, and an assembly hall featuring stained-glass windows showing scenes from Derry history. Check to see when tours are available—usually when civic and cultural events are not taking place inside (Mon–Fri 9:00–17:00, tel. 028/7137-7335).

Hands Across the Divide—Designed by local teacher Maurice Harron after the fall of the Iron Curtain, this powerful metal sculpture of two figures extending their hands to each other was inspired by the growing hope for peace and reconciliation in Northern Ireland (located in a roundabout at the west end of Craigavon Bridge).

Until recently, the Tillie and Henderson's shirt factory (opened in 1857 and burned down in 2003) stood on the banks of the river beside the bridge, looming over the figures. In its heyday, Derry's shirt industry employed over 15,000 workers (90 percent of whom were women) in sweathouses typical of the human toll of Industrial Revolution. Karl Marx mentioned this factory in *Das Kapital* as an example of women's transition from domestic to industrial work lives.

St. Columb's Cathedral—Marked by the tall spire inside the walls, this Anglican cathedral was built from 1628 to 1633 in a style called "Planter's Gothic." Its construction was financed by the same London companies that backed the plantation of Londonderry and was the first Protestant cathedral built in Britain after the Reformation. It played an important part in the defense of the city during the siege, when cannons were mounted on its roof and the original spire was scavenged for lead to melt into cannon shot. In the entryway, you'll find a hollow cannonball that was lobbed into the city, containing the besiegers' surrender terms. Inside, along the nave, hangs a musty collection of battle flags and Union Jacks that once inspired troops during the siege, the Crimean War, and World War II. The American flag hangs among them, from the time when the first GIs to enter the European theater in World War II were based in Northern Ireland. Check out the small chapter-house museum in the back of the church to see the original locks of the gates of Londonderry and more relics of the siege (£1 donation, Mon–Sat 9:00–17:00, closed Sun, tel. 028/7126-7313, www.stcolumbscathedral.org).

Long Tower Church—Built below the walls on the hillside above the Bogside, this modest-looking church is worth a visit for its stunning high altar. The name comes from a stone monastic round tower that stood here for centuries, but was destroyed for city building materials in the 1600s. The oldest Catholic church in Derry, it was finished in 1786, during a time of enlightened relations between the city's two religious communities. Protestant Bishop Hervey gave a generous-for-the-time £200 donation and had the four Corinthian columns shipped in from Naples to frame the neo-Renaissance altar (free, Mon–Sat 7:30–20:30, Sun 7:30–19:00, tel. 028/7126-2301). Hidden outside behind the church and facing the Bogside is a simple shrine beneath a hawthorn tree. It marks the spot where outlawed Masses were held secretly, before this church was built, during the infamous Penal Law period of the early 1700s. Through the Penal Laws, the English attempted to weaken Catholicism's influence by banishing priests and forbidding Catholics from buying land, attending school, voting, and holding office.

NIGHTLIFE

The **Millennium Forum** is a modern venue reflecting the city's revived investment in local culture, concerts, and plays (box office Mon–Sat 10:00–17:00, inside city walls on Newmarket Street near Ferryquay Gate, tel. 028/7126-4455, boxoffice@millenniumforum .co.uk, www.millenniumforum.co.uk).

The **Nerve Centre** shows a wide variety of arthouse films (inside city walls on Magazine Street near Butcher Gate, tel. 028/7126-0562, www.nerve-centre.org.uk).

SLEEPING

$$$ The **Tower Hotel** is the only hotel actually inside Derry's historic walls. It's a real splurge, with 93 modern and immaculate rooms, a classy bistro restaurant, and private basement parking (Sb-£69, Db-£89, cheaper Fri–Sun, Butcher Street, tel. 028/7137-1000, fax 028/7137-1234, www.towerhotelderry.com, reservations@thd.ie).

$$ **Travelodge** has 40 comfortable rooms, a great location, and a handy adjacent parking garage (Db-£45 Sun–Thu, Db-£50 Fri–Sat, full Irish breakfast-£6, continental breakfast-£4.50, two

---

Sleep Code

(**£1 = about $1.70, country code: 44, area code: 028**)
S = Single, **D** = Double/Twin, **T** = Triple, **Q** = Quad, **b** = bathroom, **s** = shower only. Breakfast is included, and credit cards are accepted unless otherwise noted.

To help you easily sort through these listings, I've divided the rooms into three categories, based on the price for a standard double room with bath:

$$$ **Higher Priced**—Most rooms £70 or more.
$$ **Moderately Priced**—Most rooms between £40–70.
$ **Lower Priced**—Most rooms £40 or less.

non-smoking floors, 22–24 Strand Road, tel. 028/7127-1271, fax 028/7127-1277, www.travelodge.co.uk).

$$ **Merchant's House**, on a quiet street a 10-minute stroll from Waterloo Place, is a fine Georgian townhouse with marble fireplaces, ornate plasterwork, and a grand, colorful drawing room (S-£25, Sb-£30, D-£45, Db-£50, 16 Queen Street, tel. 028/7126-9691, fax 028/7126-6913, www.thesaddlershouse.com, Joan and Peter Pyne).

$$ **Saddler's House,** run by the owners of Merchant's House, is a charming Victorian townhouse with seven rooms located a couple blocks closer to the old town walls (Sb-£30, Db-£45, 36 Great James Street, tel. 028/7126-9691, fax 028/7126-6913, www.thesaddlershouse.com).

$ **The Palace Hostel Derry**, located in the city center (across from a fortress-like police station), rents 40 decent beds for £10 a night with breakfast (4–6 beds per room, family rooms with private bathroom for up to four-£35, free Internet access, laundry facilities, kitchen, nightly movies, 1 Woodleigh Terrace, Asylum Road, tel. 028/7130-9051, www.paddyspalace.com, info@paddyspalace.com, Stephen McPhilemy).

EATING

The front window of **Mange 2** declares that "cuisine is when things taste like what they are." They deliver on that promise, serving casual £5–7 lunches and filling £10–16 dinners in a lighthearted atmosphere (daily 11:30–15:00 & 17:30–22:00, Clarendon Street, tel. 028/7136-1222).

The **Mandarin Palace** dishes up good £8–13 Chinese dinners in a crisp dining room that faces the river. Their £10 early-bird three-course deals are available from 16:30 to 19:00 (daily 16:30–23:00, buffet lunch Mon–Fri 12:00–14:00, Queens Quay at Lower Clarendon Street, tel. 028/7137-3656).

The hip, trendy **Exchange Restaurant and Wine Bar** offers £4–6 lunches and quality dinners with flair for £10–15, in a central location near the river behind Waterloo Place (Mon–Sat 12:00–22:00, Sun 17:00–21:30, Queen's Quay, tel. 028/7127-3990).

Easygoing **Fitzroy's,** tucked below Ferryquay Gate, serves good £5–7 lunches and £8–13 dinners (Mon–Tue 10:00–20:00, Wed–Sat 10:00–22:00, Sun 12:00–20:00, 2–4 Bridge Street, tel. 028/7126-6211).

Try the **Leprechaun Restaurant and Bakery** for a dependable £3–5 cafeteria-style lunch (Mon–Sat 9:00–17:30, closed Sun, 21–23 Strand Road, tel. 028/7136-3606).

Austins Department Store, right on the Diamond in the center of the old city, is Ireland's oldest department store and has a top-floor café with some nice views and £5 lunch specials

(Mon–Sat 9:30–17:30, Sun 13:00–15:30, 2–6 The Diamond, tel. 028/7137-7727).

Chat with locals in pubs that rarely see a tourist. Try **Peadar O'Donnell's** pub on Waterloo Street for Derry's best nightly ballad sessions (53 Waterloo Street, tel. 028/7137-2318).

Supermarkets: **Tesco** has everything for picnics and road munchies (Mon–Thu 9:00–21:00, Fri 8:30–21:00, Sat 8:30–20:00, Sun 13:00–18:00, corner of Strand Road and Clarendon Street). **Super Valu** meets the same needs (Mon–Sat 8:30–18:30, Thu–Fri until 20:30, closed Sun, Waterloo Place).

TRANSPORTATION CONNECTIONS

From Derry, it's less than an hour's drive to Portrush.

From Derry by train to: Portrush (9/day, 1 hr, change in Coleraine), **Belfast** (8/day, 2 hrs), **Dublin** (7/day, 5 hrs). In July and August, consider a £6.50 "Day Tracker" ticket, good for all-day train use in Northern Ireland (see page 245).

By bus to: Galway (4/day, 6 hrs), **Portrush** (5/day, 1.25 hrs), **Belfast** (16/day, 1.75 hrs), **Dublin** (5/day, 4.5 hrs).

Useful updated schedules and prices for both trains and buses in Northern Ireland can be obtained from Translink (tel. 028/9066-6630, www.translink.co.uk).

Route Tips for Drivers:
Sights Between Derry and Galway

If you're driving into Northern Ireland from Galway, Westport, or Strokestown and don't have time to explore Donegal, consider the two following interesting interior stops.

Belleek Pottery Visitors Centre—Just over the Northern Ireland border (30 miles northeast of Sligo), is the cute town of Belleek, famous for its pottery. The Belleek Parian China factory welcomes visitors with a small gallery and museum (Mon–Fri 9:00–18:00, Sat 10:00–18:00, Sun 11:00–18:00, less off-season), a 20-minute video, a cheery cafeteria, and fascinating 30-minute tours of its working factory (£4, Mon–Sat 9:30–16:15, call to confirm schedule and reserve a spot, tel. 028/6865-8501, www.belleek.ie).

Ulster American Folk Park—North of Omagh (5 miles on A5), this museum shows life before emigration, on the boat, and in America for the many Irish who left their homeland during the hard times of the 19th century (£4, April–Sept Mon–Sat 10:30–16:30, Sun 11:00–17:00; Oct–March Mon–Fri 10:30–15:30, closed Sat–Sun; tel. 028/8224-3292, www.folkpark.com).

County Donegal

Donegal is the most remote (and perhaps the most ruggedly beautiful) county in Ireland. It's not on the way to anywhere, and it wears this isolation well. With more native Irish speakers than in any other county, the old ways are better preserved here than in any other county. The northernmost part of Ireland, Donegal remains connected to the Republic by a slim, five-mile-wide umbilical cord of land on its southern coast. It's also Ireland's second biggest county, with a wide-open, "big sky" interior and a shattered-glass, 200-mile jagged coastline of islands and inlets.

This is the home turf of St. Colmcille (Irish for "Dove of the Church"), born here in 521 and revered second only to St. Patrick in the hierarchy of Irish saints. A proud Gaelic culture held out in Donegal to the bitter end, when its two famous clans (the O'Donnells and the O'Dohertys) were finally defeated by the English in the early 1600s. After their defeat, the region became know as Dun na nGall ("the fort of the foreigner"), which was eventually anglicized to Donegal.

As the English moved in, four friars (certain that Gaelic ways would be lost forever) painstakingly wrote down Irish history from Noah's Ark to their present. This labor of love became known as the Annals of the Four Masters, and without it, much of our knowledge of early Irish history and myth would be lost. An obelisk stands in their honor in the main square of Donegal town.

The hardy people of County Donegal were famous for their quality tweed-weaving, a cottage industry that has lost ground to modern industrial production in far-off cities. An energetic fishing fleet still churns offshore. The traditional Irish musicians of Donegal play a driving style of music, with a distinctively fast and choppy rhythm. Meanwhile, Enya (local Gweedore gal made good) has crafted languid, ethereal tunes that glide from mood to mood. Today, emigration has taken its toll, and much of the trickle of tourism comes from neighboring Northern Ireland.

SIGHTS

Donegal Loop Trip

Here's my choice for a scenic mix of Donegal highlands and coastal views, organized as a day-long circuit (150 miles) for drivers based across the border in Derry. If you're coming north from Galway or Westport, you could incorporate parts of this drive into your itinerary.

Route Summary: Drive west out of Derry (direction of Letterkenny) on Buncrana Road, which becomes A2 (and then N13, across the border in the Republic). Follow the signs into Letterkenny

County Donegal

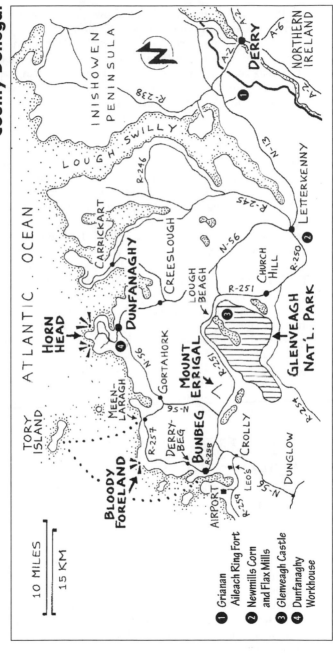

NORTHERN IRELAND

A-2

A-6

DERRY

A-2

A-2

INISHOWEN PENINSULA

R-238

1

R-13-N

LETTERKENNY

LOUGH SWILLY

R-246

R-245

2

R-250

ATLANTIC OCEAN

CARRICKART

CREESLOUGH

N-56

CHURCH HILL

R-251

3

DUNFANAGHY

LOUGH BEAGH

GLENVEAGH NAT'L. PARK

R-251

HORN HEAD

4

N-56

GORTAHORK

MOUNT ERRIGAL

R-251

R-254

MEEN-LARAGH

N-56-N

CROLLY

DERRY-BEG

BUNBEG

R-257

R-258

LEO'S

DUNGLOW

TORY ISLAND

BLOODY FORELAND

R-259

AIRPORT

N-56-N

10 MILES

15 KM

1 Grianan Aileach Ring Fort

2 Newmills Corn and Flax Mills

3 Glenveagh Castle

4 Dunfanaghy Workhouse

and take R250 out the other (west) end of town. Veer right (north) onto R251 and stay on it through Churchill all the way across the highlands, until you link up with N56 approaching Bunbeg. After a couple of miles on N56, take R258 another four miles into Bunbeg. Depart Bunbeg going north on R257 around Bloody Foreland, and rejoin N56 near Gortahork. Take N56 through Dunfanaghy (possible Horn Head mini-loop option here), and then south back into Letterkenny. Retrace your route from Letterkenny via N13 and A2 back into Derry.

Helpful Hints: An early start and an Ordnance Survey map are essential. It's cheapest to top off your gas tank in Letterkenny. Consider bringing along a picnic lunch to enjoy from a scenic roadside pullout along the Bloody Foreland R257 road, or out on the Horn Head loop. Bring lots of film, and remember—not all who wander are lost.

Once you cross into the Republic of Ireland, all currency is in euros, not pounds. For B&B rates, sight fees, and all other costs in Donegal, keep this exchange rate in mind: €1 = about $1.20.

The Tour Begins: The sights along this route are well-marked. Don't underestimate the time it takes to get around here, as the narrow roads are full of curves and bumps. Dogs, bred to herd sheep, dart from side lanes to practice their bluffing techniques on your car. If you average 30 miles per hour over the course of the day, you've got a very good suspension system. Folks wanting to visit more than a couple of sights will need to slow down and consider an overnight stop in Bunbeg or Dunfanaghy.

Grianan Aileach Ring Fort—This dramatic, ancient ring fort perches on an 800-foot hill just inside the Republic, a stone's throw

from Derry. It's a late Iron Age fortification, built about A.D. 500, and was once the royal stronghold of the O'Neill clan, which dominated Ulster for centuries. Its stout, drystone walls (no mortar) are 12 feet thick and 18 feet high, creating an interior sanctuary 80 feet in diameter.

Once inside, you can scramble up the stairs built into the walls to enjoy panoramic views in all directions. Murtagh O'Brien, King of Desmond, destroyed the fort in 1101 (the same year he gave the Rock of Cashel to the Church). He had his soldiers each carry away a stone to make it tough for the O'Briens to rebuild. What you see today is mostly a reconstruction from the 1870s. You'll find a sign for the fort well-posted just a mile off N13, not far from the junction of R239 (entry is free and unattended). If you plan on doing the whole Donegal day loop today, skip the mediocre visitors center (€5) in the converted church at the base of the hill, near N13.

Newmills Corn and Flax Mills—Come here for a glimpse of the 150-year-old Industrial Revolution, high-tech Ulster style. Linen, which comes from flax, was king in this region. The 15-minute film does a nifty job of explaining the process, showing how the

common flax plant ends up as cloth. Working conditions in a mill were noisy, unhealthy, and exhausting. A veteran mill worker often braved respiratory disease, deafness, lost fingers, and extreme fire danger. For his trouble, he usually got to keep about 10 percent of what he milled.

The Corn Mill is still in working condition, but takes a skilled miller to operate it. This mill ground oats—"corn" means oats in Ireland. (What we call corn, they call maize.) The huge waterwheel, powered by the river Swilly, made three revolutions per minute and generated eight horsepower.

The entire operation could be handled by one miller, who knew every cog, lever, and flume in the joint. Call ahead to see when working mill demonstrations are scheduled, otherwise tours last 20 minutes and are available on request (€2.75, covered by Heritage Card—see page 4, mid-June–mid-Sept daily 10:00–18:30, 5 miles west of Letterkenny on R250, Churchill Road, tel. 074/25115).

Glenveagh Castle and National Park—One of Ireland's five National Parks, Glenveagh contains pristine Lough Veagh. This jewel of a lake is three miles long, occupying a U-shaped valley scoured out of the Derryveagh mountains by powerful glaciers during the last Ice Age.

In the 1850s, this scenic area attracted the wealthy land speculator John George Adair, who bought the valley in 1857. Right away, Adair clashed with local tenants, whom he accused of stealing his sheep. After his managing agent was found murdered, he evicted all 244 of his bitter tenants to great controversy, and set about to create a hunting estate in grand Victorian style.

His pride and joy was his country mansion, Glenveagh Castle, finished in 1873 on the shore of Lough Veagh. After his death, his widow added to the castle and introduced rhododendrons and rare red deer to the estate. After her death, Harvard art professor Kingsley Porter bought the estate, and promptly disappeared on the Donegal coast (he is thought to have drowned). The last owner was Philadelphia millionaire Henry McIlhenny, who filled the mansion with fine art and furniture while perfecting the lush surrounding gardens. He donated the castle to the Irish nation in 1983.

Take the 45-minute castle tour, letting your Jane Austen and

Agatha Christie fantasies go wild. Antlers abound on walls, in chandeliers, and in paintings by Victorian hunting artists. A table crafted from rare bog oak (hundreds of years old, found buried in the muck) stands at attention in one room, while Venetian glass chandeliers illuminate a bathroom. A round, pink bedroom at the top of a tower is decorated in Oriental style, with inlaid mother-of-pearl furnishings. The library displays paintings by George Russell, and has the castle's best lake views.

Afterwards, stroll through the gardens and enjoy the lovely setting. A lakeside swimming pool had boilers underneath it to keep it heated. It's no wonder that Greta Garbo was an occasional guest, coming to visit whenever she "vanted" to be alone.

The castle is only accessible by 10-minute shuttle-bus rides (€2, 4/hr, depart from the park visitors center). The visitors center, located beside the parking lot and tea room, explains the region's natural history. Hiking trails in the park are tempting, but beware of tiny midges that seem to want to nest in your nostrils (€2.75, covered by Heritage Card—see page 4, mid-March–early Nov daily 10:00–18:30, last admission 17:00, early Nov–mid-March Sat–Sun only, tel. 074/37090).

Mount Errigal—This mountain (2,400 feet) dominates the horizon for miles around. Rising from the relatively flat interior bog land, it looks taller from a distance than it is. Beautifully cone-shaped (but not a volcano), it offers a hearty non-technical climb with panoramic views (4 hrs round-trip, covering 5 miles via the tower on the south shore of Lough Altan). Hikers should ask for a weather report (frequent mists squat on the summit) and get a trail map from the TI in Letterkenny, or at the nearby Dunlewy Lakeside Centre (tel. 074/953-1699). The trailhead is southeast of the mountain, starting at the small parking lot right beside R251, on the lower slope of the mountain.

Bunbeg—This modest town lies along R257, offering a fine sandy beach. But take the trouble to seek out the quaint little hidden fishing harbor at the rocky south end of town. The harbor access road is directly in front of you as you approach the town from the east on R258 and pull up to the stop sign beside Tigh Bhreisleain B&B (on your right). At the dead end of the half-mile access road is a cute, watercolor-worthy harbor, with an old stone warehouse and a great guesthouse (see below).

Turasmara operates a limited ferry service from Bunbeg harbor. It's a 90-minute voyage to ultra-remote and rugged Tory Island (€22-round-trip, departs at 9:00 and returns at 18:00, leaves June–Sept daily, weather permitting, tel. 074/953-1340).

The couple of miles of road north, from Bunbeg to Derrybeg, is (strangely) one of the most densely populated sections of this loop tour. Modern holiday cottages pepper the landscape in what the newly affluent Irish have come to call "Bungalow Bliss" (or "Bungalow Blight" to nature-lovers).

Sleeping in Bunbeg: **$$ Tigh Bhreisleain B&B** surveys the crossroads where R257 and R258 meet. Georgina Breslin hosts five crisp, colorful rooms with cushy carpets (Sb-€30, Db-€56, Tb-€75, cash only, non-smoking, parking, tel. 074/953-1329, fax 074/953-2625, breslins@hotmail.com). **$$ Bunbeg House** overlooks the snug and charming Bunbeg fishing harbor with simple, spacious rooms and a tiny, inviting pub downstairs. Jean Carr knows about fun rib-boat sightseeing excursions, too (Sb-€35–40, Db-€60–70, Tb-€80–100, Qb-€100, parking, tel. 074/953-1305, fax 074/953-1420, www.bunbeghouse.com, bunbeghouse@eircom.net).

Eating in Bunbeg: Try the **Seaview Hotel Bistro,** which specializes in fish dishes (€24–28 meals, June–Sept daily 18:30–21:30, Oct–May Fri–Sat only 18:30–21:30, on R257, tel. 074/953-1159). You'll find a fun pub dinner, plus a late-evening traditional-music session, at **Leo's Tavern**, run by Enya's dad. To get there from Bunbeg, hop on N56 going south through the nearby hamlet of Crolly. Take a right onto R259 (sign says "Aerphort"), and go a half mile, following signs to Leo's, which will bring you to a sharp turn right, and the pub will be 100 yards up on the left (Mon–Sat 13:00–20:30, Sun 13:00–15:30, tel. 074/954-8143).

Bloody Foreland—Named for the shade of red that backlit heather turns at sunset, this scenic headland is laced with rock walls and forgotten cottage ruins. Pull off at one of the roadside viewpoints, and savor a picnic lunch and rugged coastal views.

Dunfanaghy Workhouse—Opened in 1845, this structure was part of an extensive workhouse compound (separating families by gender and age)—a dreaded last resort for the utterly destitute of coastal Donegal. There were once many identical compounds built across Ireland as a rigid Victorian solution to the spiraling riddle of Ireland's rapidly multiplying poor. But the system was unable to cope with the starving homeless multitudes caused by the famine.

The harsh workhouse experience is told through the true-life narrative of Wee Hannah Herrity, a wandering orphan and former resident of this workhouse. She survived the famine by taking refuge here, and died at age 90 in 1926. You'll visit three upstairs rooms, where hokey papier-mâché figures relate the powerful episodes in her life (€4.75, April–Sept Mon–Fri 10:00–17:00, Sat–Sun 12:00–17:00; Oct–March call to confirm hours, good bookstore and coffee shop, on N56 a half mile south of Dunfanaghy town, tel. 074/913-6540).

Dunfanaghy—This planned town, founded by the English in the early 1600s for local markets and fairs, has a prim and proper appearance. You can grab a pub lunch here, or some picnic fixings from the town market. Enjoy them from a scenic viewpoint on the nearby Horn Head Loop (see below).

Sleeping in Dunfanaghy: **$$$ The Mill Restaurant and Accommodation** is a diamond in the Donegal rough. Susan Alcorn nurtures six wonderful rooms with classy decor, while her husband, Derek, is the chef in their fine restaurant downstairs (Sb-€50, Db-€80, Tb-€120, non smoking, parking, tel. & fax 074/913-6985, www.themillrestaurant.com, info@themillrestaurant.com).

$$ Corncrakes Rest B&B is an unpretentious, friendly place with five comfy rooms and expansive views from the breakfast terrace (Sb-€40, Db-€60, Tb-€75, cash only, non-smoking, parking, 5-min walk from town off the Horn Head road, tel. 074/913-6501, Gertie McKinley).

Eating in Dunfanaghy: **The Mill Restaurant and Accommodation** is gourmet all the way, specializing in memorable lamb or lobster dinners worth booking days ahead of time (€35, Tue–Sun 19:00–21:00, closed Mon, tel. 074/913-6985). The central **Danny Collins Pub** serves affordable pub grub (€8–12, daily 12:00–20:00, tel. 074/913-6205).

Horn Head Loop—As you approach Dunfanaghy (if your schedule allows), take an hour and embark on a lost-world plateau drive.

This heaving headland, with few trees, has gripping coastal views. Consult your map and get off N56, following the Horn Head signs all the way around the eastern lobe of the peninsula. There's less than eight miles of narrow, single-lane road out here, with very little traffic. But be alert and willing to pull over at wide spots to cooperate with other cars.

A short spur road leads to the summit of the headland, where you can park your car and walk another 50 yards up to the abandoned lookout shelter. The views from here are dramatic, looking west toward Tory Island and south to Mount Errigal. Some may choose to hike an additional 30 minutes across the heather, to the ruins of the distant signal tower (not a castle), clearly visible near the cliffs. The trails are not maintained, but it's easy bushwhacking, offering rewarding cliff views. Navigate back to your car using the lookout shelter on the summit as a landmark.

IRISH HISTORY
AND CULTURE

A surprising aspect of Ireland is the richness of its history, art, and language. And the country continues to transform and grow today, building on an ever-stronger economy, searching for peace, and reexamining some of its long-held social customs.

PAST AND PRESENT

Hunters, Farmers, and Mysterious Mounds (Prehistory)

Ireland became an island when rising seas covered the last land bridge (7000 B.C.), a separation from Britain that the Irish would fight to maintain for the next 9,000 years. By 6000 B.C., Stone Age hunter-fishers had settled on the East Coast, followed by Neolithic farmers (from the island of Britain). These early inhabitants left behind impressive but mysterious funeral mounds (passage graves) and large, Stonehenge-type **stone circles**.

The Celts: Language and Legends (500 B.C.–A.D. 500)

Perhaps more an invasion of ideas than of armies, the Celtic culture from Central Europe (particularly that of the most influential tribe, called the **Gaels**) settled in Ireland, where it would dominate for a thousand years. A warrior people with over a hundred petty kings, they feuded constantly with rival clans and gathered in ring forts for protection. The island was nominally ruled by a single high king at the **Hill of Tara** (near Dublin), though there was no centralized nation.

Druid priests conducted pagan, solar-calendar rituals among the megalithic stones erected by earlier inhabitants. The Celtic people peppered the countryside with thousands of Iron Age monuments. While most of what you'll see will be little more than rock piles that

What's a Celt?

The Irish are a Celtic people. The Celts, who came from Central Europe, began migrating west around 1500 B.C. Over time, many settled in the British Isles and Western France. When the Anglos and Saxons came later, grabbing the best land in the British Isles (which became Angle-land...or England), the Celts survived in Brittany, Cornwall, Wales, Scotland, and Ireland. Today, this "Celtic Crescent" still nearly encircles England. The word Celtic (pronounced with a hard C) comes from the Greek "Keltoi," meaning barbarian.

From about 700 B.C. on, various Celtic tribes mixed, mingled, and fought in Ireland. The last and most powerful of the Celtic tribes to enter the fray were the Gaels, who probably came from Scotland. The Irish language, Gaelic, is named for them. The fact that the Celts never had a written language meant that they had to pass their history, laws, and folklore down verbally from generation to generation. This may well account for the "gift of gab" attributed to today's Irish.

Celtic society revolved around warrior kings, who gathered groups of families into regional kingdoms. These small kingdoms combined to make the five large provincial kingdoms of ancient Ireland (whose names survive on maps today): Leinster, Munster, Connacht, Ulster, and the Middle Kingdom (now County Meath).

For defensive purposes, these early Irish lived in small thatched huts built on man-made islands, or on high ground surrounded by ditches and a stone or earthen wall. A strictly observed hierarchy governed Celtic societies: the king on top, followed by poets, Druid priests, doctors, legal men, skilled craftsmen, freemen,

take a vigorous imagination to reconstruct (ring forts, wedge tombs, monumental stones, and so on), just standing next to a megalith that predates the pharaohs is evocative.

The Celtic world lives on today in the Gaelic language and in legends of Celtic warriors, such as **Finn McCool**—the "Gaelic King Arthur"—who led a merry band of heroes in battle and play. Tourists marvel at large ritual stones decorated with ogham (rhymes with "poem") script, the peculiar Celtic-Latin alphabet that used lines as letters. The **Tara Brooch** and elaborately inscribed, jewel-encrusted daggers attest to the sophistication of this warrior society (see the National Museum in Dublin, page 57).

In 55 B.C., the Romans conquered the Celts in Britain, but Ireland remained independent, its history forever skewed in a different direction—Gaelic, not Latin. The Romans called Ireland **Hibernia**, or Land of Winter; it was apparently too cold and bleak to merit an attempt at colonization. The biggest non-event in Irish history is that the Romans never invaded. While the mix of Celtic and Roman is part of what makes the French French and the and slaves. Rarely did a high king rule the entire island. Loyalty to one's clan came first, and alliances between clans were often temporary, until a more advantageous alliance could be struck with a rival clan. This fluid system of alliances ebbing and flowing across the Celtic-warrior cultural landscape meant that the Celts would never unite as a single nation.

While Celtic society was male-dominated, a king needed a warrior-goddess queen to ensure the kingdom's fertility and power. One major goddess was Brigit, later adopted by Christians as St. Brigid. She was worshipped as goddess of healing, fertility, and poetry. Her sacred fire burned in Ireland (on a site in modern-day County Kildare) from ancient times until the English extinguished it.

Unlike the Celtic tribes living in Western Europe and Britain, the Celts in Ireland were never conquered by the Romans. This gives Ireland a cultural continuity and uniqueness rare in Europe. Their culture—which evolved apart from Europe—remained strong and independent for centuries. Then, in the 12th century, English dominance began leading to suppression of Gaelic language and Celtic traditions. With Irish independence—won only in the 20th century—Irish ways are no longer threatened. The most traditional areas (generally along the West Coast, such as the Dingle Peninsula) are protected as *Gaeltachts*. *Gaeltachts* (literally, places where the Gaelic language is spoken) are a kind of national park for the traditional culture. If much of Ireland's charm can be credited to its Celtic roots, you'll find that charm most vivid in a *Gaeltacht*.

English English, the Irish are purely Celtic. If France is *boules* and England is cricket, then Ireland is hurling. This wild Irish national pastime (like airborne hockey, with no injury time-outs) goes back more than 2,000 years to Celtic days, when it was played almost as a substitute for warfare.

Christianity: Monks and Scholars (A.D. 500–800)

When Ancient Rome fell and took the Continent with it, Gaelic Ireland remained. There was no Dark Age here, and the island was a beacon of culture for the rest of Europe. Ireland (population c. 750,000) was still a land of many feuding kings, but the culture was stable.

Christianity and Latin culture arrived first as a trickle from trading contacts with Christian Gaul, then more emphatically in A.D. 432 with **St. Patrick**, who persuasively converted the sun-worshipping Celts. (Perhaps St. Patrick had an easy time converting the locals because they had so little sun to worship.) Patrick (c. 389–461), a Latin-speaking Christian from Roman Britain, was kidnapped as a teenager and carried off into slavery for six years in Ireland. He escaped back to Britain; then, inspired by a dream, returned to Ireland, determined to convert the pagan, often-hostile Celtic inhabitants. Legends say he drove Ireland's snakes (symbolic of pagan beliefs) into the sea, and explained the Trinity with a shamrock (three leaves on one stem).

Later monks (such as St. Columba, 521–597) continued Christianizing the island, and foreign monks flocked to isolated Ireland. They withdrew to scattered, isolated monasteries, living in Celtic-style beehive huts, translating and illustrating (illuminating) manuscripts. Perhaps the greatest works of art of Dark Age Europe are these manuscripts, including the 9th-century **Book of Kells**, which you'll see at Dublin's Trinity College (see "Irish Art," page 309). Irish monks—heads shaved crosswise from ear to ear, like former Druids—were known throughout Europe as ascetic scholars.

St. Columbanus (c. 600) was one of several traveling, missionary monks who helped to bring Christianity back to Western Europe, which had reverted to paganism and barbarism when Rome fell. The monks established monastic centers of learning that produced great Christian teachers and community builders. One of the monks, St. Brendan, may have even sailed to America (see page 170).

By 800, **Charlemagne** was importing Irish monks to help run his Frankish kingdom. Meanwhile, Ireland remained a relatively cohesive society based on monastic settlements, rather than cities. Impressive round towers from those settlements still dot the Irish landscape—silent reminders of this glorious age.

Viking Invasion and Defeat (800–1100)

In 795, Viking pirates from Norway invaded, the first of many raids that wreaked havoc on the monasteries and shook Irish civilization. In two centuries of chaos, the Vikings raped, pillaged, and burned Christian churches. Monks stood guard from their round towers to spy approaching marauders, ring the warning bells, and protect the citizens. In 841, a conquering Viking band settled inland, building Ireland's first permanent walled cities, Dublin and Waterford. Viking raiders slowly evolved into Viking traders, who, among other things, introduced the concept of coinage to the Irish.

Finally, **High King Brian Boru** led a Gaelic revival, defeating a mercenary Viking army allied with rebellious Leinster clans at the Battle of Clontarf (1014), near Dublin. Boru died in the battle, however, and his unified kingdom quickly fell apart. Over the centuries, Viking settlers married Gaelic gals and slowly blended in.

Anglo-Norman Arrival (1100–1500)

The Normans were Ireland's next uninvited guests. In 1169, a small army of well-armed and fearless soldiers of fortune invaded Ireland under the pretense of helping a deposed Irish king regain his lands. A Welsh conquistador named **Strongbow** (c. 1130–1176) took Dublin and Waterford, married the local king's daughter, then succeeded his father-in-law as king of Leinster. This was the spearhead of a century-long invasion by the so-called Anglo-Normans—the French-speaking rulers of England, descended from William the Conqueror and his troops, who had invaded and conquered England a hundred years earlier at the Battle of Hastings (1066).

King Henry II of England soon followed (1171) to remind Strongbow who was boss, proclaiming the entire island under English (Anglo-Norman) rule. By 1250, the Anglo-Normans occupied three-quarters of the island, clustered in walled cities surrounded by hostile Gaels. These invaders, who were big-time administrators, ushered in a new age in which society (government, cities, and religious organizations) was organized on a grander scale. They imposed feudalism, and scoffed at the old Gaelic clan system that they intended to replace. Riding on the coattails of the Normans, monastic orders (Franciscans, Augustinians, and Cistercians) came over from the Continent and eclipsed Ireland's individual monastic settlements, once the foundation of Irish society in the **Age of Saints and Scholars**.

But English rule was weak and distant. Preoccupied with the Hundred Years' War with France and its own internal Wars of the Roses, England "ruled" through deputized locals, such as the earls of Kildare. Many English landowners actually resided in England, a pattern of absentee-landlordism that would exist for centuries. England's laws were fully enforced only in a 50-mile foothold around Dublin (**the Pale**—from the Norman-French word for "ditch"). A couple of centuries after invading, the Anglo-Normans saw their area of control shrink to only The Pale—with the rest of the island "beyond the Pale."

Even as their power eroded, the English kings considered Ireland to be theirs. They passed the **Statutes of Kilkenny** (1366), which outlawed all things Gaelic, including intermarriage with the English settlers, the Gaelic language, and the sport of hurling. In practice, the statutes were rarely enforced.

The End of Gaelic Rule (1500s)

In 1534, angered by Henry VIII's break with Catholicism (and taking advantage of England's Reformation chaos), the **earls of Kildare** rebelled, led by Silken Thomas. Henry crushed the revolt, executed the earls, and confiscated their land. Henry's daughter, Queen Elizabeth I, gave the land to colonists ("planters"), mainly English Protestants. The next four centuries would see a series of rebellions by Catholic, Gaelic-speaking, Irish farmers fighting to free themselves from rule by Protestant, English-speaking landowners.

Hugh O'Neill (1540–1616), a noble angered by planters and English abuses, led a Gaelic revolt in 1595. The rebels were joined by the Spanish, who were fellow Catholics and England's archrival on the high seas. At the Battle of Yellow Ford (1598), guerrilla tactics led to an Irish victory.

But the **Battle of Kinsale** (1601) ended the revolt. The exhausted Irish, who had marched the length of Ireland in winter, arrived to help Spanish troops, who were pinned down inside the town. But the English crushed the Irish before they could join the Spanish, who then surrendered. O'Neill knelt before the conquering general, ceding half a million acres to England. Then he and other proud, Gaelic, Ulster-based nobles unexpectedly abandoned their land and sailed to the Continent (The **Flight of the Earls**, 1607), an event seen as the symbolic end of Gaelic Irish rule.

English Colonization and Irish Rebellions (1600s)

King James I took advantage of the Gaelic power vacuum and sent 25,000 English and Scottish planters into the confiscated land (1610–1641), making Ulster (in the northeast) the most English area of the island. The Irish responded with two major rebellions.

In 1642, with England embroiled in civil war between a Catholic king and a Protestant Parliament, Irish rebels capitalized on the instability. Tenant farmers took up pitchforks against their English landlords, slaughtering 4,000 in the **Massacre of the Planters** (1641). Irish society was split between an English-speaking landed gentry (descendants of the first Anglo-Norman invaders, called "Old English") and the local, Irish-speaking, landless—or nearly landless—peasantry. But with Catholicism as their common bond, the Irish forces allied with the Old English against the Protestant Parliament of **Oliver Cromwell**.

Cromwell responded by invading Ireland (1649–1650) with 20,000 men. He conquered the country—brutally. Thousands were slaughtered, priests were tortured, villages were pillaged, and rebels were sold into slavery. Most Catholic Irish landowners, given the choice "to hell or to Connaught," were exiled to the rocky land west of the River Shannon. Cromwell confiscated 11 million acres of Catholic land to give to English Protestants. (In 1641, Catholics owned 59 percent of Ireland—by 1714, they owned 7 percent.) Cromwell's scorched-earth invasion was so harsh (the "curse of Cromwell"), it still raises hackles in Ireland.

In 1688–1689, rebels again took advantage of England's political chaos. They rallied around Catholic **King James II**, who was deposed by Parliament in the "Glorious Revolution" of 1688, then fled to France and wound up in Ireland, where he formed an army to retake the crown. In the **Siege of Londonderry**, James' Catholic army surrounded the city, but some local apprentice boys locked them out, and after months of negotiations and a 105-day standoff, James went away empty-handed.

The showdown came at the massive **Battle of the Boyne** (1690), north of Dublin. Catholic James II and his 25,000 men were defeated by the 36,000 troops of Protestant **King William III** of Orange. From this point on, the color orange became a symbol for pro-English, pro-Protestant forces.

As the 17th century came to a close, England had successfully put down every rebellion. To counter Irish feistiness, English legislation became an out-and-out attack on the indigenous Gaelic culture. The English punished the mostly Catholic nation with the **Penal Laws**. Catholics couldn't vote, hold office, buy land, join the army, play the harp, or even own a horse worth more than £5. Catholic education was banned, and priests were outlawed. But the Penal Laws were difficult to enforce, and many Catholics were taught at hidden outdoor "hedge schools," and worshipped in private or at secluded "Mass rocks" in the countryside.

Protestant Rule (1700s)

During the 18th century, Ireland thrived under the English. Dublin in the 1700s (pop. 50,000) was Britain's second city, one of Europe's wealthiest and most sophisticated. It's still decorated in Georgian (neoclassical) style, named for the English kings of the time.

But beyond the Pale surrounding Dublin, rebellion continued to brew. Over time, greed on the top and dissent on the bottom led to more repressive colonial policies. The Enlightenment provided ideas of freedom, and the Revolutionary Age emboldened the Irish masses. Irish nationalists were inspired by budding democratic revolutions in America (1776) and France (1789). Increasingly, the issue of Irish independence was less a religious question than a political one, as poor, disenfranchised colonists demanded a political voice.

In Dublin, **Jonathan Swift** (1667–1745), the dean of St. Patrick's Cathedral, published his satirical *Gulliver's Travels*, with veiled references to English colonialism. He anonymously wrote pamphlets advising, "Burn all that's British, except its coal."

The **Irish Parliament** was an exclusive club, and only Protestant, male landowners could be elected to a seat (only 1 percent of the population qualified). In 1782, led by Henry Grattan (1746–1820), the Parliament negotiated limited autonomy from England (while remaining loyal to the king) and fairer treatment of the Catholics. England, chastened by the American Revolution (and soon preoccupied by the French Revolution), tolerated a more-or-less independent Irish Parliament for two decades.

Then, in 1798, came the bloodiest Irish Rebellion. The **United Irishmen** (who wanted to substitute the word "Irishman" in place of the labels Protestant or Catholic) revolted against Britain, led by

Wolfe Tone (1763–1798), a Protestant Dublin lawyer. Tone, trained in the French Revolution, had gained French aid for the Irish cause. (Though a French naval invasion in 1796 already had failed due to a freakish "Protestant wind" that blew the ships away from Ireland's shores.) The Rebellion was marked by bitter fighting—30,000 died over six weeks—before British troops crushed the revolt.

England tried to solve the Irish problem politically by forcing Ireland into a "Union" with England as part of a "United Kingdom" (**Act of Union**, 1801). The 500-year-old Irish Parliament was dissolved, becoming part of England's Parliament in London. Catholics were not allowed in Parliament. From then on, "Unionists" have been those who oppose Irish independence, wanting to preserve the country's union with Britain.

Votes, Violence, and the Famine (1800s)

Irish politicians lobbied in the British Parliament for Catholic rights, reform of absentee-landlordism, and for **Home Rule**—i.e., independence. Meanwhile, secret societies of revolutionaries pursued justice through violence.

Daniel O'Connell (1775–1847), known as the Liberator, campaigned for Catholic equality and for the repeal of the Act of Union (independence). Having personally witnessed the violence of the French Revolution in 1789 and the 1798 United Irishman Rebellion, O'Connell chose peaceful, legal means. He was a charismatic speaker, drawing half a million people to one of his "monster meeting" demonstrations at the Hill of Tara (1843). But any hope of an Irish revival was soon snuffed out by the biggest catastrophe in Irish history: the famine.

The **Great Potato Famine** (1845–1849) was caused by a fungus *(Phytophthora infestans)* that destroyed Ireland's main food crop. Roughly a million people starved to death or died of related diseases (estimates range between 500,000 and 1.1 million). Another one to two million emigrated—most to America, and others to Canada and Australia.

The poorest were hardest hit. Potatoes were their main food source, and any other crops were far too expensive—grown by tenant farmers on their landlords' land to pay the rent, and destined for export. (If this makes you mad at the English landlords, consider American ownership of land in Central America, where the landlord takes things one step beyond by not growing the local staple at all. He devotes all the land to more profitable cash crops for export, and leaves the landless farmer no alternative but to buy his food—imported from the United States—at plantation wages, in the landlord's grocery store.)

Britain—then the richest nation on earth, with an empire stretching around the globe—could seemingly do nothing to help its starving citizens. A toxic combination of laissez-faire economic policies, racial bigotry, and self-righteousness conspired to blind the English to the plight of the Irish. While the English tend to blame the famine on overpopulation (Ireland's population doubled in the 40 years leading up to the famine), many Irish say there actually was no famine—just a calculated attempt to starve down the local population. Over the course of five long years, Ireland was ruined.

The population was cut by nearly a third (from 8.4 million to 6 million), many of their best and brightest had fled, and the island's economy—and spirit—took generations to recover. The Irish language, spoken by the majority of the population before the famine, became a badge of ignorance and was considered useless to those hoping to emigrate. Ireland, which remained one of Europe's poorest countries for over a century, was slow to forget Britain's indifference. Ireland's population has only recently begun to grow again. Irish Nationalists point out that Britain's population, on the other hand, has grown from 12 million in 1845 to around 60 million today.

Before the famine, land was subdivided—each boy got a piece of the family estate (which grew smaller with each generation). After the famine, the oldest son got the estate, and the younger siblings, with no way to stay in Ireland, emigrated to Britain, Australia, Canada, or the United States. Because of the huge emigration to the United States (today, there are 45 million Irish Americans), Ireland began to face west, and American influence increased. (As negotiations between Northern Ireland and the Irish Republic continue, American involvement in the talks is welcomed and considered essential by nearly all parties.)

Occasional violence demonstrated the fury of Irish nationalism, with the tragedy of the famine inflaming the movement. In 1848, the Young Ireland armed uprising was easily squelched. In 1858, the **Irish Republican Brotherhood** was formed (the forerunner of the IRA). Also called the Fenians, they launched a never-ending campaign for independence by planting terrorist bombs. Irish Americans sent money to help finance these revolutionaries. Uprising after uprising made it clear that Ireland was ready to close this thousand-year chapter of invasions and colonialism.

On the political front, Home Rule Party leader **Charles Stuart Parnell** (1846–1891), an Irishman educated in England, made "the Irish problem" the focus of London's Parliament. Parnell lobbied for independence and for the rights of poor tenant farmers living under absentee landlords, pioneering the first boycott tactics. Then, in 1890, at the peak of his power and about to achieve Home Rule for Ireland, he was drummed out of politics by a scandal involving his mistress, scuttling the Home Rule issue for another 20 years.

Culturally, the old Gaelic, rural Ireland was being swamped by the Industrial Revolution and dominated by Protestant England.

The **Gaelic Athletic Association** was founded (in 1884) to resur-
rect pride in ancient Irish sports, such as hurling. Soon after, in
1893, writers and educators formed the Gaelic League to preserve
the traditional language, music, and poetry. Building on the tradition
of old Celtic bards, Ireland produced some of the great early modern
writers: **W. B. Yeats**, **Oscar Wilde**, **G. B. Shaw**, and **James Joyce**,
whose rambling, stream-of-consciousness *Ulysses* chronicles a day in
the life of 1904 Dublin and set new standards for the modern novel.

Easter Rising, War of Independence, Partition, and Civil War (1900–1950)

As the century turned, Ireland prepared for the inevitable showdown
with Britain.

The **Sinn Fein** party (meaning "We, Ourselves") lobbied politically for independence. The **Irish Volunteers** were more Catholic
and more militant. Also on the scene was the **Irish Citizens Army**,
with a socialist agenda to clean up Dublin's hideous tenements.

Of course, many Irish were Protestant and pro-British. The
Ulster Volunteers (Unionists, and mostly Orangemen) feared that
Home Rule would result in a Catholic-dominated state that would
oppress the Protestant minority.

Meanwhile, Britain was preoccupied with World War I, where
it was "fighting to protect the rights of small nations," and so delayed
granting Irish independence. The increasingly militant Irish rebels,
believing that England's misfortune was Ireland's opportunity,
decided to rise up and take independence on their own.

On Easter Monday, April 24, 1916, 1,500 Irish "Volunteers,"
along with members of the Irish Citizens Army, marched on
Dublin, occupied the General Post Office, and raised a green-white-
and-orange flag. The teacher and poet **Patrick Pearse** stood in front
of the Post Office and proclaimed Ireland an independent republic.

British troops struck back—in a week of street fighting and
intense shelling, some 300 died. By Saturday, the greatly outnum-
bered rebels had been arrested. The small-scale uprising—which
failed to go national and was never even popular in Dublin—was
apparently over.

However, the British government overreacted by swiftly execut-
ing the 16 ringleaders, including Pearse. Ireland was outraged, no
longer seeing the rebels as troublemakers, but as martyrs. From this
point on, Ireland was resolved to win its independence at all costs. A
poem by W. B. Yeats, "Easter 1916," captured the struggle with his
words: "All changed, changed utterly: A terrible beauty is born."

In the 1918 elections, the Sinn Fein party won big, but the new
Members of Parliament refused to go to London, instead forming
their own independent Irish Parliament in Dublin. The following
year, Irish rebels ambushed and shot two policemen, sparking two

years of confrontations called the **War of Independence**. The fledg-ling Irish Republican Army faced 40,000 British troops, including the notorious "Black and Tans" (named for their uniforms). A thou-sand people died in this war of street fighting, sniper fire, jailhouse beatings, terrorist bombs, and reprisals.

Finally, Britain agreed to Irish independence. But Ireland itself was a divided nation—the southern three-quarters of the island was mostly Catholic, Gaelic, rural, and for Home Rule; the northern quar-ter was Protestant, English, industrial, and Unionist. The solution? In 1920, in the **Government of Ireland Act**, the British Parliament partitioned the island into two independent, self-governing countries within the British Commonwealth: **Northern Ireland** and the **Irish Free State**. While the northern six counties (the only ones without a Catholic majority) voted to stay with Britain as Northern Ireland, the remaining 26 counties became the Irish Free State. (For a review of the ongoing Troubles between the North and the Republic, see the Northern Ireland chapter.)

Ireland's various political factions wrestled with this compro-mise solution, and the island plunged into a yearlong **Civil War** (1922–1923). The hard-line IRA opposed the partition, unwilling to accept a divided island, an oath of loyalty to the queen, or the remaining British Navy bases on Irish soil. They waged a street war on the armies of the Irish Free State, who supported the political settlement. Dublin and the southeast were ravaged in a year of bitter fighting before the Irish Free State emerged victorious. The IRA went underground, moving its fight north and trying for the rest of the century to topple the government of Northern Ireland.

In 1937, the Irish Free State severed more ties with the British Commonwealth, writing up a new national constitution and taking an old name—**Eire** (pronounced AIR-uh—a Gaelic word possibly derived from the early Greeks' name for the island, Ierne). In 1949, the separation was completed, as the country officially became the **Republic of Ireland**.

Celtic Tiger in the South, Troubles in the North (1950–2000)

Beginning in 1960, the Republic of Ireland—formerly a poor, rural region—was transformed into a modern economic power, thanks to foreign investors and, in 1973, membership in the European Union. Through the mid-1990s, Ireland's booming, globalized economy grew a whopping 40 percent, and property values tripled (between 1995 and 2003), earning the Republic the nickname "The Celtic Tiger."

Meanwhile, Northern Ireland—with a 55 percent Protestant majority and a large, 45 percent disaffected Catholic minority—was plagued by the Troubles. In 1967, the Northern Ireland Civil Rights Movement, inspired by America's black Civil Rights Movement, organized marches and demonstrations demanding equal treatment for Catholics (better housing, job opportunities, and voting rights). Protestant **Unionist Orangemen** countered by marching through Catholic neighborhoods, flaunting their politically dominant position in the name of tradition, and thus provoking riots. In 1969, Britain sent troops to help Northern Ireland keep the peace and met resistance from the IRA, which saw them as an occupying army supporting the Protestant, pro-British majority.

From the 1970s to the 1990s, the North was a low-level battlefield, with the IRA using terrorist tactics to achieve their political ends. The **Troubles**, claiming some 3,000 lives, continued with bombings, marches, hunger strikes, rock-throwing, and riots (notably Derry's **Bloody Sunday** in 1972), interrupted by cease-fires, broken cease-fires, and a string of peace agreements.

Then came the 1998 watershed settlement known as the **Good Friday Peace Accord** (to pro-Irish Nationalists) or the **Belfast Agreement** (to pro-British Unionists). It has proven to be a flawed but durable breakthrough in the process of getting bitter, hard-line opponents to seek common ground.

Global Nations (2000 and Beyond)

Today, both Northern Ireland and the Republic of Ireland have every reason to be optimistic about the future, as their economies boom and the political and cultural Troubles lessen. The formerly isolated island is welcoming tourists with open arms and reaching out to the rest of the globe. In 1999, the number of tourists visiting Ireland topped the six million mark, exceeding for the first time the actual native population on the island (5.6 million).

Visitors returning to Ireland are amazed at the country's transformation. Although there are still some tense areas in the North— as there are in all big cities—the peace process is grinding forward.

Now, for the first time in history, the Irish are importing labor, and they've surpassed the English in per-capita income. Since 1980, when Apple Computer set up shop here, a stream of multinational and American corporations have opened offices in Ireland. Ireland has one of the youngest populations in Europe. And these young Irish, beneficiaries of one of Europe's best educational systems, provide these corporations with a highly skilled and educated workforce. Powered by this youthful and energetic workforce, Ireland's pharmaceutical, chemical, and software industries are booming. In fact, little Ireland is second only to the United States in the exportation of software.

Of course, this rapid growth comes with problems. Urban sprawl, rising housing prices, water and air pollution, and the homogenous nature of globalization have all left their mark. In 2003, the rising economic tide had lifted Ireland to float beside Finland as one of the two most expensive countries in the European Union. Per capita consumption of alcohol has also tripled since 1970 (the dark side of recent prosperity). Still, the Celtic Tiger, although slightly muffled by the tech bubble bursting, continues to roar.

The challenges of immigration (new arrivals into Ireland) have replaced problems associated with the generations of emigration (young people leaving Ireland). Until recently, Ireland had the most liberal citizenship laws in the European Union, granting Irish citizenship to anyone born on Irish soil (even if neither parent had an Irish passport). This led to a flood of pregnant immigrant women arriving from Eastern Europe and Africa to give birth in Ireland for their children to gain EU citizenship. Families with a child born in an EU country face fewer border restrictions, increasing their chances of moving into one of the 25 EU nations. In 2004, the Irish people closed that legal loophole in a referendum vote.

While the Irish are embracing the new economies and industries of the 21st century, when it comes to sex and marriage, they still see their island as an oasis of morality and traditional values (homosexuality was decriminalized only a decade ago). The Catholic Church continues to exert a major influence on Irish society. But since the Church no longer controls the legislature, the Irish government—driven by the popular demands of the youngest population in Europe—will undoubtedly push for some changes on the following issues.

Birth Control: Americans take for granted that birth control is readily available. But Ireland only began allowing the widespread sale of condoms in 1993.

Abortion: In Ireland, women who choose to terminate their pregnancies must go to England for help. Abortion is still illegal in Ireland. And it's only been legal since 1993 to counsel Irish women to go to England for abortions. This was a big issue in 2001, when the Dutch anchored their "abortion ship" in Dublin's harbor, and again in 2002, when a referendum legalizing abortion was narrowly defeated. Watch for more referendums proposing the legalization of abortion. Locals refer to this as their next Civil War.

Divorce: Ireland voted to legalize divorce in 1995—but only on very strict conditions, and with little compensation offered to Irish women who work as homemakers.

IRISH ART

Megalithic tombs, ancient gold and metalwork, illuminated manuscripts, high crosses carved in stone, paintings of rural Ireland, and provocative political murals—Ireland comes with some fascinating art. To best appreciate this art in your travels, kick off your tour in Ireland's two top museums (both in Dublin): the **National Museum** (see page 57) and the **National Gallery** (see page 58). Each provides a good context to help you enjoy Irish art and architecture—from ancient to modern and both rural and urban. Here's a quick survey.

Megalithic Period: During the Stone Age, 5,000 years ago, farmers living in the **Valley of the Boyne,** north of Dublin, built a "cemetery" of approximately 40 **burial mounds**. The most famous of these mound tombs is the passage tomb at Newgrange. More than 300 feet in diameter and composed of 200,000 tons of loose stone, Newgrange was constructed so that the light from the winter solstice sunrise (December 21) would pass through the eastern entrance to the tomb, travel down a 60-foot passage, and illuminate the inner burial chamber. (Not bad engineering for Stone Age architects.) The effect is now recreated daily, so visitors can experience this ancient ritual of renewal and rebirth (see page 84 of Near Dublin chapter).

Some of Europe's best examples of megalithic (big rock) art are at **Newgrange**. Carved on the tomb's stones are zigzags, chevrons, parallel arcs, and concentric spirals. Scholars think these designs symbolize a belief in the eternal cycle of life and the continuation of the life force, or that they pay homage to the elements in nature on which these ancient peoples depended for their existence.

Exploring these burial mounds (only Newgrange and Knowth are open to the public), you begin to understand the reverence that these people had for nature, and the need they felt to bury their dead in these great mound tombs, returning their kin to the womb of Mother Earth.

Bronze Age: As ancient Irish cultures developed from 2000 B.C., so did their metalworking skills. Gold and bronze were used to create **tools**, **jewelry**, and **religious objects**. (The National Museum in Dublin houses the most dazzling of these works—see page 58.) Gold neck rings worn by both men and women, cufflink-like dress fasteners, bracelets, and lock rings (to hold hair in place) are but a few of the personal adornments fashioned by the ancient Irish.

Most of these objects were deliberately buried, often in bogs, as votive offerings to their gods, or to prevent warring tribes from stealing them. Like the earlier megaliths, they're decorated with geometric and organic motifs.

Iron Age: The Celts, a warrior society from Central Europe, arrived in Ireland perhaps as early as the 7th century B.C. With their metalworking skills and superior iron weaponry, they soon overwhelmed the native population. And, though the Celts may have been bloodthirsty, they wreaked havoc with a flair for the aesthetic. **Shields**, **swords**, and **scabbards** were embellished with delicate patterns, often enhanced with vivid colors. The dynamic energy of these decorations must have reflected the ferocious power of the Celts.

The Age of Saints and Scholars: Christianity grew in Ireland from St. Patrick's first efforts in the 5th century A.D. In the 6th and

7th centuries, its many great saints (such as St. Columba) established monastic settlements throughout Ireland, Britain, and the Continent, where learning, literature, and the arts flourished. During this "Golden Age" of Irish civilization, monks, along with metal-workers and stonemasons, created imaginative designs and distinctive stylistic motifs for **manuscripts**, **metal objects**, and **crosses**.

Monks wrote out and richly decorated manuscripts of the Gospels. These manuscripts—which preserved the written word in Latin, Greek, and Irish—eventually had more power than the oral tales of the ancient pagan heroes.

The most beautiful and imaginative of these illuminated manuscripts is the **Book of Kells** (c. A.D. 800), on display in the Old Library at Trinity College in Dublin (see page 51). Crafted by Irish monks at a monastery on the Scottish island of Iona, the book was brought to Ireland for safekeeping from rampaging Vikings. The skins of 150 calves were used to make the vellum, which is painted with rich pigments from plants and minerals. The entire manuscript is colorfully decorated with flat, stylized human or angelic forms and intricate, interlacing animal and knot patterns. Full-page illustrations depict the life of Christ, and many pages are given over to highly complex yet symmetrical designs that resemble an Eastern carpet. Many consider this book the finest piece of art from Europe's Dark Ages.

The most renowned metalwork of this period is the **Ardagh Chalice**, dating from the 8th century. Now on display at the National Museum in Dublin, the silver and bronze gilt chalice is as impressive as the Book of Kells. Ribbons of gold wrap around the chalice stem, while intricate knot patterns ring the cup. A magnificent gold ring and a large glass stone on the chalice bottom reflect the desire to please God. (He would see this side of the chalice when the priest drank during the Mass.)

The monks used Irish high crosses to celebrate the triumph of Christianity and provide a means of educating the illiterate masses through simple stone carvings. The **Cross of Murdock** (Muiredach's Cross, A.D. 923) is 18 feet tall, towering over the remains of the monastic settlement at Monasterboice (north of Dublin, see page 88). It is but one of many monumental crosses that visitors will discover throughout Ireland. Typically, stone carvers depicted Bible stories and surrounded them with the same intricate patterns seen in the Book of Kells and on the Ardagh Chalice.

Early Irish art focused on organic, geometric, and linear designs. Unlike Mediterranean art, Irish art of this early period was not preoccupied with a naturalistic representation of people, animals, or the landscape. Instead, it reflects Irish society's rituals and the elements and rhythms of nature.

The Suppression of Native Irish Art: The English, after invading Ireland in 1169, suppressed Celtic Irish culture. English traditions in architecture, painting, and literature replaced native styles until the late 19th century, when revivals in Irish language, folklore, music, and art began to surface.

Painters in the late 19th and early 20th centuries went to the west of Ireland, which was untouched by English dominance and influence, in search of traditional Irish subject matter.

Jack B. Yeats (1871–1957, brother of the poet W. B. Yeats), Belfast-born painter **Paul Henry** (1876–1958), and **Sean Keating** (1889–1977) all looked to the west for inspiration. The National Gallery in Dublin holds many of these artists' greatest works, with an entire gallery dedicated to Jack Yeats. Many of his early paintings illustrate scenes of his beloved Sligo. His later paintings are more expressionistic in style and patriotic in subject matter.

Henry's paintings depict the rugged beauty of the Connemara region and its people, with scenes of rustic cottages, mountains, and boglands. Keating, the most political of the three painters, featured patriotic scenes from Ireland's struggle against the English for independence.

Contemporary Irish art is often linked to the social, political, and environmental issues facing Ireland today. Themes include the position of the Church in the daily lives of the modern Irish, the effects of development on the countryside, the changing roles of women in Ireland, and the Troubles. Look for this provocative art at the Irish Museum of Modern Art in Dublin, and at city galleries.

In Northern Ireland, murals in sectarian neighborhoods (such as Shankill and Falls Roads in Belfast) are stirring public testaments to the martyrs and to the heroes, to resistance and to confrontation, and to the reconciliation that continues to elude the people of Northern Ireland. (For more on these murals, see the Derry chapter).

IRISH LITERATURE

Since the Book of Kells, Ireland's greatest contributions to the world of art have been through words. As there was no Irish Gaelic written language, the inhabitants of Ireland were illiterate until Christianity came in the 4th century. Far from ignorant, Celtic society maintained a complex set of laws and historical records and legends...verbally. The druidic priests and bards who passed this rich oral tradition down from generation to generation were the most respected members of the clan, next to the king. After Christianity transformed Ireland into a refuge of literacy (while the rest of Europe crumbled into the Dark Ages), Charlemagne's imported Irish monks invented "minuscule," which became the basis of the lowercase letters we use in our alphabet today. The cultural importance placed on the word (spoken, and for the past 1,500 years, written) is today reflected in the rich output of modern Irish writers.

Three hundred years ago, **Jonathan Swift** created his master-piece, *Gulliver's Travels,* as an acidic satire of British colonialism, which has ironically survived as a children's classic. **William Butler Yeats** dedicated his early writings in the 1880s to the "Celtic Twilight" rebirth of pride in mythic Irish heroes and heroines. His early poems and plays were filled with fairies and idyllic rural inno-cence. His later poems reflected Ireland's painful transition to inde-pendence, as "a terrible beauty" was born. His Nobel Prize for literature (1923) was eventually followed by three more prize-winning Irish authors: **George Bernard Shaw** (1925), **Samuel Beckett** (1969), and **Seamus Heaney** (1995).

Oscar Wilde wrote the darkly fascinating novel *The Picture of Dorian Gray* and the witty play *The Importance of Being Earnest*, making him the toast of London in the 1890s—before the scandal of his homosexuality turned Victorian society against him. Meanwhile, **Bram Stoker** was conjuring up a Gothic thriller called *Dracula*. Most inventive of all, perhaps, was **James Joyce**, who broke new ground and captured literary lightning in a bottle when he developed his complex stream-of-consciousness style in his masterpiece novel, *Ulysses.*

The **Abbey Theatre** (championed by Yeats) was the world's first national theater, built to house plays intended to give a voice to Ireland's flowering playwrights. When **J. M. Synge** staged *The Playboy of the Western World* there in 1907, his unflattering comic portrayal of Irish peasant life (and mention of women's underwear) caused riots. Twenty years later, **Sean O'Casey** provoked more riots at the Abbey when his *Plough and the Stars* production depicted the 1916 Uprising in a way that was at odds with the audience's cher-ished views of their heroes.

In recent decades, the bittersweet Irish literary parade has been inhabited by tragically volcanic characters like **Brendan Behan**, who exclaimed, "I'm not a writer with a drinking problem...I'm a drinker with a writing problem." Bleak poverty experienced in childhood was the catalyst for **Frank McCourt**'s memorable *Angela's Ashes*. Among the most celebrated of today's Irish writers is **Roddy Doyle**, whose feel for working-class Dublin resonates in his novels of contempo-rary life, like *The Commitments*, as well as in historical slices of life, like *A Star Called Henry*.

IRISH LANGUAGE

The Irish have a rich oral tradition that goes back to their ancient fireside storytelling days. Part of the fun of traveling here is getting an ear for the way locals express themselves. Ask an Irish person for directions, and you'll more often than not have an interesting, mem-orable experience. Being verbal is a fundamental part of being Irish: "How do I know what I think until I hear what I say?"

Irish Gaelic is one of four surviving Celtic languages, along with Scottish Gaelic, Welsh, and Breton (spoken in parts of Brittany). A couple of centuries ago, there were seven surviving Celtic languages, but three have died out: Manx (the Isle of Man), Cornish (spoken in Cornwall), and Galician (spoken in Northern Spain). Some proud Irish choose to call their native tongue "Irish" instead of "Gaelic" to ensure that there is no confusion with what is spoken in parts of Scotland.

Two hundred years ago, the majority of the Irish population spoke Irish Gaelic. But most of the speakers were of the poor laborer class that, during the famine, either died or emigrated. After the famine, Irish Gaelic was seen as a badge of backwardness. Parents and teachers understood that English was the language that would serve children best when they emigrated to better lives in America, Canada, Australia, or England. Children in schools wore a tally stick around their necks, and a notch was cut by teachers each time a child was caught speaking Irish. At the end of the day, the child received a whack for each notch in the stick. It wasn't until the resurgence of cultural pride, brought on by the Gaelic League in 1884, that an attempt was made to promote use of the language.

These days, less than five percent of the Irish population is fluent in their native tongue. However, it's taken seriously enough that all national laws passed must first be written in Irish, then translated into English. Irish Gaelic can be heard most often in the western counties of Kerry, Galway, and Donegal. Each of these three counties has a slightly different dialect. You'll know you're entering an Irish Gaelic speaking area when you see a sign saying "Gaeltacht" (GAIL-tekt).

In Irish Gaelic, there is no "th" sound—which you can hear today when an Irish person says something like "turdy tree" (33). There is also no equivalent of the simple words "yes" and "no." Instead, answers are given in the affirmative or negative rephrasing of the question. For example, a question like "Did you mail the letter today?" would be answered with "I did (mail the letter)," rather than a simple "yes." Or "It's a nice day today, isn't it?" would be answered with "It is," or "'Tis."

Irish Place Names

Here are a few words that appear in Irish place names. You'll see these on road signs or at tourist sights.

Alt		cliff
An Lar		city center
Ard		high, height, hillock
Baile	(BALL-yah)	town, town land
Bally	(BAH-lee)	town, town land
Beag	(beg)	little
Bearna	(bar-na)	gap
Boireann	(burr-en)	large rock, rocky area
Bothar	(boh-er)	road
Bun		end, bottom
Caiseal	(cash-el)	castle, circular stone fort
Caislean		castle
Cathair		circular stone fort, city
Cill	(kill)	church
Cloch		stone
Doire	(DER-ry)	wooded area
Droichead	(DROH-ed)	bridge
Drumlin		small hill
Dun	(doon)	fort
Fionn	(fin)	white, fair-haired person
Gaeltacht	(GAIL-tekt)	Irish language district
Gall	(gaul)	foreigner
Gaol	(jail)	jail
Garda		police
Gort		field
Innis	(in-ish)	island
Kil		church; monk's cell
Mileac	(mec-luch)	low, marshy ground
Mor		large
Oifig an Phoist	(UFF-ig un fwisht)	post office
Poll		hole, cave
Rath		ancient earthen fort
Si	(shee)	fairy mound, bewitching
Sli	(slee)	route, way
Sliabh	(sleeve)	mountain
Sraid	(shrawd)	street
Teach	(tagh)	house
Trá	(thraw)	beach, strand
Tur		tower

Irish Pleasantries

When you reach the more remote western fringe of Ireland, you're likely to hear folks speaking Irish. Although locals in these areas can readily converse with you in English, it's fascinating to hear their ancient Celtic language spoken. Here are some basic Irish phrases:

Dia dhuit	(JEE-a dich)	Good day, hello
Dia's muire dhuit	(JEE-as MWUR-a dich)	response to *dia dhuit*
Fáilte	(FAHLT-shuh)	Welcome
Conas ta tu?	(CUNN-us thaw too)	How are you?
Go raibh maith agat	(guh roh moh UG-ut)	Thank you
Slán agat	(slawn UG-ut)	Good-bye

Irish Pub and Music Words

The Irish love to socialize. Pubs are like public living rooms, where friends gather in a corner to play tunes, and anyone is a welcome guest. Here are some useful pub and music words:

Poitín	(po-CHEEN)	moonshine, homemade liquor
Craic	(crack)	fun atmosphere, good conversation
Bodhrán	(BOUR-ohn)	traditional drum
Uilleann	(ILL-in)	elbow (*uilleann* pipes are elbow bagpipes)
Trad	(trahd)	traditional Irish music
Ceili	(KAY-lee)	Irish dance gathering
Fleadh	(flah)	music festival
Slainte	(SLAWN-chuh)	cheers, to your health
Táim súgach!	(thaw im SOO-gakh)	I'm tipsy!
Lei thras	(LEH-hrass)	toilets
Mná	(min-AW)	women's room
Fir	(fear)	men's room

Irish Politics

Politics is a popular topic of conversation in Ireland. Whether you pick up a local newspaper or turn on your car radio, you'll often encounter these Irish political terms in the media:

Taoiseach	(TEE-shock)	Prime Minister of Irish Republic
Seanad	(SHAN-ud)	Irish Senate
Dáil	(DOY-ill)	Irish House of Representatives
TD, Teachta Dála	(TALK-ta DOLL-a)	Member of Irish Parliament

APPENDIX

Let's Talk Telephones

Here's a primer on making phone calls. For information specific to Ireland, see "Telephones" in the introduction.

Making Calls within a European Country: About half of all European countries use area codes (like we do); the other half uses a direct-dial system without area codes.

To make calls within a country that uses a direct-dial system (Belgium, the Czech Republic, Denmark, France, Italy, Portugal, Norway, Spain, and Switzerland), you dial the same number whether you're calling across the country or across the street.

In countries that use area codes (such as Austria, Britain, Finland, Germany, Ireland, the Netherlands, and Sweden), you dial the local number when calling within a city, and you add the area code if calling long-distance within the country.

Making International Calls: You always start with the international access code (011 if you're calling from the United States or Canada, or 00 from Europe), then dial the country code of the country you're calling (see chart below).

What you dial next depends on the phone system of the country you're calling. If the country uses area codes, drop the initial 0 of the area code, then dial the rest of the number.

Countries that use direct-dial systems (no area codes) vary in how they're accessed internationally by phone. For instance, if you're making an international call to the Czech Republic, Denmark, Italy, Norway, Portugal, or Spain, simply dial the international access code, country code, and the local phone number. But if you're calling Belgium, France, or Switzerland, drop the initial zero of the phone number. Example: To call a Paris hotel (tel. 01 47 05 49 15) from Dublin, dial 00, 33 (France's country code), then 1 47 05 49 15 (phone number without the initial zero).

European Calling Chart

Just smile and dial, using this key:
AC = Area Code, LN = Local Number.

European Country	Calling long distance within...	Calling from the U.S.A./ Canada to...	Calling from a European country to...
Austria	AC + LN	011 + 43 + AC (without the initial zero) + LN	00 + 43 + AC (without the initial zero) + LN
Belgium	LN	011 + 32 + LN (without initial zero)	00 + 32 + LN (without initial zero)
Britain	AC + LN	011 + 44 + AC (without initial zero) + LN	00 + 44 + AC (without initial zero) + LN
Czech Republic	LN	011 + 420 + LN	00 + 420 + LN
Denmark	LN	011 + 45 + LN	00 + 45 + LN
Estonia	LN	011 + 372 + LN	00 + 372 + LN
Finland	AC + LN	011 + 358 + AC (without initial zero) + LN	00 + 358 + AC (without initial zero) + LN
France	LN	011 + 33 + LN (without initial zero)	00 + 33 + LN (without initial zero)
Germany	AC + LN	011 + 49 + AC (without initial zero) + LN	00 + 49 + AC (without initial zero) + LN
Gibraltar	LN	011 + 350 + LN	00 + 350 + LN From Spain: 9567 + LN
Greece	LN	011 + 30 + LN	00 + 30 + LN

European Country	Calling long distance within ...	Calling from the U.S.A./ Canada to ...	Calling from a European country to ...
Ireland	AC + LN	011 + 353 + AC (without initial zero) + LN	00 + 353 + AC (without initial zero) + LN
Italy	LN	011 + 39 + LN	00 + 39 + LN
Morocco	LN	011 + 212 + LN (without initial zero)	00 + 212 + LN (without initial zero)
Netherlands	AC + LN	011 + 31 + AC (without initial zero) + LN	00 + 31 + AC (without initial zero) + LN
Norway	LN	011 + 47 + LN	00 + 47 + LN
Portugal	LN	011 + 351 + LN	00 + 351 + LN
Spain	LN	011 + 34 + LN	00 + 34 + LN
Sweden	AC + LN	011 + 46 + AC (without initial zero) + LN	00 + 46 + AC (without initial zero) + LN
Switzerland	LN	011 + 41 + LN (without initial zero)	00 + 41 + LN (without initial zero)
Turkey	AC (if no initial zero is included, add one) + LN	011 + 90 + AC (without initial zero) + LN	00 + 90 + AC (without initial zero) + LN

- The instructions above apply whether you're calling a fixed phone or mobile phone.

- The international access codes (the first numbers you dial when making an international call) are 011 if you're calling from the U.S.A./Canada, or 00 if you're calling from anywhere in Europe.

- To call the U.S.A. or Canada from Europe, dial 00, then 1 (the country code for the U.S.A. and Canada), then the area code and number. In short, 00 + 1 + AC + LN = Hi, Mom!

Country Codes

After you've dialed the international access code (00 if you're calling from Europe, 011 if calling from the United States or Canada), dial the code of the country you're calling.

Austria—43	Ireland—353
Belgium—32	Italy—39
Britain—44	Morocco—212
Canada—1	Netherlands—31
Croatia—385	Norway—47
Czech Rep.—420	Poland—48
Denmark—45	Portugal—351
Estonia—372	Slovenia—386
Finland—358	Spain—34
France—33	Sweden—46
Germany—49	Switzerland—41
Gibraltar—350	Turkey—90
Greece—30	U.S.A.—1

Dial Away...

Note that the Republic of Ireland (country code: 353) has a different country code than Northern Ireland, which is part of Britain (country code: 44). The Republic of Ireland has a special way to call Northern Ireland: dial 048, then the local number without the area code.

From the United States/Canada to the Republic of Ireland: Dial 011-353, then the area code without its initial 0, then the local number.

From European countries (including Northern Ireland) to the Republic of Ireland: Dial 00-353, then the area code without its initial 0, then the local number.

From the United States/Canada to Northern Ireland: Dial 011-44-28 (28 is Northern Ireland's area code without its initial 0), then the local number.

From the Republic of Ireland to Northern Ireland: Dial 048, then the local number. (In this case, Northern Ireland's area code, 028, is omitted entirely.)

From any European country (except the Republic of Ireland) to Northern Ireland: Dial 00-44-28 (Northern Ireland's area code without its initial 0), then the local number.

From anywhere in Ireland (north or south) to the United States or Canada: 00-1, then the area code and local number.

Useful Numbers in the Republic of Ireland
Emergency: tel. 999
Operator Assistance: tel. 10 for Ireland, tel. 114 to call outside Ireland
Directory Assistance within Ireland: tel. 11811 (free from phone booth, or 34p from anywhere else)
International Info: tel. 11818 (free from phone booth)
   Note that calls beginning with 1-800 are free throughout Ireland, but 1-850 calls cost the same as local calls.

Useful Numbers in Northern Ireland
Emergency (police and ambulance): tel. 999
Operator Assistance: tel. 100 for Britain, tel. 155 to call outside Britain
Directory Assistance within Britain: tel. 192 (20p from phone booth, otherwise £1.50)
International Info: tel. 153 (20p from phone booth, otherwise £1.50)

Airlines
These are phone numbers for the Republic of Ireland. (To call the special 1-800 numbers from the States, dial 011-353, then the 800 number without the initial 1).
Aer Arann: tel. 01/814-1058 (www.aerarann.com)
Aer Lingus: tel. 01/886-8888 (www.aerlingus.com)
American: tel. 01/602-0550 (www.aa.com)
bmi british midland: tel. 01/407-3036 (www.flybmi.com)
British Airways: tel. 1-800-626-747 (www.ba.com)
Continental Airlines: tel. 1-890-925-252 (www.continental.com)
Delta: tel. 1-800-768-080 (www.delta.com)
Lufthansa: tel. 01/844-5544 (www.lufthansa.ie)
Ryanair (cheap fares): tel. 0818-303-030 (www.ryanair.com)
Scandinavian Airlines System (SAS): tel. 01/844-5888 (www.scandinavian.net)
United Airlines: tel. 01/819-1760 (www.united.com)
Virgin Atlantic: tel. 01/500-5500 (www.virginatlantic.com)

Car Rental Agencies
All of these car rental agencies are located in Dublin.
Avis: 1 Hanover Street East, tel. 01/605-7502, airport tel. 01/605-7500, www.avis.ie
Budget: 151 Lower Drumcondra Road, tel. 01/837-9611, airport tel. 01/844-5150, www.budget.com
Europcar: Baggot Street Bridge, tel. 01/614-2840, airport tel. 01/812-0410, www.europcar.ie
Hertz: 158 South Circular Road, tel. 01/660-2255, airport tel. 01/844-5400, www.hertz.com

U.S. Embassies

In the Republic of Ireland: 42 Elgin Road, Dublin, tel. 01/668-7122 or 01/668-8777, www.usembassy.ie

In Northern Ireland: Danesfort House, 223 Stranmillis Road, tel. 028/9038- 6100, www.usembassy.org.uk

Public Holidays and Festivals

This is a partial list of holidays and festivals. Some dates have yet to be set. For more information, contact **Tourism Ireland** in New York (tel. 800/223-6470 or 212/418-0800, www.tourismireland.com, info@shamrock.org) and check out these Web sites: www.whatsonwhen.com, www.whatsgoingon.com, and www.festivals.com.

Jan 1–3	New Year's weekend (banks closed on Mon)
March 16–21	St. Patrick's Day celebration throughout Ireland (parades, drunkenness, 5-day festival in Dublin, www.stpatricksday.ie)
March 25	Good Friday (banks closed)
March 27–28	Easter Sunday and Monday (banks closed Mon)
March 29–April 3	Pan Celtic International Festival, Tralee, Kerry (festival rotates locations every year, www.panceltic.com)
May 2	May Day (banks closed), Ireland and U.K.
June 6	June Holiday (banks closed), Ireland and U.K.
June 16	Bloomsday (James Joyce festival, www.jamesjoyce.ie), Dublin
July 11–24	Galway Arts Festival, Galway (www.galwayartsfestival.com)
July 12	Battle of the Boyne anniversary (Protestant marches, protests), Northern Ireland
Aug 1	August Holiday (banks closed), Ireland
Aug 5–14	Féile an Phobail, West Belfast Irish cultural festival, Northern Ireland (www.feilebelfast.com)
2nd weekend in Aug	Dingle Races (boat races), Dingle
2nd weekend in Aug	Puck Fair, Killorglin, Kerry ("Ireland's Oldest Fair" and drink-fest, www.puckfair.ie)
3rd weekend in Aug	Dingle Regatta, Dingle
Likely Aug 19–23	Rose of Tralee International Festival, Tralee

2005

JANUARY

S	M	T	W	T	F	S
						1
2	3	4	5	6	7	8
9	10	11	12	13	14	15
16	17	18	19	20	21	22
23/30	24/31	25	26	27	28	29

FEBRUARY

S	M	T	W	T	F	S
		1	2	3	4	5
6	7	8	9	10	11	12
13	14	15	16	17	18	19
20	21	22	23	24	25	26
27	28					

MARCH

S	M	T	W	T	F	S
		1	2	3	4	5
6	7	8	9	10	11	12
13	14	15	16	17	18	19
20	21	22	23	24	25	26
27	28	29	30	31		

APRIL

S	M	T	W	T	F	S
					1	2
3	4	5	6	7	8	9
10	11	12	13	14	15	16
17	18	19	20	21	22	23
24	25	26	27	28	29	30

MAY

S	M	T	W	T	F	S
1	2	3	4	5	6	7
8	9	10	11	12	13	14
15	16	17	18	19	20	21
22	23	24	25	26	27	28
29	30	31				

JUNE

S	M	T	W	T	F	S
			1	2	3	4
5	6	7	8	9	10	11
12	13	14	15	16	17	18
19	20	21	22	23	24	25
26	27	28	29	30		

JULY

S	M	T	W	T	F	S
					1	2
3	4	5	6	7	8	9
10	11	12	13	14	15	16
17	18	19	20	21	22	23
24/31	25	26	27	28	29	30

AUGUST

S	M	T	W	T	F	S
	1	2	3	4	5	6
7	8	9	10	11	12	13
14	15	16	17	18	19	20
21	22	23	24	25	26	27
28	29	30	31			

SEPTEMBER

S	M	T	W	T	F	S
				1	2	3
4	5	6	7	8	9	10
11	12	13	14	15	16	17
18	19	20	21	22	23	24
25	26	27	28	29	30	

OCTOBER

S	M	T	W	T	F	S
						1
2	3	4	5	6	7	8
9	10	11	12	13	14	15
16	17	18	19	20	21	22
23/30	24/31	25	26	27	28	29

NOVEMBER

S	M	T	W	T	F	S
		1	2	3	4	5
6	7	8	9	10	11	12
13	14	15	16	17	18	19
20	21	22	23	24	25	26
27	28	29	30			

DECEMBER

S	M	T	W	T	F	S
				1	2	3
4	5	6	7	8	9	10
11	12	13	14	15	16	17
18	19	20	21	22	23	24
25	26	27	28	29	30	31

Aug 29	Late Summer Holiday (banks closed), U.K. only
Late Aug–early Sept	Blessing of the Boats (maritime festival), Dingle
Late Sept	Galway Oyster Festival (4 days), Galway (www.galwayoysterfest.com)
Late Oct	Belfast Queens Festival (music, 12 days), Belfast (www.belfastfestival.com)
Oct 31	October holiday (banks closed), Ireland
Dec 25–28	Christmas holiday, Ireland and U.K.
Dec 26	St. Stephen's Day (religious festival), Ireland; Boxing Day, U.K.

Dublin Climate

The first line is the average low, the second line is the average high, and the third line is the number of days with no rain. Note that temperatures are moderate throughout the country, so use the Dublin temperatures listed below as a model. For more detailed weather statistics for destinations throughout Ireland (as well as the rest of the world), check www.worldclimate.com.

J	F	M	A	M	J	J	A	S	O	N	D
34°	35°	37°	39°	43°	48°	52°	51°	48°	43°	39°	37°
46°	47°	51°	55°	60°	65°	67°	67°	63°	57°	51°	47°
18	18	21	19	21	19	18	19	18	20	18	17

Numbers and Stumblers

- Europeans write a few of their numbers differently than we do. 1 = $\prime$, 4 = $\prime$, 7 = $\prime$. Learn the difference or miss your train.
- In Europe, dates appear as day/month/year, so Christmas is 25/12/05.
- Commas are decimal points, and decimals are commas. A dollar and a half is $1,50, and there are 5.280 feet in a mile.
- When pointing, use your whole hand, palm down.
- When counting with fingers, start with your thumb. If you hold up your first finger to request one item, you'll probably get two.
- What Americans call the second floor of a building is the first floor in Europe.
- Europeans keep the left "lane" open for passing on escalators and moving sidewalks. Keep to the right.

Metric Conversion (approximate)

1 inch = 25 millimeters   32 degrees F = 0 degrees C
1 foot = 0.3 meter   82 degrees F = about 28 degrees C
1 yard = 0.9 meter   1 ounce = 28 grams
1 mile = 1.6 kilometers   1 kilogram = 2.2 pounds
1 centimeter = 0.4 inch   1 quart = 0.95 liter
1 meter = 39.4 inches   1 square yard = 0.8 square meter
1 kilometer = .62 mile   1 acre = 0.4 hectare

Converting Temperatures: Fahrenheit and Celsius

For Weather   For Health

Making Your Hotel Reservation

Faxing or e-mailing are the preferred methods for reserving a room. They're more accurate than telephoning and much faster than writing a letter. Use this handy form for your fax or find it online at www.ricksteves.com/reservation. Photocopy and fax away.

One-Page Fax

To: _____ @ _____
      hotel   *fax*

From: _____ @ _____
        name   *fax*

Today's date: _____ / _____ / _____
                    day   month   year

Dear Hotel _____ ,
Please make this reservation for me:

Name: _____

Total # of people:_____ # of rooms: _____ # of nights: _____

Arriving: _____ / _____ / _____   My time of arrival (24-hr clock): _____
         day month year   (I will telephone if I will be late)

Departing: ____ / ____ / ____
          day month year

Room(s): Single _____ Double ____ Twin _____ Triple ____ Quad_____

With: Toilet _____ Shower _____ Bath _____ Sink only _____

Special needs: View____ Quiet ____ Cheapest ____ Ground Floor ____

Please fax, mail, or e-mail confirmation of my reservation, along with the type of room reserved and the price. Please also inform me of your cancellation policy. After I hear from you, I will quickly send my credit-card information as a deposit to hold the room. Thank you.

_____
Signature

_____
Name

_____
Address

_____
City   **State**   **Zip Code   Country**

_____
E-mail Address

Irish-Yankee Vocabulary

advert–advertisement
afters–dessert
anticlockwise–counterclockwise
aubergine–eggplant
banger–sausage
bang on–correct
bank holiday–legal holiday
bap–hamburger-type bun
beer mat–coaster
billion–a thousand of our billions
    (a trillion)
biro–ballpoint pen
biscuit–cookie
black pudding–sausage made from
    dried blood
blather–rambling, empty talk
bloody–damn (adj)
bog–slang for toilet
bonnet–car hood
boot–car trunk
braces–suspenders
bridle way–path for walkers, bikers,
    and horse riders
brilliant–cool
bum–bottom, or "backside"
busker–street musician
candy floss–cotton candy
caravan–trailer
car boot sale–temporary flea
    market with car trunk displays
    (a good place to buy back your
    stolen goods)
cat's eyes–road reflectors
champ–mashed potatoes and
    onions
cheap and nasty–cheap and bad
    quality
chemist–pharmacist
chicory–endive
chips–french fries
chipper, or chippie–fish-and-chips
    shop
chockablock–jam-packed
cider–alcoholic apple cider
clearway–road where you can't stop
coach–long-distance bus
concession–discounted admission
cos–romaine lettuce
cotton buds–cotton swabs
courgette–zucchini
crisps–potato chips
cuppa–cup of tea

deadly–really good
dear–expensive
dicey–iffy, risky
digestives–round graham crackers
dinner–lunch or dinner
diversion–detour
done and dusted–completed
donkey's years–until the cows
    come home
draughts–checkers
draw–marijuana
dual carriageway–divided highway
    (four lanes)
Dubs–people from Dublin
eejit–moron
en suite–bathroom attached to
    room
face flannel–washcloth
fanny–vagina
fell–hill or high plain
first floor–second floor
fluthered–drunk
football–Irish football
fortnight–two weeks
full monty–the whole shebang;
    everything
GAA–Gaelic Athletic Association
gallery–balcony
gammon–ham
gangway–aisle
gargle–to have an alcoholic drink
give way–yield
giving off–complaining
glen–narrow valley
gobsmacked–astounded
goods wagon–freight truck
grand–good, well ("How are you?"
    "I'm grand, thanks.")
gurrier–hooligan
half eight–8:30 (not 7:30)
heath–open, treeless land
holiday–vacation
homely–likable, cozy
hoover–vacuum cleaner
hurling–Irish field hockey/rugby
ice lolly–popsicle
interval–intermission
ironmonger–hardware store
jacket potato–baked potato
jars–drinks (alcohol)
jelly–Jell-O
jumble–sale, rummage sale

jumper–sweater
just a tick–just a second
keep your pecker up–be brave
kipper–smoked herring
knackered–exhausted
knickers–ladies' panties
knocking shop–brothel
knock up–wake up, or visit
ladybird–ladybug
left luggage–baggage check
let–rent (vb)
lorry–truck
mac–mackintosh (trench) coat
mate–buddy (boy or girl)
mean–stingy
mews–courtyard stables, often used as cottages
minced meat–hamburger
mobile (MOH-bile)–cell phone
nappy–diaper
natter–talk and talk
norn iron–Northern Ireland
nought–zero
noughts & crosses–tic-tac-toe
off license–store selling take-away liquor
paralytic–passed-out drunk
pasty–savory (usually meat) pie with crust
pavement–sidewalk
petrol–gas (fuel)
pissed (rude), paralytic, bevvied, wellied, popped up, ratted, pissed as a newt–drunk
pitch–playing field
plaster–Band-Aid
publican–pub manager
punter–partygoer
put a sock in it–shut up
quay–waterside street, ship offloading area
queue–line
queue up–line up
quid–pound (money in Northern Ireland, worth about $1.70)
ramps–speed bumps
randy–horny
redundant, made–fired
return ticket–round-trip
ring up–call (telephone)
roundabout–traffic circle
RTE–Irish Republic's broadcast network

rubber–eraser
sanitary towel–sanitary pad
sausage roll–sausage wrapped in a flaky pastry
Scotch egg–hard-boiled egg wrapped in sausage meat
self-catering–apartment with kitchen
sellotape–Scotch tape
serviette–napkin
shag (rude)–to have sex
single ticket–one-way ticket
slag–to ridicule, tease
smalls–underwear
snogging–kissing, cuddling
solicitor–lawyer
starkers–buck naked
starters–appetizers
stick–criticism
stone–14 pounds (weight)
strand–beach
subway–underground pedestrian passageway
sultanas–golden raisins
surgical spirit–rubbing alcohol
sort out–figure out
swede–rutabaga
taxi rank–taxi stand
theatre–live stage
tick–a check mark
tight as a Scotsman–cheapskate (water-tight)
tights–pantyhose
tipper lorry–dump truck
tin–can
to let–for rent
top up–refill a drink
torch–flashlight
towpath–path along a river
Travellers–itinerants, once known as "tinkers" (rude)
turf accountant–bookie
underground–subway
verge–grassy edge of road
victualler–butcher
way out–exit
wee–urinate
Wellingtons, wellies–rubber boots
whacked–exhausted
witter on–gab and gab
your man–that guy, this guy
zebra crossing–crosswalk
zed–the letter "z"

INDEX

Start your trip at
www.ricksteves.com

Rick Steves' website is packed with over 3,000 pages of timely travel information. It's also your gateway to getting FREE monthly travel news from Rick — and more!

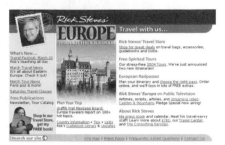

Free Monthly European Travel News

Fresh articles on Europe's most interesting destinations and happenings. Rick will even send you an e-mail every month (often direct from Europe) with his latest discoveries!

Timely Travel Tips

Rick Steves' best money-and-stress-saving tips on trip planning, packing, transportation, hotels, health, safety, finances, hurdling the language barrier. . .and more.

Travelers' Graffiti Wall

Candid advice and opinions from thousands of travelers on everything listed above, plus whatever topics are hot at the moment (discount flights, packing tips, scams. . .you name it).

Rick's Annual Guide to European Railpasses

The clearest, most comprehensive guide to the confusing array of railpass options out there, and how to choo-choose the railpass that best fits your itinerary and budget. Then you can order your railpass (and get a bunch of great freebies) online from us!

Great Gear at the Rick Steves Travel Store

Enjoy bargains on Rick's guidebooks, planning maps and TV series DVDs—and on his custom-designed carry-on bags, wheeled bags, day bags and light-packing accessories.

Rick Steves Tours

Every year more than 5,000 lucky travelers explore Europe on a Rick Steves tour. Learn more about our 26 different one-to-three-week itineraries, read uncensored feedback from our tour alums, and sign up for your dream trip online!

Rick on TV

Read the scripts and see video clips from the popular Rick Steves' Europe TV series, and get an inside look at Rick's 13 newest shows.

Respect for Your Privacy

Ordering online from us is secure. When you buy something from us, join a tour, or subscribe to Rick's free monthly travel news e-mails, we promise to never share your name, information, or e-mail address with anyone else. You won't be spammed!

Have fun raising your Travel I.Q. at
www.ricksteves.com

Travel smart...carry on!

The latest generation of Rick Steves' carry-on travel bags is easily the best—benefiting from two decades of on-the-road attention to what really matters: maximum quality and strength; practical, flexible features; and no unnecessary frills. You won't find a better value anywhere!

Convertible, expandable, and carry-on-size:

Rick Steves' Back Door Bag $99

This is the same bag that Rick Steves lives out of for three months every summer. It's made of rugged water-resistant 1000 denier Cordura nylon, and best of all, it converts easily from a smart-looking suitcase to a handy backpack with comfortably-curved shoulder straps and a padded waistbelt.

This roomy, versatile 9" x 21" x 14" bag has a large 2600 cubic-inch main compartment, plus three outside pockets (small, medium and huge) that are perfect for often-used items. And the cinch-tight compression straps will keep your load compact and close to your back—not sagging like a sack of potatoes.

Wishing you had even more room to bring home souvenirs? Pull open the full-perimeter expando-zipper and its capacity jumps from 2600 to 3000 cubic inches. When you want to use it as a suitcase or check it as luggage (required when "expanded"), the straps and belt hide away in a zippered compartment in the back.

Attention travelers under 5'4" tall: This bag also comes in an inch-shorter version, for a compact-friendlier fit between the waistbelt and shoulder straps.

Convenient, durable, and carry-on-size:

Rick Steves' Wheeled Bag $119

At 9" x 21" x 14" our sturdy Rick Steves' Wheeled Bag is rucksack-soft in front, but the rest is lined with a hard ABS-lexan shell to give maximum protection to your belongings. We've spared no expense on moving parts, splurging on an extra-long button-release handle and big, tough inline skate wheels for easy rolling on rough surfaces.

This bag is not convertible! Our research tells us that travelers who've bought convertible wheeled bags never put them on their backs anyway, so we've eliminated the extra weight and expense.

Rick Steves' Wheeled Bag has exactly the same three-outside-pocket configuration as our Back Door Bag, plus a handy "add-a-bag" strap and full lining.

Our Back Door Bags and Wheeled Bags come in black, navy, blue spruce, evergreen and merlot.

For great deals on a wide selection of travel goodies, begin your next trip at the Rick Steves Travel Store!

Visit the Rick Steves Travel Store at
www.ricksteves.com

Rick Steves

COUNTRY GUIDES 2005

France
Germany & Austria
Great Britain
Ireland
Italy
Portugal
Scandinavia
Spain
Switzerland

CITY GUIDES 2005

Amsterdam, Bruges & Brussels
Florence & Tuscany
London
Paris
Prague & The Czech Republic
Provence & The French Riviera
Rome
Venice

BEST OF GUIDES

Best European City Walks & Museums
Best of Eastern Europe
Best of Europe

More *Savvy*. More *Surprising*. More Fun.

PHRASE BOOKS & DICTIONARIES

French
French, Italian & German
German
Italian
Portuguese
Spanish

MORE EUROPE FROM RICK STEVES

Easy Access Europe
Europe 101
Europe Through the Back Door
Postcards from Europe

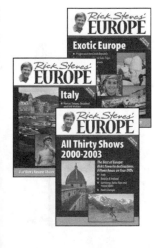

DVD RICK STEVES' EUROPE

Rick Steves' Europe All Thirty
   Shows 2000–2003
Britain & Ireland
Exotic Europe
Germany, The Swiss Alps
   & Travel Skills
Italy

For a complete list of Rick Steves' guidebooks, see page 9.

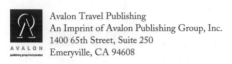

Avalon Travel Publishing
An Imprint of Avalon Publishing Group, Inc.
1400 65th Street, Suite 250
Emeryville, CA 94608

Text © 2005, 2004, 2003, 2002 by Rick Steves
Maps © 2005, 2004, 2003, 2002 by Europe Through the Back Door

Printed in the U.S.A. by Worzalla
First printing December 2004

Thanks to Rozanne Stringer for her writing on the Celts, Celtic Tiger, St. Brendan, and Irish art. Thanks also to Gene Openshaw and Mike Kelly for their help.

For the latest on Rick's lectures, guidebooks, tours, and public television series, contact Europe Through the Back Door, Box 2009, Edmonds, WA 98020, tel. 425/771-8303, fax 425/771-0833, www.ricksteves.com, rick@ricksteves.com.

ISBN 1-56691-677-1
ISSN 1538-1587

Europe Through the Back Door Managing Editor: Risa Laib
ETBD Editors: Cameron Hewitt, Jennifer Hauseman, Lauren Mills
Avalon Travel Publishing Editor & Series Manager: Roxanna Font
Avalon Travel Publishing Project Editor: Patrick Collins
Copy Editor: Mia Lipman
Indexer: Judy Hunt
Production Coordinator: Amber Pirker
Interior Design: Jane Musser, Laura Mazer, Amber Pirker
Cover Design: Kari Gim, Laura Mazer
Maps & Graphics: David C. Hoerlein, Zoey Platt, Lauren Mills, Mike Morgenfeld
Photography: Pat O'Connor
Front Matter Color Photos: page i and iv, © Pat O'Connor
Cover Photos: front © Oliver Strewe/Lonely Planet Images;
  back © David Toase/Getty Images
Avalon Travel Publishing Graphics Coordinators: Justin Marler and Deborah Dutcher